T0113835

Praise for *Skeleton Key*

"A modern-day Joycean epiphany . . . colorful, witty and persuasive . . . One can't help but be lulled into the feeling that if you're not a Deadhead, you're missing out on a good time."

—Bob Kelly, *Wired*

"Replete with a healthy sense of humor and an obvious love for its subject . . . the mix of concrete and the absurd reminds you of the Dead's music itself."

—Steve Futterman, *Rolling Stone*

"This indispensable guide to all things Grateful Dead–related is the only dictionary you can laugh your way straight—or not so straight—through from beginning to end."

— Matt Groening, creator of "The Simpsons" and "Life in Hell"

"*Skeleton Key* is an elegantly written, one-size-fits-all passport to Deadhead culture's rich, weird pageantry."

—Richard Gehr, *Village Voice*

"Indispensable . . . captures the essence of the Grateful Dead experience, both enriching it for experienced Deadheads and explaining it for 'newbies.' "

—Gersh Kuntzman, *New York Post*

"Loaded with more jargon, humorous slang terms, anecdotes and minutiae than you can shake a kind veggie burrito at! . . . this book is way entertaining."

—*Terrapin Times*

"The *Key* to understanding our subculture . . . truly the Rosetta Stone of the Deadhead scene."

—Mike Maynard, *Unbroken Chain*

"A thoroughly enjoyable guide to practically everything you might want to know about Grateful Dead lore and mythology. It examines the subculture from a plethora of vantage points—from onstage, in the crowd, in the parking lot, on the Internet; from 'Acid Tests' to 'the Zone' . . . Die-hard Deadheads and novices alike will find this infinitely fascinating."

—Jay Trachtenberg, *Austin Chronicle*

Trademark Grateful Dead Merchandising, Inc.
Used with permission.

SKELETON KEY

A DICTIONARY FOR DEADHEADS

DAVID SHENK

AND

STEVE SILBERMAN

DOUBLEDAY

NEW YORK   LONDON   TORONTO   SYDNEY   AUCKLAND

A MAIN STREET BOOK
PUBLISHED BY DOUBLEDAY
a division of
Bantam Doubleday Dell Publishing Group, Inc.
1540 Broadway, New York, New York 10036

Main Street Books, Doubleday, and the portrayal of
a building with a tree are trademarks of Doubleday,
a division of Bantam Doubleday Dell Publishing Group, Inc.

Book design by Julie Duquet

Library of Congress Cataloging-in-Publication Data
Shenk, David, 1966–
Skeleton key : a dictionary for deadheads / David Shenk and Steve Silberman.
p.   cm.
"A Main street book."
Includes bibliographical references (p.).
1. Grateful Dead (Musical group) — Dictionaries. 2. Grateful Dead
(Musical group) — Humor. I. Silberman, Steve, 1957– . II. Title.
ML421.G72S5   1994
782.42166'092'2 — dc20
[B]   94-9192
CIP

ISBN 0-385-47402-4

For Charley Wilkins,
dear friend and crispy critter

CONTENTS

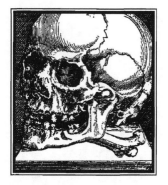

FOREWORD

Of the trips I've known, most getting long now, and a few exceeding strange, among the fattest is the curious cult(ure) that you Deadheads have spun up out of music and adversity.

Well into his eighties, the late mythologist Joseph Campbell became one of you, by his own description, and called Deadheads the most recently developed tribe on the planet.

I know what he meant by that. Never mind that most of you are straight from the heart of Generica and were brought up about as far from oogum-boogum bone-in-the-nosedness as Judeo–Christianity could coerce you. Never mind that a lot more of you are writing writs than fashioning crafts from animal parts. Never mind your BMWs or cumulative SATs in the middle teens. Deadheads are as tribal as the Tasaday.

You have your own codes (most of them sweetly old-fashioned), myths (most of them astonishing to those on my side of the Laminated Curtain), and totemic gestures (though I still sometimes wonder if those people with their fingers in the air aren't just waiting for doughnuts from Heaven).

You appear to have your own divination system buried somewhere in your obsessive scrutiny of concert play lists. (It looks to me like a cross between the *I Ching* and baseball statistics . . . the solace of a found Order in the Cosmos abstracted from an arbitrary data set.)

Somewhere in that vicinity, you even have what I consider one of the most positive developments in the history of spirituality: a religion without beliefs.

Well, that's not quite true. There are a few beliefs in there, but they are so benign and diffuse that someone used to the linear architecture of conventional religious practice might miss them altogether. It seems most of you believe that people are inherently good and to be trusted, that strangers are friends and friends brethren.

Indeed, it seems most of you are what I call *pronoids*, believing, as I do, that the universe is a conspiracy on your behalf. If you didn't, how could so many of you willingly fling yourselves into the *terra incognita* of a month on the road, setting out with little more than eighteen dollars in change, three working cylinders in the Microbus, a quarter ounce of killer bud, and faith in your goofy hearts?

But that's the key. You know the most important thing. You know that faith is all you really need. That, and a willingness to use the synchronicity that seems as common in your lives as causality is in everyone else's. Because of this, you get to enjoy the essential human experience so central to the life of tribes and so rare in America: The Quest. The Walkabout. The Road.

So arises from this shared experience your lingo, the core of whose lexicon can be found in this helpful book. I think of tribes as mind-fields. Collective organisms. Coral colonies of thought. Coursing through their organic structure, like shared nutrients, are bundles of special meaning and belonging, wrapped in words which others may use, *but not in the same way*. By these signs, ye shall know us, they say.

I'm sure many of you will contest some of the definitions and lore found between these covers. You will write (or as likely, e-mail) the authors with your own versions, and the collective story will grow and weave into itself with even more energy and complexity. This object in your hands will come alive. And you know it's gonna get stranger.

You're a good lot, you Deadheads. I'm proud to be one of you.

— *John Perry Barlow*
Somewhere over America,
April 13, 1994

OPENERS

I

In song and in dance, man expresses himself as a member of a higher
community; he has forgotten how to walk and speak and is on the way
toward flying into the air, dancing. His very gestures express enchantment . . .
a mystic feeling of oneness.

—Friedrich Nietzsche,

The Birth of Tragedy, 1871

My high school English teacher, Bob Moses, took me to my
first show, in Morgantown, West Virginia, on April 10, 1983. I
was sixteen. If I knew where he was now, I'd thank him personally. It was also his first show. "The Grateful Dead," he declared the next morning in his office, "is the best thing the
United States has to offer."

That morning, I couldn't disagree.

A week later, I dubbed some tapes given to me by the older
brother of a friend—the New Jersey Meadowlands 9/2/78 and
Pittsburgh's Stanley Theatre 12/1/79. "Drums" into "Not Fade
Away" taught me something I didn't yet know about music—
that it could take you somewhere.

Now we call that THE ZONE. I didn't know what to call it
then.

My friends Adam and John and I spent the summer patching together tape decks, unwrapping cassettes, setting levels,

popping the plastic tabs, and intently creating personalized tape labels and covers for our burgeoning collection. We also printed t-shirts, pored over *The Official Book of the Deadheads*, and caught a few more shows in the Midwest.

The recording quality of the live tapes wasn't so hot back then, but we weren't picky. We listened right through the hiss. And what we heard—well, it's still hard to describe, even after writing this book. It was music, but what kind? We heard country, bluegrass, folk, blues, gospel, rock, a little jazz. We heard weirdness. We heard *noise*. We heard the effervescent ruminations of Jerry Garcia's guitar, and the rhythmic stylings of Bob Weir's guitar. We heard—"is that just *two* drummers?"— Mickey Hart and Billy Kreutzmann sounding out complex rhythms.

And then there was Phil Lesh. Adam picked up on his innovative bass sound right away—a "Phil Phan" right from the start. It took me a little longer, but I got there too, eventually.

The music was also a vehicle for something else. We couldn't quite see it then, but our tape collection wasn't the only thing changing, growing. We sat around *thinking* a lot. With the volume up, we'd lounge around in the basement and come up with theories about life. Mine was the Giant Disco Mirror Ball in the Sky Theory: *the* explanation for ESP, déjà vu, synchronicity, and all other unexplainable phenomena.

Adam had his Pod Theory, an idea that consciousness takes place on an infinite number of distinct levels. He scratched it out one night on a yellow legal pad, and I saved it.

My Pod just interlocks with other Pods for a space of time so short it's beyond any sort of comprehension . . . Everything is not even REAL!←I did this in my explanation point Pod.←I did this in my "Pod" Pod.←I did this in my "my" Pod.←I did this in my (I did this in my "my" Pod) Pod!

Neither theory was going to cause any philosophy texts to go into a new edition. But the effect on us was profound. We were getting excited about ideas. The music of the Dead and the Dead scene had awakened us intellectually.

"People say Deadheads are throwbacks," says sociologist Rebecca Adams, who has been thinking deeply about the Deadhead experience for several years. "I think they're *pioneers*. They recognize that reality is subjective—there is no *right way*—and have been cognizant of these multiple realities for a lot longer than most other people. This is post-modernism. It's the cutting edge."

Multiple realities . . . so maybe Adam was onto something . . .

The smartest person I've ever met is a Deadhead, and so is the kindest. I don't socialize or work in an exclusively Deadhead world, but every time I come back to that home, I'm dazzled by the good-heartedness and utter intelligence at work there. In my "other" life, I've done some work with satirists and political analysts. But there's nothing that outclasses the Dead scene for wit or wisdom. I've never laughed harder or learned more than during the time spent with other Heads.

Have you ever met someone who didn't feel much enthusiasm for anything? Some people go through a whole life like that.

Not us. Deadheads have Ph.D.'s in exuberance. The enthusiasm for the music spills into our enthusiasm for *the scene*, which in turn spills into our friendships, the books we read, the food we cook, and so on.

And the stories. Ask a Deadhead about his or her first show or favorite tape. You'll hear a great story. You'll hear things that you probably won't quite believe—until another Head relates a similar experience.

If you gather together the stories, as we have, you'll see that they start to fit together and make sense on a larger scale. It's hard to understand how the Deadhead scene is a religion when you listen to one person describe it. But after a few more perspectives, it starts to make sense.

Similar expressions keep coming up. The stories and the phrases start to fit together. That's why we wrote this book. There's a community out there, a subculture. It's no fan club. It's more a way of life, a way of thought.

And a way of speaking. With this book, we have sought to understand more about our community by examining the language that we speak, the phrases that we use. Language is one window into the Deadhead spirit. This book, I hope, shows why we listen, why we dance, why we give away free tickets.

Lend a copy to your parents. Read it aloud in the family room. While this book has been written primarily by Deadheads about Deadheads for Deadheads, we'd like to think it is accessible enough to serve as a gateway for those who are curious but admittedly clueless. For if there's one thing this extraordinary American ethnic group/religion/subculture is, it is *inviting*. The bus is waiting. Climb aboard.

—*David Shenk*
New York City,
March 1994

II

It was Kerouac's insistence that they were on a quest, and that
the specific object of their quest was spiritual. Though they rushed back
and forth across the country on the slightest pretext, gathering kicks
along the way, their real journey was inward; and if they seemed to
trespass most boundaries, legal and moral, it was only in the hope of
finding a belief on the other side. "The Beat Generation," he said,
"is basically a religious generation."

—John Clellon Holmes,
"The Philosophy of the Beat Generation," 1958

You're with your best friends in a great big room. The air is
electric with the presence of 10,000 people. You're talking
about the things you love best—music, and seeing the beautiful
places on Earth before you get old. Maybe you've been waiting
on line outside the arena all day (or driving, or working) in order to be standing in this room. You know one of the great
things of your life is about to happen.

When the houselights go down, and the bandmembers walk
out of the twilight at the side of the stage, the whole room explodes in a roar that makes the hair on your neck stand on end.
If you could wish to be anywhere at that moment, you'd want
to be right where you *are*. Being at a Grateful Dead show, to a

Deadhead, is like waking up and realizing it's Christmas morning.

The Dead have been on the road for almost three decades, and some of their fans have been with them for almost as long. Some of the old folks remember when the Dead were young, and they were young too, seeing it all with the eyes of a teenager. They look at the younger Heads around them, and recognize their own younger selves—before they themselves became mothers and fathers.

The personal methods of celebration—and the size of the party—may change over the years, but Dead shows are still about what a lot of Deadheads say when you ask them how they're doing. Not "just OK," but *loving life.*

When the spotlights sweep down, all eyes turn toward the stage, but a Dead show (Deadheads rarely call them "concerts") is not another thing to be *consumed,* like TV. At the Acid Tests, there was no distinction between the guys playing the tunes and the folks dancing to them. Everybody paid a dollar, and everybody got off. Even the young Heads in the room know that the band plays the music (and on the really good nights, "the music plays the band"), but Deadheads make the big room come alive.

The magic of the Grateful Dead is collaborative magic.

Deadheads have been the best audience a band could wish for—passionate, critical, and "deadicated," eager to travel thousands of miles to sell out nearly every show the band plays, and the Dead and their organization have worked hard to make the shows places where old and young can celebrate together.

While the band was working to keep the next song fresh, Deadheads were busy inventing their own culture in America's backyard.

This is a book about that culture.

💀

Imagine that the houselights have come up again after the first half of the show is over (the "first set"), and during the break between sets, you're walking around in the hallways. People have dressed for the occasion, in hand-dyed shirts adorned with roses and skulls. Women and men wear beads, bells, and flowing cotton skirts. The air is softened by the smoke of sage and "kind bud." Drums in the hallways keep the life-giving pulse of the music alive while the band takes a break, and people are dancing. Other Heads sit in circles passing pipes, or snuggle, or sprawl, going over scraps of paper ("setlists"), containing their own records of the songs just played. Some are quiet, but most are talking excitedly, greeting old friends and meeting new ones, guessing what the band might play next, catching up on what everyone's been doing since the last show. "I'm *jonesin'* for a "Dew,' bigtime!" someone might say, and the words have that taut snap of road talk, language that's alive.

This book is a dictionary for Deadheads. We believe in the beauty and depth and humor of Deadhead language, because it is our language. Even in a community where music communicates more than many things spoken, words help make us what we are. Through them, our histories pass down.

What we have attempted is a deep view into our community—which Jerry Garcia once called "the Grateful Dead outback"—by looking at the words by which our culture is made. Some of these words may illuminate some corner of the Grateful Dead universe you have always been curious about, where we found a story hidden. Where possible, we have allowed Deadheads to speak for themselves.

There is a new kind of art some Deadheads enjoy that is based on fractals, shapes generated by mathematical equations, derived by Benoit Mandelbrot. A fractal may appear simple on first glance, but on close inspection, fractals reveal themselves to be of nearly infinite complexity.

Though some of the words in SKELETON KEY are simple, we hope the sum of their perspectives hints at the world, infinitely complex, that arose in the Grateful Dead outback—a fractal American beauty.

We humbly offer this book to those who have passed through the gates of the arenas, stadiums, coliseums, theaters, and dance halls of America in search of that good time we all set out for when we were young—and found, over and over again.

Let the words be yours.

—*Steve Silberman*
San Francisco,
March 1994

KEY TO THE KEY
(How to Read This Book)

Skeleton Key is a record of Deadhead jargon, lore, and culture.

🔹 Terms are arranged in alphabetical order, with people listed according to their last names (like CASSADY, NEAL).

🔹 A word or phrase appearing in SMALL CAPS is defined elsewhere in the book.

🔹 The words "Head" and "Deadhead" are used interchangeably in this book.

🔹 A 🔖 symbol appearing next to a term indicates that the term is used primarily by the community of Deadhead tapers and tape collectors.

🔹 A 📖 symbol appearing next to a term indicates that the term has been invented by the authors, simply because we couldn't find a term in use to describe that particular phenomenon. We know that jargon does not come from the authors of dictionaries, but from the way people talk. If a term is amusing or useful, feel free to use it. If not, pass it on.

🔹 Many of the sources of terms, definitions, and usage examples can be found in the Notes section beginning on page 371.

🔹 We have endeavored to capture and transmit something of the values of our extended family while highlighting the diversity within it. To stay true to this breadth of expression, we've invited scores of Heads to add their voices to this book. The 🌹 symbol is used to indicate places where Heads speak for themselves, including twenty-six brief essays, written especially for *Skeleton Key,* on each of the Dead's album releases (omitting "best of" collections like *Skeletons From the Closet*).

Have a good show!

SKELETON KEY

THE DICTIONARY

ACID TESTS • Events hosted by novelist Ken Kesey and the Merry Pranksters in the Bay Area and Los Angeles in '65 and '66, featuring improvised music, strobes and black lights, films and projections, tape loops, hidden microphones, and LSD—which was still legal—dissolved into Kool-Aid.

The Acid Tests developed out of parties fueled by LSD-fortified venison chili at Kesey's bungalow on Perry Lane in Palo Alto. These parties were a magnet for the best bohemian minds around Stanford University and the local coffeehouses, including Jerry Garcia, then living four blocks away in a communal household called the Chateau. Kesey had been introduced to psychedelics as a paid volunteer in CIA-funded experiments at the local V.A. hospital. ROBERT HUNTER, later a lyricist for the Dead, was another volunteer.

Admission was a dollar, even for the musicians, and "everyone was involved," explains Dick Latvala, the Dead's tape archivist. "It wasn't 'audience' and 'performer'—those distinctions were deliberately blurred. *You* are *it*, you are the experience you're witnessing—that was what it was all about." And "it" often lasted until dawn.

The musicians—including assorted Pranksters, and THE GRATEFUL DEAD—played for hours, or just a few minutes. NEAL CASSADY—the inspiration for Dean Moriarty, the hero of

Jack Kerouac's novel *On the Road*—was often the "announcer," space-rapping alone or in tandem with WAVY GRAVY, or dancing, while Ken Kesey, dressed like Captain America, played a kazoo, or made apocalyptic noises on the Thunder Machine, built by metal sculptor Ron Boise. People crawled on the floor, stirred fingers in Day-Glo paints and pressed their hands to the walls, tossed toilet paper streamers that fluttered down in the strobe lights, and glued jewels and sequins to each other's faces, while PIGPEN riffed down-and-dirty on "Midnight Hour," or Ken Babbs delivered a rap about going into orbit.

"The occasions vibrated between being intensely boring and intensely interesting, each causing the other," says Stewart Brand, who organized a similar event shortly afterwards called the TRIPS FESTIVAL. Flyers passed out in advance and at the door said, "Can You Pass the Acid Test??" "Passing the Acid Test," Brand says simply, "meant lasting all night."

Combining freeform jamming, garage science-fiction weirdness, participation by everyone, and psychedelics, "the Acid Test," as Garcia reflected, "was the prototype for our whole basic trip." *See* LSD.

Acid Tests with the Dead:

🕱 12/4/65 at biker Big Nig's house, San Jose, CA (the first show ever billed as "the Grateful Dead")

🕱 12/11/65 at the Big Beat in Palo Alto

🕱 12/18/65 at the Muir Beach Lodge

🕱 1/66 at Beaver Hall in Portland

🕱 1/8/66 at the Fillmore West

🕱 1/29/66 the "Sound City Acid Test" in San Francisco (just Garcia and Pigpen)

🕱 the "Watts Acid Test," 2/12/66, at the Youth Opportunities Center in Compton, L.A.

🕱 the "Pico Acid Test," 3/12/66, at the Danish Center in L.A.

🕱 3/19/66 at the Carthay Studios in L.A.

ALEMBIC • An adventurous sound research-and-development company founded by OWSLEY Stanley, Ron Wickersham, Bob Matthews, DAN HEALY, Betty Cantor-Jackson, and Rick Turner in 1968, with the goal of improving the primitive electronics and P.A. equipment available to musicians at that time.

"The problem was primitive gear," Owsley explained to *Grateful Dead Hour* host David Gans in 1991. "It seemed as though the technology could be pushed a little further . . . I got them together and said, 'We've got to build better instruments.' I thought it should be called the Alembic [an ancient alchemical term] because that was the vessel in which chemical verification takes place. First everything breaks down, and then it's built back up, and distilled into the right thing. We were trying to take all of the technology, and all of the experience, and put it into a vessel."

The first Alembic workshop was in a shed behind the band's rehearsal hall near the Hamilton Air Force base in Marin County. "All of us would go out there to try building our own pickups, guitars, and amplifiers," sound man Dan Healy told *One More Saturday Night* author Sandy Troy. "Garcia would come in and tear his guitar apart in the afternoon. It was a great place."

"We called ourselves the 'one-stop shop for rock and roll,' " recalls Doug Irwin, who cut his guitar-designing teeth at Alembic in the early '70s. "It was the one place where you could be sure they had the most advanced guitars and electronics and techniques they were using in the recording studios. We were really shaking the industry up, doing work for the Dead; the Airplane; the Who; Emerson, Lake & Palmer; Santana, all sorts of people. The Who had an equipment guy who used to come in and pour these broken guitars out of paper bags that they had destroyed on stage, and we'd put them back together.

"Our basses were great. Before us, when you went to hear a band, you could feel the bass, but you couldn't hear it. It was an instrument that never really got any attention. 'Oh, it's just a *bass* player, don't worry. You don't really hear him anyway.' Alembic is definitely responsible for changing the quality of the sounds you hear today." *See* THE WOLF.

"ALTHEA" AT 3:1, "BUCKET" AT 1:1, "ST. STEPHEN" AT 500:1 • Informal, low-stakes Deadhead gambling, wagers pitched on the band's song selection at an upcoming RUN of shows. Deadheads use all kinds of strategies to figure out, or "call," what the band might play, and though there are parameters that can inform the band's structuring of a set—what the band's been playing lately, or which lead singer sang the OPENER the night before, for instance—even the Dead don't know, most often, what they are going to play before they step onto the stage.

"The way we do it," explains Brian Bothun, "is to pick ten songs we each think they will play, and then everybody throws in ten bucks. Whoever gets the most correct takes the pot." ROCK MED volunteer Rick "Noodles Romanoff" Clayton has dubbed his years of betting for tapes "parimutuel Dead." "I used to be pretty good at it when I spent more time in the audience. You can get to where you can predict the next five tunes, but you have to make a career out of it." *See also* BOBBY-TUNES/JERRY-TUNES; OPENER; PICKY DEADHEADS.

AMERICAN BEAUTY • Album #6, released in November 1970. David Grisman plays mandolin on "Ripple" and "Friend of the Devil."

🍄 *Robert Hunter, lyricist, on American Beauty:*

American Beauty shows the GD playing, singing and songwriting skills in full stride. We had the confidence of a successful record *Workingman's Dead* behind, plus a shared sense of direction that was in tune with the times—The Band, The Byrds, Poco, CSNY & Dylan were all exploring traditional music augmented by the power of rock & roll. Psychedelia had had its moment (marking the GD forever in the public perception) and we were continuing to evolve what we believed to be the logical next step in American music, hence the title. There is an underlying tone of sadness to *American Beauty* (Phil's father had just passed away, Jerry's mother was dying in the hospital as the result of an auto accident) reflected in the colors of such tunes as "Box of Rain," "Brokedown Palace," "Attics of My Life" and "Ripple." On the upside, "Sugar Magnolia/Sunshine Daydream" reaffirmed the important business of just getting stupid and being in love, while "Truckin' " announced, as early as 1970, what a long, strange trip it already seemed to have been. This didn't refer only to the GD, but to the ten years of bluegrass, old timey & jug band configurations leading up to the rock & roll departure. *Grateful Dead Live*

'71, *Europe '72* & the Garcia solo release (also '72) staked out the GD's musical territory in a definitive way. It wouldn't be until 1975 and *Blues for Allah* that we would break with that feeling and extend the territory into less definable musical spaces, neither psychedelic nor traditional based. This amorphous state of transition lasted until 1985, when *In the Dark* once again found us in command of our direction in a way comprehensible to the public. *American Beauty* remains the favorite studio record of many fans and members of the band, mustering, as it does, all the resources at our command in a futile but game response to the rising tide of commercially safe music which had already begun a counter-mission to recover its monopoly of the American airwaves and record racks in the '70's.

AMERICAN REALITY • Artists Stanley Mouse and Alton Kelley's alternate title for *American Beauty,* visible in the etching on the rose mirror on the cover. Deadheads also see in the cloud above the reaper on *Wake of the Flood* both a joint and a skull, and there's a stealth "Acid" hiding in the uppermost quarter of the word "Dead" on the back of *Live/Dead.* The Dead have usually avoided loading "messages" into their music and art, secret or otherwise.

ANALY HIGH SCHOOL • The site of Garcia's first public performance, in Sebastopol, California. His band won a contest and got to record the Bill Doggett song "Raunchy."

ANTHEM OF THE SUN • Album #2, released in July 1968.

The title is the name of a piece of ancient Egyptian music found by Lesh in a report by archaeologist Paul Schliemann, describing the discovery of a tomb containing the remains of an orchestra of sixty-five instruments, eighty singers, and a single bleached skull.

The striking fire-wheel mandala on the cover of this album was painted by Bill Walker, a friend of keyboardist Tom Constanten's. On New Year's Eve, '67, the two went to a desert area of Nevada called the Valley of Fire, and took LSD and a hallucinogenic South American vine called *yagé.* The painting was the result of that experience and a series of meditations on each of the bandmembers' "subtle energy patterns" while watching them play, says Walker. The bandmembers, clockwise from the right of the beast's head in the center, are: Lesh, Pigpen, Hart, Kreutzmann, Weir, and Garcia.

The album was remixed by Lesh in '72 and rereleased, and the remix was released briefly in '76 with a white instead of a purple cover. The CD has the original mix.

☙ *David Gans, host of the Grateful Dead Hour, on* **Anthem of the Sun:**
Anthem of the Sun is an ambitious and highly enjoyable *tour de force* of psychedelic record-making. Combining studio and live tapes and employing techniques of contemporary electronic music, the band's second album is an early peak of collective composition and production, with virtually every musician contributing tunes, changes, lyrics, vocals, and multiple instrumental roles.

One of Robert Hunter's first lyric efforts for the band, "Alligator," is featured; Phil's pal, the late Bobby Petersen, contributed some lyrics, and Weir and Garcia wrote some of their own, too.

Spacey and earthy, delicate and crazed in turn—from Weir's primally psychedelic rose that "rainbow spiral round and round and trembles and explodes," to Pigpen's raunchy asides in "Caution"—someone once suggested that *Anthem of the Sun* was the Dead's answer to the Beatles' *Sgt. Pepper.*

The album opens in the studio, with Jerry singing quietly, "And all the children learning/From books that they were burning/Every leaf was turning/To watch him die" (his only lead vocal, by the way: Jerry is mostly just one hell of a guitar player on this record). Cut to concert tapes—several of them at once, in fact. When "The Other One" kicks in after a short drum intro, there are four Grateful Deads happening, as many performances intertwine and overlap throughout the suite that ensues. Drum kits and other groups of sounds wander back and forth across the stereo horizon, as exotic instrumental tracks, primitive electronic music, acoustic guitars and other flavors come and go in a delicious maelstrom of multiple musics.

Pianist Tom Constanten, Phil's partner in "serious" music going back to their UC Berkeley days, drops a toy gyroscope onto the sounding board of his piano, creating a buzz-saw roar that shocked producer Dave Hassinger right out of his chair. This swirling MUSIQUE CONCRÈTE passage includes a taped electronic music piece of TC's: "Electronic Study #3," from 1962. (The two-and-a-half-minute piece was released on its own on TC's 1992 album, *Out-*

Sides). Then the smoke clears, and "New Potato Caboose" ambles sweetly in, again overlapping pieces of similar music, and resolving into a single coherent performance.

Does "Born Cross-Eyed" make a little more sense to you if you know that it starts on the second beat, rather than the usual downbeat? That's Lesh playing trumpet, which was his instrument before he joined the Warlocks and took up the bass guitar.

Side two is all Pigpen. "Alligator" moves from composed song to a freeform percussion jam with vocal histrionics by Pig, Bob, and Jerry, and then on into a major instrumental rave-up; the multitrack experimentalism surrenders to a nice long passage of just one band jamming very, very hard (including a bar or two of the melody that came to be known—when played by the Allman Brothers—as "Mountain Jam") and then cuts abruptly to a less-sparkling recording just before the "reprise," which fades into some nonspecific feedback, and on into "Caution (Do Not Stop on Tracks)."

"Caution" is pure Pigpen high-test heartache, deeply involved with the band's most tribal groove. It's a classic display of the Dead's musical groupmind, but Pig wasn't in full command of his powers yet. To hear Pig the singer really take charge, check out *Bear's Choice* and *Live/Dead*.

In the late '60s, it was big recording news to be able to continually adjust the speed of a tape deck from half speed to full. The band took one tape of "Caution," and started speeding it up gradually to double speed, while at the same time taking another tape of "Caution" down from speed to normal. It's delightfully disorienting! A couple of unfortunate splices link some fine musical passages, and the whole affair screams to a close with three and a half minutes of wicked feedback.

Of the material on *Anthem of the Sun*, only Weir's "Spanish lady" section of "That's It for the Other One" remains in the Dead's repertoire today, one of the band's major improvisational vehicles, and a mainstay of the active rotation since late 1967. Like "Dark Star," the structure is minimal, so the possibilities are limitless.

While revisiting the album for this review, I heard something I had never heard before: Phil playing the signature notes of his "Dark Star" intro at a brisk pace during the feedback near the end of the album. Just a hint going by—either he was making that musical suggestion in the course of the jam, or it was just a random pattern in the notestream, and

I was reading too much into it. But this record can still surprise you after twenty years. How many friends and family members can you say that about?

ANTON ROUND • A fictional executive at the Dead's own Round Records circa '75, who signed business mail authorizing goofy projects such as the ill-fated *Mars Hotel* promotions to ship slabs of soap ("Mars bars") and ceramic joint holders ("Superstones") to radio stations, along with promo singles.

AOXOMOXOA • Album #3, released in June 1969. The title is one of artist Rick Griffin's lysergic palindromes. The band's original title was *Earthquake Country*.

This album is a raucous mix of haunting folk forms and busy experiments, with many layers of overdubbed guitars and keyboards. "What's Become of the Baby?" began as a simple twelve-string guitar track by Garcia that was transformed into high weirdness as the band sucked nitrous oxide from hoses in the studio.

There are two versions of *Aoxomoxoa*, the later one marked "remixed" on the back of the LP. The CD is the remix. The original release features a glockenspiel on "St. Stephen," choirs of angels on "Mountains of the Moon," and an a capella reprise after "Doin' That Rag."

🌿 *Tom Constanten, keyboardist, on the making of* **Aoxomoxoa:**

Aoxomoxoa was the first album the band did using sixteen-track technology. *(Anthem of the Sun* had been done on eight-track.) This had several consequences. First, to secure greater control of the individual parts of the mosaic, it was decided to record them separately. About a half dozen tracks were dedicated to the drums, and at least two to the bass. Next, the guitars, and then my keyboard. Then came whatever trimmings—glockenspiel, cowbell, whatever—we'd thought of after Phase I was complete. Finally the vocal tracks were added.

What with the newness of the technology, no one had any experience with this way of working, so it was make-it-up-as-you-go-along. A nuance in a basic track could have a disproportionate influence on later tracks. In "St. Stephen," for instance, there was a beat missing, that was only discovered after much of the work had been done. Too much of a hassle to redo, impossible to undo, it was left in.

Mixing sixteen-track was another brand-new game. Even when it didn't sound loud, it sounded dense, and the VU needles were bouncing off the pins. The mixdown became a performance in its own right, with three or more pairs of hands on the soundboard, minding their cues. It was a good day when as many as three tunes got done.

There were two exceptions to this. "Rosemary," which Jerry had done on a four-track, and "Mountains of the Moon," which had no drums. For the latter, Jerry, Bob, Phil, and I recorded the basic tracks in the same room at the same time. The Neupert harpsichord at Pacific Recorders in San Mateo wouldn't tune up to concert pitch, so I had it tuned a whole step lower. This put the piece, normally in G, in A for me, and meant that when Bob asked for an E to tune by, I gave him an F. Meanwhile, Phil was wrestling with an upright bass, literally.

Having played the music in concert so many times helped, but still this style of recording was a very different experience. The aforementioned real-time ensemble was the exception. Even the remixed version has a rough-cut quality to it, like you'd expect from an avant-garde theater in SoHo. I like *Aoxomoxoa* because it reflects the thrill of discovery before the groove is worn down into a rut of blasé excellence.

AUDIENCE TAPES (AUDs) ☜ • Recordings of shows made by Heads in the audience using microphones, as opposed to SOUNDBOARD TAPES (SBDs) and those taped over the radio (*see* FMs).

Audience tapes are generally recorded in the TAPER'S SECTION, or—illicitly—in front of the soundboard, where taping is not permitted (*see* F.O.B.). There is an ongoing discussion among Heads about the virtues of audience tapes versus those of soundboard tapes. There is, of course, more audience noise on audience tapes—clapping, screaming, talking during the music, and so on—but an excellent audience tape can give the listener more of the "feel" of being at a show than a soundboard tape. The sound on the very best audience tapes is faithful to the Dead's P.A. ambience, hailed by the staid audiophile journal *The Absolute Sound* as "the finest large-scale High End audio system" in the world. Because of the uncluttered clarity of soundboard tapes, however, and the muddled quality of many audience tapes made with bad equipment in the '70s and '80s, soundboards (called "SBDs" on traders' LISTS) are generally more desired by tape traders than AUDs.

Incidental sounds on an audience tape can increase the excitement of listening to it. Near the beginning of one of the crispest audience tapes ever made, recorded by Bruce Harvie and Bob Marx on 8/6/71 at the Hollywood Palladium, Weir says, "Hey, you down there with the microphone—if you want to get a decent recording, you've got to move back about forty feet. It sounds a lot better that way." ("Right here!" someone says, as the taper slides into the "sweet spot.")

For many dedicated tapers, who take professional pride in their equipment, and spend years refining their methods to "lay it down clean," recording Dead shows is a way to participate in the making of history and the moment of creation.

AVALON BALLROOM • A small, ornate dance hall at Van Ness and Sutter Street in San Francisco, where the Dead played thirty times from the spring of '66 through '69. The Avalon was operated by Chet Helms and the Family Dog cooperative, a loose-knit group of bohemians who had spent the summer of '65 in Virginia City, Nevada, fixing up an Old West saloon called the Red Dog, taking LSD, dressing up like cowboys, shooting pistols, and setting off dynamite. A swing ballroom in the '30s, the Avalon was not commercially successful compared to Bill Graham's FILLMORES, but it was much beloved. Its wooden dance floor with spring suspension bounced in rhythm when enough people danced on it. "The pure hippie of the day," reflected Bill Graham, "thought of the Avalon as the *real* church. Mine was the commercial church."

The Dead played many nights there starting in the spring of '66, including the shows released on the BOOTLEG records *Historic Dead* and *Vintage Dead*. The version of "Hard to Handle" from the video *Backstage Pass* is from the Avalon, as is "Death Don't Have No Mercy" on LIVE/DEAD, recorded in January of '69. The Avalon was shut down in '69 because of noise complaints. It is now a Regency movie theater.

BACKROADS TOUR 📖 • "Freeways are the worst," wrote Robert Pirsig in *Zen and the Art of Motorcycle Maintenance.* "Roads free of drive-ins and billboards are better, roads where groves and meadows and orchards and lawns come almost to the shoulder, where kids wave to you when you ride by, where people look from their porches to see who it is." Heads agree, and those with the spare time often put some effort into making the trip from venue to venue a memorable *journey.* More than a few Heads have, by way of TOUR, become passionate sponsors of their own personal Ph.D.'s in American Studies, digging the roads less traveled before the malls eat them up.

BACKSTAGE PASSES • Much sought-after colorful stickers, sometimes called "stick-ons," that let you join the hordes milling around where you can't see the band, hear the music, hang out with friends, eat the food, or drink the beer. The passes do, however, look great pasted into TOURBOOKS. *See* LAMINATES.

BALAFON • Also spelled "bailophone," this West African xylophone-like instrument has been a part of Mickey Hart's onstage garden of percussion since the late '70s. The instrument is built of carved wooden keys mounted on a wooden frame, with resonating gourds under each key. Its warm wooden chiming can be heard embellishing the studio version of "Fire on the Mountain," and the balafon was one of the instruments that contributed to the evolution of DRUMS into a highly melodic segment of the show. In recent years, Hart has played a custom MIDI-compatible balafon that uses the keys to trigger other sounds *(see* MIDI).

The balafon is a descendant of Stone Age instruments, and oral history has it that its modern form was revealed to its tenth-century inventor, Sumanguru Kantey, in a dream. It's "watery" tones are said to resonate with water in the human belly, and call down rain. Among the Minianka people in West Africa, the balafon is used to make contact with the "invisible world," and draw spirits from their hiding places. So many different kinds of spirits find the music of the balafon irresistible — including the spirits of poisonous snakes — that players wear protective amulets when they strike it.

There is a balafon on the back cover of the RHYTHM DEVILS' *Apocalypse Now Sessions,* under the round photograph of Hart.

BALLOONS • 1. Released into the hall in exuberant confetti cascades from the ceiling by Bill Graham Presents crew on special occasions such as Mardi Gras or New Year's Eve, and by Deadheads at every show. Many Heads derive great pleasure from bouncing them back and forth in time to the music, but some are annoyed by balloons' uncanny ability to float to and remain in spots where they block views of bandmembers. Balloons are anathema to tapers, because they bump into microphones and knock over mic stands. (They frequently account for the strange thudding sounds during the midnight OPENER on New Year's audience tapes.)

Heads have passed elaborate balloon sculptures around the venues, like the lengthy "Unbroken Chain" that made its way around many West Coast shows in the late '80s. An inflatable Gumby and Bozo made a spectacular appearance at the 4/30/88 show at Frost Amphitheater, spacedancing frenetically through "Shakedown Street" until the wind bore them aloft.

2. "To do balloons" is to inhale nitrous oxide. *See also* DEAF-HEADS; NITROUS OXIDE.

THE BARDO REALM • Name given by veteran hall-dancer — and author of the Deadhead guide *Outside the Show —*

Paul Hoffman to the venue corridors that come alive during the music with dancers and SPINNERS. The word "bardo" comes from the *Tibetan Book of the Dead*, where it refers to the passages or transitional states a spirit moves through on its way to the next incarnation. The implication of this term is that the different areas of the audience at a show constitute different realms of being. *See also* HALLDANCING.

BARLOW, JOHN PERRY • Lyricist. Born on October 3, 1947, in Jackson Hole, Wyoming.

A close friend of Weir's going back to high school, Barlow has been Weir's primary lyricist since the early '70s, when they teamed up to write a batch of songs for Weir's first solo album, *Ace.* Many of the Weir/Barlow compositions from that era, including "Black-Throated Wind," "Looks Like Rain," and "Cassidy," along with many other subsequent collaborations over the years—including "Weather Report Suite"/"Let it Grow," "The Music Never Stopped," "Lost Sailor," "Saint of Circumstance," "Estimated Prophet," "Feel Like a Stranger," "Throwin' Stones"—are regarded by Heads as essential Dead. They bring to fore celebrations of companionship; lamentations of lost love; and explorations of alienation, freedom, and the frontier. In the '80s, Barlow also wrote a number of songs with Brent Mydland, a collaboration cut short by Mydland's death in July '90.

Though he's always spent most of his time living and working elsewhere, Barlow is also a member of the Grateful Dead family. A self-described "knee-jerk moralist," he has occasionally taken it upon himself to act as the Grateful Dead's conscience, imploring members of the organization to do the right thing. It is Barlow who has written and spoken most eloquently about the tragic losses of Bill Graham and Brent Mydland.

The scion of farmers and ranchers "clear back to the genealogical horizon," Barlow was raised on Bar Cross cattle ranch in Pinedale, Wyoming. "I had the sort of childhood which parents of the nineteenth century used to use as guilt food for their twentieth-century children," he writes in an unpublished memoir. "I really *did* ride horseback three and a half miles through deep snow in order to attend a one-room log schoolhouse. I really *was* putting in twelve-hour days on a tractor by the time I was eleven.

"Such a background might have prepared me to be President one day," he continues, "had it not been for Mr. Honda, who, in 1961, started shipping cheap little motorcycles to the United States. These hit my Mormon Boy Scout troop like a moral virus."

By the time he was a high school freshman, Barlow had become, by his own account, a "miscreant," a vandal, and a failing student—putting his father, a state senator who was coming up for reelection, in a bit of a political pickle. "To the great and mutual satisfaction of both Pinedale and myself, he sent me off to prep school in Colorado." Bob Weir, an equally mischievous teen who had just been kicked out of his freshman year at Menlo Park School, in California, was serendipitously sent to the very same place—Fountain Valley High, in Colorado Springs, Colorado. The two formed an instant bond. "We were thick as thieves," Barlow says. "We were easily the most unpopular kids in the school. We had each other and that was about it. We were miscreants, and they kicked Weir out after one year, but for some reason they didn't kick me out. I thought this was a miscarriage of justice, so I quit in protest and made plans to go with Bobby to Pacific High School, and live with his family. Bobby came and drove a tractor on my ranch that summer of '62. But at the last minute—one week before school started—I got cold feet and decided that there was something safer about staying at Fountain Valley."

They kept in touch, but didn't see each other for five years. While Weir got deep into the Palo Alto music scene in the early '60s, Barlow sublimated his hoodlum instincts, bucked himself up academically, and got accepted to Wesleyan, a small liberal arts university in Connecticut. "I started out wanting to be a physicist, but ground to a halt on arithmetic." He went on to devise an independent studies major in literature and theology. "Wesleyan in those days was filthy rich, and I had courses with people like Jerzy Kosinski, John Cage, Karl Popper. These were seminars, not lecture courses. I was so burnt out by the time I was a senior that I was just kind of starving at the banquet, because I had just done it too fast."

He also became a devout East Coast acidhead. "I'm convinced that the best thing I ever did was to take LSD," says Barlow. "It changed everything."

There were basically two psychedelic camps—the West Coast Ken Kesey manifestation, and the East Coast Timothy Leary manifestation. I got involved with the Leary scene early. Leary had actually taught at Wesleyan, before he went to Harvard. By the time I was a senior, the whole damned school was psychedelic. My junior year, there were 186 psychological discharges out of a student body of 1100. It was insane. People really losing it, having psychotic breaks, trying all kinds of drugs.

I went crazy like everybody else. But I was student body president, and they were very careful not to let me lose it completely. When I started to crack up, they sent me packing off to this private sanitarium. They had me building ship models for a while.

Like the others, I got detached. You've got to understand that in 1966 and '67, it felt to those of us on the leading edge of that movement that everything was about to be different. I mean, *really* different. When, after the initial flush of excitement, it turned out that things were not going to be as different, right away, as we thought—that it was going to take longer, that society had lots of immune response—a lot of people had a hard time with it. I was certainly one of them. Then I adapted to the slow course, realizing that, in order to change consciousness, you've got to be willing to put in a lifetime at it. It's not just getting a few of your friends to drop acid.

There were two main strains of politics at that point. One was the new Marxist, SDS (Students for a Democratic Society) anti-war politics, and there was the politics of consciousness. I was more inclined to believe that if you could change consciousness, the politics would take care of itself. The problem was the way people looked at things, the way in which they structured reality. They needed to understand that reality is an opinion. Once you understand that, authority takes on an entirely different character, because so much of authority is based on the idea that reality is fixed.

In June '67, after equally profound but completely separate psychedelic experiences, Barlow and Weir reunited for the first time in five years, at a Grateful Dead gig in New York City. After introducing them all to Leary, Barlow followed the band back to San Francisco, where he shacked up with them for the summer at 710 Ashbury Street. A few years later, as Weir was attempting to pen some songs, he approached Barlow and asked him if he'd be interested in writing lyrics. Barlow first obliged with "Mexicali Blues," and an old friendship soon evolved into a fruitful artistic collaboration that has lasted more than two decades.

In the mid-'80s Barlow's life reached a turning point, precipitated by a financial failure of his family ranch in Wyoming. In '86, at the prompting of David Gans, he took a virtual tour of the electronic bulletin board THE WELL, and was enthralled by what he saw as the next frontier of human existence.

"There was a weird kind of recognition there. I could see that it was a lot of the small town that I came from in some thin, virtualized way. I'd been worrying about where those kinds of small towns are going to come from in the absence of agriculture or physical locus. I started to think that the information environment was a place where you could find community."

A radical career change took place over just a few years time, from rancher to online activist and pundit. "I now spend a good deal of time writing and thinking about how information works," he says. "I'm trying to develop a sense of the ecology of information."

In June 1990, Barlow co-founded the Electronic Frontier Foundation with software developer Mitchell Kapor. The organization quickly evolved from a "hacker defense fund" into the central think tank and political organizing body on issues surrounding the "information superhighway."

Barlow divides his time between New York City and Pinedale, Wyoming. He has three daughters—Leah, Anna Winter, and Amelia. *See* BOB WEIR; WEIR/BARLOW.

BASS GREAT, LESH PHILLING • A playful appropriation of the Lite beer advertising slogan, "Tastes Great, Less

Filling" by devout Phil Lesh fans, and one of many spunky *Phil*-ifications of the English language to make it onto bumperstickers and t-shirts, along with "I'm a Lesh Lush and I Can't Get My Phil!," "Lesh Is More," "I'm a Phil Phan."

BATHROOM MIRROR • A source of endless visual fascination during the break.

BATHROOM TUNES • Songs claimed by picky (or jaded) Deadheads to be played too often or less than engagingly, allowing for a visit to the lavatories. The unappreciated tunes themselves are often given snide nicknames: "Don't Ease Me In" becomes "Don't Sleaze Me In," for example, and "U.S. Blues" becomes "Useless Blues," "U.S. Snooze," or "U.S. Blahs." "Corinna" becomes "Bore-eena," "Tennessee Jed" becomes "Tennessee Dread," and so on. Some also consider Weir's "cowboy songs" ("Mexicali Blues," "Me and My Uncle," etc.) an ideal opportunity for a pit stop; the DRUMS and SPACE portions of the show are also lost on some Heads.

Over the desk of Grateful Dead Ticket Sales chief Steve Marcus, a cartoon mailed in by a Deadhead shows a row of urinals with Heads in front of them groaning with relief, under the caption "Sometimes Rhythm Devils doesn't come soon enough!" *See also* PICKY DEADHEADS.

THE BE-IN • A "gathering of the tribes" held on January 14, 1967, in the Polo Field of Golden Gate Park in San Francisco, featuring the Dead, Quicksilver Messenger Service, Janis Joplin and Big Brother and the Holding Company, as well as poets Allen Ginsberg, Michael McClure, and many others. The Dead played "Morning Dew," "Viola Lee Blues," and "Good Morning Little Schoolgirl" with jazz flautist Charles Lloyd.

The Be-In was conceived by *San Francisco Oracle* editor Allen Cohen as an "ecstatic union of love and activism" between Berkeley antiwar activists and the psychedelic revolutionaries of THE HAIGHT-ASHBURY. The event was conducted as a *mela* — a meeting of spiritual leaders — with a ritual purification of the Polo Field beforehand, and friends of LSD manufacturer OWSLEY Stanley walking through the crowd handing out thousands of doses of "White Lightning" acid, Owsley's strongest vintage. Tens of thousands of people spent the afternoon in the sun under fluttering banners, sharing fruit and turkey sandwiches provided by Owsley and THE DIGGERS, enjoying the music, and marveling at how large the hip community had become. The Be-In was the last flowering of the original Haight spirit before the Summer of Love hype taxed the neighborhood's resources and overwhelmed its sense of purpose.

THE BEAM • A ten-foot aluminum girder strung with piano strings, tuned to extremely low pitches in octaves and fifths, fitted with a giant magnetic pickup. Played by Hart during DRUMS, the Beam was developed by Hart and Tom Paddock. Hart has played it with a section of pipe, his fingers, and his feet, drawing out of it long, rolling arcs of slow thunder.

"It illustrates the ancient perception that the divine was contained in certain mathematical relationships that could be turned into sound," writes Hart. "One of the most powerfully ethereal instruments I have ever played. The Beam can be an instrument of war or an instrument of peace. It can purr like a Tibetan choir or it can explode like napalm. . . . You can go lower and deeper with the Beam than with anything else I know, descending into vibrations that are perceived less by the ear than felt as shockwaves throughout the body." The Beam can be heard rumbling on "Psychopomp" on Hart's *Dafos*, and during "Victim or the Crime" on *Built to Last*.

BEAR • *See* OWSLEY.

THE BEAST • Hart's circular array of massive bass drums that became a familiar sight at shows in the late '80s. The Beast was developed for the RHYTHM DEVILS' soundtrack to *Apocalypse Now*, inspired by Japanese *taiko* drums, especially the *o-∂aiko*, the great drum, often four or more feet across (Hart calls his *o-∂aiko* "home plate"). The striking of the *o-∂aiko* by a traditional *taiko* drummer is preceded by respectful bowing and meditation. At Dead shows, Hart raises his mallets before striking the big drum, encouraging the audience to send power up to the stage. *See* DRUMS.

BETTYBOARDS ☜ • A cache of 250 hours or so of soundboard master tapes of the Dead, Kingfish, the New Riders of the Purple Sage, Hot Tuna, and various Garcia bands — on large and small reels and cassettes — recorded by sound engineer Betty Cantor-Jackson, and kept in a storage locker until 1985, when the contents of the locker came up for auction due to delinquent storage fees. A small group of tape collectors and associates made the winning bid for the contents, copied the tapes, and distributed them to traders.

Such an enormous volume of highest-quality tapes caused a mass upgrade of trading standards. "It was like opening up a garage, and finding a '71 Corvette that had never been driven," explains taper Ihor Slabicky. Many of the shows had not been previously available as soundboards, and shows like the 8/27/72 Veneta, Oregon, show ("Kesey's farm") are considered to be among the finest the Dead ever played. The word "bettyboard" appears on tape traders' LISTS as a rating of distinction.

A partial list of the bettyboards:

2/18–24/71	The Capitol Theater, Port Chester, New York
4/5–6/71	Manhattan Center, New York City (end of 2nd set only)
4/7–8/71	Boston Music Hall, Massachusetts
12/14/71	The Hill Auditorium, Ann Arbor, Michigan
8/21, 22, 25/72	Berkeley Community Theater, California
8/27/72	Old Renaissance Faire Ground, Veneta, Oregon
3/16/73	Nassau Coliseum, Uniondale, New York
3/21, 22/73	Memorial Auditorium, Utica, New York
3/24/73	Spectrum Arena, Philadelphia
5/26/73	Kezar Stadium, San Francisco
6/22/73	Pacific Exhibition Coliseum, Vancouver, B.C.
6/10, 11/76	Boston Music Hall, Massachusetts
6/14, 15/76	The Beacon Theater, New York City
6/29/76	The Auditorium Theatre, Chicago
2/26/77	The Swing Auditorium, San Bernardino, California
5/5/77	New Haven Coliseum, Connecticut
5/7/77	Boston Gardens, Massachusetts

5/8/77	Barton Hall, Cornell University, Ithaca, New York
5/9/77	War Memorial Auditorium, Buffalo, New York
9/29/77	The Paramount Theater, Seattle
10/2/77	The Paramount Theater, Portland, Oregon
10/28/77	Soldiers & Sailors Memorial Hall, Kansas City, Missouri
10/29/77	Field House, Northern Illinois University, Dekalb
10/30/77	Assembly Hall, Indiana University, Bloomington
11/1/77	Cobo Hall, Detroit
11/5/77	War Memorial, Rochester, New York (end of show)
11/6/77	Broome County Arena, Binghamton, New York
4/7/78	Sportatorium, Pembroke Pines, Florida
4/10, 11/78	The Fox Theater, Atlanta, Georgia
4/12/78	Duke University, Durham, North Carolina
4/14/78	Virginia Polytechnic, Blacksburg
4/15/78	William and Mary College, Williamsburg, Virginia
7/7, 8/78	Red Rocks, Morrison, Colorado
10/18/78	Winterland, San Francisco—"From Egypt With Love"
4/22/79	Spartan Stadium, San Jose, California

BIG HAIR • Applied to the sound of the DRUMS on particular nights by Hart and crew during the '80s. "It was big hair tonight," Hart might say after a particularly intense set, and the phrase found its way onto Deadheads' setlists and tape covers (*see* J-CARDS). Bob Bralove credits studio tech Tom Paddock (who designed the pickup for THE BEAM) with coining the term. *See also* THE BEAST; X-FACTOR.

BIOSPHERE 2 • The scientists involved in this attempt to create an enclosed, self-sufficient ecosystem under a dome in the Arizona desert were invited to participate in the New Year's festivities at Oakland Coliseum in '91, via telephone link. Inside the biosphere, the dawn of the new year was toasted with papaya juice and home-brewed banana wine.

BIRTHDAY SHOWS • Along with New Year's Eve, April Fools' Day, Halloween, and other festival holidays, bandmembers' birthdays tend to arouse high anticipation among Deadheads. Aside from the occasional "Happy Birthday" at the beginning of a set (as for Brent Mydland on 10/21/88 or Bill Walton on 11/5/85), *musically* spectacular things rarely happen (one notable exception was Weir's thirty-fourth, at the Melk Weg hash bar in Amsterdam, where the band revived "Love-light" and "Gloria," on borrowed instruments). But small moments of recognition and celebration go a long way toward upping the energy level in a hall. As the band vamped a verse of "Happy Birthday" to Mickey Hart on 9/11/87, in Landover, Maryland, Hart stood up and gave Kreutzmann a long hug. The next year, Kreutzmann hit Hart in the face with a birthday pie at the end of DRUMS. *See also APPENDIX I: THE DEADLINE.*

Bandmember birthdays:

Jerry Garcia: August 1

Mickey Hart: September 11

Bill Kreutzmann: May 7

Phil Lesh: March 15

Bob Weir: October 16

Vince Welnick: February 2

BISCUIT • A very low note or chord played by Lesh. "The Philsbury doughboy pumps out the biscuits." Also known as a "bomb." *See* PHIL BOMBS.

BLACK T • Jerry Garcia's customary stage apparel. Size known to fluctuate. See TROUBLE AHEAD, JERRY IN RED.

BLUES FOR ALLAH • Album #12, released in September 1975.

♣ *Blair Jackson, editor of* The Golden Road, *on **Blues for Allah:***

Blues for Allah is unique among the Dead's studio albums in that it consists entirely of material that was developed in the studio for the record, rather than being a hodge-podge of songs worked out in advance on the road and then recorded. Two things happened that allowed the group to make the album that way: In October 1974, the Dead began an indefinite hiatus *(see* THE LAST ONE) that gave them the opportunity to not only work on solo projects, but record a GD album at a more leisurely pace. And in early '75, work was completed on Bob Weir's recording studio, built adjoining his beautiful A-frame house on the wooded slopes of Marin County's majestic Mt. Tamalpais. That meant an end to worrying about costly recording studio time. "The whole idea was to get back to that band thing, where the band makes the main contribution to the evolution of the material," Garcia said of the album. "So we'd go into the studio, jam for a while, and then if something nice turned up we'd say, 'Well, let's preserve this little hunk and work with it, see if we can do something with it.' " Most of Hunter's lyrics were written after the jams had gelled into song form; the major exception was "Crazy Fingers," which Garcia set in its lilting, slow reggae arrangement (after first trying a much harder attack) from finished words. Perhaps this modus operandi explains in part why Hunter's lyrics are so elliptical throughout the record—they are mainly short bursts unconnected to any sort of story or larger whole; a collection of aphorisms rather than character-driven situations and narratives. (A few of the more "conventional" Hunter-Garcia tunes from this period turn up on the Garcia solo album *Reflections.*)

The magical core of *Blues for Allah* is a series of remarkable instrumental pieces that showcase a remarkably high level of intraband collaboration: "Slipknot!" the amazing bridge between the sharp, angular "Help on the Way" and the loping, melodic "Franklin's Tower"; the fiery, Latin-sounding "King Solomon's Marbles"; Weir's Bach-inspired "Sage & Spirit"; and the long, ultra-spacey exposition on the title tune. The component pieces of the title track represent perhaps the strangest music the Dead had recorded in the studio since *Aoxomoxoa*'s "What's Become of the Baby?"; then and now I find it a tough listen, perhaps more successful in its intention than its execution. The remaining song on the record, "The Music Never Stopped," was just the third Weir–John Barlow tune to make it onto a Dead album. Musically, it shows a clear gospel influence (especially on Donna Godchaux's solo vocal parts). Lyrically it paints a fanciful portrait of the Dead on the road—"There's a band out on the highway, high-steppin' into town . . ." A tad self-conscious perhaps, but it worked.

Blues for Allah sounds completely unlike any other Dead album. There is an intimacy to it—the sense that you're right there in the studio with the instruments and singers—that's somewhat disarming. It's also a pretty laid-back affair, not surprising given the fact that the songs did not evolve onstage. All the vocal pieces on the record (except "Blues for Allah") developed tremendously once the band started touring again in mid-'76, but there is an endearing charm to these studio versions that somehow allows them to escape comparisons with what they became. Garcia sings in "Crazy Fingers," "Something new is waiting to be born." Listening to this album is a little bit like hearing the birth of these songs, and that carries with it all the excitement (and messiness) of new creation.

BOARDS ☜ • *See* SOUNDBOARD TAPES (SBDs).

BOBBY HI-TEST AND THE OCTANE KIDS • A Dead cover band that turned out a working member of the band: Bruce Hornsby. In the spring of '74, Hornsby's brother Bob—who was in a Deadhead frat at the University of Virginia, Beta Theta Pi—formed the Octane Kids to play frat ragers, featuring Bruce on Fender Rhodes and vocals.

"We used to play college grain-alcohol parties," remembers Hornsby. "We did a little Allman Brothers, a little Band, but almost all Dead. We used to do 'Jack Straw,' 'Sugar Magnolia,' 'Truckin',' 'Not Fade Away,' 'Goin' Down the Road Feelin' Bad' . . . lots of *Europe '72* and *Skull and Roses*. We didn't do a whole lot of money gigs, but it was more about just going to this country house that my brother lived in with all these hippies, and sitting around playing." *See also* BRUCE HORNSBY; HOUSE OF JERRY.

BOBBY-TUNES/JERRY-TUNES • One distinction made at shows by setlist-conscious Heads. Garcia and Weir are the primary composers of Grateful Dead melodies, and also sing their own songs. The typical procedure at shows is to alternate between Garcia and Weir-sung tunes in a set. *See* "ALTHEA" AT 3:1, "BUCKET" AT 1:1, "ST. STEPHEN" AT 500:1; OPENER.

THE BOGUS BOBBY • Randall Delpiano, first-class con man and Weir look-alike. In 1988, Delpiano was arrested in Oakland for fraud and theft after impersonating Bob Weir as a means of conning people out of food and thousands of dollars in cash. After serving twenty-five months in prison, Delpiano apparently resurfaced in August 1990, again impersonating Weir, and employing a story about being badly shaken by Brent Mydland's recent death and wanting to lie low for a while. Two impressionable businessmen near Sacramento took him into their resort community home and spent $1,500 indulging his whims before a veteran Deadhead spotted the imposter. Delpiano does closely resemble Weir, but one giveaway is that he plays a lot of harmonica, which Weir doesn't. *See* FALSE JERRIES.

BOOTLEGS • 1. Grateful Dead concert recordings made by Heads. *See* TAPES.

2. Unofficial recordings sold for profit. For suburban Heads in the '70s, before SOUNDBOARD TAPES and AUDIENCE TAPES were easily available for trade, bootleg LPs purchased at the local headshop were often the only source of alternate versions of songs. Two favorites were *Make Believe Ballroom/Deedni Mublasaron* (which was actually 8/13/75 from the Great American Music Hall in San Francisco—*see* ONE FROM THE VAULT), and *Double Dead* (Harpur College 5/2/70), both distinguished by volcanic performances and soundboard fidelity.

Heads frown on bootlegging for profit, but old-timers recall with smiles finding the crate marked "Collector's Items" in the rear of dusty small-town record stores. Unofficial Dead discographer Ihor Slabicky notes that bootlegs would notoriously be marketed under several different names, and would omit the long jams—say, "Dark Star"—in favor of shorter songs, which was a sure sign to Slabicky that the bootlegs were not being made by Deadheads.

In the '80s, digitally mastered bootlegs came out of Italy and Germany. Many of these CD sets—such as a triple-disc set of the beloved Cornell 5/8/77—are manufactured by small deregulated companies associated with Italian radio stations.

BOTA BAGS • A relic of primitive Deadhead culture from the '60s. These flask-shaped, ornately stitched leather pouches enabled Heads to carry sangria and other refreshments into venues where no carry-in bottles were permitted. On the rare occasions that a Head received an unintended mouthful of some PSYCHEDELIC substance, a "dosed" bota was often the culprit.

THE BOYS • Affectionate nickname for the band, which, save for singer Donna Godchaux's '72–'79 tenure, has been all male. "The Boys were on fire tonight." Sometimes spelled "Boyz."

BREAKOUT • A song's stage debut. The term is also used as a synonym for REVIVAL, playing a song again after not playing it for a long time. Also called a "bustout."

Breakouts are enjoyed as historic occasions, the night a new song joins the repertoire. One of the most spectacular breakouts was the premiere of Bob Dylan's "All Along the Watchtower" at the Greek Theater on 6/20/87. There were few, if any, rumors that it would be played, so it took the hometown audience by surprise; and the thunderous announcement of the "Watchtower" theme out of "Gimme Some Lovin' " was greeted by a roar of recognition and approval.

BRIGHTMAN, CANDACE • Lighting designer for the Dead since the Europe '72 tour.

Brightman's lighting is extraordinarily sensitive to subtleties in the band's interactions, shunning bombastic effects for a vivid focusing of attention that is as much a part of the jam as the music itself. Brightman's lights create landscapes that are as naturalistic and intense as the jams, passing over the stage like bright sun, lightning, starlight.

Brightman grew up in Winnetka, Illinois, and graduated from the St. John's College "Great Books" program, where, as she says, she trained "to be an enlightened, well-educated member of the unemployed." In the mid-'60s, she moved to New York and joined the theater scene in Greenwich Village, which was undergoing a cultural awakening similar to that in THE HAIGHT-ASHBURY. She applied for a cashier's job at the Yiddish American Theater, which was beginning to book rock bands at night. When promoter Chip Monck asked Brightman what she wanted to do at the theater, she said lighting, though she had never done it. On her first night, Monck wasn't there, so she ended up lighting the show: "I just randomly hit a circuit breaker and the stage went RED, and everyone around me looked at me and said, 'Wow!' "

Soon Brightman was across the street at Bill Graham's Fillmore East, working in tandem with the artists of the golden age of light shows. "The Fillmore East was the hub of the whole rock scene," Brightman recalled to Blair Jackson in '86. "It wasn't mellow. It wasn't relaxed. It had an exciting, magical quality. Jimi Hendrix used to come by the lighting booth."

After Garcia saw some work Brightman did for the Mahavishnu Orchestra, he asked her to go out on the Europe '72 tour. "The most wonderful experience for me, in my early days with the Dead, was lighting a Pigpen tune," she recalls. "You could light him and really make it look like he was sweating. Or you could have the lights pull him out from the rest of the group, and make the guys look like they were in a smoky club . . . Finally, I was able to do lighting that wasn't gross or frenetic or meant to make the band look like superstars."

Brightman's equipment, techniques, and sensibilities evolved with the band's as she worked intimately with DAN HEALY's sound (Healy's "zoned" treatment of the vocals on "The Other One" was inspired by her lights). Brightman breaks down the barriers between the Dead and its fans by lighting the band so they can still see the audience, or by lighting the audience itself. She may ease the lights down low during meditative jams, and then shine headlight-bursts through "rain" for the breakthrough fanfares of "I Know Your Rider." More than anything, her lighting is extraordinarily *honest*. When the band is cooking, so are the lights.

"The audience shouldn't be separated, they should be *celebrated*," says Brightman. "Everyone should feel like they're in that room together."

BUILT TO LAST • Album #21, released in October 1989.

This is Mydland's last studio album with the band before his death. On "Just a Little Light," he sings wearily, "I had a lot of dreams once, but some of them came true"; and the lullaby "I Will Take You Home" is a tender, fatherly defense of innocence for his daughters Jennifer and Jessica.

"Victim or the Crime" is the album's foray into apocalyptic dissonance, with lyrics by actor Gerrit Graham. "SHIT

HAPPENS" and "Believe It or Not" were recorded for the album, but not released.

☙ *Bob Bralove, associate producer, on **Built to Last:***

Built to Last was the second album I worked on with the Dead, and the first album where I shared songwriting credits, on "Picasso Moon," with Bobby and John Barlow.

For some reason, the band had decided not to play any of the songs in concert before recording them. This was unusual for them, because most of the songs for previous albums found their maturity in front of an audience, and then were recorded for release. This time, they wanted to try to perfect the songs before playing them in concert, and be able to present them as mature pieces.

There was a great deal of effort put into developing this album sonically. Everyone was recorded in full isolation from each other, allowing anyone to replace a part they didn't like. This gave the bandmembers a great deal of freedom to experiment with new sounds. Brent and I worked extensively on his keyboard sounds, often recording his performances via MIDI on a computer, and experimenting with different synth orchestrations. On "I Will Take You Home," Brent played an acoustic piano fitted with MIDI triggers. I then went back and doubled some of the parts with samples of a music box; adding the winding of the music box was an afterthought that seemed to fit.

Mickey also did intensive experimentation with samples, recording on his own at his studio, on "slave reels" of the master tapes. "Victim or the Crime" has crashing light bulbs and samples from the Beam playing the rhythm; "Foolish Heart" has a full array of shakers and Latin percussion, sampled and played back through MIDI instruments.

It was a production whirlwind until the very last minute, doing the mixes while a private plane waited for Bobby and Jerry and John Cutler to take them to the East Coast for a Garcia Band tour. Brent walked in at 4 A.M. while we were doing the mix of "I Will Take You Home," and said he wanted strings. Jerry and Bobby and John left so they could make the gig, and Brent and I added "strings" from the computer recording of his own performance, and did the final mix. We finished at 6 A.M., which was just enough time for me to take a shower, catch a plane to Los Angeles, master the record, and make our deadline. I can't listen to a note of the record without "hearing" these events.

BUMPERSTICKERS • *See* EVERYTHING I NEEDED TO KNOW ABOUT LIFE I LEARNED FROM READING THE BACK OF A VOLKSWAGEN VAN.

CALLING THE OPENER • *See* OPENER.

CAPTAIN TRIPS • Garcia's "handle," given to him by the Merry Pranksters, that has stuck with him among Heads to the present day.

The Garcia-as-guru rep became an institution in 1967, when Garcia was listed on the back of Jefferson Airplane's *Surrealistic Pillow* as "musical and spiritual adviser." Garcia has never liked the tag, or the responsibility it implies, and has assiduously resisted all efforts to brand him "captain" of anybody's trip but his own, or even bandleader. "I'm not the leader of the Grateful Dead," Garcia said in '72. "There isn't any leader. I mean, I can bullshit you press guys real easy, but I can't bullshit Phil and Pigpen. Everybody is the leader when it's the time for them to be the leader."

Garcia's role as a "lead" vocalist and guitar player in a band that plays music used as a compass for psychedelic exploration has encouraged successive generations of youthful audiences to regard him as a father figure and guide. (Heads occasionally refer to Garcia affectionately as "the Old Man.") Lyricist Robert Hunter notes that some fans are disappointed when they discover that Garcia didn't write the lyrics he sings.

Garcia is astute and engaging in interviews, and one explanation—beyond his power as a musician—for the guru status
that has been foisted on him is that, as he puts it, he is "a com-
pulsive question answerer. I'm just the guy who found myself in
the place of doing the talking every time there was an interview
with the Grateful Dead. But as for coming to me for advice,
that's ridiculous. 'Captain Trips'—that's bullshit." *See* JERRY IS
GOD.

❧ *Lyricist John Barlow on Jerry Garcia:*
Garcia's got an aura, an enormously charismatic personality. He has something that even those of us who have been around him all these years are still
somewhat cowed by. People who are like brothers to Garcia still deal with
him the way a fan treats a celebrity. It's not just that he's so quick. He's just
so big somehow. And you can be aware of his frailties, which are many, and
still have that awe.

CAROUSEL BALLROOM • A small venue at Van Ness
and Market Street in San Francisco, operated cooperatively
from January through the spring of '68 by the Dead, Quicksilver Messenger Service, and the Jefferson Airplane. The idea
was to provide a less commercial alternative to shows produced
by Bill Graham, and the Dead played most of their eight shows
there without paying themselves. It was a noble experiment,
but the Carousel's lax admission policies and financial disorga-
nization forced it to close in June of '68. The space was subsequently rented by Bill Graham, who renamed it the FILLMORE
WEST.

CARRIER WEIGHT LAW • Passed in 1986 as part of a
severe mandatory minimum sentencing statute, requiring federal judges to take into account the weight of the blotter paper,
sugar cubes, liquid, or other "carrier" substance for LSD when
sentencing.

As part of the Reagan and Bush administrations' "War on
Drugs," judges were obliged to calculate lengths of sentences as
if the drug carrier were also made of pure LSD. Hence, a person caught with 1 gram of LSD dissolved into a bottle filled
with 10 grams of water was charged and sentenced as if he had

been selling 11 grams of LSD, leading to a substantially longer jail sentence.

In the fall of '93, under pressure from Deadheads, Families Against Mandatory Minimums (FAMM), and Attorney General Janet Reno, the carrier weight law was abolished, and replaced with a standard carrier weight measurement for each dose: 0.4 gram. The change is retroactive, meaning many Heads currently in jail doing hard time—most of them first-time offenders—will be free to walk in the sunshine sooner. The band has been active against unconstitutional drug laws, donating Rex Foundation money to FAMM and other groups, and speaking out on the subject. "I'd like to say to the thousands of Heads who are currently serving maximum sentences that there's still hope for a miracle in America, so keep the faith," Lesh said in January '94, on the occasion of the band's induction into the Rock & Roll Hall of Fame. *See* DRUG CHECKPOINT AHEAD!

CASSADY, NEAL • Born on February 8, 1926, in the back of a jalopy. Along with writers Jack Kerouac, Allen Ginsberg, and William Burroughs, Cassady was one of the original members of the Beat Generation—an enormous cultural and literary influence on the band members and their audience in the early days. In the '60s, Cassady was also the driver of the Merry Pranksters' bus, "Furthur." Cassady's Prankster name was "Speed Limit." He is celebrated as "Cowboy Neal" in the Weir song "The Other One," and is one of two subjects of the song "Cassidy," the other being Cassidy Law, daughter of Eileen Law (who is not named after Cassady, but Butch Cassidy in the film *Butch Cassidy and the Sundance Kid*—*see* THE OFFICE).

Cassady grew up in the '40s in the hobo jungles of Denver, hot-wiring cars to drive women up to the mountains to make love to them, and educating himself about philosophy and literature by reading Proust and Schopenhauer in the public library between his car-washing job and paper route. After bouncing in and out of reform schools, Cassady impressed a local high school guidance counselor with his energetic sincerity and good looks, and the counselor suggested he meet two former students of his at Columbia University—the young writers Jack Kerouac and Allen Ginsberg—and their friends.

Cassady drove to New York City with his fifteen-year-old bride LuAnne Henderson, and met Ginsberg and Kerouac. Cassady's effect on the two men was dramatic. Cassady became the prototype for heroic characters in several of Kerouac's novels, most notably as Dean Moriarty, the jazz-loving, sexually athletic, Zen-rapping "wild, yea-saying overburst of American joy" in *On the Road*. Cassady also became Ginsberg's muse and occasional lover, celebrated in Ginsberg's breakthrough poem "Howl" as "N.C., secret hero of these poems, cocksman and Adonis of Denver." These three men—with Burroughs as mentor—laid the foundation for what became known as "the Beat Generation" in the late '40s, in all-night conversations marked by frankness, passionate brotherhood, a faith in the redeeming power of writing and creativity, and a conviction that everyday life is sacred.

When *On the Road* was published in 1957, Cassady both enjoyed and suffered his sudden notoriety as a literary hero in the awakening counterculture, and became known as "Johnny Potseed" in the cafés of San Francisco's North Beach. In '58, Cassady was set up by narcotics agents, and drew two years for possession of marijuana in San Bruno County Jail and San Quentin. When he got out, he was unable to resume the brakeman's job with the Southern Pacific that had allowed him to support his family, and lived out his parole in Los Gatos as a tire recapper.

By 1962, Cassady was partying with coeds at Stanford at the same time that Garcia, Hunter, and Pigpen were gigging at local coffeehouses and KEPLER'S BOOKS & MAGAZINES. Ken Kesey had been having acid parties at his bungalow on Perry Lane for a couple of years, while three blocks away, Garcia and others were jamming in a big house called the Chateau. One night at a party, Robert Hunter met Cassady, and soon after that, Cassady met Carolyn Adams in a coffeeshop, and introduced her to Kesey. Adams became a Prankster and was given the handle "Mountain Girl."

Cassady had introduced himself to Kesey after reading his just-published novel *One Flew Over the Cuckoo's Nest*. He recognized a reflection of himself in the novel's hero, Randle Mc-Murphy, drove to Kesey's bungalow, and introduced himself. Kesey was pleased to meet the real-life Dean Moriarty, and Cassady became a welcome participant in the parties at Perry Lane that shortly thereafter moved up to a ranch in nearby La Honda, where Cassady met Garcia. (Garcia was already familiar with Cassady's rep, having hung out in North Beach at the Co-Existence Bagel shop when he was a kid, where there were poetry readings by poets like the black surrealist Bob Kaufman.)

Cassady—who would pilot Furthur over mountain passes with a "bomber" (a fat joint) in one hand and a kazoo in the other—was a guiding influence on the MERRY PRANKSTERS. ("Cassidy [sic] gets things done," read a sign on the back of his driver's seat on the bus.) His athletic embodiment of freedom, stamina, sparking unfettered intelligence, and telepathic aptitudes in THE ZONE greatly impressed the Dead, who invited him to rap with them while they jammed at the opening of the Straight Theater on Haight Street in September of '67.

Garcia credits Cassady with changing the course of his life from graphic artist to Acid Test guitarist: "It wasn't as if he said, 'Jerry, the whole ball of wax happens here and now.' It was watching him move, having my mind blown by how deep he was, how much he could take into account in any given moment and be really in time with it. He helped us be the kind of band we are, a concert, not a studio band . . . He presented a model of how far you could take yourself with the most minimal resources. Neal had no tools. He didn't even have work. He had no focus, really. His focus was just himself and time."

Cassady was a frequent visitor to 710 Ashbury, where he would hold forth for hours in the kitchen, speedrapping on several levels at once while Weir sat reflectively, soaking it all in. Cassady was supplementing his diet of LSD with green hearts of Mexican Dexedrine, which took their toll on Cassady's powerful constitution.

Cassady was nominated to drive the Dead's equipment truck on their first cross-country tour in early '68, but by then, he had become increasingly uncommunicative and estranged from his friends. On February 3, 1968, he left the house of a young lover in San Miguel de Allende, Mexico, to pick up his "magic bag"— containing a Bible, and letters from Ginsberg and Kerouac— that he had left at the train station. He met up with a Mexican wedding party, washed down some Seconals with alcohol, and set off on a fifteen-mile walk along the railroad tracks to Celaya in a hard rain. He was found in a coma the next morning by a group of Indians, and died later that day.

The melody of "Cassidy" was composed by Weir in 1970, while Eileen Law was in labor with her daughter. The lyrics were written by Barlow two years later, as he plowed deep snow on his ranch in Wyoming, before going to a hospital in Salt Lake City to tend to his dying father.

❦ *Selections from Cassady's rap at the Straight Theater, September '67:*

I knew I should've worn more paisley. I said I'm serious about America . . . Three things I had: a flat tire, a place to stay, and a joint . . . Don't eat when you're angry. Who was ever happy angry? . . . You are all surrounded . . . The embryo, you know, goes through the fish stage, but we didn't enter until ape-late. Christ-Adam-Higher Soul help us out through so the cyclops don't win the unicorn brew. We're here to experience . . . and finally evolution the little toe. We'll beat it though—the odor of sanctity.

CAT DICTATION 📖 • One of Robert Hunter's more esoteric sources of lyrical inspiration. "A cat dictated 'China Cat Sunflower' to me," he explains. "It was just sittin' on my stomach, purring away, and sayin' this stuff. I just write it down. I guess it's plagiarism." "Talkin' Money Tree," Hunter's preamble to "Friend of the Devil" (released on Hunter's *Jack O'Roses*), has been attributed to the same feline oracle.

CAUTION: MINDS AT LARGE • Friendly warning painted onto the back of the bus "Saratoga" in the spring of '84, as a dozen or so Evergreen College students made their way around the country following the Dead and fulfilling academic contracts with Evergreen's Native American Studies program. Explains participant Leslie Gowell, "it meant that our minds were roaming, so people better beware." The journey was originally conceived as an effort to explore the state of face-to-face communication in the wake of rapid technological advances in non-face communication. "But there were so many Deadheads on the bus," Gowell says (she includes herself), "that we ended up following the spring tour."

THE CHANT 📖 • The anthem of DEADICATION: the refrain of one of the most popular Dead cover tunes, Buddy Holly's "Not Fade Away," "You know our love will not fade away."

On New Year's Eve '85, at Oakland Coliseum, leaflets were passed out in line beforehand requesting Heads to express their love for the band by chanting the refrain as the band came onstage. The band acknowledged the salute by opening the show with "Not Fade Away."

Often, if the chant is still alive when the band returns for an encore, they will sometimes go back into "Not Fade Away"— taking the handoff from the audience. *See also* WE WANT PHIL!

CHERRY GARCIA • Ben & Jerry's salute to the Great One—a designer ice cream, infused with flakes of dark chocolate and Bing cherry slivers soaked in amaretto, which made its debut in February '87. "At least they didn't name a motor oil after me," Garcia is reported to have quipped when sent a sample to taste. Half of Garcia's royalties go to the band's in-house charitable group, the REX FOUNDATION.

"Nothing really rhymed with 'Grateful' or 'Dead,'" explains Jane Williamson MacDonald, the 100-show veteran who came up with the idea in '84, in a Ben & Jerry's store on Exchange Street in Portland, Maine. "So I said, 'For me, Garcia is the heart of the band,' and within fifteen seconds, out popped 'Cherry Garcia.' We wrote it down and laughed hysterically for ten minutes, and then put it up on the suggestions board."

As luck wouldn't have it, that store burned down soon afterward, the idea literally going up in smoke. "So I sent them a postcard," MacDonald says. "But I didn't sign it. I just put a heart at the end. It was a political postcard—that's what Ben liked most about it. It was a drawing of Ronald Reagan as 'Ronnie Reggae,' with dreadlocks; it said, 'Fire up the Sky,' and there were missiles exploding everywhere."

At the behest of a friend, MacDonald phoned Ben & Jerry's headquarters to identify herself a few months after the flavor came out. "I told her who I was, and she said, 'Wait a minute—could you say that again?' I started to repeat myself, but before I finished, she put her hand over the phone and started screaming, 'I found her! I found her!' She went wild. In June, I was the guest of honor at their annual shareholders' meeting. They sent us shirts and plane tickets. I got a year's worth of ice cream. You know how Andy Warhol said everybody gets their fifteen minutes of fame? I've had *way* over fifteen minutes. This has been one of the most hysterical things I've ever experienced in my life."

In 1988, Cindy Scott, arts editor for the *California Aggie* at the University of California at Davis, took the cue and ran with it, conjuring up "Eyes Cream of the World," a fantasy ice-cream parlor with Dead flavors *only*. Some of her flavors:

Touch of Grape • Blackberry Peter • Sugar Mango • Jack Strawberry • In the Mint Chip Hour • He's Gone Bananas • Fudge Ripple • Wharf Raspberry • Gimme Some Lemon • Looks Like Rainbow (also available as Box of Rainbow) • Rocky Road to Unlimited Devotion • Beat It on Down the Lime • China Cat Sundae • Mocha Stack Lightning • Amaretto Getaway • Might as Watermelon • U.S. Blueberry • Mexicali Blueberry • Minglewood Blueberry • Walkin' Blueberry • Dupree's Diamond Blueberry • Stella Blueberry

Scott also suggests some flavors that might not go over too well in THE PARKING LOT, such as **Jack-A-Roe** (a caviar swirl), **Stagger Beet, Cucumberland Blues, Friend of the Deviled Egg,** and **Uncle John's Clam.**

Says Scott, "There'd be a choice of **Casey Cones, Sugaree,**

Throwin' Cones, or **The Other Cone. Row Jimmies** optional."

CLAMS • Blown cues, sour or flat notes.

CLOSER • 1. The last song in a set. "The first set was a short but sweet seven songs, with a 'Might As Well' closer."
2. The last show in a tour. The tender, elegiac "Brokedown Palace" has often been played as a tour closer since 1980.

CLUB FRONT • The band's nickname for their studio on Front Street in the factory district of San Rafael, where the Dead have been rehearsing since '74. The first full album recorded and mixed there was the Jerry Garcia Band album *Cats Under the Stars,* in '78. *Shakedown Street* was recorded there, and tracks for every Dead studio album since then, with the exception of *In the Dark,* recorded a couple of miles away, at the Marin Veteran's Auditorium. Front Street is also the home of THE VAULT, the Dead's tape archives.

There's no identifying sign on the outside of the building. Just inside the front door, there's a shelf of books belonging to Willy Legate, a friend of the band since the pre-WARLOCKS days, and maintenance man at Club Front—including *Hindu Manners, Consciousness Explained, The Oxford Book of Royal Anecdotes, The Beatles' Illustrated Lyrics,* and *Joe Bob Goes to the Drive-In.* (Legate's album credits don't say "janitor," but "sage.")

A sign over the door to the studio reads "Shakedown Street." Though photographs taken in the big room tend to focus on the drums or the dramatic murals on the walls, the recording area is a humble clearing surrounded by fertile clutter, with cardboard crates and equipment cases stacked to the rafters. The instruments, amps and music stands are there, on Turkish carpets thrown over the red cement floor.

Front Street is an unusually intimate place to lay down tracks, as there is no glassed-in control room, and the producer sits in the same room as the players, listening through headphones. When there are no Dead sessions in progress, the studio is used for projects like Rob Wasserman's *Trios,* and producer/engineers John Cutler, Jeffrey Norman, and Bob Bralove pursue their own inspirations there.

THE VAULT is up at the top of some wooden stairs. A collection of percussion instruments collected by Hart over the years is stashed above the roadies' rooms, one of which has a sign on it that says "M.V.P. Club, Members Only, Proper Attire Please." A five-foot buzz-saw blade Hart used as a gong on one tour rusts by that door. On the wall, there's a Marines' bumpersticker, cut to say "Marin," next to an old hotel saloon card forbidding use of the words "hell" and "damn," and a collection of license plates—THE DEAD from California, DARKSTAR from N.Y.—under a sign: "Ask for Realtor *Bob Weir.*" There's a five-foot ball of gaffer's tape among snaking cables, zipped up from the floor of every stage on the last tour—the kind of inspired goof that hardworking professionals keep around to drive themselves sane.

Club Front is not for show, but a retreat, far from the crowds, to invent and refine sounds without distraction.

🐾 *Dick Latvala, official Dead tape archivist, on being a Deadhead on the other side of the "rail":*

I came in here with a lot of naïve assumptions. I can't imagine how anyone tolerated me eight years ago, how I was. I loved the Grateful Dead, and I was a fan, and wore Dead shirts all the time. I was a *flaming* Deadhead. Working here was a process of grooming myself into a part of the machine of the Grateful Dead. I contribute to its day-to-day functionality. They may want me here because I love the music, but they don't want me here saying, 'WOW, what a great show!' "

They don't gravitate toward compliments *or* negative statements. They *work.* Everybody has a job. It's us fans that put all the mojo on it—how spiritual, how revelatory, how *transportational.* So I am of two heads. Half of me has to be immersed in that Deadhead perspective, of witnessing the magic. And half of me has to work here. Which is two opposite things.

THE COMEBACK SHOW • Garcia's triumphant return to the stage with the Dead on 12/15/86 at the Oakland Coliseum, after a three-day, near-fatal diabetic coma in July '86. He was released from Marin County hospital after a few weeks, and subsequently underwent what doctors called a remarkable recovery. With the assistance of Merl Saunders and other longtime musician friends, Garcia learned how to play guitar again. "It changed me," Garcia says about his illness. "I came out a little scrambled. It was as though all my information and my memories and everything had been dumped into the random access tank and stirred up. I haven't been able to find any huge open holes, so I don't think there's anything permanent involved. It was one of those things—a reminder of my own mortality."

The band opened the first set of the comeback show with "A Touch of Grey," the audience joining in for joyous sing-alongs on the chorus, "We will survive." During "Candyman," when Garcia sang the line, "Won't you tell everybody you meet that the candyman's in town," he raised a fist in the air, while the audience cheered. Garcia says, "There wasn't a dry eye in the house, man. It was great to be able to play again. The Grateful Dead is like nothing else. I think it was the longest we'd ever laid off. 'What's it gonna be like, what's it gonna be like?' The first night, Weir forgot maybe 80 percent of the lyrics. But the next couple of nights were great." *See* THE ICK; WE WILL SURVIVE.

THE COMMUNITY • A spiritual family that follows the East Coast tours in a double-decker bus called *Oseh Shalom* ("Peacemaker") offering free medical aid and handing out newspapers called "freepapers" as missionary work.

Though the bus is a familiar sight in the parking lot, Community members rarely venture into the hall to enjoy the show. "We're not fans of the Grateful Dead," explains Community member Simaick, "we're fans *of the fans* of the Grateful Dead." Community brothers and sisters are often referred to as "Yahshuas" by Heads, but "Yahshua"—the Hebrew name of Jesus—is used by Community members to refer only to Jesus, not to themselves.

The Community was founded in 1972 in Chattanooga, Tennessee, as the Vine Christian Community. The group began ministering to Deadheads after brother Aharon, an ex-tour-head who writes for the freepapers, suggested to Community elders that there might be "many lost brothers and sisters" among Heads.

Santa Cruz brother Michael explains how he joined the Community after being disappointed that the feeling of family that nourished him at shows was temporary: "The question has been through thousands of people's minds: Why do we have to go home after the show? Why doesn't everyone just stay together? But it's on to the next show, the next town, or back to work, or back to school—back to 'reality.' I was looking for a *life* that was beyond society, not just an experience."

The Community has about 1,000 members at centers in Island Pond in Vermont, Brazil, Ontario, and elsewhere. The brothers and sisters hold possessions in common, and believe that the hierarchy of Community elders is a reflection of the dominion of Yahshua over humankind, as is the authority of men over women in decision-making in the Community businesses, which include health food stores and futon frame shops.

The Community frowns on psychedelics as a means of spiritual search. "LSD is like a tornado," Aharon explains. "People do it because they're trapped in spiritual death. You can't claw your way out of Adam's casket. Love is the life that people are looking for."

"Yahshua is our teacher, and we hear Him in one another, from the least to the greatest," says Aharon. "How wise a person is, is how well they listen."

COMPLETISM VS. PERFECTIONISM • An ongoing debate among Deadheads about whether the Dead should treat its live releases as untouchable documentations of history, preserving the original events precisely as they occurred ("completism"), or—in the case of a recording with technical glitches, out-of-tune instrumentation, or rhythmic unevenness—edit or amend performances to produce a "perfected" piece of music.

"A song, a set and a show are all entities unto themselves," argues Walter Keeler. "To subdivide any of them unnecessarily is to sacrifice the integrity of the whole."

Dick Latvala, keeper of THE VAULT, argues the perfectionist stance. "It became apparent to me and John Cutler and Jeffrey

Norman that each CD should have a life of its own," he explained about his work assembling DICK'S PICKS, VOLUME ONE. "This isn't an attempt to recapture the total picture of the total show. It's *a* picture, an entity of its own. So the first disc has the feel of a first set, but you'll notice that 'Weather Report Suite' is thrown in there though it is actually from a second set." (There is also a two-minute splice in "Weather Report Suite" because of a gap in the source tape.)

Both sides admit that hot spots in a show may not come alive on tape, while a flat note barely noticed in concert will stand out loud and clear. But for completists, there is the "integrity of the whole," as Keeler puts it—meaning, most broadly, the evolution of the band's career as a whole, which includes "mistakes."

CONSTANTEN, TOM (T.C.) • Keyboards. Born March 19, 1944, in Long Branch, New Jersey.

Constanten joined the Dead in November '68, adding his piano, organ, harpsichord, and taped electronic music to the band's sound at a time when the music was its most experimental, the era of ANTHEM OF THE SUN, LIVE/DEAD, and AOXOMOXOA. It's Constanten's warm, filigreed organ that drives toward the crescendo after the first verse of the *Live/Dead* "Dark Star," and his bright, calliope-like sound adds an element of festivity and humor (while staying in outer space) to "China Cat Sunflower" and "Dupree's Diamond Blues" on *Aoxomoxoa*. Constanten had the widest range of musical reference of anyone who has ever occupied the Dead's keyboard HOT SEAT.

Constanten met Lesh in the fall of '61, while they were both students at the University of California at Berkeley, where Constanten was not studying music, but astronomy. (At the founding meeting of Constanten's astronomy club in Las Vegas, the proto-psychedelic rapper Lord Buckley had shown up and gamely suggested calling the club the "Star Diggers.") Lesh introduced Constanten to his friends in the South Bay—Garcia, Hunter, Willy Legate, and Bobby Petersen. T.C. (as his friends call him) and Lesh shared a love for the new music that was being made by living composers like John Cage, Stockhausen,

Schoenberg, and the energetic and influential Terry Riley, with whom Constanten had improvised variations on Bach in his home studio. Another composer the two young *avant gardistes* adored was Luciano Berio, who was teaching at Mills College nearby. Lesh and Constanten enrolled.

The apartment shared by the two became, in Constanten's words, "an avant-garde music factory." While Lesh composed a concerto for four orchestras playing simultaneously, called *Foci,* T.C. applied his efforts to *Three Pieces for Two Pianos*—to be played by *one* pianist. Lesh and Constanten were riding personal crests of creativity coinciding with a flourishing of new culture—what Ken Kesey termed "the Neon Renaissance"—in bohemian enclaves all over the Bay Area, and in places like Greenwich Village in New York, where a young folk singer named Bob Dylan was playing the Gaslight Café. When Berio invited his two promising students to tour Europe with him, Constanten went along.

T.C. rejoined Lesh, and the ongoing renaissance, in the summer of '63, and continued developing his compositions. In '65, T.C. avoided the draft by enlisting in the Air Force. He'd hoped to be stationed at Hamilton AFB—next to the Dead's rehearsal hall—but was sent to Nevada. T.C. saw the Dead at California Hall on Memorial Day '66, and "it was clear that the guys were having the time of their lives." T.C. added his prepared keyboards and taped electronics to *Anthem of the Sun.* Instead of the "one, two, three" that kicks off most recording sessions, Robert Hunter would recite sections of James Joyce's *Finnegans Wake* by heart.

Pigpen and T.C. roomed together on the road, playing chess, but T.C. had a harder time contributing to the music onstage than he did in the studio. Plagued by undependable equipment, repossessed instruments, "my dynamic range consisted of *triple forte* and *double forte,* and [anything below that] inaudible," he lamented in his autobiography, *Between Rock & Hard Places.* "I began to suspect that some of the band members themselves didn't have that clear an idea of the keyboard's role in a guitar band context."

Though, as T.C. writes, "it was gratifying for Jerry to tell me to play 'more like a source and less like a sideman,'" from Lesh's perspective, his friend "never got over a certain stiffness." T.C. left the band after a show in Honolulu on January 26, 1970 (with at least one guest appearance on April 28, 1971, at the Fillmore East, sitting in for the second set).

T.C. teaches piano in the Bay Area, and performs solo and in ensembles. He has remained a prolific composer and a witty and vital performer. Constanten was commissioned by Robert Moran, along with Philip Glass and Virgil Thomson, to compose a contemporary piano waltz for Moran's Waltz Project. His contribution, "Déjavalse," was given high praise by critics when the recording was released in '81, and again in '88, when Peter Martins used it for an inventive new ballet of the same name. T.C. continues to shine in diverse musical contexts, from rock bands like Zero, Merl Saunders's Rainforest Band, and Dead Ringers (with members of Kingfish and New Riders founder David Nelson), and on his own recordings, which include solo variations on DARK STAR and other Dead tunes. From '86 on, T.C. was the house pianist on Sedge Thomson's innovative, eclectic radio show *West Coast Weekend.*

Constanten's memoir, *Between Rock & Hard Places,* was published by HULOGOSI PRESS in 1992.

A selected Tom Constanten discography:

U—the Incredible String Band (Constanten composes and play piano); Elektra, 1970

Tarot—Music from the off-Broadway play *Tarot;* United Artists, 1972

The Electric Guitar Quartet—(Constanten composed "Alaric's Premonition, A Gothic Fugue en Rondeau on a Theme by J. Garcia"); EGQ Cassettes, 1983

Fresh Tracks in Real Time—Includes "Dark Star," "Cold Rain and Snow," "Hesitation Blues," and others; home release, 1989

Heart's Desire—The Henry Kaiser Band. Includes Tom Constanten on a live version of "Dark Star"; Reckless Records, March 1990

OutSides—Includes "Electronic Study #3," which was used in the track "We Leave the Castle" on *Anthem of the Sun;* home release, November 1990

Nightfall of Diamonds — Includes "Dark Star"; Relix Records, 1992

Duino Elegies — Rainer Maria Rilke, translated from German by Robert Hunter. Block prints by Maureen Hunter. This was released as a joint paperback/tape edition: On the forty-minute-long tape, Hunter reads with Tom Constanten's accompaniment on piano of pieces by Brahms, Chopin, and Scriabin; Hulogosi Press, 1988

COSMIC CHARLIE CAMPAIGN • *See* REVIVAL.

COUNTERFEIT TICKETS • A longtime problem for the band — 2,000 counterfeits turned up at the opening of New York City's FILLMORE EAST in '68 — and for Heads, who may spend $50 on a "fittie," only to be turned away at the door.

GRATEFUL DEAD TICKET SALES is involved in a constant battle to stay one technological step ahead of counterfeiters. "Glitter" tickets, tickets on thermal or layered paper, and ultraviolet inks have all been mimicked successfully by counterfeiters.

Sophisticated counterfeits can be difficult to detect, as 200-show vet Tony Beers found out the hard way one night in Chapel Hill in '93. "This one was a work of art," Tony marvels. "A counterfeit mail order with all the sprinkles. It looked great. I've been around the scene for twenty years, and *this* was a real ticket. But I was burned." The only surefire protection against counterfeits is for Heads to buy tickets only via mail order, or through legitimate (if pricey) ticket services (*see* TICKETBASTARD).

As of the late '80s, Steve Marcus, the head of Grateful Dead Ticket Sales, has set up a ticket verification table in the parking lot, so that anyone buying a ticket in the lot can bring the ticket in question to Marcus himself for examination. (Those trying to sell an authentic ticket should have no problem with this request.) *See also* SCALPERS.

🗝 *Steve Marcus, of Grateful Dead Ticket Sales, on counterfeits:*

There have been counterfeits from the very beginning. I got hired by Bill Graham Presents in '77 to check for counterfeits at the Days on the Green. It really got hairy after the "Day of the Dead" on MTV. On New Year's of '87, we confiscated over 300 fake tickets. My personal feeling is that it's organized crime. If we play three shows in a city, and one show gets hit, and we confiscate 1,500 counterfeits at $30 to $50 dollars a pop—and that happens ten times—that's $350,000. I think one organization does the whole tour.

The FBI got involved in '91, and there was a big bust. They busted the place a week before the Giants Stadium shows, and they had tickets on the press. Some of the main people who led to that bust were scalpers who called me up and said, "How can I help you? They're ruining my business."

COWBOY SONGS • Tunes from the range—"Mexicali Blues," "Me & My Uncle," "El Paso," and others—that Weir often plays as the fourth or fifth song of the first set. This portion of the set is sometimes known as the "cowboy slot." *See* DYLAN SLOT; the JERRY BALLAD SLOT.

🍃 *John Barlow, lyricist, on cowboy "Ace" Weir:*
The first thing I wrote for Weir was "Mexicali Blues." He was in a cowboy phase, doing "El Paso" and "Big River," and dressing up and thinking of himself as some kind of a cowboy. So I thought, "Well, I'll write him a cowboy song."

There was something that Weir found very appealing about the cowboy. His cowboy thing is about the mythical cowboy, not the real cowboy. He'd *seen* the real thing, but when he was on my ranch in '62, he was never a cowboy. He was a tractor driver. He was around some cowboys, and he dug them, but I don't think his cowboy thing came from that. There was a huge cowboy thing going on inside the Grateful Dead culture, largely the result of a major cowboy influx in the road crew—Rex Jackson, Ram Rod, and all these guys from Pendleton—and, to a certain extent, me.

CRANKING • 1. Playing hard. "Phil was *cranking.*"

2. Turning up the volume. "Crank this 'Sugaree'—it smokes."

3. To play or copy tapes tirelessly. "Let's crank THE KILLS."

CREDIT CARD HIPPIES • *See* TRUSTAFARIANS.

CRISP; CRISPY • 1. Said admiringly of ultra-"clean" tapes, usually soundboards, with no hiss, no saturation, no distortion, or other unwanted noise. "Those Veneta BETTYBOARDS are so *crisp!*"

2. A crisp show or set is distinguished by superb sound and intense playing.

3. Also said of people who have maybe had "too much too

fast" of tour and hotel-room activities. "A *crispy* critter looks
like Timmy when he was flung from the electric fence in *Juras-
sic Park,* and the paleontologist said, 'Timmy, you look like a
piece of toast.' "

CRUNCHY • *n.* "A crunchy is a '90s hippie," says Scott
Blasik, a young poet from Durham, New Hampshire. "A hik-
ing-boot-wearing, granola-eating, Grateful Dead/Blues Traveler–listening type of person. Kids don't say 'hippie' around
here anymore."

"Crunchy" is also used as an adjective, especially with "gra-
nola," which means the same as "crunchy"—earthy, unslick.
Similarly, "D.T.E."—"down to earth."

THE CURSE • Garcia's tongue-in-cheek term for the
surge in Deadhead interest in a musician after he or she performs with the Dead. "You've got the curse," Garcia joked to
Bruce Hornsby when Hornsby started to notice a big influx of
Heads at his own shows—"They'll never leave."

For the majority of these musicians, the curse is actually a
blessing. "We love it when the Deadhead crowd comes to our
show," says Hornsby. "It makes for a more boisterous show."
The scores of soloists and ensembles who have ventured onstage with the Dead might agree:

A partial list:

Duane & Gregg Allman • Joan Baez • The Beach Boys • John
Belushi • Jack Casady • Neal Cassady • John Cipollina •
Clarence Clemons • Billy Cobham • Ornette Coleman • David
Crosby • Dirty Dozen Brass Band • Gary Duncan • Bob Dylan •
Hamza El Din • Ramblin' Jack Elliot • Martin Fierro • Bela Fleck •
John Fogerty • Peter Green • David Grisman • Daryl Hall •
David Hidalgo • Zakir Hussain • Etta James • Janis Joplin •
Jorma Kaukonen • Matthew Kelly • Ken Kesey • Kitaro • Huey
Lewis • Charles Lloyd • Branford Marsalis • Airto Moreira •
Maria Muldaur • David Murray • Neville Brothers • New Riders of
the Purple Sage • Ken Nordine • Baba Olatunji • Buffalo Philhar-
monic Orchestra • John Popper • Flora Purim • Bonnie Raitt •

Carlos Santana • Boz Scaggs • Grace Slick • Stephen Stills • Mick Taylor • Tower of Power horns • Pete Townshend • Suzanne Vega • Steve Winwood • Chris Wood • Neil Young

D-5 ☜ • Short for Sony TCD-5M, a highly sophisticated portable analog recording tape deck which, up until the advent of DAT (digital audio tape), was the Deadhead taper's deck of choice. Many of the "crispy" AUDIENCE TAPES in circulation were originally spun on D-5s.

In the early '90s, the first portable DAT players came onto the market, and were embraced by many tapers as the next step up in taping, with no FLIP necessary and no loss of fidelity during copying. *See* DAT.

DANCING BEARS • A Deadhead icon popularized by Jonathan Marks's Grateful Graphics, a vendor of t-shirts and other merchandise since 1985. Marks's distinctive design—five bears in a row, each in a different posture of jubilation—were adapted from Bob Thomas's cover art for the album *Bear's Choice*, which may have been modeled after bears printed on blotter acid manufactured by OWSLEY, also called "Bear." Other companies, such as Liquid Blue, have also marketed t-shirts and bumperstickers with bears.

"I'll never forget the day in 1985 that I rolled out of my waterbed, and my first thought was that I'd always wanted a dancing bear shirt," Marks recalls. With help from friends, Marks silkscreened and handpainted ninety shirts, went to a show at Hampton Coliseum, and sold fifty shirts in the first hour.

"It was a phenomenal acceptance of a new icon," says Marks. "The skeleton and skull imagery had been proliferating for a long time, and the bears gave people a chance to show their Deadhead colors in shirts that didn't offend or exclude anyone who couldn't make the Dead connection." After Marks placed an ad in THE GOLDEN ROAD, his shirts became extremely popular.

After Peter Barsotti and Jan Simmons of Bill Graham Presents emblazoned one of Marks's bears on a flag at Cal Expo, the bears started appearing on GDTS mail-order tickets and on official Grateful Dead merchandise, and Grateful Graphics is now a licensee of Grateful Dead Mercantile. The bears danced from official into unofficial Deadhead iconography and back.

Grateful Graphics sells its cheerful wares to Deadheads and non-Deadheads all over the world, including Japan, where they are sold at two stores called Bear's Choice. "The bears are my children," Marks says. "Even the one in the middle, just standing there, is saying that it's OK just to be still, and it's also OK to flip your arms and legs and have a ball. If you wake up in the morning and look in your drawer and you have these bears looking up at you, and a black t-shirt, chances are you're going to want to put on something more positive. I want the exuberance of these bears to live forever, as timeless as the music."

DARK STAR • The first collaboration between lyricist Robert Hunter and the Dead, written while the band woodshedded in Rio Nido, north of San Francisco on the Russian River, during the summer of '67.

"It was the first time I'd seen them in some time, and they were working on 'Dark Star,' and I just started writing words for it then," Hunter recalls. "That's when it became obvious to all of us that the collaboration was going to work." (Hunter cites the poetry of T.S. Eliot as an influence on the haunting lyric.)

"Dark Star" is considered by many Heads to be the ultimate Grateful Dead song, but the word "song" doesn't do it justice. "Dark Star" is more an approach, a platform for exploration, a gate swinging open to THE ZONE.

🦋 *Jim Powell, poet and translator, on the history of "Dark Star":*

"Dark Star" is the kernel of wide open possibility at the core of the Dead's repertoire, the essential seed promising unlimited intergalactic space journeys at the speed of total mindwarp: "Shall we go,/you and I/while we can?" It is the most exploratory of Dead tunes and it is the trippiest, the one where the acidic whistle of the dark interstices is heard most starkly, where you might turn any corner and step off into the void. It is the Dead's spirit of musical adventure at its strangest, wildest, most vehement, weirdest, dreamiest, and the place where the leading wave of the Dead's music is most often audible being created in mid-air.

Or it *was* the place, from December '67 through October '74, and again from October '89 through at least '91. The earliest "Dark Star" tapes circulating are from a studio session in Los Angeles on 11/14/67. The Warner Bros. single "Dark Star" probably comes from this; it consists of a brief instrumental intro, the first stanza ("Dark star crashes . . ."), a twenty-second instrumental jam on the theme, the second stanza ("Mirror shatters . . ."), and a quick instrumental fade. The first live version circulating (Crystal Ballroom, Portland, Oregon 2/3/68) is nearly twice as long. The evolution of "Dark Star" consists in the elaboration of these two spaces for jamming, one before the first vocals and the other after. The tune's first maturity is audible in the version on *Live/Dead* [FILLMORE WEST 2/27/69]. The first jam inclines to stay fairly close to the "Dark Star" theme, while the second tends to involve impromptu jams on other themes as well. The jamming after the first vocals also tends to move further out into space (by "space" here I mean a passage where there is no steady beat or key or riff, but instead metamorphosing noises coexisting in a less linear or directional, more multidimensional sound space).

As "Dark Star" continues its evolution after *Live/Dead*, the first jam becomes more adventurous, more oblique and fragmentary in its relations with the "Dark Star" theme, while the second absorbs new jams ("Feelin' Groovy" jam, "Mind Left Body" jam, Allmans jam, "The Tiger," "Insect Dread," "Martian Blues," countless unnamed others) and drives ever further into Deep Space and Total Weirdness. The second vocals fall out of regular use after '71, replaced by the emergence of other songs at the far end of space jams reaching ever outward. By '72, other jams and spaces sometimes occur before the first vocals as well as after. The pace of 1970 "Dark Stars" is markedly slower than '69's, and in '73 it slows down even more, resulting in the dreamy "Dark Stars" of October through December '73. "Dark Star" is also the largest scale work in the Dead's repertoire, and between '72 and '74 it sometimes reaches truly monumental proportions. The longest known is Civic Hall, Rotterdam 5/11/72 (48:38).

The Dead played "Dark Star" five times between '75 and '84, but the results must not have been encouraging or the signs inauspicious, since nothing came of these isolated versions. But on 10/9/89 at the Hampton Coliseum, they began a revival which has enjoyed better fortune. (Nearly anybody on the bus at the time can tell you where they were when they heard the news.) These new "Dark Stars" return to the basic architecture of the original version (usually without the second vocals), but they haven't yet begun to absorb other jams much, tending to go off into Drums →Space instead. They are most remarkable for the effects of MIDI, which has opened innumerable and astonishing new dimensions for exploration. Since '91, however, the Dead seem to work on the leading wave of their music more in space than in "Dark Star."

DAT 🎞 • Digital audio tape, a late '80s technological boon to tapers, who instantly embraced the technology and began snapping up Sony D-3s (later, D-7s), declaring them the successors to the legendary analog D-5. DAT technology all but eliminates hiss, by recording a stream of on-off pulses rather than an electronic facsimile of the sound waves. For tape traders, this introduces the radical notion that a high-generation tape—a "hi-gen," the previously undesirable copy of a copy of a copy of a copy of a copy—will be essentially the same tape as the first dub off the master. Consequently, some of the politics of tape trading—networking for closer access to the source tapes—is made more democratic, with social hierarchies mattering less, and the development of efficient means of disseminating more or less equal quality tapes mattering more (*see* TREES AND VINES).

DAT decks are also more suited to Dead shows because their continuous running time is two hours, eliminating the stressful FLIP. Tapers can "set and forget," leave their decks, wander, and even dance.

DAY OF THE DEAD • *See* TOUCHHEADS.

DAY OFF • The travel day between shows, for both band and fans. For tourheads, it is a day to sleep late, eat, update TOURBOOKS, read, bathe, and *drive.*

Garcia has said that all he needs is one day off a week, and that in an ideal world he'd be playing six gigs weekly: two with the Dead, two with the Jerry Garcia Band, and two playing with an acoustic group like the Black Mountain Boys.

DBA • "Dead Buddhists of America," a group formed by Ken Sundowner "for those distinguished individuals appreciating Grateful Dead and Buddhist cultures and meditation." Sundowner also edits the DBA newsletter, *The Conch-Us Times.* One sample issue features a review of the Chinese New Year's shows, the passing of His Eminence Jamgon Kongtrul Rinpoche, the Food and Drug Administration's drive to limit over-the-counter dietary supplements, and word that Garcia was dating a Tibetan Buddhist. "If we must be labeled," writes Sundowner, "we prefer to call ourselves Dead Buddhistheads."

♣ *Dogen Zenji, first Japanese Zen patriarch, on enlightenment:*

To study the self is to forget the self. To forget the self is to be enlightened by all things.

♣ *Jerry Garcia, guitarist, on getting high:*

To get really high is to forget yourself. To forget yourself is to see everything else. To see everything else is to become an understanding molecule in evolution, a conscious tool of the universe . . . I'm not talking about unconscious or zonked out. I'm talking about being fully conscious.

DEAD AIR • A Grateful Dead radio show that went on the air in the early '80s, originally on Dan Healy's own radio station in Garberville, California, KERG. Much appreciated by Deadheads in the Pacific Northwest, the show is hosted by Dead extended-family member Downtown Deb, and features soundboard tapes and tour information. Since '86, it has been broadcast on KLCC-FM in Eugene, Oregon.

DEAD BOARDS • Electronic bulletin board systems (BBS), accessible by personal computer and modem, run by and for Heads to share information and ideas.

Tape traders and other Heads ravenous for information have come to depend on these boards, local and national, which have timely and reliable upcoming tour info, as well as recent SETLISTS and show reports. They also serve as a haven for exchange of ideas, rumors, jokes, and gripes. There are more than a dozen of these boards scattered throughout the country, including Brian Davidson's "Sugar Magnolia BBS," Klaus Bender's "Dead Board," and James Scofield's "Terrapin Station," which has approximately 650 users. (A list of known boards with modem access numbers appears in *APPENDIX III: HOW TO BECOME A NETHEAD.) See also* DEAD-FLAMES; NET-HEADS; THE WELL.

DEAD DREAMS 📖 • "Hasn't everybody had them?" asks Gwyn McVay. Dreams are the ultimate venue, in which Heads finally get to meet the bandmembers, have dinner—or share a joint—with them, hear rare or never-before-played tunes, or play in the band themselves.

There's a familiar closeness between Heads and the band that can't exist in waking life, with bandmembers often offering advice or direction.

🍃 *Zack Kasprzak's cheese dream:*

It was the soundcheck. I was up in the stands on Jerry's side, and there were people hanging out and smoking pot. The band came out and started tapping their mics and playing with MIDI boxes and stuff. I was leaning over the rail and, at the top of my lungs, screamed, "Phil likes cheese on his cauliflower!" Bobby yelled back, "Hey, you in the stands, that was rude and uncalled for."

Phil says, "Know what? I *do* like cheese on my cauliflower. And if you can guess what kind, I'll see to it that you get tickets for the rest of the tour." So I yell, "CHEDDAR!" "WRONG!" retorts Phil. "I'm partial to Monterey Jack." I guess I'm just JONESIN' for a show.

DEADBASE • The complete guide to setlists from every show the band has played, compiled and annotated by John Scott, Mike Dolgushkin, and Stu Nixon. Known among tapers, tourheads, and members of the Dead organization as "the Bible."

An invaluable resource to tape traders and scholars, the first edition of *DeadBase* was published in 1987. With successive editions, the scope of *DeadBase* has widened beyond setlists to include a complete catalog of the composers and all recorded versions of every song the Dead have performed (thirteen pages in *DeadBase VI)*, a discography, venue statistics, and detailed recollections of shows by Dick Latvala, Blair Jackson, Rob Bertrando (one of the first tapers), and many others. *DeadBase* has also begun annotating lyrics by content, noting the recurrences of certain images like "reptiles" ("Alligator," "Mister Charlie," "Fire on the Mountain," etc.) and "eyes" ("Eyes of the World," "Alabama Getaway," "Weather Report Suite," and thirty-three others.)

DeadBase began as editor John Scott's graduate-school term project in computer science. Scott met with band spokesperson Dennis McNally at Cumberland County Civic Center in '86 to get official approval for the project, and McNally put Scott in touch with database expert Stu Nixon, and with Mike Dolgushkin, who had been compiling his own meta-list from friends' lists since '73. Dick Latvala offered assistance, and Lesh championed the project at a band meeting. Keeping *Dead-Base* up to date is a sixty-to-eighty-hour-a-week job for Scott, who supplements the hard info with diversions like computer recombinations of words like "Grateful Dead" ("regulated fad," "dreadful gate").

DeadBase sells out its "big book" editions of six thousand copies, and also offers smaller annual editions of the year's shows and notes. An important addition to later editions of *DeadBase* is a Deadhead survey section, listing the results of questionnaires sent out to readers on everything from favorite tapes (5/2/70, 5/8/77, 3/29/90, 2/13/70, and so on) to favorite after-show activities (food, beer, sleep, party, sex, etc.). "Our aggregate Deadhead is 31.1 years old," says *DeadBase VI,* "having attended 69.6 shows, owning 617 hours of Dead on tape, and a $2,308.05 stereo system to play them on."

🐌 *John Barlow, lyricist, on* DeadBase:

It's like baseball statistics. There is this feeling that if you can get on top of all the statistical information, you can understand it. Also, Deadheads know

on an instinctive level that it's them that control the setlists and the song order. The Dead really don't know what they're going to play before they go
on. It really is the GROUPMIND that guides that.

DEAD-FLAMES • An electronic mail digest of the In-
ternet-wide electronic discussion group, also called "rec.mu-
sic.gdead," read by approximately 70,000 NETHEADS online.

Though "flame" in Net-speak means merciless criticism,
Dead-Flames is not all incendiary dissent. Its virtue is that it is
everything — song lists, tour schedules, ticket "grovels," rumors,
questions, band history, tribal philosophy, debates about Weir's
new guitar, best or worst venues, hottest versions of songs — all
cascading past the reader's eye in five or six batches of new
postings every day. (When the conversation strays *too* far from
the "subject," Netheads remind each other to heed the ODC:
the "obligatory Dead content.") If The WELL is an ongoing salon, polite and scholarly, Dead-Flames is what the thought-
reading angels in *Wings of Desire* would hear if they walked
through the parking lot at a show.

Dead-Flames is the rowdy great-grandchild of an online
mailing list for Heads in the '70s kept by Paul Martin, who was
working at the Stanford Artificial Intelligence lab. By the time
Usenet came online in late '79, the new keepers of the list were
getting swamped with postings. The list keepers split over what
constituted relevant mailings, and the result was two different
lists: Dead-Flames and Dead-Heads. Dead-Flames was also
called "Jerrys-breakfast" (its tongue-in-cheek description was,
"Discussion of what Jerry Garcia eats for breakfast"), to dis-
tinguish it from Dead-Heads, which described itself as "Just
the tix, ma'm."

When the Usenet music newsgroup filled up with Dead-related postings, the "gods" of the Net were persuaded (by a
Deadhead "philibuster") to create the first Deadhead village in
cyberspace: the original net.music.gdead, which became
rec.music.gdead and was linked with Dead-Flames and Dead-
Heads a year later. *See also* DEADBOARDS, THE WELL.

DEAD FREAKS UNITE! • Before there were DEAD-
HEADS, there were "Dead Freaks," early fans of the band in-

vited to join a mailing list on the inside cover of the 1971 live album SKULL AND ROSES. "Dead freaks unite. Who are you? Where are you? How are you? Send us your name and address and we'll keep you informed."

According to Eileen Law, who took charge of the mailing list in '71, the "Dead Freaks" ad was a last-minute insert. Garcia and ICE NINE PUBLISHING lexicographer Alan Trist soon preferred the phrase "Dead Head."

(The word "freak" was used by the original hippies, who hated the word "hippie." In theater circles in the nineteenth century, "freak" meant an actor who took a part in a second-rate show. By 1967, London journalist Robert Pitman was writing in the *Daily Express* about "these curious way-out events, simulating drug ecstasies, which are known as 'freakouts,' in which girls writhe and shriek and young men roll themselves naked in paint or jelly.")

Though "Dead Head" has been the "official" term since the printing of a second mailing list invitation in *Europe '72*, some Heads still prefer the term "Dead Freak."

"For better or worse," says Deadhead discographer Ihor Slabicky, "I still think of myself as a Dead Freak. 'Deadhead' to me sounds too mellow, too laid-back, and does not reflect the intensity of my involvement with the Dead."

🐾 *Steve Brown, Round Records employee, on "Dead Freaks":*

"Freak" was used in '68 and '69 for those really outrageous people who'd come modestly dabbling in the Mod era in '66 and '67, and become full-blown grizzly. The term "Dead Freak" had a hard edge to it, because of the harder edge in society at the time. It was a slightly scary term, for the followers of this particularly notorious, *illegal* band [the Dead were busted for possession of marijuana at 710 Ashbury on October 2, '67]. It was worn with the same pride that a biker might take in earning a certain color. A lot of the edge came because they had Pigpen in the front. As much as everybody loved Jerry's guitar, the image that stuck in everyone's mind was Pigpen. Here was a guy from the bar or the garage, who was out there doing this gutsy, bluesy stuff, and railing the audience in a way the band has never had since. "Hippie" didn't describe Pigpen. Pigpen was a freak.

DEAD HEADS' DIRECTORY • In 1983, Phil Davidson and David Michelson made an early effort to compile a directory of Heads' names and addresses "to aid Deadheads traveling long distances to Dead shows." The *Directory* came with a plea that a listing in its pages was "not an open invitation for house guests!"

DEAD IN WORDS • The short-lived "Southern-based Dead newsletter," a periodical for tapers published in Chapel Hill, North Carolina, in '73. One of the earliest Dead-related periodicals published by fans, the magazine sold out to *Dead Relix* after one or two issues. (*The Olompali Sunday Times*, published by the Dead family, preceded them both.)

The centerfold of the first issue was dedicated to a "Grateful Dead convention" planned for the weekend of July 5 and 6 of that year. "There has been one Grateful Dead appreciation class," advised the editors, "held at King Niles' Invisible University, and featuring the best of his extensive collection of Dead tapes." *See* RELIX.

THE DEAD IN YOUR HEAD 📖 • For many Heads, the music becomes the soundtrack of life, even when they are unable to play tapes. Certain songs, such as "Tennessee Jed" and "Ramble on Rose," have rhythms that synch up with an easy loping stride, making each step a dance at the show that never ends. "It happens a lot when I'm hiking," says Texan Head Barney Issen. "The song in my head changes as my pace changes. Slow songs like 'He's Gone' when I'm climbing steep slopes; faster ones like 'One More Saturday Night' when going downhill."

"The Dead's music is a vibrational plane that certain people are able to attune themselves to, and resonate with," says John Dwork, editor of *Dupree's Diamond News*. "For Deadheads, the constant subvocal recitation of songs is akin to Tibetan chanting of a mantra."

DEAD SET • Album #18, released August 1981.

This is the electric sister-album to the acoustic RECKONING, each culled from live material recorded at shows in September/October '80 at the Warfield Theater in San Francisco and New York City's Radio City Music Hall.

🍀 *Roy Kreitner on **Dead Set:***

As a historical document, this album works. The song selection faithfully reflects the period (no one-timers or breakouts), and the performances register a time of transition for the band: while "Passenger" has an even, rolling, '70s-rock feel, with all the sections bleeding into one another, "Feel Like a Stranger" has that snaky groove and abruptness that foreshadowed a funkier sound to come in the '80s. Garcia's voice is also in transition—from his boyish crooner's voice, crying sweetly on "Loser," to a new gruffness coming through on much of his backup singing.

Dead Set also serves up a nice mix, treating Deadheads to a crystal-clear sampling of every instrument and every voice, including backups (listen for Mydland on "Stranger" and everybody on "Passenger"). Weir's guitar—the most underrated sound in the band, and the one most often obscured on recordings—comes through extraordinarily well (listen for rhythm changes on "Friend of the Devil"). Lesh's and Mydland's playing also come through distinctly. The only weakness here is the drums, which sound muffled for most of the album, with the exception of "Greatest Story."

My assessment of the album's musicality is less upbeat. Maybe it's the inorganic setlist, maybe the severe editing of some of the tunes and transitions ("Friend of the Devil" was cut by about 25 percent). Clearly, this album doesn't do justice to the band in general and to that year in specific, as compared with other tapes I've heard from that period. The X-FACTOR ain't here. And while "Loser" and "Fire on the Mountain" are gems, most of the other tunes fall a bit flat ("Little Red Rooster" being especially sleepy). "Brokedown Palace," the final cut, can be seen as a microcosm of the album: Sweetly sung, the playing never takes any risks and consequently doesn't take us very far either.

DEAD SLED • *See* DEADMOBILE.

DEAD THREADS • Show wear. Dressing for shows is like dressing for sport. Versatility is key: layers (it's cold in the parking lot, hot on the rail) and freedom of mobility (spacedancing in a binding brassiere is no party). T-shirts bought in the parking lot acquire sentimental value as they are worn to more and more shows.

DEADER-THAN-THOU SYNDROME 📖 • The temptation to try to one-up other Heads with esoteric knowledge of band history, ability to recite SETLISTS from memory, call the opener, remember lyrics better than the singers, or predict which color guitar Weir will come out with after SPACE.

🐾 *The final word from Eileen Law, liaison between the band and Dead Heads:*

We get some funny letters, where kids will say, "My friend says that I am not a true Dead Head, because I haven't gone to enough shows." That's *awful.* They have their own little game among themselves. And I always write back, "As far as I know, to be a true Dead Head, all you need to do is be on our mailing list. I'll put you on. You're now a Dead Head!"

DEADHEAD • Someone who loves — and draws meaning from — the music of the Grateful Dead and the experience of Dead shows, and builds community with others who feel the same way.

The earliest meanings of the word "deadhead" predate the Grateful Dead by centuries, but have intriguing resonances. The original Latin term, *caput mortuum,* was used by alchemists to describe the residue "remaining after the distillation or sublimation of any substance, 'good for nothing but to be flung away, all vertue being extracted.' " By the mid-1850s, a "deadhead" had become "one who travels free, hence eats free, or, especially, goes free to a place of entertainment." An 1883 review of Donizetti's opera *Lucia di Lammermoor* panned it by saying it was so "stale," even "the most confirmed deadhead" wouldn't try to scam in to the Opera House. "Deadheadism" was the practice of letting people into a show for free, and in 1860, Oliver Wendell Holmes wrote that one of his characters "had been 'dead-headed' into the world some fifty years ago, and had sat with his hands in his pockets staring at the show ever since." (SPACEDANCING was still one hundred years away.)

There is some debate among Heads as to whether being a Deadhead is a lifestyle, a set of progressive social values, a religion, or strictly a musical preference. To Eileen Law, the official liaison between the fans and the band, being a Deadhead means one thing: being on the Dead Head's mailing list, an effort to keep Deadheads and the Dead in touch with one another that she has tended with care since '71. The DEAD FREAKS UNITE! campaign elicited 350 letters; by '74, the Office had gotten 40,000. With the help of Mary Ann Mayer, Law sent out a series of Dead Head Newsletters to those on the list, playful communiqués from the band and family that kept fans informed about tour schedules and record releases.

When the Dead took a year off in '75, most of the Office staff was laid off, including Law, who was sorry to note that a huge batch of Dead Head mail was just coming in. The list was maintained by the short-lived Grateful Dead Records, and when the band went back on the road in '76, Law was offered her job back. There was a "Dead Heads Only" tour of SMALL HALLS in the late '70s, with tickets available by mail order. The original list has grown to 71,000 names in this country, and has never given out or sold to other organizations. Mailings fell off during the '80s. The spirit of the newsletters has been resurrected by Grateful Dead Mercantile's Gary Lambert, who edits a combination merchandising catalog and informative newsletter called *The Grateful Dead Almanac.*

The Dead-related meaning of "deadhead" is beginning to infiltrate standard dictionaries. "A follower of the Grateful Dead rock group" is meaning number 3 in the National Textbook Company's 1993 edition of the *Dictionary of American Slang and Colloquial Expressions,* with these examples of usage: "What do these deadheads see in that group?" and "My son is a deadhead and travels all over listening to these guys."

🐞 *Blair Jackson on Deadheads:*

I wish I had a dollar for every person I've met who said, "I like the Grateful Dead, but I'm not a Deadhead," as if the word "Deadhead" was a synonym for "leper." That's because these people have bought into the straight media's portrayal of Deadheads as stoned, tie-dye-wearing, VW-van-driving, stringy-haired, patchouli-scented, weirdly-named, monosyllabic crazies who sell veggie burritos and crystals. Of course there actually *are* a fair number of Deadheads who fit that description, but anyone who bothers to look even the slightest bit beneath the Day-Glo veneer finds so much more: doctors and dentists and lawyers and geologists, students, computer programmers, jocks, jewelers, organic farmers, Congressional aides, teachers.

It's not really accurate to say that the Deadhead world is like a microcosm of the Real World, because the surface anarchy of the scene is so threatening to so many people, that you instantly have to eliminate 98 percent of the general population from any possibility of embracing the Dead, much less calling themselves Deadheads.

It's not about how many shows you've been to, or how many stickers you have on your car, or whether you know when the band last played "The Eleven." You don't have to know the lyrics to every Dead song (the band messes 'em up half the time anyway), you don't have to own a Nakamichi Dragon tape deck, or even have been to a show in the past five years.

I was thinking that what it *is* about is a certain openness in spirit and attitude—a communal celebration of the band and scene—but that's not really it either, because there are loads of folks who go to shows, collect tapes, and call themselves Deadheads, but *hate* the scene, almost never have fun at a show, and maybe dislike a bandmember or two! It takes all kinds, and that, of course, is the BIG SECRET. Is it too much of a cop-out to suggest that if you say you're a Deadhead, you are? And that if you're not willing to admit it, you're not?

DEADHEAD-IN-UTERO 📖 • Viable tourhead in waiting, accompanying Mom to the show for free *(the utero scam!)* in the warmest, safest reserved seat of all.

(Once they're born, they get complimentary access to shows for two years. As the hotline says, "Children of walking age, two years or older, must have their own ticket to enter a Grateful Dead concert.")

"My daughter Hadley was one of those," recalls Deadhead sociologist Rebecca Adams. "When I went to get my ultrasound the day after a show at Hampton in '87, the gynecologist said, 'What's going on in there? She's *spinning.*'"

DEADHEAD SHUFFLE • The jive used by Heads to subvert a gratuitous exercise of authority. "It's when you appear to be complying with the request of those in charge, while actually doing what you wanted to do all along," explains John Lee. Kris Nyrop adds, "My friends and I use it in reference to those folks who shuffle around the ushers and manage to stay in the aisles all night." *See* SEAT SURFING.

DEADHEAD SOCIOLOGY • A pair of advanced undergraduate courses taught by sociologist Rebecca Adams at the University of North Carolina at Greensboro in the summer of '89. Though there have been myriad independent academic studies on the band and the Deadhead subculture over the years, Adams's may have been the first university course offered on the subject. On top of the requisite classroom instruction and reading material, course work for her twenty-one students consisted of an eight-show tour by bus, meetings with band publicist/biographer Dennis McNally and social theorist Michael Kaern, and a final paper. *See* CAUTION: MINDS AT LARGE; DEADBASE.

🌹 *Rebecca Adams on her Academic Tour '89:*

By the time the bus left our third show at JFK Stadium, the class had solidified into a show family. My husband, Steve, and daughter, Hadley, later joined the group for the Deer Creek show and Alpine Valley run. Hadley uttered her first sentence while on tour: "Go bus!"

The class motto was: "You Ain't Gonna Learn What You Don't Want to Know." Fortunately, they wanted to know a lot. The students wrote papers on a variety of topics: gender roles, tapers, vendors, how children are treated by their Deadhead parents, becoming a Deadhead, the concert as a spiritual experience, cooperation and survival, social control, the phenomenon as a pilgrimage, and so forth. One paper, by Paul Durham, received an honorable mention in the North Carolina Sociological Association's Undergraduate Paper Competition. Another, by Robert Freeman, was presented at the annual meetings of the American Folklore Society, and one written by the two graduate assistants (Jon Epstein and Robert Sardiello) was published in a scholarly journal.

As a result of the experience with my class, I decided to begin research for a book which I am currently writing: *Deadheads: Community, Spirituality, and Friendship.*

Although the class was officially over at the end of August 1989, it lives on in the minds and lives of the participants. We are scattered all over the country, but at shows, many of us find ourselves together again. The distinction between professor and student became blurred long ago. Many Deadheads assume that I have taught the class repeatedly, but it was a unique experience.

Other academic Dead projects:

Dollar, N. J. "The Development of a Strong Musical Taste Culture: The Deadheads." Master's Thesis, Arizona State University, Tempe, 1988.

Kolker, A. *Dead Life* (a novel about four Deadheads on tour). Dissertation for Ph.D. in English, University of Kansas.

Kotarba, J. "The Rave Scene in Houston, Texas: An Ethnographic Analysis." University of Houston, Department of Sociology. Published by the Texas Commission of Alcohol and Drug Abuse, October 1993.

Lieberman, F. "Fieldwork Among the Dead: Portrait of a Marin Rock Band." Presentation at University of California at Santa Cruz.

Paterline, B. "Community Reaction to the Deadhead Subculture." Master's Thesis, University of North Carolina at Greensboro, 1993.

Pearson, A. "The Grateful Dead Phenomenon: An Ethnomethodological Approach." Master's Thesis, 1987. Related article published in *Youth and Society*, June 1987.

Rayle, J. M. "Dead Serious." Interdisciplinary studies course, Appalachian State University, Boone, North Carolina, spring, '92. ("This sophomore-level course included a look at the political and social context in which the Dead came about; group dynamics surrounding Deadheads; the history of psychedelics; and some examination of spirituality.")

Ritzer, J. "Deadheads in Contemporary American Society: Mediated and Negotiated Readings." Presented to national meeting of the Popular Culture and American Culture Association, New Orleans, 1993.

Sardiello, R. "The Ritual Dimensions of Grateful Dead Concerts." Master's Thesis, University of North Carolina at Greensboro, 1990.

Skaggs, S. "The Transitive Nightfall of Diamonds: Eco and the Aesthetics of Trancendence." University of Louisville, Kentucky. Presented at the Conference of the Semiotic Society of America, St. Louis, Missouri, 1993. ("A Jacob Obrecht mass and 'Dark Star' both lead to a transcendent mysticism because the music, continually violating norms and expectations, avoid a clear marking or denotation of a signified. What is left is a state of ambiguity in which the listener is enticed into closer attention of momentary detail.")

Strugatz, E. "The Grateful Dead Phenomenon: A Qualitative Approach." Master's Thesis, Kent State University, Ohio, 1991.

Sutton, Shan C. "The Deadhead Community: A Popular Religion in Contemporary American Culture." Master's Thesis, Wright State University, 1993. ("The Deadhead community is a vivid example of a 'popular' religion, created and guided by common people rather than specialists. It is based on a communal pursuit of the mystical experience centered around Grateful Dead concerts and featuring a combination of transformative agents: music, dance, and hallucinogens. In their ritual activities, Deadheads combine methods of achieving mystical states that are found in some practices of shamanism and spirit possession. Powerful emotional states, inspired by the aesthetic appeal of the music, differ markedly from ordinary states of consciousness and are enhanced by the emergence of *communitas*, the state of union among ritual participants. In communities in which members consistently achieve mystical experience, the members' beliefs and values are influenced by their shared encounters with mystical reality.")

DEADHEADS OF COLOR • Though the Grateful Dead river is fed by many streams out of African music (R&B, jazz, the blues), and the DRUMS are energized by the spirits of Latin *congeros* and Japanese *taiko* drummers, many have noticed that the Deadhead community itself is predominantly, though not exclusively, Caucasian. Though the Heads pride themselves on being inclusive, nonwhite Heads can feel alienated. "Whenever I'm listening to the Dead," says Erik Fortune, "I find myself *encompassed* by the white community. It can really take a toll. I love the music, but I don't want to lose my identity."

"I've gotten my share of strange looks from fellow African-Americans," says Crystal Fisher. "I think even white people think hippies are weird, but to see a black hippie—that can be shocking."

The tide may be turning, however. "I'm seeing more and more Deadheads of color at every show I go to," says Fortune. The toughest challenge, he suggests, may be in reaching a critical mass of nonwhites at shows so that Heads of color won't feel as alone.

✿ *Erik Fortune, on being a Deadhead of color:*

I grew up in Roxbury, a ghetto area near Boston. And when I was seven, my dad and I moved to a Jewish upper-middle-class part of Newton. I met all these kids who were getting into the Dead because their older brothers and sisters were into the scene. The ideology of pitching in, communal living, and learning from other people's situations—the Deadhead community represented a big part of that coming true. I used to walk through shows, and see this other black kid, and he'd be with four or five white people, and it was like, "Is he here for the same reasons I'm here?" I was there because I felt the music was a part of *me*.

I have a friend, an Irish-Catholic kid from the South Shore of Boston, the guy who took me to my first show. He's a genius, but he's such an outcast that even white people feel uncomfortable around him. They don't understand his rap. That's the way I see Pigpen. He was so much of his own wild person, his own self, that he was a nigger. He was a "minority," wherever he went. When a lot of people think of the Grateful Dead, they think of white, middle-class music. Jerry Garcia is a Latino—but people look at him as white. That is really an irony.

I had a girlfriend who I met at a book signing by Mickey Hart, and a big part of our relationship was that we were both going through this transformation. She was coming from a traditional Chinese family, and was really getting into touring, and she suddenly found herself surrounded by non-Asians. There was frustration that she was losing her identity. It was really hard to get anyone else to take that stuff seriously. We needed to do it together.

I don't really care who I go to the show with, or who I see at the show. What I care about, is that when the lights go down, I'm *there*.

DEADIFICATION 📖 • The appropriation by Heads of an icon or scrap of jargon from mainstream American culture. Deadified slogans and pictures on t-shirts turn the parking lot into a living museum of cultural parody. The Deadhead appetite for these transformations is insatiable, as if every commercial slogan could eventually be read as a comment on the band or scene; deadification is Deadhead alchemy, making the unhip hip. *See also* EVERYTHING I NEEDED TO KNOW ABOUT LIFE I LEARNED FROM READING THE BACK OF A VOLKSWAGEN VAN; JUST DEW IT!

GRAPHIC	SLOGAN
Jerry on a box of cornflakes	"Win a free trip anywhere!"
Drawing of a Mountain Dew soda can	"Morning Dew"
Laurel and Hardy as skeletons	"Another fine show you've gotten us into!"
Tweety bird	"Shakedown Tweet!"
Bugs Bunny smoking a joint	"Toke up, Doc!"
Calvin and Hobbes hugging one another	"Our love is real—not fade away."

DEADMOBILE • A road-worn jalopy barely visible under a découpage of rose-crowned skulls, smilin' Jerries and STEALIES. Sometimes called a "Dead sled." A "tourmo" is not the grand TOURBUS for long hauls, but the sturdy little escape pod for quick sprints to nearby venues. When driving without any visible Dead paraphernalia, you're DRIVIN' STEALTH.

DEAFHEADS • Nonhearing Deadheads who, with the aid of paper cups, balloons, and other resonating props, enjoy the music by feeling the harmonious vibrations from the sound system. "They sense the sound as it hums up the spine, rattles the jaw, and resonates in the imagination," writes Laura Blumenfeld in an excellent *Washington Post* story on the phenomenon.

Thanks to the efforts of British Deafhead Paddy Ladd, Rob and Carol Bruce, Annette Flowers from THE OFFICE, and soundman DAN HEALY (whose father is deaf), an official "Deaf Zone" was established in the late '80s, close to the stage and staffed with an American Sign Language interpreter. Interpreter Lori Abrams told the *Post* that she tries as best she can to keep up with the lyrics, but then the band will break into something like "China Cat Sunflower"—"*Coppertone bodhi drip a silver kimono like a crazy quilt stargown through a dream nightwind*"—"at which point," she said, "I just get off the platform."

"Here in the Deaf Zone," writes Blumenfeld, "people mix, hug and laugh, signing giddy, rapid conversation. A guy hugs a balloon to pick up bass notes. A girl stands riveted by the pur-

ple flash of stage lights. A hearing guy sneaks into the zone, because he likes 'the party spirit.' Other hearing guys hang over
the metal barricades, body-language-flirting with some young
deaf women. They offer squirts from water bottles, kiss their
hands and ask them to teach them sign language."

Hart, of course, thrives on the notion that the band is reaching beyond the hearing world. "Music is vibration," he told Blumenfeld. "It's great to share the vibes with everybody, especially those who can't usually share it."

DECEMBER 31, 1999 • The date of the next New Year's
show, according to band sources. After Bill Graham's death, the
band decided to forgo playing on what had become his annual
signature event.

DECHEADS • Deadheads who work at Digital Equipment Corporation, a computer company that is one of an increasing number of businesses attempting to humanize corpo-
rate life by encouraging their employees to fraternize according
to hobbies and special interests. DECheads stay in close touch
via an in-house "Grateful Dead Notes File" on their VAX computer system.

DICK'S PICKS, VOLUME ONE • Album #26, released in
1993.

Dick's Picks is a two-CD set, available by mail order only.
"Dick" is Dick Latvala, the official tape archivist for the band.
It is a live recording, from 12/19/73, Tampa, Florida.

🐌 _Gary Burnett, writer on The WELL, on **Dick's Picks, Volume One:**_

The Florida show preserved on these discs happened right between my
first two shows at Winterland. I've carried something of those shows with me
all this time: bits of visual and auditory memory, snatches of melody, physical
memories of a body in motion with the music, an overwhelming sense of the
immediacy of the occasion. That feeling is what I find recovered on these
discs. The jamming is marked by unity of intent and imagination; no matter
how far afield it gets — and it can go very far — the band plays as a unit, weaving five distinct musical strands into the workings of a single passion. It can
be heard almost everywhere here — most of all, in the jam between "The
Other One" and "Stella Blue," called "Space" by most of us, that is the habi-
tation which most fully belongs to the Dead.

12/19/73 was not the best show of that magical year. Still, these discs translate those structures of meaning that the Dead have always been able to build
out of the inspirations of a moment, more than twenty years after they first
took shape. It's a wonderful gift.

DIGA RHYTHM BAND • An all-percussion group, including Mickey Hart, that released an album called *Diga* in
1975. "Diga" is a sound used by Indian drummers to denote a
stroke on the bass side of a *tabla*, a hand drum.

The drummers of Diga were Jordan Amarantha on congas;
Zakir Hussain, Joy Schulman, Peter Carmichael, Aushim
Chaudhuri, and Tor Dietrichson on tablas; Vince Delgado on
dumbec and tablas; Arshad Syed on folk drums; Jim Loveless
on marimbas; Ray Spiegel on vibraphone; and Mickey Hart on
traps (the traditional drum kit, called a "contraption" by the
early jazz drummers) and gongs.

The seed of Diga was planted in '67, when Hart met
tabla master Alla Rakha. A year later, Hart was taking
tabla lessons from Shankar Ghosh, who was showing Hart
how to play the complex cycles that lit a blaze of polyrhythms
under early Dead jams like "The Eleven." Hart shared his
lessons with Kreutzmann, and in exchange, the two drummers taught Ghosh how to play traps. During "Alligator" at
the Berkeley Community Theater on 9/20/68, the onstage
amps parted, and Ghosh and Vince Delgado were rolled out
on a riser playing *tals*, long cycles of strict time, that wound
their way into a closing composition by Ali Akbar Kahn himself.

In '70, Hart met Zakir Hussain, Alla Rakha's son, who
formed a group of his most gifted students, and when the Jefferson Starship asked the group to open a concert, they christened themselves the Diga Rhythm Band. Diga played two concerts at Winterland in May of '75, a concert in Golden Gate
Park with Garcia on 5/30/75, and recorded an album in Hart's
Barn studio.

Hart kept the players on a salary for six months, so they
could concentrate on the sessions. During one four-day period
of continuous playing, the bandmembers followed each other

around the Barn—even to the bathroom—to make sure the pulse was never dropped.

Diga featured Garcia on two cuts, including an early lilting version of "Fire on the Mountain" with no vocals, called "Happiness Is Drumming." *See* DRUMS; RHYTHM DEVILS.

THE DIGGERS • The Diggers were one of the first communes in the original HAIGHT-ASHBURY, and very influential in shaping the hippie ethos that was the rootstock of Deadhead culture. Named after a religious group in seventeenth-century England which advocated that unused areas of good land in parks and on estate grounds should be farmed—dug—as a commonwealth by poor people, the Diggers kept the pre–Summer of Love Haight fed and clothed by scoring food from local supermarkets and restaurants, and serving it up from pots every afternoon in the Panhandle of Golden Gate Park. (This tradition is carried on in the modern-day Haight by a group called Food Not Bombs. The Dead played several Digger benefits.

The Diggers ran a store where everything was free at 1090 Cole Street, and free was their bottom line—*"It's free because it's yours."* Much of the seed vision of the Diggers was articulated by Emmett Grogan, author of *Ringolevio,* who believed that life was lived most keenly by those who dared to be "life actors." The Diggers were the practical-minded antagonists of "flower power" naïveté, publishing mimeographed newspapers, called the Digger Papers, aimed at rousing the Haight community to address its ills.

Grogan died of a heroin overdose on a New York City subway in '78; another founding Digger, Peter Coyote, became a student of Zen, and a well-known actor and writer; and Peter Berg went on to found the Planet Drum Foundation, a group that advocates precise awareness of the watersheds and native plants in one's home place. *See* THE HAIGHT-ASHBURY.

DIRT SURFERS • Heads who have relaxed their standards of personal grooming to the extreme. The joys of living on a TOURBUS are many, but hot showers aren't one of them.

THE DISCO BUS • A white bus with a glitter ball and a destination sign that dared Heads to "Be Free!" that was the landmark for after-show boogie in the parking lot of West Coast shows in the late '80s. The groove was carried into the Rave Era by the free house-music parties called the Atomic Rooster and the Atomic Dog in the north lot of Oakland Coliseum on 12/19/93 and 2/27/94, featuring live DJs.

DOORWAYS AND SPLICES • Metaphors used by Garcia to describe two types of transition from one song to another. Doorways are the seamless jams (e.g., "China Cat Sunflower"→"I Know You Rider") and splices the brusque jumpcuts ("Stella Blue"→"Around & Around").

"It used to be that a lot of what we were doing was going from one song into a wholly different kind of song where the transition itself would be a piece of music," Garcia told Blair Jackson in 1988. "Lately it's much less that, and more that we're able to come up with transitions that are very graceful in a short amount of time, because we've tried almost everything by now, in terms of going from one thing into another. It's not that the transitional music doesn't exist anymore. It's just that we've worn the pathways."

DRIVIN' STEALTH • Going down the road with no potleaf flags or "Just Say N_2O" bumperstickers—that is, incognito—to avoid attracting the attention of the local authorities. If Dad's car, the "Stealth Beamer." *See* DEADMOBILE.

THE DROUGHT TOUR • The Midwest tour during the dry summer of '88. "It didn't rain at all," explains New York tourhead David Pelovitz. "The daytime temperature never dropped below eighty-eight. Crops died, and farmers sold camping space in cornfields to recoup losses. We had never been so tan, so dehydrated, or so popular with the Midwest locals before."

DRUG CHECKPOINT AHEAD! • This sign, posted by police on roads surrounding arenas, has emerged as a popular and effective East Coast tactic for nabbing Heads after shows. Since cops don't really intend to stop traffic and impose a consistent search of drivers—the only method ruled constitutional—the signs are not for information but propaganda: The intention is to frighten Heads into chucking THE KIND out of windows (at which point the cops can nab them) or pulling off at the nearest exit, where the *real* and lawful drug checkpoint is set up. "To avoid the hassle," says Klaus Bender, "I usually go the backroads." *See also* BACKROADS TOUR; JOHNNY LAW.

DRUM CIRCLES • Impassioned assemblies of drummers and dancers in the parking lot and in the halls of shows, reaching peaks of thunderous intensity just before showtime, during the set break, and afterward.

At West Coast shows, conch shells are sounded to convene the circles, with drummers standing at the center playing congas, tars, *djembes*, and shakers or blowing clay whistles, and the dancers contributing to the driving rhythm by clapping. The dancers often break out in spontaneous chants and howls.

Drum circles are one of the oldest ways of bringing people together and arousing the spirit, and in many cultures, drumming accompanies ordeals of transformation, possession, and initiation. Heads on psychedelic journeys are especially drawn toward the drum circles. Drum circles are a vital example of a Deadhead social form that doesn't depend on the band to produce the magic.

DRUMS • Percussionists Hart and Kreutzmann's opportunity in the second set to groove on their own terms, and explore THE ZONE. "We start on our drum sets," Hart explains, "locking in the groove, and once we've sunk to a deep enough level, one of us will usually head for the part of the stage where THE BEAST and THE BEAM await . . . Once in the zone, the point is to go somewhere where you've never gone before." For roughly ten minutes at almost every show, generally after the third or fourth song in the second set, the Rhythm Devils work primal magic without having to be the spine of the full ensemble.

The drums may begin with Kreutzmann and Hart taking the heartbeat of "Eyes of the World" or "The Other One" farther and farther out, until they are sharing and superimposing rhythms from many different cultures of the world, quick beasts stalking a pulse. Some of the instruments played during drums are folk instruments that Hart has collected over the years, and guest drummers from various world traditions may walk onstage for a drum summit—like Airto, shouting the songs of his fathers as he rings a metal skeleton, or Hamza El Din, playing the dry winds of Nubia on a tar. Evolving out of drum breaks during "The Other One" and "Alligator" at THE FILLMORE and THE AVALON, the highly melodic form of the drums segment became a standard feature of second sets in the late '70s.

Since '86, Hart and Kreutzmann's co-composer has been Bob Bralove, working behind Hart, adding his own percussion, layering in prerecorded sounds, and sculpting holographic soundscapes in QUAD SPACE with help from sound man Dan Healy.

For some Heads, the drums are a profound spiritual experience. In the hallways, SPINNERS may bow toward the stage when the low rumblings of the Beam shiver the walls of the arena. For others—since there are no familiar landmark "songs"—drums is a respite from intense involvement in the music, a time to get off their feet, or glance over setlists. Like all improvised music, sometimes the mojo works and sometimes it doesn't, but Heads who always talk through drums, or head for the bathroom, may miss out on some of the most vital music the Dead play, where the thunder of jazz masters, *capoeiristas*, and the lords of funk meld together under a groove. Says Bralove, "As I told Ram Rod last tour, 'My goal during drums is to have *everybody* dancing.'" *See* BALAFON; THE BEAM; THE BEAST; RHYTHM DEVILS; SPACE.

DSL (DEAD SIGN LANGUAGE) 📖 • Hand jive used by the bandmembers to cue one another to the next song. When Weir flashes seven fingers to the drummers, it means "Estimated Prophet"; eight fingers is "Samson & Delilah," as is a flex of the biceps; ten is "Playin' in the Band." ("Samson" is in an eight-beat time signature, and "Playin' " is in ten.) A thumbs-up from Lesh means "Tom Thumb's Blues," and for "Box of Rain," Lesh may trace a box in the air.

DTV (DEAD HEAD TV) • The first nationally distributed television show produced by and for Deadheads. Created by Kathleen Watkins and Scott Wiseman in the spring of '88, DTV produced eighteen half-hour shows from spring '88 to fall '90, and eventually gained audiences in more than three hundred cities, via distribution to local cable outlets. Viewing of the shows in a group became weekly parties in some places. The lively, engaging broadcasts included tour reports, occasional concert footage, scenes from the parking lot, and interviews with Deadheads and notables such as Robert Hunter, Stanley Mouse, Alton Kelley, Merl Saunders, David Gans, Dan Healy, and Rebecca Adams.

DUNKELSTERN! • "Dark Star!" in German; a cry heard at the shows in Berlin '90.

As with many other nations (Japan, England, Italy, Israel, etc.), Germany has a small but devoted contingent of Deadheads, many of whom are serious tapers. *Mutterband*—"mother tape"—is German for "master," reports Ralph Metzger from Bonn, and similarly, dubs or successive "generations" of copies are "children"—*Kinder.* "A new tape, fresh from the USA, gets soon a lot of *Kinder* here in Germany," Metzger explains.

There are equivalents in German for many American Deadhead words, but many German Heads avoid them, says Metzger. "Instead, we use the American words, which no one else can understand here." *See also* EURAIL HOTEL; SETLIST SHORTHAND.

DUPREE'S DIAMOND NEWS (DDN) • A quarterly magazine "documenting the Deadhead experience" since 1986, edited by John Dwork and Sally Ansorge Mulvey. *DDN* also publishes a free flyer distributed at every venue, with recent setlists and excerpts from the quarterly.

The seed of *Dupree's* was the magazine *Dead Beat,* published by the Hampshire College Grateful Dead Historical Society, founded in 1978 by Dwork. The society hosted parties, and established a tape archive and a library of articles on the band going back to '68. Dwork recalls, "This was before *DeadBase,* back when there were hundreds of tapes that were mislabeled or had parts of different shows on them, and very few soundboards in circulation. It was a whole other ballgame—you needed to be an archaeologist." In 1984, *Dead Beat* merged with another early periodical, *Terrapin Flyer*, edited by Peter Martin, and in '86, Dwork and Mulvey renamed both the quarterly and the concert handout with its current title.

There is much discussion among Heads as to whether or not being a Deadhead is a "lifestyle"—with implications of an identifiable set of beliefs and attitudes—or only a musical preference. Dwork and Mulvey have chosen to articulate the Deadhead experience as a compassionate and socially aware view of the world, supplementing setlists and show reports with articles on environmental action (including Dwork's rainforest preservation fund, the "Garden of the Gratefully Deadicated"), interviews with Wavy Gravy and psychedelic theorist Terence McKenna, collections of DEAD DREAMS, and features on myth and spirituality, including David Prem Meltzer's column, "Truckin' to a Higher Consciousness."

Dwork's essay from *DDN* #23, "The Most Important Grateful Dead Concert of All Time," is the most in-depth show report in general circulation, an analysis of the 8/27/72 concert on Kesey's farm in Veneta, Oregon, as a ritual journey of death, transformation, and rebirth.

🐾 *David Prem Meltzer, columnist, on vehicles and the Path:*

There's an old saying in mystical traditions, "the raft is not the shore." This means not to get caught up in the method, in the specific form which brought you to a greater vision. Don't get stuck thinking that meditation, or dance, or yoga, or drugs, or any old band are the destination. The forms themselves are only vehicles of transportation. The whole purpose is to take you someplace. Don't forget to get off! Let us take the visions that we have shared at those all so special times when the Grateful Dead was happening, and manifest those visions for the benefit of all sentient beings and Mother Earth.

DYE PARTY • A gathering to TIE-DYE a mountain of t-shirts, dresses, scarves, and baby clothes in preparation for tour, to be sold or bartered for food, tickets, floor space, and tour goodies. You know who your real friends are when you see them with blue elbows—and they're not even *going* on tour because they can't get time off from work. *See* APPENDIX II: HOW TO TIE-DYE.

DYLAN AND THE DEAD • Album #20, released in January 1989; recorded on the tour with Dylan in July of '87.

Four out of the six shows on that tour were three-set shows: two Dead sets, followed by a dozen or so Dylan songs. Garcia played pedal steel onstage for the first time since concerts in the early '70s.

Tapes of the rehearsals at Club Front recapture some of the burnish of *Workingman's*-era Dead, with Garcia and Dylan strumming banjos and mandolins and swapping verses on a number of songs that were never played on tour, including the poignant "Ballad of Ira Hayes" and a raucous version of Paul Simon's "The Boy in the Bubble."

♣ *Mike Dolgushkin, editor of* DeadBase, *on **Dylan and the Dead**:*

The final selection of tracks on the album was the result of much sending of tapes back and forth between the Dead and Dylan. The songs are very well performed, showing the Dead's skills not only as a backup band, but as interpreters; and the interplay between the musicians is breathtaking, giving Dylan some of the most sensitive support he has ever had. As with other live Dead albums, one may quibble endlessly over the selection of songs, but this collection manages to capture some of the finest moments of an admittedly spotty collaboration.

Both the Dead and the Garcia Band have covered Dylan songs since the beginning, and the rehearsals at Front Street gave the band a chance to try their favorites with a playfulness and a sense of adventure lacking during the tour.

THE DYLAN SLOT • The point about five or six songs into the first set where, since the tour with Bob Dylan in July of '87, Bob Weir has frequently "pulled out" a cover of a multi-verse Bob Dylan ballad like "Desolation Row," "Queen Jane Approximately," or "When I Paint My Masterpiece" (*see* DYLAN AND THE DEAD).

"During some tours," says Deadhead discographer Ihor Slabicky, "the Dylan song became so omnipresent that the song statisticians developed a new stat called 'the Dylan factor,' which 'was a measure of how many Dylan songs were performed per show, city, or tour."

Some songs tend to fall into a "slot" for compelling reasons.

Weir has said "Sugar Magnolia" has to go at the end of the show because it thrashes his voice to sing it. *See also* THE JERRY BALLAD SLOT.

EAST COAST DEADHEADS/WEST COAST DEAD-HEADS • One demographic distinction often made about Heads by Heads. The clichés—each containing some truth—are of a more boisterous, enthusiastic East Coast crowd, and a patient, quieter West Coast crowd. East Coast Deadheads are said to sing along more, and drive the band to play harder, whereas West Coast Heads—who are older than East Coast Heads on the average, according to Grateful Dead Ticket Sales' Steve Marcus—are quieter during jams and SPACE.

"Crowds are more respectful out west," affirms Erez Kreitner, a New Yorker who has seen shows in Giants Stadium and Oakland Auditorium. "No one is yelling 'Dark Star!' or 'St. Stephen'! They're more interested in letting the band do what they want to do."

"On the West Coast," adds sociologist Rebecca Adams, "people aren't as likely to lead two different lives. Deadheads on the West Coast exchange business cards at shows. That doesn't happen as much on the East Coast. People leave the rest of their life behind when they go to shows here."

ECSTASY • *See* MDMA.

EGYPT '78 • The live album planned to defray the $500,000 expenses of the tour to Egypt, but never completed, to have been culled from the Dead's three performances at the Gizah Sound and Light Theatre on 9/14, 9/15, and 9/16/78, beside the Great Pyramid. (Alton Kelley designed a cover for the posters and the album.)

Hamza El Din, playing the *oud* (a lute), and other Nubian musicians on *tars* (frame drums), singing and clapping hands, joined the band on all three nights for the OPENER, the twelve-beat Nubian folk tune "Ollin Arageed." Healy attempted to use the King's Chamber of the Great Pyramid as an echo chamber, but ran out of cable. Though the music did not surpass the setting—Kreutzmann was playing with a broken hand—the dates were a profound experience for the band and family, the realization of many hopes.

The concerts benefited the Cairo Museum of the Antiquities, and the Faith and Hope Society, a charity for deaf and blind children.

On the final night, there was a complete lunar eclipse. *See also* FANTASY VENUES.

❧ *Bill Graham on the Egypt experience:*

If we had nine hours, perhaps we could tap into what it was all about for me. And you know, I've never really taken the time to say, "Thanks, you've given me one of the most special experiences of my life." The music and the place and that ride across the desert after that last show. I mean seeing Kesey and Bill Walton having a camel race across the desert is not exactly an everyday occurrence!

They didn't think they played well enough to put the tape out, but for me, it was the most moving musical event. There have been great New Year's Eves, where they were great and jammed with all these people. But the first night's show in Egypt, with Hamza El Din and other Nubian musicians playing on tars—they started to play, and I was on the side of the stage feeling no pain, and then very gently came these notes. It was Jerry's picking, like this bird that was flying over the stage, amongst the tar playing. Then there was the bass line. One by one the guys picked up their instruments and they just tapped into what the Nubians were doing. They were as one for twenty minutes, and then the Nubians left the stage and the Dead played.

That twenty minutes can't ever be equaled for me. It was everything. Here's the Sphinx, and here's the pyramid. And here I am. I can't begin to describe it. But if the Dead gave me the highest experience of my life, they also gave me the seventh, the nineteenth, the twenty-sixth—so many separate experiences with the Dead are part of my top fifty or one hundred experiences.

EJECTED • Worse than being fired: the quick exit from the arena under duress. First stage of post-ejection: *anger*—"Those assholes." Second stage: *self-doubt*—"Did I really deserve this? . . . well, maybe." Third: *weather*—"It's cold out here. Where'd I park the tourmobile?"

ENCORE • The last song of the night, when the band returns to the stage for its ovation. The send-off for enthusiastic Heads, often chanting THE CHANT, can be a song that either drives the audience to such a peak—like "Sugar Magnolia"—that the exhausted throngs are willing to go home; or a meditation on what's been said and the meaning of farewell, like "Black Muddy River," "Brokedown Palace," or "Knockin' on Heaven's Door."

Second encores are rare. Heads who lingered after "U.S. Blues" at the Greek Theater on 6/22/86 were surprised with a "Box of Rain" sung for the few hundred people still gathered around the stage. "The encore is the completion of a journey. Not just the second set, but a whole day," says Southern California tape trader Tom Bellanca.

ENDANGERED MUSIC PROJECT • A cooperative effort by Mickey Hart, the Library of Congress, and Rykodisc to use music to highlight the importance of preserving indigenous cultures. For the series' first title, *The Spirit Cries: Music from the Rainforests of South America and the Caribbean* (released in March '93), Hart assisted ethnomusicologists Kenneth Bilby and James McKee in distilling more than ninety hours of music from the Library's archives into one CD.

Spirit gathers together a Choco Indian healing ritual (Panama), Ashaninka folk songs (Peru), music from the *punta* dance (Belize), and drumming from Suriname. "By restoring and repatriating these musics, and by rewarding the performers for their efforts," McKee explains, "the Endangered Music Project seeks to provide traditional peoples of the world, threatened by ecological and cultural compromise, with a newly restored glimpse of their collective pasts to carry into the next century." *See* PEACE; REX FOUNDATION; SEVA.

ENERGY BALLS • Spheres of vital energy, or *ch'i*, seen especially by psychedelically sensitized Heads, that can be moved, played with, or passed around the audience.

Greg Collis, veteran of shows since Magoo's Pizza Parlor '65, says he became aware of this phenomenon at a show at Winterland in 1974 during "Dark Star," when someone tossed him a ball of glowing energy that he caught and then threw up to the balcony, where he saw another Head pass it on.

ESTIMATED PROFIT • Pregnant misspelling of the Weir/Barlow tune "Estimated Prophet" by the Muzak Corporation — "we are more than just music" — in their formal request to ICE NINE PUBLISHING to purchase, arrange, and pipe said tune into elevators and malls. Muzak was also interested in acquiring the "Greatful [*sic*] Dead" tunes "Uncle John's Band" and "Easy to Love You." The final word from Ice Nine's Annette Flowers to Muzak: "Hunter says NO!"

Muzak licensing manager Alan Peterson expresses his dismay at the notion that the Dead and Muzak wouldn't be a good fit. "Muzak has changed," he insists. "You haven't heard us recently, have you? We would *not* do injustice to a Dead tune. We do Doors tunes, we do Steely Dan tunes. We've updated our sound. We're out of that '1,000 string' image. *Bruce Springsteen* is considering giving us permission!"

EUROPE '72 • Album #8, released in November 1972.

☙ *Dan Levy, editor, on **Europe '72**:*

Europe '72 was the Dead's third major live album, and introduced a number of Garcia/Hunter songs still living in the standard repertoire. A sunnier, jauntier recording than the brooding and elegant *Live/Dead*, it is the sole official record of one of the band's most interesting periods of instrumentation. These were Pig's last officially released recordings, and Keith and Donna Godchaux's first with the Dead. Keith had only months before he introduced the grand piano into the band's sound, and his open-eared and spritely playing created new spaces for the band to inhabit. Mickey Hart was on a hiatus, and Kreutzmann's swing provided a more nimble rhythmic anchor than the two-drummer formation.

With "Brown-eyed Woman," "Jack Straw," "Ramble on Rose" and "Tennessee Jed" joining other songs like "Cumberland Blues" and "China Cat Sunflower"→"I Know You Rider," the Dead continued to use the traditional American song form to create mythopoetic landscapes onto which listeners could graft their experiences onto personal reckonings of American culture and history. The first and second discs are full of these new songs. The fifth and sixth sides feature gorgeous, sparse improvisations out of "Truckin' " and into "Morning Dew." Pigpen is featured on "Mr. Charlie" and on the Elmore James blues classic "Hurts Me Too." The recording captures the sound of the elegant and small European venues with proscenium stages, like London's Lyceum and Paris' Olympia Theater. Unlike many other Dead live albums, the performances are a good representation of the shows on that tour (though the tapes, as usual, are worth getting).

It is hard for CD listeners to fully appreciate the aesthetic impact of the album's original LP release. There hadn't been many triple albums, and one from the Dead, coming at the heels of two previous double live albums, seemed absurdly indulgent to non-Heads. To early true believers, *Europe '72* was a further sign that the Dead had evolved irretrievably past the days of *Live/Dead's* radical spontaneity. To nascent Dead Heads—without today's easy access to live tapes—it seemed an act of generosity.

The double gatefold featured THE ICE CREAM KID, the Rainbow Foot, and song titles on one side, and three panels of pure white on the other. Inside, there was an eight-page booklet with color photographs of the band on tour. The band and family—forty-three of them—were clearly on alien turf. Bundled against the chill, the queue of folks waiting to board a ship on the back page look like they're sticking together out of faith in the power of numbers. Misfit power indeed.

Freaks bringing San Francisco psychedelia to the Continent, the touring party got goofy. Jerry wearing a clown nose and fake Bozo hair? Bobby in ponytail and Groucho glasses? The liner notes hint at an arcane rivalry between the two busloads of Heads. Apparently there was a rise of "hypnocracy" during this tour, but the liner notes caution that the differences between the vibes of the two buses were subtle and "so profoundly hidden and enigmatic that you could never possibly understand it." The entire package was enticing for those willing to accept the Dead's newly displayed levity. Who the hell was the Ice Cream Kid? Contemporary Dead Heads can only imagine a tour of *anywhere* that is not overrun by tour rats. But do you know anyone who was on the *Europe '72* tour? *See* OVER THERE.

EURAIL HOTEL • Tourhead accommodations on wheels. Since a Eurailpass was good for unlimited train travel, some Heads on the tour of Europe in '90 would sleep on the train all night—regardless of where it was going. In the morning, they'd hop on a train headed to that night's show. *See* DUNKELSTERN!

EVERYTHING I NEEDED TO KNOW ABOUT LIFE I LEARNED FROM READING THE BACK OF A VOLKSWAGEN VAN • A Deadhead bumpersticker that expresses both the self-deprecating wit that is essential to Deadhead spirit, and a deep appreciation for bumperstickers as a means of group identification and communication.

Each tour, scores of new stickers appear on Deadmobiles, proclaiming Heads' "deadication" ("A Bad Dead Show Is Better Than a Good Day at Work"), silliness ("Jerry Wobbles and He Won't Fall Down"), politics ("Space Is for Deadheads, Not for Warheads"), and insiders' wit. For a group of people who spend a significant amount of their time on the road, it's a way of showing pride in their calling. (The stickers can also come in handy for Heads lost on the way to a show—"Just follow that van with 'Pound Us Again, Phil!' on the back.")

Bumperstickers, unfortunately, also give JOHNNY LAW an easy target, and stories of policemen hassling drivers of "Dead sleds" are legion. What makes flying the colors worth it for most Heads are the smiles, thumbs-up, and letters on the windshield that show up in the strangest of places.

Are You Kind?

Bass Great—Lesh Philling

Don't Blame Me—I Voted for Jerry!

Don't Worry, Be Hippie

Grateful Fred: A Modern Stoned Aged Family—Yabba Grabba Doob

Have a Jerry Christmas and a Happy Bob Weir

Hippies With Haircuts

I've Tripped and I Can't Get Down!

If He Plays We Will Come

Leave the Bombs to Phil

Make Tapes, Not War

My Other Car Is on Tour

Nothing Left to Do but :-):-):-)

Question Reality

Same Happiness . . . Different Tour

The Fat Man Rocks

The Thin Man Spits

WARNING! DRIVER MAY BE EXPERIENCING AN AWESOME
CHINA→RIDER!

Weir Everywhere

When You Absolutely Positively Have to Be at Every Show

Who Wants a President That Doesn't Inhale?

Yo! It's a Dead Thing . . . You Wouldn't Understand

You Wouldn't Drive Any Better if You Were as High as I Am

You've Been Selected for Jerry Duty

EXTRA • *n.* An extra ticket for the night's show. "Cash for your extra."

EYES OF CHAOS/VEIL OF ORDER • A radio program created and hosted by Phil Lesh and Gary Lambert (who also edits the *Grateful Dead Almanac* for Grateful Dead Mercantile, the band's merchandising arm). The program has aired monthly on listener-supported KPFA in Berkeley, California, since June of '87.

Eyes of Chaos is a logical adjunct to Lesh's longtime advocacy of adventurous, "difficult" twentieth-century music that falls through the cracks of conventional categorization. The show has featured a wide spectrum of music, from the world music-influenced big-band jazz of Peter Apfelbaum and the Hieroglyphics Ensemble, to symphonic works by Harrison Birtwistle and Havergal Brian. Lesh has been largely responsible for the REX FOUNDATION's frequent grants to composers and improvisers of such music. In 1992, the BBC produced a film called *The Grateful & the Dead*, which documented Lesh's work in this area. A national edition of *Eyes of Chaos* is in the works.

FALSE JERRIES • Garcia look-alikes who catch Heads' eyes at shows. Hair color and weight can be used to date *faux* Garcias to a specific vintage. "Did you see that guy? He looked *a lot* like Jerry—the *'82* Jerry."

FAMILY • 1. Used by some Deadheads as a more intimate synonym for the community of Heads.

"Many Deadheads consider themselves to be a part of the same extended family," explains sociologist Rebecca Adams, "and sometimes refer to one another as 'brother' and 'sister.' With kinship comes certain obligations such as running interference when there is 'trouble ahead,' offering comfort when there is 'trouble behind,' and sharing resources even when it would not normally cross your mind."

Deadheads who enjoy going to shows together over a period of time often call themselves a "show family." Show families can develop within formally organized groups, such as the Wharf Rats, or The WELL. Many last for years, and grow as the members fall in love inside and outside the circle, and spouses and children become part of the extended show family.

The assumed intimacy implied by words like "family" is a turnoff to some. Danielle Mattoon enjoys the music, and is friends with several Heads, but is made uncomfortable by what she regards as artificial closeness. "I don't think that because someone nods at you at a concert, they know what you're thinking, or how you feel," she says. "I don't like being clumped in a group. I'm aware that there's a mass out there cleaving to every note that Phil or Jerry plays, but I'd just as soon not be part of it. Some people love it, but the assumption that by buying some tape I immediately have 70,000 siblings makes me cringe."

2. The word is also used specifically to describe close associates of the band. "That was where the original 'family groove' came from," said longtime soundman Dan Healy to Sandy Troy, author of *One More Saturday Night*, describing the genesis of the Dead organization around the time of the Acid Tests. "A network began, of light shows and all. A production company formed so we could produce shows. Everyone functioned as an individual, but in those days you all would come, and it would fit together as a whole when you got there. There was not a whole lot of consideration given to whether it was part of one company or not. It didn't work like that." Children of the bandmembers occasionally take jobs in the "family business," working at GRATEFUL DEAD TICKET SALES, or in THE OFFICE.

🍄 *Tom Bellanca, tape trader, on Deadhead families:*

That's what struck me at my first show. Everyone was there for the same purpose, a ritualistic family gathering. You get there as a group, you wait in line together, you make plans to sit either on Phil's side or Jerry's side, and all of that is part of the fun, the process, and the experience.

Your "family" isn't only the people that you go to shows with, but the people you know are going to be there. I have friends from out of state who I know will be in the same spot on the floor—it's like a reunion every couple of months. When you come to the next run, you want to see the same people, because they're a reminder of all of the wonderful experiences you've had together.

I look up to older Heads as family elders who can help me find out about the past, and teach me how to have the best time at a show. There is nowhere else that I have as many older friends who I can talk to and relate with in such a personal way.

I'm sure that's what turns lots of people on. People find a family on tour.

FAMILY SHOWS • What people on the West Coast used to call shows at small outdoor venues like the GREEK THEATER and Frost Amphitheater, where older Deadheads, with their loved ones and children, could bring a picnic for a show in the sun.

After three decades, second- and even third-generation Deadheads have become an integral part of the scene. "I think that there's a certain kind of kid for whom we say something," Garcia told Mary Eisenhart in '87, "and it's been that way each generation. Back when we started, it was the people who were our age, and we've been picking them up younger and younger every decade. Now parents are bringing their kids, kids bringing their parents, people are bringing their *grandparents*. I mean, it's gotten to be really stretched out now.

"It was never my intention to say this is the demographics of our audience," Garcia said. "I was delighted the first time that people didn't *leave*. Everything beyond that is pure gravy." *See* TRIPPING ON DNA.

✿ *John Barlow, lyricist, on second-generation Deadheads:*

Rebellion is part of the way in which you create yourself. At some point, you've got to differentiate yourself from your parents. One funny twist on this is that second generation Deadheads get really straight for a while. But they come back around, usually. There's a kid who was raised in the larger Grateful Dead family, whose name was Chay. When he got to be about twelve, he decided he wanted to be called Johnny. He was Johnny until he was about twenty-one. I met him one night backstage at a concert and I said, "Are you still Johnny, or are you going back to Chay yet?" And he said, "I hadn't considered it—but Chay *is* kind of a cool name." And he went back to Chay.

FANNING • Garcia's rapid strumming at the crests of solos and jams. Also called "scrubbing," "the tuck" (because of the way Garcia tucks the guitar close to his body, leaning over it in intense concentration), "the machine gun," and "the butterfly." Fanning is an element of Garcia's stylistic vocabulary that signals a PEAK for many Deadheads. The crescendo of the Cornell 5/8/77 "Morning Dew" is a prime example of the power of this technique.

FANTASY VENUES 📖 • Nominations for future show sites, given no practical limitations. "Imagine," offers Mitch Gilbert, " 'Stella Blue' in the house of great Italian operatic acoustics—La Scala, in Milan!" Such fantasies, inspired by some of the far-out places the Dead have actually played (most notably the three September 1978 gigs at the Gizah Sound and Light Theatre, beside the Great Pyramid of Giza in Egypt), are a popular Deadhead pastime. "On occasion," admits Gail Edwards, "my friend Chiefy and I fantasize about a 'Grateful Cruise'—a hundred or so Deadheads on a luxury liner, with the Dead jamming each night in the ship's ballroom. Bobby would wear a white tuxedo and stroll by our table serenading us— 'Ooeee, oooee baby, won'tcha let me take you on a sea cruise?' Afternoons would be spent relaxing in lounge chairs on the deck, sipping cool drinks, and chatting with the roadies about memorable moments in their career." *See* SMALL HALLS.

Stonehenge—Proposed by Garcia in the London *Times*. "I don't see why they wouldn't let us play there. It'd be *fun*!"

The Great Meteor Crater, Arizona—That would make for a nice in-the-round show," muses Matthew Reed Templeton. "Plenty of lawn seats too—it's about half a mile across."

Machu Picchu, Peru

Herod Atticus Theatre—At the base of the Acropolis, in Athens.

Sea of Tranquility, the Moon—The ultimate venue for SPACEDANC-ING, suggests *Dupree's Diamond News*—a coproduction of Bill Graham Productions and NASA. "Personal oxygen required."

Hawaii's Diamond Head Crater; NYC's Metropolitan Opera House; Mount Rushmore; Old Faithful; a New Year's Eve show on Alcatraz Island—Suggestions depicted on the back of a 1986 t-shirt entitled "U.S. Dream Tour, 1987."

My backyard, the 4th of July—Christian Crumlish.

FEEDBACK • An early name for SPACE, used on the cover of *Live/Dead*. (*DeadBase* lists the last "Feedback" as 5/2/70.)

The early explorations of space at shows often passed through extremely dissonant realms, with the band literally turning their backs to the audience to feed the guitars back through the amps. "I remember one Fillmore East show in '68 or '69," recalls musician Michael Bobrik, "where people were actually saying, 'Enough! We can't handle this anymore.' So they stopped and walked off the stage, and then of course the audience said, 'Come back—we're sorry!' And they came out and finished the show."

🎵 *Mickey Hart on feedback:*

They loved feedback. First one would feed back, then all of them would be feeding back madly, until the song disappeared beneath torrents of noise. It was like someone tossing a bloody chicken into a school of piranha. Phil would almost be foaming at the mouth, throwing his guitar into his amp. And Jerry would just drop everything and run at his amp, as if he couldn't get back there to start feeding back fast enough. God, it was exciting. For a few minutes, you'd be out on the edge with this roaring animal all around you, and it was always an open question whether it was going to go back into its cage or not. Pigpen hated it. He would hide behind his organ, and we'd have to call him to come back out and play.

FILLER ▪ Songs tacked onto the end of a tape of a show.

Using a ninety-minute cassette, there might be twenty minutes of extra blank space on a tape of a FIRST SET (first sets generally run about an hour or less), while second-set tapes rarely have enough extra tape for one tune, if that. (Often, a second-set tape won't even have enough room for the encore, which will then be tacked onto the end of the first set.)

Choosing filler is a subtler art than it might appear. Some traders insist that the filler be chosen from the same tour as the main set, so the band's sound is consistent for the duration of the tape. Filler is a good way of preserving good single tunes from lackluster sets, or of calling attention to an especially juicy NUGGET. Radio shows like the GRATEFUL DEAD HOUR are goldmines of soundboard-quality filler.

THE FILLMORE AUDITORIUM (THE "OLD FILL-MORE") • The primal venue. A dance hall at Fillmore and Geary streets in San Francisco, operated by BILL GRAHAM from the fall of '65 to June '68.

With Graham's organizational skills and chutzpah, the Fill-

more became the showcase for the new generation of psychedelic rock groups, enhanced by slide shows, black lights, a mirror ball, and balloons. The first "light shows" at the Fillmore
were created by colored footlights wired to the keys of an accordion in the balcony.

The Dead's first show at the Fillmore, on December 10,
1965, was both their first appearance as "the Grateful Dead"
(billed as "formerly the Warlocks"), and the beginning of an extraordinarily fruitful twenty-six-year relationship with Graham. One year later, on December 31, 1966, the tradition of Bill
Graham–sponsored Dead New Year's bashes was born at the
Fillmore, with Graham's friend Jim Haynie in a diaper as the
New Year's Eve baby, a role he would play for the next decade.

The Dead played many great shows at the Fillmore during
the PIGPEN era, often on double bills with groups like Quicksilver Messenger Service and Jefferson Airplane. The high point
of the shows was usually a ripping version of "In the Midnight
Hour," with a long rap by Pigpen, starting at midnight. Other
bands — notably the Who — were challenged musically by playing the Fillmore, where long jams were expected. "There was
very much a whole kind of Fillmore energy coming off the audience that combined with the band," recalls Eric Clapton, who
played the Fillmore with his primordial power trio, Cream. "I
was encouraged to get outside of the format. I was encouraged
to experiment."

Many of the ideas that Bill Graham used to produce shows at
the original Fillmore were adopted from the TRIPS FESTIVAL
notion of rock show-as-multimedia, polysensual banquet.
Though Graham did not approve of it, marijuana was smoked
openly at the Fillmore, including one event hosted by THE DIG-
GERS called "Roll Your Own, Stone Your Neighbor," where
bricks of marijuana and hashish were heaped onto charcoal
grills.

Graham took pride in the fact that the reputation of the Fillmore was such that people would come to shows there without
even knowing who was on the bill. He took advantage of the
drawing power of bands like the Dead to introduce deserving

acts to wider audiences—especially blues and soul acts like Lightnin' Hopkins and Big Mama Thornton.

In the wake of the Martin Luther King assassination and subsequent racial unrest in the predominantly black neighborhood surrounding the auditorium, Graham closed the Fillmore, and renamed the CAROUSEL BALLROOM the "Fillmore West." The "old Fillmore" was reopened by Graham briefly in '89, and closed again after being damaged by the powerful Bay Area earthquake that fall.

The Fillmore reopened on 4/27/94 with a show by the Smashing Pumpkins, Ry Cooder, and David Lindley, refurbished, reinforced, and lovely as ever, with apples at the top of the stairs.

THE FILLMORE EAST • A 2,400-seat theater on the Lower East Side of New York City, formerly known as the Village Theater, and rechristened the Fillmore East by Bill Graham in 1968.

The Dead played the old Village Theater twice in December '67; then came to the Fillmore East for shows in June of '68; February, June, and September of '69; January, February, May, July, September, and November of '70; and finally closing out the theater with a celebrated five-night run in April '71.

☙ *Blair Jackson, editor of* THE GOLDEN ROAD, ON THE FILLMORE EAST:

The Grateful Dead took New York the old-fashioned way in the late '60s and early '70s, by playing there often, and *really well.* The Jefferson Airplane and Country Joe & the Fish were the first San Francisco bands to make waves in the Big Apple, but the Dead had little trouble establishing a loyal following there that quickly eclipsed both bands. They were viewed in the East as the total embodiment of San Francisco hippiedom—from the long, organic jams in the music, to the large, freewheeling family scene that seemed to surround them.

In '67–'68, the only part of New York that was at all analogous to San Francisco's Haight-Ashbury was Greenwich Village, which became a magnet for East Coast hippies lured by the affordable housing, nightclubs, head shops, and cheap restaurants. The Village never quite had that *glow* that emanated from the Haight in its prime (there was always more edge to the street scene in the Village, and more ingrained neighborhood poverty; not just hippie poverty), but when the Dead came to town, it was like they trucked in the Spirit of San Francisco with them.

The scene right outside the theater at Dead shows was completely crazed. Everyone was decked out in their countercultural finery, and either rapping with each other, or wandering up and down the line. There were always dealers snaking through the throng muttering "acidhashgrass, acidhashgrass" like it was their personal mantra, and there were all sorts of colorful characters that seemed to turn up whenever the Dead were in town. My favorite was a tall, skinny African-American dude everyone called Super Spade: He wore a black and purple cape, dark granny glasses down his nose, and always had a wide grin, and stoned-red eyes.

Once inside the theater, you were transported into a magical world that was completely under Graham's control. It was cleaner and more plush than anything you'd expect to see in the heart of the Lower East Side. The sound and sightlines were phenomenal. There were *no* bad seats. Everything seemed special about the Fillmore East, from the concessions to the completely transporting light show (the legendary Joshua Light Show, that later became Jo's Lights), worth the trip to the Fillmore all by itself.

My strongest memory is seeing one of the July '70 "Dead at Midnight" concerts, with the New Riders opening, then an acoustic Dead set, followed by a long electric set. At the one I attended (alas, there's no known setlist for 7/10/70) they raised the giant light show screen during the "Lovelight" closer and projected the lights onto the crowd. When they opened the side doors at the very end, morning light streamed in—it was 5 A.M.

Neither tapes nor setlists exist from many of the late '60s shows, so we can only imagine what sort of inspired madness went on. But various GD Fillmore East shows from '70 to '71 rank among their best ever. Clearly there was something about the (apparently) oil-and-water mix of California and New York countercultures that brought out the best in both within the rococo walls of that hallowed space. There's never been anything like it since.

THE FILLMORE WEST • The name that Bill Graham gave to the Carousel Ballroom—a 2,800-capacity venue at Market and Van Ness streets in San Francisco—when he rented it in June of 1968. Graham inaugurated the Fillmore West the night after closing the old Fillmore (see FILLMORE AUDITORIUM), with a concert by the Paul Butterfield Blues Band and Ten Years After.

The Fillmore West had a flocked velour ceiling, pillars, and a large parquet dance floor, with risers along the sides. Graham installed glass cases in the hallways with corkboards where he would post community news and clippings, and there were free apples at the door—a Graham trademark that continued through Winterland and beyond. "It was a great laboratory," recalled Graham in his autobiography. "A place where people could let their hair down."

The Dead had already played the venue fifteen nights or so as the Carousel Ballroom, but the first run the Dead played in the room as "the Fillmore West" was 8/20 to 8/22/68, three nights of PRIMAL DEAD featuring multiple combinations of "Dark Star," "St. Stephen," "The Other One," and "Alligator." "And We Bid You Goodnight" made its first appearance during this run, as a jam the second night, and a full version, with vocals, to close the third night.

It was also at the Fillmore West that Owsley and the Dead, via their road manager, were finally successful in slipping LSD to Bill Graham, by putting a drop of liquid on the rim of his can of 7-UP. When Graham figured out that he had been dosed, he confronted Hart, and Hart said, "We're going on, Bill. You want to play?" and handed Graham a drumstick. Graham was onstage for four hours, bashing gongs and kettledrums.

The band's last show at the Fillmore West was on 7/2/71, two nights before it closed, and featured a fierce version of the complete "(That's It for) the Other One" dedicated by Lesh "to our friend Owsley, who's in jail." The entire show was filmed and broadcast on three FM stations in San Francisco.

❧ *Mickey Hart on the night Bill Graham was gratefully Dead:*

The next thing I knew, he was hanging over the gong on stage. And he had no mercy. He was beating the gong *wildly*. He was smiling and just whacking that gong and foaming at the mouth. I said, "Bill! This is a *ballad!*" Then he started playing the cowbell. He was *in* the band. He became one with the universe. We couldn't stop him. We were in for the groove and we were *flying*. And this guy was flying with us.

Afterward, I gave him a gold-plated cowbell to commemorate the night.

"FINANCE BLUES" • The working title in the studio for "Money Money," the tongue-in-cheek Weir/Barlow song that never came across as wryly as intended, with lines such as, "The Lord made a lady out of Adam's rib/Next thing you know you got (*ooh ooh*)—women's lib!"

THE FIRST SET • The first half of a show, before the SET BREAK. Though first sets can come on strong (a "Shakedown Street" OPENER can get the band jamming hard five minutes after the houselights go down), even bandmembers call the first set "the warm-up set." The band is often occupied in finding an ensemble sound, smoothing technical glitches, and easing their way into a groove that will come into its own in the more improvisational SECOND SET.

The last or second-to-last song of the first set, however —"Cassidy," "Let It Grow," "Bird Song," "Lazy Lightnin' "— can open up into the freeform conversations typical of the second set, and be a harbinger of what's to come. *See* THE DYLAN SLOT.

THE FIRST SHOW • First shows are milestones: the beginning of a Deadhead's long strange trip. Often the tale of the first show is qualified by a confession that the Head-to-be didn't really "get it" until the second or third show; but a Head's first show gives him or her a foothold in the band's history, transforming setlists into the signposts of an individual journey.

☙ *John Holzman,* REFORMED DEADHEAD, *on his first show:*

It was in Morgantown, West Virginia, 4/10/83. Our high school English teacher, Bob Moses, took us in his van, forgoing his vehicle of choice, a motorcycle. Later, he told us we probably saved his life. He had this philosophy about taking curves on country roads. It was to take whatever the recommended speeds and double them.

My first impression of the parking lot was that it was like finding something that made total sense to me, without having any prior knowledge of it. I had been listening almost exclusively to Grateful Dead albums for almost a year, and had no idea about the Dead scene, or tapes, or the parking lot. I just knew that I was into this music. So driving into the parking lot was like finding a whole world of people just like me. It was pretty much a dream come true.

It was a nice spring day. I remember being amazed by all the colors, smells, tie-dye, ponchos, people walking barefoot. Smoking pot was still a new, fun activity—still a very special thing to do. I was just blown away at seeing this vastly different lifestyle that I had never been consciously desirous of, but could immediately imagine joining.

I remember going into the show and being overjoyed at every song that I knew. Every song felt like a gift—"Oh my God, I can't believe they're playing *that!*" Which was ridiculous in retrospect, but when they played "Uncle John's"—which was my first favorite Grateful Dead song—I thought they were playing it for me. They played "Sugar Magnolia," which later became passé, but at that show, to me, it was spectacular. I couldn't believe they were playing it. They ended the first set with "Might As Well," which was one I didn't know, but the song felt instantly familiar.

My friend Dave Shenk had scammed us all down onto the floor, which was general admission, and we ended up getting pretty close to the stage—as close as I ever got. I had only seen one glimpse of a show, footage of the previous New Year's on the news. You could see this writhing crowd on the floor, and I thought, "That's where we should be." And there we were. I thought, "I'm finally in that place where I've been wanting to be for so long."

THE FLIP ✏ • Ejecting and turning a cassette from side A to side B to continue recording the show in progress—a challenge presented to non-DAT tapers especially during THE SECOND SET, where the playing is relatively continuous. Typically, the second-set flip is made between DRUMS and SPACE, which means that the moment when the guitarists come back onstage, after the drummers exit, is a convenient moment—the so-called "Jerry flip."

The improvisatory nature of the band's performances, however, means that a fearsome jam might erupt before the first side of the tape runs out, or bandmembers might even linger for the entire set. A flip made during a passage of music is called a "bad flip." An analog tape collector might apologize for a bad flip in a jam when trading a tape.

This problem plagued the earliest tapers, who taped on seven-inch reels at 7½ i.p.s. for good sound quality, which meant that the reels would have to be flipped after forty-five minutes. The ideal setup was to use ten-inch reels, which would usually last the set, but they, and the machines that used them, were very expensive. The entire problem was solved by the invention of DAT decks, which use two-hour tapes that don't need to be flipped. *See* DAT; TAPER'S SECTION.

FLOOR SPACE • 1. The area of the arena floor near the stage, staked out by RUNNERS from the moment the doors are opened. *See* RAILRATS.

2. A place to unroll a sleeping bag, or at least lie down in relative peace. What TOUR RATS need most. "Floor space!" is an oft-heard plea in the parking lot after the show. *See* EURAIL HOTEL; MAXING OUT; REAL ESTATE.

FMs ↩ • Tapes recorded from the band's live radio broadcasts, or from Dead-specific radio programs like David Gans's GRATEFUL DEAD HOUR. Up until the late-'80s influx of the BETTYBOARDS and other soundboard tapes, these radio recordings were for years the highest quality tapes that were easily available for trade. Though they're not as rich in fidelity as a direct SOUNDBOARD (because the music is squeezed through a narrower bandwidth), FMs do have great clarity and stereo separation. The broadcasts also often come with the added perk of colorful commentary from friends or relatives of the band—folks like Bill Walton, Ken Kesey, and Paul Krassner. Occasionally the announcers themselves become an amusing part of the tape, as when the KSAN announcer for New Year's Eve '71–'72 at Winterland informed his audience, "All sorts of people are dropping by—David Crosby, Joni Mitchell, on and on. Everyone's smiling and taking off their clothes. I'm barely sane."

"In-house" FMs were a mid-'80s experiment in which soundman DAN HEALY reinforced the feed to some speakers in the arena through a low-power FM signal from the soundboard. Tapers found that they were able to pick up these signals on portable receivers and tape directly from them, obtaining near-soundboard quality tapes. The experiments were discontinued, however, after Healy realized even his low-wattage, extremely local broadcasts were in violation of FCC regulations.

F.O.B. • A tape made by illicitly recording in Front of the Board—the SOUNDBOARD—where taping is no longer permitted.

Before the TAPER'S SECTION was established behind the soundboard in July '84, most tapers set up their rigs in the so-called sweet spot of the audience, about forty to seventy-five feet back from the stage. (This is sometimes called taping "in the mouth.") Though F.O.B. taping is now officially forbidden, there is still a sizable group of tapers who attempt it—risking confiscation of tapes and equipment—because of the superior presence and three-dimensionality of F.O.B. recordings.

To conceal their activity, F.O.B. tapers take advantage of the latest developments in microphone miniaturization, hiding high-fidelity mics under shirts, in eyeglasses, in hats, etc. F.O.B. tapers have developed their own lingo and sign language to avoid detection. A taper might point index and pinky fingers to the stage to indicate that he or she has "Neuumanns in the hat" (Neuumanns are easily concealable high-fidelity mics), or use a hand signal to remind their partner to TWEAK the levels or flip the tape. *See also* GETTING YOUR DECK IN.

☙ *From a letter from taper Clay Brennecke to taper Jeff Silberman on the F.O.B. spirit:*

Blessed brother, take up electronic arms, and like a mighty vacuum cleaner, suck up all there is. Twenty years from now, when you are scraping to remember what it was like, or when your grandchildren come across the curious chest of immortality in your attic into which your life's blood and vigor have been poured, you will answer their youthful questions by saying, "Thank God I recorded EVERYTHING I possibly could, and had big enough balls to dispel my fears and run spread omnis with a kamikaze-buccaneer mentality, for every show which I did not push myself to record is a world less complete."

Upon your proclamation, your family will have had any doubts removed as to the seriousness of your senility. But you will know the truth.

FOUR-TWENTY (420) • Said to be police radio or civil statute code for a bowl of marijuana "in progress." Used as a justification to smoke pot at 4:20 in the afternoon (or morning). The term has become so widespread that hats and bumperstickers have appeared in the parking lot reading, "It's 4:19 — you're late!"

THE FOX'S DEN • A clandestine Deadhead tradition among seniors at St. Paul's school, in Concord, New Hampshire, based on appreciation of a tape recorded from the balcony of the Fox Theater in Atlanta on 11/30/80. (The show was distinguished by a titanic "Scarlet→Fire" transition, as well as unusual song-choices and a fearsome level of jamming throughout.) The tape was passed down from senior to senior at St. Paul's from '80 to '85, along with a scroll inscribed with a credo that gave the possessor of the tape — whose room was given the honorary title "the Fox's Den" — a set of conditions: You had to listen to the tape every day. You couldn't stop the tape in the middle. You had to smoke pot while listening to it.

FROM THE MARS HOTEL • Album #11, released in June 1974.

This album captures the band's sound just before its year-long touring hiatus. The long workout on "Unbroken Chain" stands as one of the most extended and dynamic Dead jams in the studio, alongside the version of "Playing in the Band" on Bob Weir's *Ace.*

As the Dead were recording the album at the CBS Studio in San Francisco, the band and crew would walk past a rehabilitation center in the Mars Hotel on Fourth Street, and "ugly roomers" — i.e., the residents of the hotel — became the subtitle of the album. Round Records executive Ron Rakow nixed the subtitle on the grounds that it would offend the Mars residents, and the more acceptable phrase, "ugly rumors," appears upside down and backwards on the cover. *See* THE LAST ONE..

🌺 *Steve Brown, production coordinator, on* **From the Mars Hotel:**

In March of '74, the band went into the old CBS Studios in San Francisco to record their second album for their own label. With "Uncle Roy" Siegel at the helm, the band was able to synch up two sixteen-track tape machines, and record up to thirty tracks on each song.

"U.S. Blues" was the Dead's State of the Union address for '74, a great opener with a fat, bouncy bass line and a chorus that's become a sing-along favorite at shows: "Summertime done come and gone, my oh my."

"China Doll," a moody reflection on the fragility of our lives in the face of personal traumas, is draped with Keith's delicate Victorian harpsichord and punctuated by Garcia's searing sustains. Phil's never-performed-live "Unbroken Chain" is a river of hot lava that filled up all thirty tracks, even doubling up on a few tracks, with synthesizer enhancements by Ned Lagin and Phil. "Scarlet Begonias," though not the full-blown swinging version of today, bounces along like the perky muse of the tune, with Donna's vocals adding a texture now long gone.

Phil's "Pride of Cucamonga" could have spun out of the *American Beauty* or New Riders of the Purple Sage sessions. Marin County musician John McFee played the pedal steel on this track, because Garcia had not played steel in a while (McFee, by the way, also played steel on Elvis Costello's *My Aim Is True*). The lyric was written by Phil's buddy Bobby Petersen.

Even if no one knew what to think about Bob's "Money Money," the vocal riff—inspired by Motown songwriter Barrett Strong's "Money"—kept things cooking. "Ship of Fools," one of Hunter's most poignant meditations on personal and societal affairs, brought the album to a close in stately fashion.

FUKENGRÜVEN • Say, *"fuckin' groovin!"* A bumper-sticker conceived during the summer of '90 by Geoffrey Miller, when he found himself on tour with no money. "I was in the parking lot and saw the stickers that said 'Darkstarvergnugen' and 'Philvergnugen.' I thought of *groovin'*, which was something people could relate to."

Miller's original plan was to make "Fukengrüven" t-shirts, but they would have been too bulky to hitchhike with, so he brought a Volkswagen Farvergnugen decal to Walt Fedorich, a sticker-and-sign printer in Binghamton, New York, who promised he could print high-quality stickers in a few days. Miller altered the design of the VW original, adding the lines to the left of the letters to look like TRAILS.

"I was doing face painting on tour, not making a lot of money," Miller recalls. "I ordered one thousand stickers. I went that afternoon to an old swimming hole in Binghamton. I was totally broke, because I'd just spent all my money on stickers. I had no idea what I had. I grabbed the sack of stickers and walked around the lake, selling them for a dollar. I sold twenty stickers in twenty minutes. The first one went on a '71 Monte

Carlo, some old beat rusty car, a couple of high school kids who thought it was the greatest. I hitchhiked with a big box down to Giants Stadium. I walked down the first aisle of cars, and everybody started freakin', so I thought—'It's New York City, I'll sell 'em for *two* bucks.' After two shows, I'd gone from being totally broke to having eight hundred dollars. Two more shows, and I was out of stickers. Now I order ten thousand at a time."

What does "fukengrüven" mean? "It's finding a groove, finding your own thing. There's a connotation of dancing, and it's an update on *groovy*. I've had people say, 'You ought to do it on colored paper,' but it's supposed to look generic. Everybody's wearing bright screaming mismatched Guatemalan stuff and tie-dyes—and all of a sudden here comes a black-and-white sticker that just *goes nuts*. It shows that life can be a little simpler."

GARCIA, JERRY • Lead guitar, vocals, composition. Born on August 1, 1942, in San Francisco.

Jerome John Garcia was named after Broadway composer Jerome Kern. His father, Spanish immigrant Jose "Joe" Garcia, was an accomplished jazz musician who died in a fishing accident in 1952. His mother, Ruth, was a nurse.

Garcia spent his youth in the Mission district of San Francisco. His first creative inclinations were not musical, but visual. "In the third grade, I had a lady teacher who was a bo-hemian," he recalls. "She was colorful and pretty and energetic and vivacious. She had everybody in the class making things out of ceramics and papier-mâché. Art was more or less my guiding interest from that time on. I was going to be a painter."

Aside from his art class, Garcia didn't have much use for for-mal schooling. "I was a fuckup. A juvenile delinquent. My mom even moved me out of the city to get me out of trouble. It didn't work. I was always getting caught for fighting and drink-ing. I failed school as a matter of defiance."

At fifteen, Garcia discovered both marijuana—"it was just what I wanted, it was perfect"—and the electric guitar. "I was just in heaven. I stopped everything I was doing at the time. I tuned it to an open tuning that sounded right to me, and started picking and playing." His earliest influences were Freddie King and Chuck Berry.

At seventeen, Garcia quit school and enlisted in the Army. "I just wanted to be some place completely different. I lasted nine months. I was at Fort Ord for basic training and then they transferred me to the Presidio in San Francisco, overlooking the water and the Golden Gate Bridge. Neat old barracks and almost nothing to do. It started me into the acoustic guitar."

Discharged around 1960 (with a total of two court-martials and eight AWOLs), Garcia headed down to Menlo Park, thirty miles south of San Francisco. There he met Robert Hunter, just out of the National Guard, who was playing traditional music in the burgeoning coffeehouse scene around the Stanford Uni-versity campus. Steve Marcus remembers seeing "Bob & Jerry" at Peninsula School in Menlo Park. "I went up to Hunter and I said, 'I saw you and Jerry play in May of '61. You played my favorite song.' And he said, ' "Michael Row Your Boat Ashore." ' I said, 'How'd you know?' He said, 'That was *everybody's* favorite song in 1961!' I mentioned that to Jerry and he said, 'That was our first paying gig—but they never paid us.' "

The two slept in their cars, and joined the growing folk scene in clubs like the Tangent and St. Michael's Alley, where many of the musicians who would invent the "San Francisco Sound"—like Paul Kantner and Jorma Kaukonen—were woodshedding.

"I heard five-string banjo bluegrass records," Garcia recalls, remembering his first exposure to Bill Monroe and Harry Smith's Folkways Anthology, "and I thought, 'God, what is that sound? I gotta make that sound.' It became an obsession, and I learned how to learn something difficult. It was slow going and I had to listen to a lot of records slowed way down, so I could figure out the individual notes. I got a lot of respect for the individual note. When you're blasting along straight eighth notes at a quick tempo, it requires a lot of control and a lot of practice. The root of my playing is that every note counts, every note has a personality, every note has a little spirit."

Garcia bought a banjo from fifteen-year-old drummer BILL KREUTZMANN at the Dana Morgan Music store, and was soon working at the store himself, giving lessons and performing in a number of bluegrass bands, including THE WILDWOOD BOYS, the Sleepy Hollow Hog Stompers, and others.

Two of the young kids hanging out with Garcia at the back of the store between (and during) their high school classes were a handsome sixteen-year-old named Bob Weir, and a sixteen-year-old future recording engineer named Bob Matthews. "One day we told Jerry, 'We're forming a jug band,'" recalls Matthews. "And Jerry being Jerry said, 'Great—I'm in on it.'" MOTHER MCCREE'S UPTOWN JUG CHAMPIONS was formed in early '65 with Garcia, Weir, Marshall Leicester on guitars, Tom Stone on fiddle, drummer Kreutzmann, harp player Ron "Pigpen" McKernan, and Bob Matthews, as he puts it, "moving from washboard to second kazoo, and then out the door." With some inspiration from the Beatles, R&B, and lots of urging from Pigpen, the Jug Champions made the leap to electric blues-rock under their new name, THE WARLOCKS, in the spring of '65. By '66, they had changed their name to the Grateful Dead.

Garcia lived in a big house called the Chateau, where Pigpen also lived. The Chateau was only a few blocks away from where Ken Kesey was living and throwing his electric venison-chili bashes, and Garcia became one of the earliest proponents of LSD. "It just changed everything. For me, personally, the effect was that it freed me because I suddenly realized that my little attempt at having a straight life, and doing that, was really a fiction and just wasn't going to work out. That realization made me feel immensely relieved."

Garcia met his companion for many years, Carolyn "Mountain Girl" Adams, at an Acid Test. The band moved south to Los Angeles, courtesy of OWSLEY, for a crucial period of development in '66, and then back up to San Francisco, to 710 Ashbury and the Haight.

Many streams of music flow into Garcia's playing—blues, Ozark mountain fiddling, Art Tatum, Freddie King, Chuck Berry, reggae, Wes Montgomery, Duke Ellington—but his sound, the *presence* speaking in the notes, is unmistakably his own. There is a brightness, an essential optimism, and an affable humor that does not flinch away from the gravest, most desolate places blues can go.

In the Grateful Dead, Garcia has built an outlet for his talents that gives him both a loyal audience to encourage him to venture to the limits of his inspiration, and a team of collaborators which has allowed his gift to unfold over the decades, with little commercial interference.

Garcia's style has matured from the faster-than-thought explosions of notes crackling through "Viola Lee Blues," to the seasoned grandeur of an older musician who never retreated from the edge of experiment, and can endeavor to play a line he is not sure about with earned sureness. His musical gestures are heard and understood by his fans in a universe of reference to past performances that summons the deepest meaning out of every note.

Garcia's unlimited devotion to the music and to collaboration has landed him in dozens of ensembles, with musicians Howard Wales, Merl Saunders, David Grisman, Melvin Seals, John

Kahn, Ornette Coleman, and many others. In February '94, Garcia was married to Deborah Koons. He has four daughters from previous marriages: Heather, Anabelle, Theresa, and Keelin. *See* GARCIA/HUNTER; JERRY GARCIA BAND; RECONSTRUCTION.

A selected Jerry Garcia non-Dead discography:

Hooteroll — Garcia, Wales, 1971.

Garcia — "The '72 Garcia," 1972.

Heavy Turbulence — Garcia, Saunders, 1972.

Live at Keystone — Garcia, Saunders, 1974.

Garcia — "The '74 Garcia"; also known as "Compliments of Garcia," 1974.

Old and in the Way — Bluegrass band featuring Garcia, Vassar Clements, David Grisman, John Kahn, and Peter Rowan, 1975.

Reflections — Garcia, 1976.

Cats Under the Stars — Jerry Garcia Band, 1978.

Run for the Roses — Garcia, 1982.

Almost Acoustic — Jerry Garcia Acoustic Band, 1988.

Jerry Garcia Band — live album, 1991.

Garcia/Grisman — David Grisman and Jerry Garcia, 1991.

Not for Kids Only — David Grisman and Jerry Garcia, 1993.

GARCIA/HUNTER • The longtime songwriting collaboration of Jerry Garcia and Robert Hunter, born in 1966 when Hunter mailed the lyrics for "Alligator," "St. Stephen," and "China Cat Sunflower" to Garcia from New Mexico. Shortly thereafter, Garcia asked Hunter to be the Dead's lyricist in residence. Hunter has since written around one hundred songs with Garcia, including "Ripple," "Stella Blue," "China Doll," "Wharf Rat," "Mississippi Half-Step," "Bertha," "He's Gone," "Eyes of the World," "Scarlet Begonias," "It Must Have Been the Roses," "Brokedown Palace," and "Touch of Grey."

🎸 *Jerry Garcia on Garcia/Hunter:*

Our best collaborations are when we work together. He has a tendency to write in very dense rhythmic and metrical stuff that's hard to break out of the meter. When I work with him, I make him do things that are more irregular, and I give him phrases that he wouldn't normally come up with. The songs of his that I eventually turn into music — they *find* me. It has to do with an emotional quality of the words. There's something about them that I feel—"Yeah, this song speaks to me."

We've lucked out and gotten some really nice songs. I mean, I have the experience of singing those songs over the years, so I know how nice they are. It's hard to sing a song that doesn't mean something to you, and it's hard to have a song keep meaning something to you when you repeat it a lot of times. It's a testament to the power of a lot of those songs that I can still sing them and they still mean something to me.

I don't have any specific favorites. There are a few songs that I always really love. "Stella Blue" is one. More of them than not, really, because they've already gone through the editing process. The only ones that find their way into existence are ones that speak to me on some level anyway.

I rarely change his lyrics without consulting him, although I've gotten more comfortable with changing a word or a phrase here and there than I used to be.

Some things we worked on for years, before they ever came out to be performable songs. One of the ones that I thought really ended up working well on that level was "Reuben and Cherise," which is one of my favorite of our songs together. There's a song that was not a matter of inspiration. It's one of those songs that we worked on year after year. We'd bring it out. "Let's try this again . . . No, it still doesn't work—ah, forget it." The whole process took about seven or eight years.

Sometimes he rethinks what he's done and decides, "Well, this would've been a better ending." But usually he doesn't insist that I use it. Like he's got a verse that he's been wanting me to add to "Friend of the Devil" for a million years. I refuse to do it. Maybe I'll blow his mind someday and do it.

He's got his versions of "Lady With a Fan" and "Terrapin." One version has a beautiful conclusion, where everything comes together finally in the end. I prefer the open version—we don't know what happened. The storyteller makes no choice—and neither do we. And neither do you, and neither does anybody else. I prefer that. I prefer to be hanging. I've always been really fond of the fragment. The song that has one verse. And you don't know anything about the characters, you don't know what they're doing, but they're doing something important. I love that. I'm a sucker for that kind of song.

GEN ☜ • Short for "generation," used by tape traders as a ranking of tape quality. When a tape is copied, the copy is said to be a generation away from the source tape. Thus, a copy of a source tape is a "first gen," a copy of the copy is the "second gen," and so on. The sound quality of analog tapes (as opposed to DATs) decreases with each generation, as hiss, distortion, signal fading, "breakup," and other forms of "generational distortion" increases.

Tapes that are less than five generations or so away from the source tape are considered "low-gen," and tapes that are more than that are "hi-gen." Low-gen tapes are most desirable for trading. (The five-generations guideline is dependent on the quality of the tape decks used for copying. A single cheap dubbing deck with dirty heads that need demagnetization can do more damage to the sound quality of a tape than several clean Nakamichis.)

Many analog tape traders specify "low-gen SBDs"—soundboard tapes of low generation—"only." Because DAT copying entails little if any generational distortion, "gens" are not an issue among digital traders. *See* TREES AND VINES.

THE GENE POOL ☜ • Serious tape collectors view their racks of tapes not only as treasure-houses of delight for the present but as archives for the future: mini-vaults (*see* THE VAULT). The conviction that the music on the tapes will outlast the collectors themselves carries a sense of responsibility, and encourages tapers to seek out the best recordings possible and copy them on the highest-quality blanks they can afford. There are collectors who make a point of recording over inferior-quality tapes when they are certain there are better versions available, to "keep the gene pool healthy."

GETTING BUMPED • When the rightful owner of a seat appears, forcing a SEAT SURFING Head to move along. "I was six rows up on Phil's side for most of the first set, but I got bumped and ended up behind the stage."

GETTING IT • Said by Heads about the moment they became a Deadhead. "I saw two shows at Pine Knob, but I didn't really *get it* until the 'Playin'' into 'Uncle John's' at the Greek '88."

"On one level," says sociologist Rebecca Adams, " 'getting it'

is understanding shows as spiritual experiences, though Deadheads are quick to point out that many people 'get it' in places
other than a Grateful Dead show. On another level, 'getting it'
is perceiving these spiritual experiences as inseparable from the
music, the scene, and a cooperative mode of everyday existence."

"If you ask a Deadhead what the 'it' is," observes Adams, "he
or she has a hard time responding. Even when Deadheads refer to a musical understanding or a social conscientiousness,
spirituality permeates their comments. Spiritual experiences at
shows vary widely, the most common ones being self-revela-
tions and feelings of unity with specific individuals, the family
of Deadheads, or all of humanity. These experiences usually
happen during THE SECOND SET."

GETTING YOUR DECK IN ⊠ • In the late '70s and
early '80s, before THE TAPERS' SECTION was created, Heads
who wanted to sneak taping equipment into the auditorium
sometimes had to go to elaborate lengths to foil arena security.
Santa Cruz Head T'res Buika remembers women strapping
decks and mics to their thighs with duct tape to avoid detection.
"The first women into the bathrooms at the old Greek shows
were always peeling tape off their legs," she recalls. "An old
taper told me, 'Duct tape holds the world together.' "

One couple would bake a "D-5 cake" each New Year's
Eve—a hollowed-out sheet cake with the compact Sony deck
inside and frosted with "Happy New Year!" A wheelchair not
only offered hiding places, it got you in early. The hard part,
taper Jeff Silberman recalls, was finding someone to sit in it. "I
remember one night," Silberman says, "the guards asked this
guy going in what the huge tripod strapped to the back of the
chair was. 'Oh,' he says, 'that's my *IV ∂rip.*' "

GO TO HEAVEN • Album #16, released in April 1980.
This was Mydland's first album with the Dead, recorded less
than a year after his joining the band. It was produced by Gary
Lyons, who framed songs like "Alabama Getaway" and "Lost
Sailor"→"Saint of Circumstance" with a sculpted, keen-edged

sound. It has been said that the album is overproduced, but compared to *Terrapin Station, Go to Heaven* is stripped down and lean. The cover photograph depicts the band as blow-dried angels decked in white suits.

♣ *Mitchell Stein, keyboard player, on* **Go to Heaven:**

Go to Heaven is clearly one of the Grateful Dead's most successful attempts to reach a mainstream audience. Previous projects contained select tracks that showed up on radio ("Truckin'," "Casey Jones," and "Sugar Magnolia," to name a few), but Gary Lyons's production showcased the Dead at their pop-chart slickest. The album stayed on the charts for twenty-one weeks, peaking at #23. As a junior in high school who had been "on the bus" for three years when the album came out, I welcomed *Go to Heaven* with open ears.

"Alabama Getaway" stands out as one of the most hard-driving songs the band has recorded (it also hit #68 on *Billboard*'s top 100). Garcia's blistering lead lays a foundation in the first few notes, and Brent's flowing synthesizer line is definitively his own. "Far From Me," Brent's solo contribution to the album ("Easy to Love You" was co-written by Barlow), stands out for me because I chose it as my transcription assignment while attending the Berklee College of Music in 1981. What follows those first few imposing chords is a well-told tale of a man's attempt to say good-bye to a lover with whom he has become a bit too "comfortable."

"Althea" is one of Garcia and Hunter's strongest collaborations. The song's story of love misplaced ("I told Althea I'm a roving sign—that I was born to be a bachelor/Althea told me, 'Okay, that's fine,' so now I'm out trying to catch her") contains one of my favorite Dead lyrics— the first half Hunter, the second half Shakespeare: "You may be the fate of Ophelia, sleeping and perchance to dream . . ."

Weir and Barlow struck gold with the next three tunes on the album. "Feel Like a Stranger," which matured into a wall of bass-driven voodoo live (check out *Dead Set*), contains some of the more intriguing harmonic changes of the band's repertoire. While the lyrics are less deep than some of Weir and Barlow's other efforts, the song delivers an instrumental wallop reminiscent of songs like "Samson and Delilah" and "Help on the Way," due in large part to Phil's powerhouse bottom end. The song ends abruptly, as though someone forgot to fade down the mix before the tape ran out—a pranksterish touch.

"Lost Sailor" is a "power ballad," an ethereal story of a soul adrift in a sea of longing, haunted by ghostly ship's bells. The song segues perfectly into "Saint of Circumstance," with its ironic lyrics ("Holes in what's left of my reason, holes in the knees of my blues . . .") and highly danceable grooves. "Lost Sailor" and "Saint of Circumstance" made a great pairing back-to-back in concert. Mickey and Billy's "Antwerp's Placebo (The Plumber)" strikes me as an afterthought, an inside joke in which I am not included. "Easy to Love You" finds Brent in a very different mood from "Far From Me," reveling in heartfelt joy found in the company of his lover. The last track on the album, "Don't Ease Me In," is a celebration from the first note, with Brent's searing Hammond B-3 organ, and Garcia in great voice, laying down one classic lead after another.

Go to Heaven, the Dead's third album for Arista, signaled an important step in the band's evolution. The accessibility of the tracks paved the way for a significant increase in the Grateful Dead's popularity, and proved to the public at large that even a band known for obscure lyrics and extended jamming could produce vital "popular" music.

Commercial? Perhaps. Even so, *Go to Heaven* is essential Grateful Dead.

GO TO HELL • After the release of *Go to Heaven*, with its elegant cover featuring the band in all-white suits (the only Dead album that gives credit to the tailors), a rumor circulated widely that the follow-up would be called *Go to Hell*, with a cover of the band dressed as street people.

GODCHAUX, DONNA • Vocals. Born August 22, 1945. On March 22, 1972, five months after her husband Keith's debut as the band's new keyboardist, Donna Godchaux joined the Dead onstage at the New York Academy of Music to help sing "How Sweet It Is." With that, she became the first and only woman to be a member of the Grateful Dead.

"They had asked me to sing right away," when Keith joined the band, she explained to Blair Jackson in 1985. "It was just a question of when I decided it was time for me to do it." With the May '72 release of Bob Weir's solo album, *Ace*, Donna came into her own as a new and important part of the band's sound. On *Ace*, and on many subsequent Weir tunes, she complemented Weir's tenor cowboy lilt with soulful gospel-influenced upper-range harmonies. Singing with Garcia in both the Dead and the

JERRY GARCIA BAND, she brought a rhythm-and-blues verve to his sweet, somewhat fragile voice. She also contributed several tunes to the Dead's repertoire during her tenure, including "Sunrise" and "From the Heart of Me."

Godchaux grew up as Donna Jean Thatcher in Muscle Shoals, Alabama, where black musicians like Aretha Franklin, Percy Sledge, and Sam Cooke were pioneering a new sound by putting a rockabilly beat behind oldtimes blues and Negro spirituals—*rhythm and blues*. While still in her teens, Donna and her vocal group Southern Comfort became a fixture in the Muscle Shoals R&B scene, recording backup vocals for Sam Cooke and many others. After Percy Sledge's "When a Man Loves a Woman," with Donna's background vocals, went to number one in the *Billboard* pop charts in 1966, she became a hot commodity. A few years later, a Southern Comfort recording of "Suspicious Minds" caught the attention of Elvis Presley, who brought Donna's group to Memphis to record it, and several other tunes, with him. Donna also recorded with Lynyrd Skynyrd and the Rolling Stones, and, later on, sang backup on Little Feat's *Dixie Chicken*.

She gave up her music career—or so she thought—to move to the Bay Area in 1970. "I'd just always wanted to come here," she told Blair Jackson. Within one twelve-hour span in October '70, she was introduced to both future husband Keith Godchaux *and* the Grateful Dead. "A group of us took acid and went up in the mountains," she recalls. "Toward the end of the day, someone suggested we all go down to a Grateful Dead concert. We were in the very back of the balcony of Winterland. The New Riders came on and I went, 'Hmmm—this is interesting.' Then Quicksilver came on and I went, 'Hmmm!' Then the Jefferson Airplane came on and I said, 'Hmmm!!!' Then the Grateful Dead came on and I said, '*What is this?* Whatever it is, this is where I'm at!'

"I couldn't sleep that night. I kept thinking, 'How did they do that?' They weave a spell. There's this whole mystical energy that happens when you see the Grateful Dead, and you're ready to receive it. I was ready to receive it, and I got it."

After spending a year as devoted Deadheads, the couple, who by then were married and living in Walnut Creek, approached Garcia and requested an audition with the band. A week later, they were members of the Dead.

Ironically, although she was by far the most thoroughly trained and technically proficient singer the group has ever had, tapes reveal a tendency to sing off-key at live performances, for the simple reason that she had little monitor support on stage.

After some mounting marital troubles, compounded by the pressure from a life spent in hotels and recording studios, the Godchaux's eight-year collaboration with the Dead came to a mutually agreed upon end in February '79. Two months later, Brent Mydland was recruited to replace Keith and Donna.

Shortly after Keith's death in a highway accident in 1980, Donna experienced a religious awakening, and became a devoted Christian. She is now married to bassist David MacKay, who is a pastor, and lives with her two sons, Zion and Kinsman, in Petaluma, California.

GODCHAUX, KEITH • Keyboards. Born July 19, 1948, and grew up in Concord, California.

"He had a heart of music," says Kreutzmann.

Godchaux trained classically for five years as a child, but did not have the temperament for it. When he was fourteen, he joined a band that played in local country clubs, and he also played cocktail jazz in piano-bar trios. The Dixieland that he played in those years informed his playing with the Dead, which glowed with an authentic, down-home soulfulness.

Godchaux was hired in October of '71, when both Tom Constanten and Pigpen had left the band. "He was so brilliant at the beginning," recalls Lesh. With Kreutzmann as the sole drummer, Godchaux helped propel the band into its most jazz-influenced period, when the band's time was at its most elastic, and the grooves at their most relaxed, expansive, and lyrical. Godchaux is a vastly underrated player, owing partly to his laconic performances in later years.

The brilliance that Lesh refers to can be heard on his sparkling contributions on *Mars Hotel,* where Godchaux plays stately harpsichord on "China Doll"; or on *One From the Vault,* his Fender Rhodes darting between the other players' notes during "King Solomon's Marbles" and "Big River" like fleet mercury; or on *Europe '72,* where his funky/elegant lines are the ragtime heart of a quintessentially American band playing cowboy music in Paris.

Donna Godchaux started singing with the band a few months after Keith's debut, and the two performed and recorded with the Dead—and, off and on, with the Jerry Garcia Band—up until early '79.

As time went on, the band became unhappy with the way Godchaux's strictly percussive attack was inhibiting development of tone colors in the band, and Godchaux's presence on and offstage was becoming more and more disconsolate. "Keith didn't really like it here," Weir says. "He was bored with life in general, and he would freely tell anybody that. The darkness came upon him, and it pretty much took control."

After a last great show at Oakland Auditorium on 2/17/79—featuring a moving version of "The Wheel"—the Godchauxs left the band by mutual agreement, resuming their career playing with Dave Mason and in a Marin County group called The Ghosts. Godchaux was killed in a car accident near his home on July 21, 1980. He is survived by his wife and his son, Zion.

🔊 *Donna Godchaux, on how she and Keith Godchaux came to be members of the Grateful Dead, from Blair Jackson's* Goin' Down the Road:

Keith would play his rock and roll piano at home, and I was basically supporting the two of us. One day our friend Pete said, "Let's listen to some Grateful Dead." Keith said, "I don't want to listen to it. I want to play it." We were just so high and in love! We said to Pete and Carol, "Hey, guys, we're going to play with the Grateful Dead," and we really believed it. We had no doubt.

We went home, looked in the paper, and saw that Garcia's band was playing at the Keystone, and went down. At the break, Garcia was walking by, so I grabbed him and said, "Jerry, my husband and I have something very important to talk to you about."

He said "Sure," and told us to come backstage. But we were both too scared. A few minutes later, Garcia came up and sat next to Keith. I said,

"Honey, I think Garcia's hinting that he wants to talk to you. He's sitting right next to you." He looked over at Jerry, and looked back at me, and dropped his head on the table and said, "You're going to have to talk to my wife. I can't talk to you right now." He was just too shy.

So I said to Jerry, "Well, Keith's your piano player, so I want your home telephone number so we can call you up and come to the next Grateful Dead practice." And he believed me! He gave me his number.

That coming Sunday, Jerry told us to come on down, but the band had forgotten to tell Jerry that the rehearsal had been called off. So Keith and Jerry played, then Jerry called Kreutzmann and got him to come down. The next day, the Dead practiced, and by the end of the day, Keith was on the payroll.

We had no idea what joining a band of the magnitude of the Grateful Dead would mean. It's this whole extended reality. When Keith and I first got together, we wanted to write music to the Lord, because it didn't seem like there was much out there that was spiritual. When we heard the Grateful Dead, it had a quality that was magical, ethereal, and spiritual. That's part of what was so attractive about it.

A selected Keith and Donna Godchaux non-Dead discography:

Keith and Donna — Released in March '75

The Ghosts Playing in the Heart of Gold Band — Released in 1984

GOING INTO, COMING OUT OF (→) • Used by Heads to describe the improvised musical bridges that link one song to another, as in, "They jammed 'Dark Star' out of 'Mountains of the Moon' and into 'St. Stephen.' " It is in these transitional passages that the Dead have played some of their most haunting and unforgettable music, combining songs into improvised suites by what Garcia and Grisman call "fast composition," to flow gracefully from one musical realm into another.

Heads have developed a very economical notation for this process on setlists and tape covers: the arrow (→). "Scarlet→ Fire," written on a SETLIST, means the band jammed from "Scarlet Begonias" into "Fire on the Mountain" without stopping. Because the transitions are not always seamless, the meticulous authors of *Dead Base* have adopted what they call "the three-second rule" as a guideline. If the band does not pause, or retune, for more than three seconds before going into the next song, *DeadBase* lists an arrow between tunes.

The first use of this Deadhead notation on an official Grateful Dead release was on DICK'S PICKS, VOLUME ONE, the cover of which consciously emulates a collector's handwritten SETLISTS. *See also* DOORWAYS AND SPLICES; JAM.

THE GOLDEN ROAD • "The crème de la crème—the most beautiful magazine that there will ever be about the Grateful Dead," says John Dwork, who edits his own magazine on the same subject, DUPREE'S DIAMOND NEWS. *The Golden Road*, published by Bay Area journalists Blair Jackson and Regan McMahon, began as a quarterly for mail-order subscribers with a winter '84 issue.

Combining meticulous scholarship, reasoned opinion, sophisticated graphics, interviews with band and family members, and irreverent insider's wit, *The Golden Road* offered its readers a perspective that was both personal and informed. Each issue boasted a vivid cover by artists like Stanley Mouse, Gary Houston, Scott McDougall, and Dave Marrs, and offered its readers detailed reports of recent tours, lively letters from other Heads, and excavations into Dead history. Jackson's "Roots" column pinpointed the sources of the band's inspiration by unearthing original versions of cover tunes, while satiric features—like an ad for a Grateful Dead Book Club offering *The Neal Cassady Guide to Safe Driving*—leavened the deep background with humor.

Jackson's career as a Dead scholar began while he was in high school, deciphering the lyrics to "What's Become of the Baby?" *without* headphones. Jackson saw his first show at the Capitol Theater in Port Chester, New York, on 3/20/70, and in '83, he published his first book, *Grateful Dead: The Music Never Stopped*, combining an overview of band history, reportage of a concert at Ventura, and a critical discography. When the book was finished, he had a lot of unused research, access to the bandmembers, and an urge to go on tour.

Jackson recalls, "The Dead started playing lots of really nice venues in Northern and Southern California in the early '80s. It was also a time when the media was completely ignoring the band, in the wake of punk and New Wave. They weren't putting out records, there was nothing glamorous about them, so the straight media viewed them as the Over-the-Hill gang, even as their popularity was rising. It seemed like there was an opening for a well-researched West Coast perspective on the Dead." Early encouragement from friends—and eventually, from Garcia himself, who told Jackson, "We appreciates it"—persuaded Jackson that he was on the right road.

The Golden Road was a family affair. Jackson and McMahon did almost all of the writing and paste-ups themselves, and the mass mailings to up to five thousand subscribers became parties for the Jacksons' show family, longtime habitués of the Phil Zone. Certain pieces in *The Golden Road*—like a biography in issue no. 27 called "Pigpen Forever: The Life and Times of Ron McKernan"—set the standard for Dead historical writing, and a selection of *Golden Road* features was published in '92 as *Goin' Down the Road: A Grateful Dead Traveling Companion.* The magazine became an annual in '92. With the birth of Jackson's second child, and a feeling that many of the things that Jackson had set out to do had been accomplished, *The Golden Road* took an indefinite hiatus after the '93 issue.

THE GOLDEN ROAD TO UNLIMITED DEVOTION • The Dead's first official fan club, founded in '65 by the original Deadheads: Sue Swanson, Connie Furtado, and Bob Matthews. A dollar to the club got you posters, buttons, "biographies of each Dead," and the very first issue of *Rolling Stone.* For $2.50, you got one of the first Dead shirts ever made, with Pigpen on it. The club promised personal responses to all fan mail, and promised to divulge "secrets" about the band-members' lives.

Swanson became friends with Weir in World Geography class at Menlo-Atherton High School. Swanson and Furtado were Beatlemaniacs, who asked Weir to teach them how to play guitar so they could play Beatles songs. "He made us learn Bob

Dylan songs, and other morbid songs. He wouldn't teach us Beatles songs," moans Furtado.

The name of the club occurred to Swanson as she sat at her kitchen table with her friend Bruce. "It just seemed like the right thing to my sixteen-year-old mind." Swanson earned her fan-club credentials by starting the first official Rolling Stones fan club in America, in the hopes that through the Stones, she could meet the Beatles.

The first song on the Dead's first album, a tribute to a high-spirited young woman who is "a-whistlin' and a singin' and a-carryin' on"—a muse of the Haight-Ashbury spirit—was named after the club. "Hey, hey! Hey right away," invited the lyric. "Join the club and pa-a-arty, every day!"

Swanson still works in the family business.

🍀 *Sue Swanson, founder of the Golden Road to Unlimited Devotion, still on the road:*

I was the one who held the sheet music so Phil could sing at the second Warlocks rehearsal. It really was a golden time, just being on the trip.

It *is* unlimited devotion, it *is* so much fun, it *is* great, it *is* a golden road. I've had to learn to share them—a lot. But they'll always be *my* boys.

GOOD OL' GRATEFUL DEAD • This slogan—with its bluegrass flavor, and implications of the Dead as durable homeboys built to outlast pop fads—seems to refer to a band with a lot of history behind it. According to Haight-Ashbury historian Charles Perry, however, red-white-and-blue buttons emblazoned with this tribute appeared as early as 1966. "In an apartment at the corner of Stanyan and Alma," Perry writes in his book *The Haight-Ashbury,* "the tenants sold the coveted buttons . . . If the people were home, you could go in and buy one. If they weren't, you could walk in, find the upended orange crate with the dish of buttons on it, take what you wanted and leave the money on the crate."

Round Records employee Steve Brown recalls Bill Graham referring to the band with this tag from the stage at the Fillmore, where the Dead played at least twenty-four shows in the last months of '66. The good ol' Grateful Dead could always be counted on to play benefits for local causes. "There was a pride very early on," says Brown, "in both the band, and in the kind of people who were coming to see them. They were already inspiring a very special kind of loyalty."

The slogan was incorporated into Bob Thomas's cover art for *History of the Grateful Dead, Vol. 1 (Bear's Choice)* in '73.

GORBY BLOTS • A particularly potent and clean vintage of blotter LSD popular in the early '90s, illustrated with the face of Mikhail Gorbachev, the last leader of the Soviet Union. "It was my favorite acid ever," says *Golden Road* editor Blair Jackson. "We used to argue over who would get the birthmark."

GRAHAM, BILL • Concert promoter. Born Wolfgang Grajonza on January 8, 1931, in Berlin, Germany.

The man behind the Fillmore Auditorium, the Fillmores East and West, Winterland, and the annual Grateful Dead New Year's extravaganzas, Bill Graham was a charismatic and influential rock and roll businessman who helped to radically change the way live music was presented. Graham, operating in San Francisco, first helped to invent the club scene, and then, in the '70s, led the transition into mammoth venues like hockey arenas and baseball stadiums. Always controversial, Bill Graham was the man who gave Bay Area psychedelic music a place to happen and evolve.

He was also a very close associate of the Grateful Dead, going back to the early days. Graham produced countless shows for the band, including the famous New Year's shows, where he would make grand entrances into the middle of the ultimate Deadhead party atop a giant mushroom, a skull, a joint, or riding a motorcycle down from the balcony. He is the honorary thirteenth eye on the cover of the Dead's IN THE DARK. "The Grateful Dead experience gives you something we all need," Graham said, *"time out ."*

Born in Berlin just as Hitler was coming to power, Graham's father was a civil engineer who died of a blood infection when Bill was two days old. The rest of his family was subject to Nazi persecution throughout the '30s. Bill escaped from Germany with part of his family when he was nine. He spent two years in France and finally arrived in New York in September 1941.

Cared for by the Ehrenreich family in the Bronx, "Billy Grajonca" was subject, both as a Jew and a German, to yet more persecution from his American neighbors and fellow students. A fighter by necessity from an early age, Graham developed a tenacious, defiant personality.

In his teens, he worked as a waiter in the Catskills, and he later moved to Southern California to become a character actor. Leaving L.A. in disgust after being denied a television role expressly because of his Jewish appearance, Graham wound up in San Francisco, where he got involved with a progressive, left-wing theater company called the Mime Troupe. It was here that Graham made his transition from actor to entertainment businessman. "He came as an actor and he found out that there was no business manager, and that it was something that needed to be done," explains ex–Mime Trouper Judy Goldhaft.

Graham's first productions were dance benefits for the Mime Troupe at the Fillmore, featuring Bay Area bands—including, at the third benefit on 12/10/65, "The Grateful Dead—formerly the Warlocks." It was the band's first billing as the Dead.

"I seemed to have a knack for it," said Graham, "the carrying out of the details of public assemblage. Working the room, and hiring the right people to do security. Little by little, after the first and second benefits, certain things began ticking me off. I realized at that two o'clock in the morning, these people who had been dancing all night long were not yet finished with their flight. Even though the music was over. They were coming in like a glider lands. You can't glide and glide and glide and then come right down—*bang!*—on the ground. At the third benefit, I remember asking, 'Who turned the house lights on?' I told people not to do that again. When the music ended, I wanted the lights left soft. The next time, I rented a mirror ball. I started the mirror ball turning and put on slides of flowers and animals with soft, soft music going in the background, so people could land without a crash."

This was Bill Graham's signature: canny *chutzpah,* and an empathy for his audience expressed in attention paid to a thousand details. He thought of himself as the maître d' of every show he produced. Known as the "guy with the clipboard," Graham would go to every show with 3 × 5 cards, jotting down ideas on how to improve things the next time around. Unlike other promoters, Graham could always be seen floating into the crowd to check the sound, the lighting, the refreshments. He became a celebrity, and would draw suggestions and criticisms from the folks in the audience.

Graham was particularly proud of the adventurous double bills he staged in the early years of his live production career— Miles Davis and the Dead, Chuck Berry and Moby Grape, Woody Herman and the Who.

The father of rock mega-concerts was, with some hindsight, not particularly proud of everything his industry had become. "When the bands started getting popular," he explained to Blair Jackson and Regan McMahon in 1985, "it became, 'Bill, we want to play Madison Square Garden.' I'd say, 'No, play three nights at the Fillmore.' But there were finances involved, and we're all human—who doesn't want to have a nicer car or a new house? Economics came into play and I got caught up in that, and then the groups priced themselves out of the smallest places.

"Does it take away from the positive impact when you make the distance between the microphone and the last person in the audience longer and longer? Yes. Not many groups can pull that off."

Graham always had a special place in his heart for the Dead. "I always thought they were different," he told Jackson and McMahon. "Even the Warlocks were very sensual. They make my body move and feel good. They did that from day one.

"The Dead show is like an umbilical cord between the people who come. They connect at the gig, then they take their plug out and leave. There's something that happens there, and when it's over, you go back to the world and your TVs, and you punch the clock, and it's no longer 'time out.' When the people want a second encore, a lot of times I think they're just saying, 'It's nice being here.' The attempt on our part is never to forget that."

Graham, who sat on the board of the Dead's REX FOUNDA-TION, related to the band as family, and was never shy about poking and prodding them occasionally to do a second encore, when he felt the mood was right. "It's not just me that wants the second encore on certain nights. I'm just trying to transmit information from the crowd. You can feel it. The crowd isn't finished. So there I am, chasing them through the backstage, and I say, 'Listen, before you step inside that car' — 'Yeah, what is it, BILL?!' " At Frost Theater '85, Graham was able to convince the band to come back for a stunning "She Belongs to Me" second encore.

Bill Graham was killed in a helicopter crash on October 25, 1991, along with his girlfriend Melissa Gold and their friend and pilot Steve Kahn. On November 3, a public appreciation of the three, called "Laughter, Love, and Music," was held in Golden Gate Park. Performers included the Dead with John Fogerty sitting in; Robin Williams; Jackson Browne; Aaron Neville; and Crosby, Stills, Nash & Young. Jerry Pompili, a longtime friend and employee, closed the show by looking to the sky and saying, "Hey, Bill . . . *great* show." *See* FILLMORE EAST; FILLMORE WEST; UNCLE BOBO; WINTERLAND.

GRATEFUL BED & BREAKFAST • Fantasy Island meets 2/13/70.

This Puerto Rican "alternative" resort was started by Marty Soucie in February '92 as a vacation spot for other Deadheads, eco-tourists, "and anyone looking for something a little less impersonal and more in tune with the local environment and culture." His five-acre ranch in the foothills of the Luquillo Mountains is thirty minutes from the San Juan airport, five minutes from the Luquillo beach, and ten minutes from El Yunque Caribbean rainforest. For $50 a night, you get room, breakfast, savvy advice on your eco-adventure itinerary, and access to a music room with sundry musical instruments and a tape library with 350+ hours of GD, three hundred non-Dead tapes ("classical, blues, reggae, Latin music, you name it—but no rap and no disco"). Soucie reports a tally of three hundred guests in the first two years of operation, roughly two hundred of which were Deadheads. Club Dead lives! "My goal," says Soucie, "is to open up a few more around the country. I want to be the Conrad Hilton of alternative vacationing."

GRATEFUL DEAD • In 1965, the "Warlocks" (Kreutzmann, Garcia, Weir, Lesh, and Pigpen), on the verge of signing with Warner Bros., discovered that another band with the same name had beaten them to vinyl. Scores of suggestions for new names were tried on for size: "Vanilla Plumbago" (words selected from an Edward Gorey book that Weir was reading) . . . "The Hobbits" . . . "Mythical Ethical Icicle Tricycle." On November 3, 1965, the band recorded a six-song demo for Tom Donahue's Autumn Records at the Golden State Studios under the name "the Emergency Crew."

"We had a million funny names," says Garcia. But "nothing quite fit . . . We were at Phil's house one day; he had a big dictionary, I opened it up and the first thing I saw was 'The Grateful Dead.' It said that on the page and it was so astonishing. It was a truly weird moment. I didn't like it really, I just found it to be really powerful. Weir didn't like it, Kreutzmann didn't like it, and nobody really wanted to hear about it. But then people started calling us that and it just started, Grateful Dead, Grateful Dead." *The original entry in Funk and Wagnall's New Practical Standard Dictionary of the English Language, Vol. 1, 1955:*

GRATEFUL DEAD—The motif of a cycle of folk tales which begins with the hero's coming upon a group of people ill-treating or refusing to bury the corpse of a man who had died without paying his debts. He gives his last penny, either to pay the man's debts or to give him decent burial. Within a few hours he meets with a traveling companion who aids him in some impossible task, gets him a fortune, saves his life, etc. The story ends with the companion's disclosing himself as the man whose corpse the other had befriended.

The most luminous retelling of the ancient tale is family member Alan Trist's *The Water of Life: A Tale of the Grateful Dead. See* HULOGOSI PRESS.

GRATEFUL DEAD • Album #1, released in March 1967.

Record company reps swarmed into the Bay Area in the mid-'60s, looking to sign bands that embodied the new psychedelic culture that was coming out of THE HAIGHT-ASHBURY. RCA signed the Jefferson Airplane, Columbia made a deal with Janis Joplin's Big Brother and the Holding Company, and Warner Bros. landed the Dead.

Grateful Dead, originally titled *The Golden Road*, was the first of ten albums for Warner Bros., and was released in mono. The collage on the cover is by Alton Kelley. The lettering above the title had read, "In the land of the dark, the ship of the sun is drawn by the Grateful Dead" (a phrase that is—apocryphally—reported to come from the *Egyptian Book of the Dead* and is *not* the source of the group's name), but the band decided the slogan was pretentious, and the lettering was partially obscured. (When asked by Blair Jackson if Warner Bros. had any problems with the cover, Kelley recalled, "They were super pleased, because the in-house art department had been doing covers for Sinatra, and they had no idea what to do.")

🦋 *Steve Brown, Round Records employee, on **Grateful Dead**:*

We weren't even "Deadheads" yet, still "Dead Freaks," when we heard that the band would be recording their first album for a bigtime label. Warner Bros., wow! Thrusting our local heroes into the mainstream would be Dave Hassinger, who had just produced the Rolling Stones' *Out of Their Heads*. This was the Dead's opportunity to show their stuff, as the first wave of new music from San Francisco was breaking in 1967.

Although by today's standards, some of the tunes sound like speeded-up Top 40, fans felt the beginning of a new era of countercultural pride as college and "underground" FM radio carried the Grateful Dead into living rooms, dorm rooms, and even into military barracks and warships at sea. (I carried a tape of the album to Vietnam to play for sailors in the Tonkin Gulf, and in Subic Bay in the Philippines.)

The album opens with a swirling organ riff that takes you down a rabbit hole to "The Golden Road (to Unlimited Devotion)." This joyous song helped set the tempo for a Summer of Love—ending appropriately on an ominous chord. "Beat It On Down the Line" has a rush-to-get-there urgency and an upfront tambourine probably played by Pigpen, and Mr. Pen steps out with the bluesy "Good Morning Little Schoolgirl," which crackles with the band's original mojo, fading out just as Pig's harp, and the jam, takes off.

"Cold Rain and Snow" was the anthem for the band's first wave of fans, a spirit-rouser with stinging guitar licks. "Sittin' on Top of the World" has not stood the test of time by lasting in the repertoire, but Garcia gets off some sparkling runs before the song fades too soon. "Cream Puff War" is another relic of a bygone era, a pace-changing rocker that could have been written by the nearly forgotten Los Angeles band, Love.

"Morning Dew"—a lament against nuclear war written by Canadian folk singer Bonnie Dobson—was especially poignant to a generation in the agony of the Vietnam war, feeling helpless to change an older generation's warring ways.

When you wanted to impress someone with what this new Grateful Dead thing was all about, you played them "Viola Lee Blues." Garcia's spiraling lines, Pig's big Hammond organ, and Bobby's churning rhythm took you on a roller-coaster ride that started off slow, accelerated you screaming through space, and then brought you back to a place comfortable and familiar.

A taste of things to come.

THE GRATEFUL DEAD HOUR • David Gans's nationally syndicated weekly radio show, featuring live tapes from the Vault, interviews, history, and commentary. The show itself is taped faithfully by collectors and traded, and carries live Dead music to Heads in places where the Dead never tour. As of December '93, it is broadcast on more than seventy commercial and public stations. More than a wellspring of soundboard-quality tapes, the show's interviews and commentary help locate the music in context, in keeping with Gans's aim to make the show a *"National Geographic* of Grateful Deadland."

The show began in November '84, as the KFOG *Deadhead Hour* in San Francisco. Radio personality M. Dung hosted the show for a while, and Richard Raffel—a Deadhead doctor—worked on it in the first months. Gans guest-hosted a feature on the evolution of "The Pump Song" (now called "Greatest Story Ever Told") while promoting his book *Playing in the Band*, en-

joyed doing it, and eventually took over the weekly program.
By 1987, Gans had secured permission from the band to
distribute the *Hour* nationally, and also got access to Vault
tapes. He works closely with archivist Dick Latvala in choosing material from the Dead's collection. Gans does not play entire sets, in keeping with an agreement made with the band,
who may wish to release the tapes someday as live albums.
(The show's hour-long format, with a break in the middle,
wouldn't allow the broadcast of uninterrupted second sets anyway.)

"My mission is to bypass the sloppy version of so-and-so at
the beginning of the set, and realize that things clicked into focus during the song that followed," says Gans. "I choose stuff
based on what's interesting to me, but I try to embody the musical values of the Grateful Dead as I understand them, which
includes respect for diversity, and appreciating that other people like songs that I don't. I go to where the jamming action is,
so I play a lot of 'Terrapin,' a lot of 'Dark Star.' But then I'll get
a letter that says, 'Hey, man, can't you find a "Fennario" in
there?' So I'll try to mix it up, interweave the best of different
eras, to take the wheel all the way around."

Gans's first show was 3/5/72 at Winterland. "I got dragged to
the show by my roommate and songwriting partner, Stephen
Donnelly," he recalls. "We slipped a little windowpane under
our tongues, and our designated driver drove us to San Francisco from San Jose in a green VW 1500 with the throttle stuck
all the way open. We were blazing by the time we got to Winterland, and we climbed way up into the top of the balcony. It
was 180 degrees up there, and I was a little scared. There was
a guy onstage doing pyrotechnics, the flames erupting in perfect time with the music. I didn't get the jamming at first, but
the songs—'Bertha,' 'Black-Throated Wind,' 'Greatest
Story'—etched themselves in my mind." Gans's own band,
Crazy Fingers (formerly the Reptiles), has been mixing up
Dead, non-Dead, and original material in club performances
since '81, with occasional guests like Henry Kaiser.

Semi-annual fundraising marathons for KPFA, hosted by Gans, are eagerly anticipated by Bay Area Deadheads, who stock up on blank cassettes, and hunker down for long days and nights of "spinning" tapes as Gans unearths one rare nugget from the Vault after another. Marathons are also community-builders, as callers dedicate pledges to other Heads far and wide, challenging one another to support the kind of community radio that has always provided a more comfortable home in airspace for Dead music than Top 40.

GRATEFUL DEAD LIVE • *See* SKULL AND ROSES.

GRATEFUL DEAD TICKET SALES (GDTS) • The Dead's own mail-order ticket vending service, founded in 1983. With two telephone hotlines—one on the East Coast, the other on the West—to give Heads ordering information and tour schedules, GDTS dispenses roughly one third of the tickets to each show, and does not charge the extravagant service fees of TicketMaster and its ilk. "Our main thing is not to make money," says GDTS director Steve Marcus. "We're here to provide a service to Deadheads, because we're Deadheads ourselves."

The GDTS base of operations is in a house near THE OFFICE in San Rafael. While soundboard tapes play, orders are filled by workers sitting around a big table, with tickets from three piles—great seats, OK seats, and poor seats. Marcus and crew aim to ensure as fair a distribution as possible, and Heads ordering tickets for a three-night run will most likely end up with great seats for at least one night. The method also means that groups of tourheads will end up sitting next to each other for shows in different cities, encouraging new friendships.

GDTS protects Heads from scalpers by flagging multiple orders, but it can be a tricky operation, says Marcus. "Once there were fifteen envelopes from the same house on Arch Street in Berkeley," he recalls. "So I pulled them—'I'm canceling all of them!' But my friend Calico [a longtime Hog Farmer] pointed out to me that there were fifteen Heads living at that address. So you have to be careful."

Steve Marcus has been a fan of the music since May of '61,

when he saw "Bob & Jerry"—Robert Hunter and Garcia—play at the Peninsula School in Menlo Park. His career in ticketing began in '77 at the BASS agency in Oakland. In '83, the Dead hired Marcus to supervise their first attempt at mail order, for several benefit shows at the Warfield Theater in San Francisco.

The hotline began in September of that year, with a stunning demonstration of the power of Deadhead word of mouth. Marcus set up an answering machine with ordering information for the Halloween run at Marin Civic Auditorium; then, at the Grass Valley show on September 18, he and Dead Heads' liaison Eileen Law each told ten Deadheads only to "call this number on Wednesday at noon, and there will be a surprise." The phones were jammed for a week straight, until the shows sold out.

In '83, the Dead sold 24,500 tickets by GDTS mail order. The next year, they sold 115,000. After MTV's "Day of the Dead" in '87, the sales jumped from 300,000 tickets to 450,000; counterfeits increased, and for the first time, half the ticket requests had to be sent back empty. By '93, GDTS was shipping half a million tickets a year.

The upstairs rooms of GDTS are a gallery of the Deadhead art that decorates many of the envelopes that Heads send in—with pleas, portraits of the band, and goofy messages, elaborate and very colorful—hoping to catch someone's eye at the big table. "We don't give beautiful envelopes priority anymore, though some of us used to," says Marcus. "But they are definitely appreciated." *See also* TICKETBASTARD.

GRATEFUL DISC FRISBEE CLUB • Anyone who's ever walked around the parking lot at a show knows Deadheads and Frisbees have an irresistible magnetism for one another. Grateful Disc Frisbee Club founder Bill Wright explains, *"You* fly with the disc. The disc bounces around and flows with the wind, and the TRAILS are great. It's so free out there, but it's controllable. Frisbees have an inherently magical characteristic about them." Established by Colorado State University Frisbee enthusiasts at the first Red Rocks show on 7/7/78, the club is still thriving. (A group of discers in Chico, California, filed with Wham-O for the same name shortly afterward and ended up calling their club the Airheads.) The Grateful Discers played many contests in the late '70s—the most accomplished freestylers were called the Coloradicals—earning respect and awards, and winning their first tournament in Minneapolis in 1979 by freestyling to "Uncle John's Band."

"We'd take mushrooms and go out with a boom box and play all afternoon to 'The Other One,'" remembers Wright. "Our original logo was the Ice Cream Kid spinning a disc. We made a huge banner for a tournament and hung it outside our bedroom window. Our landlord hated us. One day these guys knocked on our door and said, 'You guys are the Grateful Disc? Cool! We live in the Mars Hotel in Philly—can we come in?'"

In the '80s, the club became less oriented around the Dead, but was still going strong, and an influx of younger Heads in the '90s have reconnected Wright—who named his twins (boy and girl) Marley and Cassidy—with his past. "It came full circle. These guys who started very young with the club are now *way* into the Dead and got to be really good freestylers, and I started playing with them again, so now I'm on the same campus, and the same tunes are playing, and we're out there, gettin' high and playing Frisbee. It gets me rejuvenated to play hard again. Amazing how the music moves you."

GRAVY, WAVY • *See* WAVY GRAVY.

GREAT BIG LOVE BEAST • What David Crosby says crawls out of the speakers at a really good show to "eat the audience."

THE GREEK THEATER • A 8,700-seat venue on the campus of the University of California at Berkeley where the Dead played two shows in the '60s (10/1/67 and 10/20/68), and annual runs in late summer every year of the '80s.

Built into the Berkeley foothills in 1903, surrounded by aromatic eucalyptus trees, with San Francisco glittering in the distance, the Greek Theater was one of the "temples" of PRIMAL DEAD. The steeply angled bowl shape of the arena meant that shows at the Greek felt very intimate, due to the fact that every-one could see everyone else.

Showtimes for three-day runs there were usually staggered so each show began an hour earlier than the last, which meant that the first show took place mostly in the dark, with the first set of Saturday's show happening before sunset and the second set at night, and the Sunday show in daylight.

Shows at the Greek—an increasingly "tough ticket" as the band's popularity rose—were family shows, with many oldtime Heads who went *only* to Greek shows bringing spouses and kids for picnics. Many tapes from the Greek are considered to be classic performances.

The band is no longer able to play there, because the crowds became unmanageably large. For the last couple of Greek runs, the band provided speakers in a field nearby for those unable to get tickets.

On 7/13/84, the band resurrected DARK STAR as an encore (playing it for the first time in almost three years), with NASA slides of moonscapes projected behind the band. Just before the Dead came onstage, a meteor streaked across the sky. *See also* THRONES.

GROUPMIND • The collective identity or gestalt created in the big room at Dead shows. "During the concert experi-ence," writes theology student Shan Sutton in his analysis of the community of Deadheads as a grassroots religion, "Deadheads are no longer the unique individuals that exist in the everyday social structure. Instead, they become fellow parts of a brightly colored organic entity, with thousands of tie-dyed shirts swirling together . . . A Deadhead relates that 'the participation in each dance enables my spirit to transcend my body and min-gle and rejoice and become one with the spirits of all the other participants.' "

🌸 *John Barlow, lyricist, on groupmind online:*

The French philosopher and anthropologist Teilhard de Chardin wrote about collective consciousness assembling itself. Deadheads have always been into that. They get together at a concert and they create a group-mind, and they're always looking for any environment where the groupmind can set itself up. Cyberspace is perfect for that. It doesn't have all the obstacles that physical bodies create in compartmentalizing the continuum of mind.

Deadheads are early-adopters. They're throw-forwards. They're not troubled by ambiguity or confusion, because they're acidheads. The great thing about being an acidhead is that you actually *like* being confused. That fits you very well for life in the twenty-first century. So Deadheads don't have the social resistance to computer technology that others have.

And they're big into connection. You need a village green, a physical place that's more consistent and reliable than where the Grateful Dead happen to be playing, a place where you can run into each other and exchange the kind of random information that communities have to exchange. So much happens in the Pinedale, Wyoming, post office every morning. It's the tissue of *that* community. There isn't anything like that in the Dead scene, except for that which can be provided electronically. No matter where the Dead are playing, the WELL and rec.music.gdead and America Online are always there. So if you want to get out the word about some problem, or find out where somebody is, that's where you can go.

   GRTFLDED • License plate on a DEADMOBILE in New York State.

   Deadhead "vanity" plates are almost as prevalent as bumper-stickers and t-shirts, and serve as invitations for mutual recognition on the road. The special limitations of the medium — eight letters and numbers at most — forces Heads to condense their wit.

PLATE	STATE	TRANSLATION/SONG REFERENCE
10ACJED	NC	"Tennessee Jed"
AM DEW	ME	"Morning Dew"
ANY WNDO	CA	"Look out of any window" / "Box of Rain"
BRD SNG	CA	"Bird Song"
BTWIND	NY	"Black-Throated Wind"
CZYFGRS	CA	"Crazy Fingers"
DNCNBRZ	CA	DANCING BEARS
DRKSTAR	NV	"Dark Star"
DRUMZZ	PA	"Drums"
EYE-CO	DC	"Iko Iko"

GDTRFB	WA	"Goin' Down the Road Feelin' Bad" (*See* SETLIST SHORTHAND)
GETAWAY	AL	"Alabama Getaway"
GR8FUL	CO	Grateful
HLP ONWY	CA	"Help on the Way"
IWLGETBI	CA	"I will get by"/"A Touch of Grey"
JERY ME	CA	Jerry me
JK STRAW	NY	"Jack Straw"
LUZ LUCY	CA	"Loose Lucy"
MILTNN2	CA	"My lightnin' too"/"Lazy Lightnin' "
ON TOUR	DE	On tour
OTHR ONE	PA	"The Other One"
PV3HPV3P		(turn it upside down)
ROLL OA	NY	"Roll away the dew"/"Franklin's Tower"
RUKIND	CO	"Are you kind?"/"Uncle John's Band" (*See* THE KIND)
RXR BLUS	CA	"Big Railroad Blues"
STLYRFAC	NY	Steal your face (*See* STEALIE)
VIOLALEE	VA	"Viola Lee Blues"

GUAT • Guatemalan hand-loomed cotton clothing, prized by Heads for its brilliant natural colors and flowing comfort, perfect for SPACEDANCING.

GUITAR HEROES • Hart's tongue-in-cheek term for Garcia, Weir, and Lesh, who, because of the amplification of their instruments, have always been able to make a *big* noise with a little movement of the fingers. THE BEAM is Hart's revenge.

🎵 *Elvis Costello on Garcia's guitar style:*

I really love his playing—it's very lyrical, humorous, and unpredictable. I like his use of harmonics, and the endless modulations he goes through in his solos. But my favorite thing is that sense of fearlessness. Sometimes it seems like he's never played the guitar before in his life, in a great way. It's not everyone who can forget everything they ever knew and play completely fresh each time. Many of Garcia's solos have that feel about them.

My favorite solo without question is in "Bertha." It seems to somehow get outside the mode that you're expecting it to be in, yet it's still a rock and roll solo. I think of it as running up steps. It's funny and charming.

GUNG HEY NOW! FAT CHOY NOW! • Multicultural Bob. Sung during "Man Smart, Woman Smarter" at the Chinese New Year's show at Kaiser, 2/19/85.

GYUTO TANTRIC CHOIR • A group of Tibetan Buddhist monks who specialize in sub-baritone "multiphonic" rhythmic chanting, in which each vocalist sings several notes at one time. Brought to the U.S. in 1988 with the assistance of Mickey Hart to make a record, tour, and raise funds for a new monastery in Kathmandu, the monks were embraced by Deadheads, who heard in their chants the same spiritual power that Hart did. The crimson-robed monks are seen wearing "Steal Your Face" watches in the documentary film, *Timeless Voices*.

"The chants are not designed as entertainment, but as prayer," according to the liner notes to their album, *Freedom Chants From the Roof of the World*. "I have a tape of theirs that I call my 'high' tape," Hart has said. "I used to listen to it to come down from Grateful Dead gigs."

THE HAIGHT-ASHBURY • The San Francisco neighborhood bordering on Golden Gate Park, named for the intersection of Haight and Ashbury streets at its center. 710 Ashbury—occupied by the Dead during the late '60s—is located there.

The Dead were one of several bands in the neighborhood when the Haight came to world media attention as the birthplace of the hippie counterculture just before the summer of '67, the so-called Summer of Love. (Neighborhood residents did not like the word "hippie.") From 1964 to 1966, the Haight was a laboratory for a new humane social order based on the shared enjoyment of art, music, psychedelics, and the spirituality and sensuality of daily life.

Originally an integrated working-class neighborhood, by the mid-'60s the Haight held a mix of black families, refugees from the post-Beat North Beach district, and a growing population of San Francisco State students, drawn by low rents. In 1965, one could move a whole household into a beautiful Victorian in the Haight for a pittance, a bonanza created by the defeat of a proposition to build a freeway along the Panhandle of Golden Gate Park. Many local landlords had counted on the passing of the bill, and allowed their buildings to deteriorate to the point where they were unrentable to any clients except students, artists, and a new variety of bohemian.

In the summer of '65, Chet Helms, later the impresario of the AVALON BALLROOM, held a series of jam sessions in the basement of a Victorian at 1090 Page Street. San Francisco's first electrified hippie rock band, the Charlatans, had a triumphant summer-long engagement at the Red Dog Saloon in Virginia City, and returned to live in the Haight that fall, fêted as avatars of the burgeoning psychedelic sound.

In January of 1966, THE TRIPS FESTIVAL ran for three days at the Longshoreman's Hall. Several months later, the Dead moved into the house at 710 Ashbury, joining the other musicians in the neighborhood, including Janis Joplin. Hunter S. Thompson was researching his book on the favored outlaws of the hippies—the Hell's Angels—and living a couple of blocks up from Haight Street. By the summer, both Graham's Fillmore and Helms's Avalon were in full swing, providing rock and roll to a community hungry for communal entertainment. An article

in the September '66 issue of the Haight neighborhood newspaper *P.O. Frisco* describes the atmosphere of discovery at those
shows: "A musician who was present at some of the sessions at
Minton's Playhouse during the natal throes of bebop said,
'Man, it was like being at the beginning of the world.' The situ-
ation in San Francisco today, while the atmosphere is different,
is analogous . . . It is the beginning of a new musical world."

Colorful new shops catering to acidheads—selling Mod
clothes, incense, paisley prints, and books on yoga—were moving into vacant storefronts up and down Haight Street. The
neighborhood was also becoming known as the place to buy pot
and OWSLEY's latest batch of acid.

March of '66 saw the first large drug bust in the Haight,
twenty-five arrests in a commune on Ashbury, and a lurid
write-up in the *San Francisco Examiner.* On October 6, 1966,
LSD was made illegal, and there was a free "Love Pageant
Rally" in the Panhandle, where the Dead played a tribute to
OWSLEY, "Alice D. Millionaire." (Owsley had been referred to
in a newspaper headline as the "LSD millionaire.") A week
later, THE DIGGERS began giving away free food every day in
the Panhandle.

The neighborhood became a magnet for the hip intelligentsia
from all over the world, including Allen Ginsberg and George
Harrison. A "Declaration of Independence" printed in the *Oracle,* a neighborhood newspaper edited by Allen Cohen, and
printed with rainbow inks on perfumed paper, embodies the
ambitions of the new world struggling to be born: "When in the
flow of human events it becomes necessary for the people to
cease to recognize the obsolete social patterns which have isolated man from his consciousness, and to create with the youthful energies of the world revolutionary communities of harmonious relations to which the two billion year old life process
entitles them . . . We hold these experiences to be self-evident,
that all is equal, that the creation endows us with certain in-
alienable rights, that among them are: the freedom of body, the
pursuit of joy, and the expansion of consciousness . . ."

The call was heard, and a massive influx of young people to

the tiny neighborhood began. In January of '67, THE BE-IN was held in Golden Gate Park, in some ways the last flowering of community and peaceful change that was the defining spirit of the Haight. Two months later, the Board of Supervisors of the city declared hippies unwelcome in the city, ignoring warnings of impending hordes. Scott McKenzie's Top 10 hit, "San Francisco (Be Sure to Wear Flowers in Your Hair)," turned up the hype with its refrain: "For those who come to San Francisco, summertime will be a Love-In there." DJ Tom Donahue's founding of a rock show on radio station KMPX gave a voice and an ear to the Haight for the coming summer. The Dead played spur-of-the-moment free concerts in the Panhandle and the Park that were joyous celebrations for the neighborhood residents, who shed clothes and cares to dance in the sun on Sunday afternoons.

The Monterey Pop festival held in June catapulted the city's hippie bands into the limelight, most notably Big Brother and the Holding Company with Janis Joplin.

Time magazine ran a cover story on "The Hippies" on July 7, and during the following "Summer of Love," 75,000 people—mostly kids—poured through the tiny neighborhood, straining the resources set up by the Diggers.

On October 2, 1967, 710 Ashbury was busted for marijuana possession. The Dead and their managers Rock Scully and Danny Rifkin held a press conference with media fanfare, delivering a statement warning against unrighteous laws that "create a mythical danger and call it a felony. The people who enforce the law use it almost exclusively against the individuals who threaten their ideas of the way people should look and act. The result is a series of lies and myths that prop each other up."

On October 6—the first anniversary of the outlawing of LSD—the Diggers held a symbolic wake called "the Death of Hippie," marching a cardboard coffin laden with hippie accoutrements to the Psychedelic Shop. Later that month, the shop closed. Around that time, poster artist Alton Kelley was walking down Haight Street with his friend Herbie Goldberg when they were approached by someone who said that a celebrated

Indian guru was arriving to address the throngs. "We need another holy man around here," joked Goldberg, "like we need a
twenty-mile oil slick."

On March 3 of '68, the Dead played a free concert on Haight
Street, as a gesture of gratitude to the neighborhood. Pictures
of that concert grace the inside gatefold of *Live/Dead*. The only
tape of the show in circulation was recorded by Steve Brown
with what was left of the batteries in his reel-to-reel deck after
recording Cream at Winterland the night before. Brown recalls:
"They were playin' 'Dancin in the Streets' on Haight Street,
with all the facades of the buildings festooned with freaks, and
the sun backlighting them. *Very* beautiful. At one point, Phil led
the crowd in a big 'Fuck you!' cheer for the cops. A canyon of
humanity, with the Grateful Dead as the river running through
it."

By 1969, the neighborhood was a shell of its brief glory,
wracked with speed and heroin. As one commentator put it, the
Haight died of "overpopulation, overexposure, and overex-
pectancy."

🍂 *Steve Silberman on the Haight in the '80s:*

When I moved to the Haight in May of '79, the only relic of the old Haight
was the Psalms Café at Haight and Masonic, formerly the Drogstore. The
city was still grieving the assassinations of progressive gay supervisor Harvey
Milk and liberal mayor George Moscone, and one of the original drummers
of the Jefferson Airplane was begging handouts from neighborhood restaurants. There was a glimmer of what I imagined to be the old vibe in places like
Gus's Pub, where bikers, gay people, and longhairs hung out together smoking joints, and in a club called the Shady Grove, where Garcia would occasionally be seen at the bar in a Yankees jacket.

After the Shady Grove and the Grand Piano Café closed in 1980, the
Haight was without a comfortable neighborhood hangout. Though vanloads
of Deadheads arrived hourly to take each other's pictures on the corner of
Haight and Ashbury, the economic priorities of the Reagan Revolution
slammed the neighborhood hard, and guys who had spent the Summer of
Love in Vietnam curled up in doorways at night, as the shelters overflowed.
It was hard to walk down Haight Street through the litany of
"Doses . . . doses," without feeling like you were wandering through the ruins

of what had tried to be a heaven, and ended up a hell. Someone wrote on a wall at the corner of Haight and Clayton, "This is the Dawning of the AIDS of Aquarius."

When the Dead played at the Greek Theater or Henry J. Kaiser across the Bay, however, the street would fill up with Heads, and on those sunny afternoons—and on the days of mail order for the New Year's shows when a line stretched out of the post office—it was easy to imagine the Haight in its first flowering. The neighborhood is still a thriving Deadhead ghetto, with inspired jams soaring out of windows on sunny days. There is pride in being a Haight-Ashbury Deadhead, though the bandmembers themselves haven't lived here for twenty-five years—as the stickers say, "Haight-Ashbury—Land of the Free, Home of the Dead."

The Haight shook its malaise in '89 or so, as three or four thriving new cafés gave spirited "slackers" a place to commiserate with one another, and the rave kids made the Haight a center for a new generation of psychedelic youth culture based on a vision of unity transcending race, gender, and sexual orientation.

When Brent died on July 26, 1990, neighborhood Heads built a little shrine at the corner of Haight and Ashbury, with photographs, flowers, and incense. A circle of kids, who hadn't been born yet when the Dead played for free on Haight Street, sang Brent back home.

There was a single rose on the steps of 710.

HALFTIME • The intermission between sets. Also known as "set break" or just "the break."

The Dead scene is rich with sports terminology and metaphor, and not only because many show arenas also host basketball games or other sporting events. Bay Area Heads sometimes joke about the Dead being "the home team," and it has been said that a show is like a Super Bowl where no one loses. A frequent component of postshow wrap-ups is deciding who was MVP, the Most Valuable Player of the show or the run.

HALLDANCING • SPACEDANCING in the hallways of a venue, without any view of the band, a phenomenon that has become a trademark of Dead shows.

Glenn "Raz" Raswyck, director of ROCK MED, relates an incident in San Diego, in which the fire marshal stormed backstage to loudly condemn promoters for selling standing-room-only tickets. "We didn't!" the promoters explained. "Those people are in the halls because they *want* to be there." "You should've seen the looks on their faces," says Raswyck. " 'This doesn't happen for Neil Diamond,' they said."

🐾 *Paul Hoffman, author of* Outside the Show, *on halldancing:*

At most Dead shows, the band sets up speakers outside the main auditorium but inside the show, often in a wide area of the venue's hallways. If you hang out at these speakers, you cannot see the band or the lights, and the sound isn't as good or as loud as it is inside. For those of us who are hallway dancers, the show is a completely different experience than for the vast majority of Deadheads who are inside the main arena.

What the hallways lack in audio quality, they more than make up for in visuals and community. Instead of seeing the band, we see each other—dancing, swirling, laughing, spinning, loping, crying, zooming, bouncing, toddling, shaking, and smiling. Inside, you have no idea how much the person two rows in front of you is liking the show; in the hallway, there is direct personal contact at every moment.

The hallways can turn even the shyest Deadhead into a dancer, and many long-term relationships are engendered there. After spending a few shows dancing where you can see each other, you recognize faces and dance moves. It's common to catch someone's eye ten yards away, and share a moment before dancing off in opposite directions. You can make friends without saying a word.

At any other concert, the hallways are deserted, save for a few lost souls who can't find their seats after going to the bathroom. At a Dead show, they are filled with people dancing and interacting at an incredible rate. Most "people watchers" who spend time in the hallways quickly burn out on the high level of human contact, but to the hallway dancers, that's why we're there. We thank the band for giving us such a wonderful venue for our times together. To us, the lights and sound inside the arena cannot match the people and the dancing in our hallway home.

THE HARRY SIDE • A tongue-in-cheek name for what is commonly known as THE PHIL ZONE: stage right/house left, where monitor mixer Harry Popick stands.

HART, MICKEY • Drums and percussion. Born on September 11, 1943, in Brooklyn, New York. Hart became a member of the Grateful Dead on September 29, 1967.

Hart brings to the band not only an aggressive drumming style and a highly melodic gift for accent, but a belief in the power of drumming as a healing practice and a vehicle of transport to experience the sacred. With co-drummer Kreutzmann stoking the backbeat, the two together—as the "Rhythm Devils"—are the polyrhythmic engine that keeps the Grateful Dead locomotive on track.

Michael Hart didn't so much discover the drummer's life as inherit it. Though his father Lenny, a world-champion rudimental drummer, left home before Mickey was born, the younger Hart was always "acutely aware that I was the son of a great drummer. That was my father's legacy to me, that and his drum pad, and a pair of beautiful snakewood sticks he'd won in competition."

Hart's drumming mother, Leah, provided a more active form of encouragement, sponsoring twice-weekly private lessons all through high school. "From the age of ten until forty, all I did was drum," Hart recalls in his 1990 book, *Drumming at the Edge of Magic.* "Obsessively. Passionately. Painfully. The drum took everything I had; it had all my attention." Hart would drum for hours along with Benny Goodman's 1939 Carnegie Hall performance of "Sing, Sing, Sing," entranced by drummer Gene Krupa's thunder.

Like several other members of the band, Hart dropped out of high school to join the military—in his case, the Air Force, home of the best rudimental drummers in the world. While stationed in Spain, Hart met the man who would become his first deep teacher, a judo instructor named Pogo. In eighteen months of sessions in the *dojo* with Pogo, Hart learned intense, single-minded focus.

Shortly after his discharge in 1965, he received a letter from his estranged father, inviting him to come work at Hart Music, his store south of San Francisco. At Mickey's urging, the store was renamed Drum City, as they sought to make it a focal point of the Bay Area percussion scene. Hart considered himself a big-band drummer at the time, and through the store and their occasional drum clinics, the Harts got to be friendly with a number of noted drummers traveling the circuit. Attending a Count Basie show at the old Fillmore (*see* FILLMORE AUDITO-RIUM) one night in '67 to admire the great drummer Sonny Payne, Hart was introduced to Bill Kreutzmann, drummer for the Grateful Dead.

The two went out that night with a bottle of scotch, drum-ming on cars, and quickly became "drum brothers," as Hart says. Kreutzmann invited Hart to his first Dead show at the Straight Theater on September 29, and in between sets, Kreutz-mann asked Hart to sit in. They jammed for two hours on "Al-ligator"→"Caution." "I remember the feeling of being whipped into a jetstream," Hart recalls. "Garcia later told me that every-one had felt it when I finally synched up. Suddenly, with two drums pounding away in the back, they had glimpsed the pos-sibility of a groove so monstrous it would eat the audience." (*See* GREAT BIG LOVE BEAST.)

As a member of the band from that point on, Hart added both rhythmic complexity and the ability to include sounds far beyond where rock and roll had been. Hart's breathing gongs, chittering *guiros,* and other contributions to the *Live/Dead* "Dark Star" illustrate what Kreutzmann meant in '69 when he said, "We're not trying to be two drummers, we're trying to be one drummer with eight arms." (Hart's rudimental training is audi-ble on the whipcrack snares in "Turn On Your Lovelight.")

In 1970, Lenny Hart, who had taken over the business man-agement of the band, was caught skimming money off the top. Lenny went to jail, and though no one in the band blamed Mickey, he took a leave of absence. Hart's last show before his hiatus was on February 18, '71, but he was kept on a stipend by his fellow bandmembers, who made it clear that he was wel-come back at any time. "Confused, unbalanced, I wanted to flee and hide, bury my head and cry. I stopped touring, and went to ground at the Barn [Hart's residence in Novato]."

There, with the advance from a three-record solo deal with Warner Bros., Hart built a state-of-the-art sixteen-track studio, and began to explore and record rhythms from all over the world. His first solo album, *Rolling Thunder,* begins with an invocation by the Shoshone medicine man who has been influential in shaping Hart's ideas about drumming and spirituality (Rolling Thunder's land, Meta Tantay, was where "Serengetti" on *Shakedown Street* was recorded). Hart has an insatiable appetite for collaboration, and has worked with master drummers like Babatunde Olatunji, Zakir Hussain, Hamza El-Din, and Airto on projects as diverse as the soundtrack to Francis Ford Coppola's *Apocalypse Now*, the DIGA RHYTHM BAND, a short-lived dance-rock unit called Kodo (never released), TV soundtracks, and dozens of other projects. Hart's interest in the roots of drumming, and the drum's role as a catalyst in the development of culture and religion, has led him all over the world as a field recorder and producer. He has been a one-man emissary of rhythm as universal language, and his collaborations and explorations have greatly nourished his role since rejoining the Dead in '74 (*see* THE LAST ONE). Several of the drummers that Hart met in his travels ended up joining the Dead onstage for a guest appearance during DRUMS.

Hart is also a collector of folk drums, and his widening of the Dead's percussive arsenal to include the Nubian *tar* (one of the world's oldest drums), talking drums, Brazilian *berimbaus*, kalimbas, the BALAFON, THE BEAM, and THE BEAST—and his experiments with tape loops, electronic drums, and triggered samples in the mid-'80s, which developed into collaborations with MIDI expert Bob Bralove—has helped the drums to evolve beyond traditional solos and duets (like those on *Skull and Roses* and *One From the Vault*) into almost cinematic landscapes. Hart's bearing onstage is that of a warrior, and his articulation of Grateful Dead music as "transportation" in his books *Drumming At the Edge of Magic* and *Planet Drum* has helped Deadheads find cross-cultural contexts for their spiritual experiences.

In recent years, Hart has worked with the Smithsonian in transferring their vast collection of perishable field recordings to digital format; recorded and produced Tibetan monks, klezmer wedding music, gospel, and many other groups; and signed a contract with Rykodisc to put together the "World" series of recordings, representing a broad range of cultures and rhythms. (*See* ENDANGERED MUSIC PROJECT.)

Hart lives with his wife Carol Orbach on his ranch in Sebastopol, California, called YOLO ("You Only Live Once"), and has two sons: Creek and Taro.

♣ *Mickey Hart on the spirit side of drumming:*

You might say drums have two voices. One is technical, having to do with the drum's shape, the material it's made of, its cultural context, and the standard way it's played. Technique gives you this voice—the drum's sweet spot, that point where the drummer, the drumhead, and the rhythm that arises from their interaction flow seamlessly together. It takes commitment and apprenticeship to learn how to find a drum's sweet spot. But once you do, the potential arises for contacting the drum's second voice—one I have come to think of as the spirit side of the drum.

A selected Hart non-Dead discography, as producer and performer:

Rolling Thunder, 1972.

Diga—The Diga Rhythm Band, 1976.

The Apocalypse Now Sessions—The Rhythm Devils, 1979.

Dafos—Mickey Hart, Airto Moreira, Flora Purim, 1983.

Music to Be Born By—Mickey Hart and Taro Hart. The fetal heartbeat of Mickey's son Taro, recorded from Mary Hart's womb onto sixteen-track, overdubbed with flute, percussion, and bass, 1989.

Planet Drum, 1991.

HEALY, DAN • Sound engineer—captain of the soundboard, master of the mix—for the Dead from '66 until '94 (with a sabbatical from late '69 till February '71). Healy and his colleagues were responsible for the standard-setting clarity of the Dead's concert sound in large arenas, and his distinctive processing of instruments and vocals—most noticeable during SPACE and "The Other One"—became an invaluable element of the band's sound.

Healy grew up in redwood country, near Garberville, California, close to the Oregon border. His grandfather was a folk singer, and his father was a nightclub owner and slot-machine racketeer. When Healy was in sixth grade, he wired together a couple of turntables and a transmitter, and put his own pirate neighborhood radio station on the air. "While other kids were

THE   DICTIONARY   ☠   141

out playing Cowboys and Indians," Healy recalled to Blair
Jackson, "I was learning how to use a soldering iron."

Healy dropped out of high school and moved to San Francisco in '63, and got jobs doing maintenance work at KSFO and
janitorial work at Commercial Recorders, a state-of-the-art,
three-track studio. Healy had known Quicksilver Messenger
Service guitarist John Cippolina since they were kids, and
when Healy moved to a houseboat in Larkspur, north of the
city, Quicksilver would rehearse on the houseboat next door.

Cippolina invited Healy to see Quicksilver at the old Fillmore in June of '66, and the Dead were playing when they arrived — or not playing, because Lesh's amp had broken down.
Healy promptly fixed the amp, earning the gratitude of the
band. After the show, Healy made a crack about how lousy
their sound system was; Garcia and Lesh dared him to do better, and by the time the Dead played at the Fillmore again about
a month later, Healy had put together an impressive system,
one that sounded much better than any other rock concert
sound system in use at that time. A partnership was born.

Healy would sneak the Dead into Commercial Recorders at
night, and they would record until dawn. Top 40 AM radio
wouldn't touch the tapes, because the Dead were an unsigned
band, but Healy took them down to KMPX-FM, and played
them on his late-night radio show. Word got around that
KMPX was playing some interesting music at three in the
morning, and Healy's show, and shows hosted by Tom Donahue and a couple of others, marked the beginnings of underground FM radio.

By 1969, Healy was very in demand as a record producer,
and he was wooed away from running the Dead's P.A. to produce albums by other psychedelic groups like the Charlatans,
Mother Earth with Tracy Nelson, Doctor John, Quicksilver,
and Blue Cheer, as well as by blues artists like Junior Parker.
During his absence, the Dead's sound was managed by
OWSLEY Stanley and Bob Matthews.

By December of '71, Healy and a woman named Darlene
DiDomenico were playing the Other End in Greenwich Village

as a folk duo, and Healy went to see his old friends play at the Felt Forum. "What I heard was an atrocity," Healy recalls. "So I just dropped what I was doing and told Ram Rod, Jerry, and Phil, 'I'll see you on the Coast when this tour is up. I'm restaking my old turf.' "

When Healy came back to the Dead, he began working with Owsley on the state-of-the-art speaker system that became THE WALL OF SOUND. At the unveiling of a new low-distortion tweeter array at the 2/9/73 show at Maples Pavilion, $12,000 worth of tweeters blew in the first three seconds of the show. Healy was encouraged that the Dead did not castigate him for it but gamely accepted it as the price of experimentation.

With the Dead's financial support, Healy and his colleagues—including Don Pearson, John Meyer, John Cutler, Ron Wickersham, and others—forged a working enclave of radical technological innovation that holds creative inquiry, and what writer Michael Nash calls the *"what-if?"* mindset, above all else. Healy and OWSLEY's early innovations made crystalline concert sound possible, and for three decades the Dead's P.A. has stayed at the leading edge of audio research and development.

Healy had a close relationship with the fans, asking tapers for advice on the sound, and providing occasional "patches" to the soundboard. "They're my pals. I've always been out there in the middle of 'em." Healy told Blair Jackson: "How could I do sound for the audience if I isolate myself from the audience? There are a lot of young audio freaks out there, and it would be a shame if I weren't willing to share what I know with them. These people are the future of audio!" For years in the '70s and early '80s, a banner hung from the balconies of West Coast shows that read (in cryptically psychedelic lettering): "HEALY'S A GENIUS."

Healy is fiercely proud of the priorities the band demonstrated over the years. "I really think that one of the things that cuts us apart from other bands is that we're doing it for the audience, and for ourselves, and *for the music.* Even in our deepest, darkest moments, when there was probably an easier way out, we didn't take that easy way out. We can sleep at night. We can live with ourselves."

In March of '94, Healy left the post he occupied for nearly thirty years. *See also* QUAD SPACE; SOUNDBOARD.

❧ *Healy on why we're here:*

There is something that is above all of us. There's a passion there that transcends the music. It means far more to society than what it means to the band and to me as far as music and sound. That's what it is that I'm committed to. Jerry would probably tell you the same thing, although we don't sit around and talk about that kind of stuff. But we all know it's there. Without it, none of us would be here.

HEY NOW! • The "Hello!" that says you're ON THE BUS. From the chorus of "Iko Iko."

HIPPIE CRACK • *See* NITROUS OXIDE.

THE HIPPIE HIGHWAY • The circuit of glorious spots on Earth where Heads run into other Heads between tours, enjoying a spectacular desert or good surf, a waterfall or a psychedelic canyon. Durango, Sedona, Bali, Moab, Goa, Provincetown, Arcata, Olympia, Kona . . . The same faces, familiar from the rail or the lot, met on the trail to the power spot or pueblo or hot springs or setting sun. ". . . You go to shows?" *See* GRATEFUL BED & BREAKFAST.

HISTORY OF THE GRATEFUL DEAD, VOL. 1—BEAR'S CHOICE • Album #9, released in July 1973.

❧ *Nick Meriwether, author and historian, on* **Bear's Choice:**

Bear's Choice was taken from several nights' shows in February of 1970 at Bill Graham's famed FILLMORE EAST, where the Dead were inspired or challenged by the notoriously demanding New York City crowd to turn in some of their best shows. The "Bear" in question was Owsley Stanley, who recorded the shows. The five acoustic songs and two electric on this album—both covers—serve to round out the picture of those nights, emphasizing a lesser-known side of the band. *Bear's Choice* is not to everyone's taste, but it is a distinctive piece of history, holding many treasures for aficionados.

The band's stage presence is friendly and loose. Pigpen verbally dispatches a heckler, and Bobby explains to the crowd what a capo is, calling it a "cheater" (to which Jerry eruditely adds, "That's the vulgate"). The 2,300-seat Fillmore sounds almost homey, thanks to superb digital remastering on the CD (like *Steal Your Face*, this album has been salvaged by remastering). Recorded directly to two-track, there was presumably little opportunity to tinker with the mix afterwards; some Deadheads cannot tolerate it largely for this reason. ("Where are the drums?")

It offers a good slice of the Dead in transition, away from the freeform jazz-inspired improvisations documented on *Live/Dead*, to their more country-rock early '70s persona. It begins with a rarity: Pigpen accompanying himself on bottleneck guitar, singing "Katie Mae," an old Lightnin' Hopkins blues. (Rock Scully recalled that the band had been coaxing Pigpen to do this for years.) Garcia and Weir sound marvelous on "Dark Hollow," and "Wake Up Little Suzie," a reminder that the Dead have always been willing to play songs commonly considered pure pop. "Black Peter" finishes the acoustic part of the album, the only original, treated here to a sparse, wistful rendition.

The second side of the LP is electric, with two cuts that showcase Pigpen as the blues-singing frontman, a fitting tribute to him. For fans accustomed to the band's more succinct late-'80s jams, "Smokestack Lightning" is a delightful reminder of a band with time on its hands.

H.O.R.D.E. BANDS • Named after "Horizons of Rock Developing Everywhere," two tours in '92 and '93 of bands that share a commitment to jamming and the live groove, including Phish, Big Head Todd and the Monsters, Blues Traveler, Spin Doctors, Widespread Panic, and Col. Bruce Hampton and Aquarium Rescue Unit, the Samples, Bela Fleck, and numerous unsigned bands like Xanax 25. Conceived of by John Popper of Blues Traveler as a vehicle for new bands, an alternative to "alternative" rock.

Many Heads have added live tapes of H.O.R.D.E. bands to their trading lists, and some young Heads are leaving the Dead scene to become fans (or, in the case of Phish, "phans") of the H.O.R.D.E. bands, feeling more at home at smaller shows.

🔥 *Interview with Tom Marshall, Phish lyricist:*

SS: Tom, now that Phish is ten years old, and you've been cowriting songs with Trey [Anastasio, the lead guitarist] for longer than that, isn't it time that you came out of your seclusion, removed your mask, and addressed once and for all the question of the parallels between the Dead and Phish?

TM: Yes, yes, no and, er . . . what was the middle thing?

SS: Would you say psychedelic lyrics like "China Cat Sunflower," were an influence on a song like, say, "Stash"?

TM: I didn't know "China Cat Sunflower" *had* lyrics.

SS: What inspires you to come up with lyrics like that?

TM: A castaway, asleep on a rock in the middle of the Aegean, dreams of the great flood and his polar opposite, his familiar, a goldfish named Trout. Several years later that same set of circumstances befall him again —this time, as he's packing his designer Sumatran luggage rescue-style.

SS: Could you be more specific?

TM: I take my lover by the hand
>   to stroll across the ocean strand
>   until she soaks into the sand
>   leaving me with empty hand.

SS: I hate when that happens. Is that a future Phish song?

TM: Page [McConnell, keyboardist] wouldn't like it, because of the part I left out.

SS: The Dead and Phish are both jamming bands, both play long sets that are different every night, both draw from many lineages of music in order to produce a sound that is both completely individual and thoroughly American, both bands play to seething hippie-type audiences, both allow taping and have huge underground tape trees on the Net for trading, etc. How can you tell the difference?

[*A minute passes.*]

SS: Have you ever been to a Dead show?

TM: Maybe ten times—those oversized video special effects and that booming, stadium-filling basswash that people groove to stayed with me for weeks afterward.

SS: Did you like it?

TM: At least I'm enjoying the ride.

SS: Do you have any advice for Deadheads?

TM: Drift where the current chooses.

HORNSBY, BRUCE • Keyboards, accordion, vocals. Born November 25, 1954, in Williamsburg, Virginia.

Hornsby was an official member of the band for a period of eighteen months, from September '90 to March '92. He played grand piano in conjunction with Vince Welnick's MIDI keyboards for most of the shows during that period. "Garcia called me the floating member," he recalls. "I think I helped serve as a bridge between Brent's death and the time Vince got comfortable with the band."

Hornsby is an aggressive player—he calls himself a musical "jock"—and engaged in fertile musical conversations with Garcia during ensemble passages. He was also willing to linger onstage during DRUMS and SPACE for impromptu jams, and brought a couple of his own tunes to the repertoire, including "Valley Road" and "Stander on the Mountain," as well as his earnest harmonies.

Raised in a musical family, at sixteen Hornsby got excited about the piano by seeing Leon Russell play and hearing Elton John's "Amareena" on the radio. A year later, he heard the Keith Jarrett solo album *Facing You,* and started down the path of jazz by listening to Bill Evans, Herbie Hancock, Chick Corea, and McCoy Tyner. (He was also digging Professor Longhair and Otis Spann.) He pursued formal jazz training at the Berklee College of Music and the University of Miami.

Hornsby was introduced to the Dead by his older brother Bobby, who was in a Deadhead fraternity. "What really got me," he recalls, "was when they played William and Mary College in Williamsburg (9/11/73). We were in the second row, and it was a great gig. At the end of the night, Bob Weir comes up to the microphone and says, 'We had such a great time tonight, we're gonna come back and play tomorrow night for free—take out all the chairs, and make it a party!' When you're nineteen years old, and some sonofabitch gets up there and says that, you're *sold.* I thought, 'Man—these guys are for *me.*' "

The Hornsby brothers formed a band, BOBBY HI-TEST AND THE OCTANE KIDS, that played Dead covers, mostly songs from *Europe '72* and *Skull and Roses.* Hornsby saw the Dead at the Tower Theater in Philadelphia in '77, but the band, with Keith Godchaux, was not playing well.

After struggling to break into the music business for eight years, Hornsby became an "overnight success" with his debut hit single, "The Way It Is," in 1986. "We had to become headliners with nine songs," Hornsby remembers, "so we would do other people's songs, like we would segue from 'Red Planes' into 'I Know You Rider,' the way the Dead do it. I guess Garcia and Phil became fans of the record, and heard we were playing their songs, and asked us to open a couple of shows. I was mad for that, of course, because I had been a fan."

The first time Hornsby opened for the Dead, he warmed up by playing a bitonal version of Scott Joplin's "The Entertainer," playing in the key of C in one hand and C-sharp in the other. "Phil got a big laugh out of that, and we started talking about Charles Ives." Hornsby and the Range became a favored opening act, opening a two-day triple bill with the Dead and Ry Cooder at Laguna Seca in Monterey in '87. Garcia played on a couple of tunes for Hornsby's third album, *A Night on the Town*, and Hornsby also recorded "Jack Straw" for the *Deadicated* tribute album.

When Brent died a month before the beginning of an already-scheduled fall tour in '90, Hornsby was invited onboard, coming into the band as a full-fledged member for one of the most celebrated runs in recent years at Madison Square Garden, with impromptu duets and trios with the drummers and Lesh.

On the tour of Europe in '90, Hornsby broke up the predictability of the setlists by playing variations of the themes of "Let It Grow" and "Dark Star"—the latter at Garcia's suggestion. "Garcia and I have just always connected well," Hornsby says. "We've always had a good musical bond between us. I told him I was producing a record for Leon Russell called 'Jezebel,' and he brought out the original record from the '40s, by the Golden Gate Quartet. He's a walking encyclopedia of folk music, so I've always loved getting into conversations and learning from him.

"The Dead performing my songs—that came from them. I never wanted to push it. If a song like 'Stander on the Mountain' fell by the wayside, I never brought it up again. That's not why I was there. I have an outlet for my music, my own band.

There's a kindred musical spirit between me and the Dead, coming from our mutual interests in both folk and jazz. There were lots of nights when I would get the chills onstage. I remember one night at Cap Center, playing 'Wharf Rat,' just sitting up there next to Jerry, getting off. Transcendent moments."

The tours of Hornsby's own band in '93 were wholeheartedly improvisational, sandwiching jams from "Dark Star," "Jack Straw," and "Terrapin" among Sonny Rollins and Charlie Parker covers.

"I always thought it was the best party you could go to," says Hornsby, "and I was proud to be part of that party for a year and a half. I think of myself as a cousin of the Dead."

Hornsby has a wife, Kathy, and twin sons, Keith (after Keith Jarrett) and Leon (after Leon Russell).

HOT • Father of all heat-related adjectives, employed by Deadheads to communicate the intensity of the musical experience when THE BOYS are *on*. "That was one *hot* show!" "Ooh — that 'Franklin's Tower' was *scorching.*" "They're *smokin'* tonight." "Did you listen to drums tonight? They were *on fire.*" Other related terms include "blazin'," "blistering," "raging," "sizzling," and "in flames." "Barnburner" might be used to describe a particularly intense performance of a tune like "Deal," with solos combusting at the edge of feedback.

Not all of the heat-related adjectives are interchangeable. Most Heads wouldn't say that the poignant, stately ballad "Stella Blue" was "scorching," but might admit that it "melted" them.

THE HOT SEAT • Life imitates *Spinal Tap*. Weir's name for the "curse" on the occupants of the Grateful Dead's keyboard bench. (Three of their six keyboardists over the years have died young.)

HOUSE OF JERRY [DEADHEAD FRATERNITIES AND SORORITIES] • Early-'80s nickname for a Denison University chapter of the Fijis (the Phi Gammas), one of many Deadhead frats and Head-friendly student co-ops on campuses across the land that bring collegiate Heads together and serve as informal hostels for Deadheads on tour. The fraternity and sorority system is a bit like the Deadhead subculture, offering pledges a ground of common interests, commitment to adventure, risk, and fellowship, and a body of lore that is added to by each generation of initiates.

"Where else on campus can one hear an all-ukulele band play a two-hour jam of 'The Lion Sleeps Tonight' into 'Dark Star'?" asks historian Anton Saurian of the Kappa Alphas, a literary secret society that has seen several generations of pledges go out on tour. Parties at Deadhead frats—being local, noncommercial events—often come closer to the Dionysian chaos of the original Acid Tests than latter-day Dead shows themselves.

Deadhead Greeks have also been targeted by drug enforcement officials, including a raid on a Tau Kappa Epsilon ("Teke") house at the University of Virginia (known among the brothers as "Toke") on a night that the Dead were playing two hours away, at the Capital Centre, in Landover, Maryland. There were several arrests, including an Echols Scholar on the dean's list, who was sentenced to thirteen months in prison when he refused to give the names of his brothers to the authorities in exchange for a lighter sentence.

Q: HOW DO YOU KNOW IF DEADHEADS HAVE STAYED AT YOUR HOUSE? • A: They're still there.

HUG CIRCLES • Deadheads extending the POSTSHOW GLOW as long as possible.

One especially memorable hug circle formed after the first show at Laguna Seca on 5/9/87, when a hug initiated by three ex-boyfriends of a dancer named Pam kept growing until approximately 1,500 people were included in it. After several minutes, the circle exploded in a wild dancefest that lasted until security told everyone to leave.

An article in *Relix*, written by a tourhead who had been an undercover agent for the DEA, cited the fact that agents "will never freely hug one of us" as one way of spotting a setup.

HULOGOSI PRESS • A worker-owned cooperative publishing house founded in '84 by Carolyn "Mountain Girl" Garcia, Alan Trist (who was the head of ICE NINE PUBLISHING for several years), and Hal Hartzell and Stevens Van Strum, who were Hoedads, tree planters in Oregon with the soul of Coyote. *Hulogos'i* means "yew tree" in Yahi, an extinct language once spoken by native Californians.

Hulogosi is a small, visionary press run by Dead family members and friends that published "Pride of Cucamonga" lyricist Bobby Petersen's book of poems, *Alleys of the Heart,* containing a moving tribute to Pigpen; Hunter's translations of the poetry of Rainer Maria Rilke (worked out over microwave-heated glasses of cognac while Rilke's ghost kept watch over Hunter's shoulder); TOM CONSTANTEN's "musical autobiodyssey," *Between Rock & Hard Places;* and Alan Trist's *The Water of Life: A Tale of the Grateful Dead.* Hulogosi also publishes non-Dead-related books like Hal Hartzell's *The Yew Tree,* with assistance from Weir's Furthur Foundation.

HUNTER, ROBERT • Lyrics. Born on June 23, 1941, in Arroyo Grande, California.

Hunter's lyrics are profoundly evocative of place in the same way that Bob Dylan's or Robbie Robertson's are, seeming to emanate from a half-gone America, where miners and pioneers, gamblers and jackballers endure dire tests with secret prayers for redemption, often caught by the storyteller's lamp just at a moment of decision. Hunter populated the Dead's abstract musical landscapes with unforgettable characters, like the lady who tests her lover's mettle by tossing her fan into the fire; the woodsman who invites grinning death in for a game in wastes of snow; or the desperate gambler who's "got no chance of losin'," charging Fate to deal him a queen of diamonds.

Hunter's knack for coining aphorisms that yield hard-won truths after hundreds of hearings, and his unerring ear for the syncopations of living language, give his songs the authority of folk music. Many of his lyrics—for songs like "Friend of the Devil"—are already becoming "traditional," as at home sung by a fire or along a highway as any by Elizabeth Cotten or Woody Guthrie, or the ancient unnamed balladeers.

Hunter lived in San Francisco from the fourth through the seventh grade. His parents then moved to Palo Alto, where

Hunter remained through the eleventh grade. He spent a year at the University of Connecticut studying drama.

After six months in Oklahoma with the National Guard, Hunter moved back to the Peninsula. Inspired by reading Aldous Huxley's *The Doors of Perception,* he volunteered for the same psychedelic research at the V.A. hospital that Kesey was involved in.

Hunter met Garcia in 1960, at a production of *Damn Yankees* at the Commedia Theater in Palo Alto, and the two started playing together in local coffeehouses and schools as "Bob and Jerry," and in bluegrass bands like the Hart Valley Drifters, the Thunder Mountain Tub Thumpers, and the WILDWOOD BOYS.

"We sang very well together," Hunter recalls. "Our voices matched very nicely. We thought we were ethnic, but we weren't. The *Weavers* (Pete Seeger's folk group) were ethnic to us. It wasn't until a little bit later that we ran into *Folksongs of North America* and the Harry Smith archives, and really got ethnic."

After Hunter moved to New Mexico, Garcia invited him to contribute some lyrics for his new band, the Grateful Dead. "I was writing songs on my own, in New Mexico. So I sent three songs to the band that I had been singing to be charming at parties—'China Cat Sunflower,' 'St. Stephen,' and 'Alligator.' They decided to do them, and told me to come on out and get involved."

Hunter went up to Rio Nido, where the band was rehearsing on the Russian River, north of San Francisco. "They were working on 'Dark Star,' and I just started writing words for it. That's when it became obvious to all of us that it was going to work."

Hunter's lyrics, stitched and dyed on millions of jackets and t-shirts, are kept near at hand as wise counsel on the long road by Deadheads everywhere.

Hunter is also a poet and translator, debuting with the publication of a translation of Rainer Maria Rilke's *Duino Elegies* in 1987. Since then, he has published *Night Cadre, Idiot's Delight,* and *Sentinel,* collections of poems quickened by the same wit that sparkled in the "Hypnocracy Papers," and the sayings of St. Dilbert, Hunter's acid zen communiqués to the Dead Heads' mailing list in the early '70s. *Sentinel,* published by Viking in 1993, includes "An American Adventure," a very funny metaphoric memoir of the Dead's haphazard mission.

His collected lyrics were published as a *Box of Rain.*

Hunter recounts the best compliment he ever got for a song, from a miner who had worked the Cumberland lode. Hearing "Cumberland Blues," the old miner said, "I wonder what the guy who wrote this would've thought if he'd ever known something like the Grateful Dead was gonna do it?"

🍀 *John Barlow, fellow lyricist, on Robert Hunter:*

I love Hunter's work. There are lines that make me ring like a gong. He is a brilliant poet. He listens to his muses. He knows how to *get out of the way,* to let it pass through him, which is what it's really about: getting yourself into a condition of mind where you're not trying to think about how things make sense in the physical world. You're just listening to the voices.

Every time I've done something that worked, it was like that. "Weather Report" was like that. I just let it happen. It's channeling.

Art is what happens when God speaks through a human being. The Holy, whatever that is. I'm not talking about the big guy with the beard. I don't know what it is, and I certainly don't know what it *wants.* I'm inclined to think that all world religions constitute some form of blasphemy.

Whatever it is, Hunter can hear it. Real art is revelation.

It reminds me of when we were on the road with Dylan and the Dead. Kesey and I were traveling together in this big old beat-up Cadillac. We were down in L.A., in Anaheim Coliseum. We'd been watching Dylan, and from close up, he seemed strange, twisted. We were sort of puzzling about how this character had been able to do this. I was feeling like Salieri in the presence of Mozart. "This isn't fair, Lord. Why would you give this . . . *Dylan* the gift, and not me. He doesn't *deserve* it." But that's the point, in a way.

Kesey finally turned to me and said, "I finally figured out who this guy is." I said, "Who is he?"

He said, "Same guy that wrote the Book of Revelations."

Which is about right.

Hunter is a serious student of poetry, especially Irish and Gaelic and Scottish and Welsh poetry and music. He reaches back into his own genetic core.

It's just bubbling up in him all the time. He'd write if there were no Grateful Dead. He writes because he has to.

A selected Hunter discography:

Tales of the Great Rum Runners — 1974

Tiger Rose — 1975

Jack O'Roses — 1980

Amagamalin Street — 1984

Live '85 — 1985

Rock Columbia — 1986

Liberty — 1988

A Box of Rain — Live 1990 — 1991

I EAT TOFU AND I VOTE • Successor to the popular bumpersticker "I Take Acid and I Vote," a humorous proclamation that you-are-what-you-eat can be powerful politics. Deadheads' avoidance of heavy-handed political preachiness goes back to the very beginnings of the scene. "The Airplane became political, but the Dead never came on that way," recalls Dick Latvala, of the atmosphere in the Haight in '67, when the names of the events featuring the Dead were shifting from "Love Pageant Rally" to "Week of the Angry Arts."

"The Dead were always oblique, and always going to new areas. It was always mind-blowing, and it kept evolving," Latvala says. "The only revolution that counted was the inner revolution, and the music was what was talking to that, reflecting that, and celebrating that drive to break through your conditioning and find out who you are. It became a lifelong trip then, of discovering yourself. The music was just the background for that process."

I'LL BE GRATEFUL WHEN THEY'RE DEAD • The refrain of the anti-Dead anthem, "I Hate the Grateful Dead," recorded by a band called the Violets in 1991. Other violently anti-GD rants include "Bring Me the Head of Jerry Garcia," from Iron Prostate (1991), and "Kill Jerry Garcia," by A. D. Nation and Buz Rico ("I just wanna kill the myth/I just wanna kill Jerry Garcia . . . I'd wanna kill Pigpen if he were alive").

THE ICE CREAM KID • The rainbow-haired and bucktoothed paragon of MISFIT POWER on the back cover of *Europe '72*—which found his way onto a million denim jackets and t-shirts, official and bootlegged—was a collaboration by Alton Kelley and Stanley Mouse.

🦥 *Alton Kelley on the genesis of the Ice Cream Kid:*
Stanley and I went to a costume party. I was dressed as a Nazi soldier, my girlfriend was made up like a hooker; Stanley was a priest with a bottle of wine, and his girlfriend was a deranged Girl Scout. We were thinking about the cover for OVER THERE, which was what we thought *Europe '72* was going to be called. We *were* "over there"—we'd taken some designer drug, maybe DMT, and we were lying on the floor, and couldn't get up. Then somebody told a joke about this spastic kid who won a contest by clapping "Deep in the Heart of Texas." When they gave him first prize, an ice cream cone—"*Gee, thanks!*"—he plopped it into his forehead. That's when we thought of it.

ICE NINE PUBLISHING • The band's in-house publishing company, which retains rights to all music and lyrics on behalf of the artists, grants or denies permission for use of the lyrics in movies and books (*see* ESTIMATED PROFIT), and distributes royalties to lyricists and bandmembers (present and former). The name "Ice Nine" comes from the apocalyptic super-water molecule in Kurt Vonnegut's *Cat's Cradle* that causes all the oceans on Earth to freeze. Robert Hunter is the president of Ice Nine, and the company is administered by longtime family member Annette Flowers in THE OFFICE.

THE ICK • Tour slang for a bacterial or viral infection, resembling chronic bronchitis, resulting from overexertion, overexposure, and undernourishment on tour, passed from water bottle, pipe, or "fatty" to lips, or directly from mouth to mouth. Also called "tour fever" or "tour crud."

There are many recommended folkloric means of averting the ick, including megadoses of vitamin C, zinc lozenges, osha root, and goldenseal (the latter two notable for their noxious taste, rivaling peyote, which may account for their reputed effectiveness).

After the "comeback show" following Garcia's coma in '86, many Heads got a particularly virulent strain that lingered until the New Year's run.

IN THE DARK • Album #19, released in July 1987.

With "A Touch of Grey"—both the single and the heavy-rotation MTV video—the Dead found for the first time a wide popular audience beyond the bounds of the Deadhead community. This caused problems at shows, as hordes of young people who wanted to party descended on the parking lot; the fresh Heads were labeled TOUCHHEADS and IN-THE-DARKERS by veteran Heads who suddenly could not get tickets. "Within a couple of tours," says Blair Jackson, "a natural winnowing process took over and only the new fans who'd 'gotten it' on a more profound level remained; still a huge number of people; *too many,* a lot of old-timers would argue, for the scene to comfortably bear."

♣ *Blair Jackson, editor of* The Golden Road, *on* **In the Dark:**
At the time *In the Dark* was released, there were a fair number of Heads who actually wanted the record to fail, precisely because they foresaw the problems mainstream success would bring to the always-fragile GD ecosystem. Personally, I enjoyed a sort of morbid fascination following the record's rise up the charts, reading about the Dead in the straight media, and hearing "Touch of Grey" on radios in weird places like convenience stores and at the beach. And I think the band got off on at least the beginnings of their brush

with the Big Time. After all, they and we knew the truth—that it was all a crazy aberration, a disturbance in the forcefield, a dream record company weasels dreamed long ago-o-o-o.

Another contextual distraction for Deadheads was the fact that most of the material was several years old by the time the record came out: "Touch of Grey," "West L.A. Fadeaway," and "Throwing Stones" had been introduced in 1982; "Hell in a Bucket" and "My Brother Esau" in 1983 ("Esau" appears only on the cassette version of the album); "Tons of Steel" in '84.

The Dead first took a stab at recording the material in 1984, but the sessions went nowhere. A year later, they began work on a longform video, setting up their gear on the stage of the Marin Veteran's Auditorium, and playing live with no audience, using a recording truck parked outside the hall to capture the results. While no usuable material for the eventual video (*So Far*, released the same time as *In the Dark*) came from those sessions, the band [so] enjoyed recording that way that when they got serious about making an album again—in the winter of '87, following Garcia's miraculous recovery from his near-death in the summer of '86—they went back to Marin Vets and cut the basic tracks there, adding overdubs at Club Front later.

After Garcia's comeback, the band was on such a natural high, it's no wonder that *In the Dark* is crackling with fresh energy. The group managed to invest their road-worn tunes with plenty of new ideas—subtle new arrangements, sound effects, etc.—and Garcia also came up with two new songs that were only played a few times before they were recorded: the jaunty (but ultimately disposable) "When Push Comes to Shove" and the heavy dirge "Black Muddy River" (phenomenal lyrics, dull tune). All in all, it was a slightly motley affair, but after seven years of waiting for a new studio album, and giddy with excitement just to have Garcia alive and playing, most Deadheads were happy to lay down their hard-earned scratch for *In the Dark*. Today, you probably won't find much enthusiasm for the record among the Deadhead ranks, but I think it's worn relatively well. Three tracks are classics in my view: "Touch of Grey," "Hell in a Bucket," and "Throwing Stones." Each captures a vitality that is rare for a Dead studio album. The other great song on the album, Garcia's snaky blues "West L.A. Fadeaway," unfortunately suffers from gimmicky and grating production tricks. I can't say I really play the CD much at home anymore (and I'm one of those Heads who *does* still play GD records), but when "Touch" or "Hell" or "Throwing Stones" comes onto my car radio, I crank it up and smile, remembering that now faraway, slightly scary time when the Dead ruled the pop world.

IN-THE-DARKERS • *See* TOUCHHEADS.

INFRARED ROSES • Album #24, released in November 1991.

Infrared Roses was the most experimental album the Dead had released since *Blues for Allah,* and was the return of uncompromisingly "outside" Dead for those who value the band as a laboratory of new sounds. The primary composer of the pieces was Bob Bralove, working from tapes of DRUMS and SPACE. The Hornsby/Welnick duet, "Silver Apples of the Moon," is variations on the theme of "Dark Star" from the Wembley Arena on 11/1/90, played, according to Hornsby, at Garcia's request.

🐾 *Jon C. Sievert, editor of* Guitar Player, *on Infrared Roses:*

If there is any single factor that has given the Dead its creative edge over the past quarter century, it's their continued willingness to step boldly into the netherworld of collective improvisation. Rooted in the band's Acid Test ramblings, drums/space has been a fixture of virtually every Dead concert since the beginning, providing a loose framework for freeform sound and rhythm explorations. For many veteran concertgoers, it's the high point of the show. (For others, it's time to chat with their neighbors, go to the bathroom, or get something to eat.) Curiously, however, surprisingly little drums/space has shown up on record, given the fact that it's such an integral part of the band's persona. *Infrared Roses,* released in 1991, is the first attempt to put some of these explorations into a coherent format, and it succeeds brilliantly.

The secret to the success of *Infrared Roses* is MIDI guru Bob Bralove, who waded through five years of drums/space to assemble it. And *assemble* is the right word here, because Bralove did more than simply choose a dozen interesting jams. Instead, he isolated selected passages from dozens of jams, and used them as compositional elements to create a series of four symphonic pieces of three movements each. The result is a haunting musical landscape studded with brilliant tone colors, muscular rhythms, and unearthly sounds. It could be the best headphone album ever made.

Starting with "Crowd Sculpture," an amusing sampling of Deadhead sounds in the parking lot (including pleas for tickets, bargaining, chants, car stereos, random conversations, and barking dogs), Bralove creates a compelling portrait of all the elements that make the Dead work. The portrait includes not only bandmembers but Deadheads, crew, and special guests. Lyricist Robert Hunter provided insightful titles for the jams. In the opening sequence, Bralove cleverly links Deadheads outside with the show inside by blending parking lot drummers into "Parallelogram," a powerful Kreutzmann/Hart duet. The crowd roar that bridges the gap and signals the show's opening has so much presence it bristles the hair on the back of your neck.

Every piece has a character of its own, blending a rainbow of guitars, bass, keyboards, and drums with an array of MIDI sounds such as French horn, mandolin, trumpet, flute, shakers, marimbas, vibes, bells, trombone, strings, birds, and "instruments" that don't exist. Familiar melody fragments pop up in odd places, while pieces move effortlessly and logically along toward the conclusion, "Apollo at the Ritz," a stunning eight-minute *tour de force* featuring Branford Marsalis and the rest of the band blowing their asses off at the Nassau Coliseum on 3/29/90. No matter how much of a Deadhead you think you are, if you don't have this album, your picture of the band is incomplete.

INSTRUCTIONS FROM THE MOTHERSHIP • Author Howard Rheingold's term for SPACE.

Garcia actually did play the aliens' five-note call from *Close Encounters of the Third Kind* during space in Eugene 1/22/78.

IT'S ALL OVER NOW, FIND YOUR SHOES • Postshow motto of avid HALLDANCERS, a play on the Dylan ballad, "It's All Over Now, Baby Blue," covered by Garcia for twenty-five years. "I've lost everything many times," says hyperdancer Tony Beers. "Clogs, sweaters, many pairs of shoes. In Saratoga '82, I left all my stuff in a stranger's trunk. In Hampton '84, I lost a whole duffel bag full of clothes. I take them off and very carefully put them somewhere, and then I carefully forget. I've also lost my brain at shows."

J-CARDS ✎ • The folded cards inside of cassette covers, shaped like a "j" when viewed sideways, that list the recorded contents of the tape. They have become an art form in the hands of Deadheads, using collage, marbleized papers, gold and silver inks, Day-Glo paint, colored pencils, dancing bears and skeletons, venue photographs and portraits of the band, often carefully chosen to match the era in which the show was played.

Elaborately decorated cards are given away with treasured tapes as gifts to friends and lovers. The setlists are often written in a personal calligraphy that expresses hard-to-describe movements in the music: Long jams will be represented with winding arrows, an adventuresome space may be represented by planets and stars, and songs themselves may become hieroglyphs, such as "Dark Star" and "Alligator." Stage chatter may be included in the margins, or notations of events that happened during the show, such as a sketch of the rainbow that shimmered overhead during drums at the Santa Fe Downs 9/10/83.

J. GARCIA • The name used by Garcia to sign his sketches, paintings, computer art—and neckties.

Garcia began his creative life as a painter at the California School of Fine Arts, now called the San Francisco Art Institute. "He thought of himself as an artist who played guitar," says

Roberta Weir, owner of the Weir Gallery (no relation to Robert), who sells his original works to a devoted group of collectors, most of whom are Heads.

"The first airbrushes came out after his illness in '86," says Weir. "I think the art helped him recover. Initially he was an observer. Now his personality is coming out more in the work — his enthusiasm, kindness, imagination, humor. Parts of the work that I call 'spatial excursions' develop like his music, rambling and collecting itself into various forms — mind at play, serendipitously roaming around. There are a lot of trees with strong roots, and life under the sea, little cartoon characters, and there's also a dark strain, like one called 'August West' — people in various stages of decay. But I think he likes to emphasize the whimsical aspects. The dominant thread is love of nature in spectral rich colors." Garcia claims as influences Picasso, Paul Klee, Max Ernst, Van Gogh, De Chirico, and the Expressionists.

"Jerry wanted to do some oil painting, so I had him over for a figure session with a model. I showed him how I laid out the colors, and I left him alone. I usually use two or three brushes on a painting, but when Jerry was done, he'd been through fourteen brushes. There was a student of mine there, a seventeen-year-old with a classical education who didn't know who Jerry was, so he treated Jerry like any other person, 'Hey man — can I use some of your white?' I think it was refreshing for him." (When asked by the gallery if his art had ever been displayed publicly, Garcia wrote, "No. I don't work for an audience. Not really looking for more public attention.")

Garcia sometimes makes art with bassist John Kahn, who painted the cover of the *Jerry Garcia Band* album. Like many Heads, Garcia carries a sketchbook with him on tour, sometimes sketching in bed. A book of his pen-and-inks and watercolors, edited by Art Peddler dealer Nora Sage Murray with help from Roberta Weir, was published by Ten Speed Press in 1990.

"Because of who Garcia is," says Weir, "it's important for him to continue to do his visual art, which draws attention to drawing and painting for younger artists. I'd like to think he'd be a celebrity artist who could cross over into the serious art world. The kids can't learn the traditional arts in schools anymore — it's been cut out. That's why we teach it here at the gallery. I'm very grateful that Garcia's involved."

In July 1992, Stonehenge Ltd. began marketing neckties based on patterns in Garcia's artwork, after Stonehenge presidents Irwin Sternberg and Libby Wegner saw an exhibit of his watercolors and pen-and-inks at a SoHo gallery. When an interviewer for *Magical Blend* magazine asked Garcia, "What inspired you to design a line of ties?" he replied, "I don't really have any control over them, they're just extracted from my artwork. I don't design ties, for God's sake!"

JAM • 1. *v.* "To play collectively improvised music," according to jazz clarinetist Mezz Mezzrow in *Really the Blues*, published in 1946. The word became popular among "hot jazz" players of Louis Armstrong's generation of the 1930s, who called a group of musicians playing together — especially at a party — a "jam session."

The word "jam" probably comes from the word "jama," used by the Wolof people of Africa as far back as the 1700s, to mean a large gathering or celebration. By the 1860s, a "jam" was a group of slaves getting together for fun and dancing. (The word "jam" also had sexual connotations, akin to "jellyroll," referred to in Hunter's "Dupree's Diamond Blues.")

Deadheads use the word as either a verb ("they jammed that 'Shakedown' ") or a noun ("that 'Estimated' jam was the total melt") to describe what the band does best, spontaneously composing memorable melodies and transitions. Grateful Dead music is a conversation between form and chaos. Certain songs — like "Cassidy," "The Music Never Stopped," "Playing in the Band," "Dark Star" — have jams built in, places where the band can, as jazz musicians say, "take it outside," pushing the limits of harmony and dissonance.

Melody is stretched until the song is only a key and a rhythmic feel; the downbeat floats until the bandmembers may lose the "one"; and near the fertile edge of disorder, new melodies appear, leading into another song, or back to the composition that was the starting point. *Completely* free playing, with no pre-planned changes, is also called a "jam."

Jams are an essential element of the drama of a Dead show. The places in songs where jamming begins are like points of embarkation into unmapped, wild territory. (*See* DOORWAYS AND SPLICES.)

2. *n.* Untitled themes played on numerous occasions by the band are sometimes given names by Deadheads, and these titles are sometimes cause for debate. A lilting jam that the band often played out of "Dark Star" beginning in the fall of '69 is referred to as the "Feelin' Groovy" jam, because of its slight resemblance to the Paul Simon song of that title. (This jam also appeared as a "doorway" between "China Cat Sunflower" and "I Know You Rider" in the early '70s.) Another jam, reminiscent of *Sketches of Spain*—era Miles Davis, that the band has played off and on since '68, is called "Spanish Jam" or "Bolero." (An excellent example of this jam was performed on 6/23/74 in Miami, out of "Dark Star.") Other Deadhead-derived titles for jams include "The Seven," the "Heaven Help Jam," "Milkin' the Roses," the "Darkness, Darkness Jam" (based on a Young-bloods tune), and the "Mind Left Body" jam—a *DeadBase* title taken from an only slightly related track on Paul Kantner and Grace Slick's *Baron Von Tollbooth and the Chrome Nun.* See PLANET EARTH ROCK & ROLL ORCHESTRA; THE SECOND SET; SPACE.

☙ *Michael Nash, musician, and collaborator with Weir and Taj Mahal on a musical life of Satchel Paige, on listening:*

There are constant offerings being put out there by the bandmembers, and whether or not they're picked up has to do with how much listening is going on. Sometimes there's not a lot, but amazingly often it's nearly telepathic. A phrase will be picked up, or counterpointed, or augmented into a new idea, and a door will open up. For me, "Playing in the Band" is the best representation of that voyage. Once the lyrics are done, it's like a ship setting off on open sea. In the course of a second set, you go out on the journey.

As the improvisation goes on, and little hints of the melody come back, it's like sighting land. When they play the reprise, it's like coming back to harbor.

No matter how scary it gets—no matter how high you get—you can pretty much count that they'll deliver you home again.

THE JERRY BALLAD SLOT • An informal name for one of the conventions of THE SECOND SET, the placement of one of Garcia's unhurried, sweet ballads a song or two after space—"Stella Blue," "Wharf Rat," "The Days Between," "Black Peter," "Standing on the Moon," "Attics of My Life," "Morning Dew," and so on.

The comforting melodies and philosophical introspection in these songs come as a consolation and a "returning home" for many Heads following the stripping down of melody during drums and space. Many of these songs also reach dramatic instrumental climaxes—such as "Black Peter" and "Morning Dew"—and can be the emotional highlight of a show.

🍀 *Jerry Garcia on that moment:*

I don't think of it as *my* statement. I think of it as a place where the energy goes down—whooosh! With our audience, it's not hard but it's taken a long time to get that. Ideally, there's a song in there that's so delicate that it's got a moment in it of pure silence.

🍀 *Elvis Costello on Garcia's vocal virtues:*

It's a very communicative, very human voice. He's a very underrated singer, and a great storyteller. He's very good at getting inside songs without attempting to make his voice lean out into other worlds. I always really liked his version of "When the Hunter Gets Captured by the Game." He sings it beautifully. Also, apart from all the *Europe '72* stuff, which I love, I'm fond of the vocals on "Sugaree," "Brokedown Palace," "Stella Blue," "China Doll," "Ship of Fools," "He's Gone," and "It Must Have Been the Roses." The slow tempo songs are just gorgeous.

Some of my favorite singers have no power to speak of in their voices. Maybe that's what makes them sound human. Randy Newman doesn't have a loud voice or much range, but his voice rings true. Some people who bellow don't communicate anything at all to me. There are people who have enormously powerful voices, like Stevie Wonder, who is so flexible, or Little Richard, whose voice is like a blowtorch—it sears your ears off. Then there're people with beautiful, mellifluous voices like Tim Hardin. Garcia's is right there between the two. You couldn't say it's mellifluous, and neither is it commanding. It's human sounding. He can sound very tragic, with an ache, which

I think is just as valuable as being able to hit any note. Particularly in American singing, there are a lot of people who do so much with very meager resources, examined purely from the compass of range and tone. And yet they turn their voices into the most moving thing you can imagine.

I heard a tape from one of the first shows back after his illness (*see* THE COMEBACK SHOW). It was very passionate, and kind of angry-sounding, which I'd never heard before, and liked enormously. It was really full of life.

JERRY GARCIA BAND • Garcia's other mainstay, which debuted under this name on 8/5/75, and has persisted as a touring and recording band, with changes of personnel, except for John Kahn, the bass player in every incarnation of the band. The Jerry Garcia Band, or "JGB," has been an alternate showcase for Garcia's playing and songwriting, typically playing smaller venues than the Dead until the late-'80s, when the JGB began playing larger halls.

Before the formation of the Jerry Garcia Band, Garcia and Bay Area keyboardist/vocalist Merl Saunders co-led the Garcia/Saunders band and the LEGION OF MARY. The first Jerry Garcia Band featured Nicky Hopkins on piano, known for his work with the Rolling Stones and Jefferson Airplane. A later incarnation, which lasted from 1/27/76 to 11/4/78, featured Keith and Donna Godchaux on piano and vocals. When Keith Godchaux was in good spirits, the band rocked hard, with expansive solos by Garcia alternating with crystalline lines by Godchaux that had a warm and authentic American soulfulness. Donna Godchaux's gospel stylings on songs like "Lonesome and a Long Way From Home" were more effective in the more intimate band setting than with the Dead. The JGB gave Garcia a more casual venue than the Dead for covers of Bob Dylan, Jimmy Cliff, Robbie Robertson, and others, and extended versions of his own "Sugaree" and "Friend of the Devil."

After several changes of personnel (Lesh played bass at three gigs in '81), in '84 JGB settled into a lineup of Melvin Seals on organ, John Kahn on bass, David Kemper on drums, and Gloria Jones and Jaclyn LaBranch on vocals. Seals's bright, muscular Hammond organ is the perfect rootsy complement to Garcia's abstract guitar explorations, and Jones and LaBranch (who jokingly call themselves "the Jerryettes") add celestial harmonies to "I Shall Be Released" and "The Night They Drove Old Dixie Down." The band's *Cats Under the Stars* is a studio gem, and songs like "Don't Let Go" and "Deal" on the '91 two-CD release *Jerry Garcia Band* show how far the boundaries of a club band can be stretched with Garcia at the helm.

🌿 *Melvin Seals, organist for the Jerry Garcia Band, on the audience:*

They seem to understand the music really well. They feel things that I sometimes can't feel onstage. Many times I've had people tell me that a wave of energy has gone through the audience at a certain time, but I can't sense it that much. They can feel the music and sense things so much in part, I think, because they move so much, and interpret the music that way.

JERRY IS GOD • Garcia, on being thought of as God: "Anybody who thinks I'm God should talk to my kids."

When asked in an interview for *Magical Blend* magazine if he minded being thought of as a religious figure by the SPINNERS, Garcia replied, "Well, I'll put up with it until they come for me with the cross and the nails."

When asked if he was aware of the "impact he has on people's minds," Garcia replied, "Not like that. I've made an effort to not be aware of it because it's perilously close to fascism. For the first eighteen years or so, I had a lot of doubt about the Grateful Dead. I thought that maybe this was a bad thing to be doing, because I was aware of the power, so I did a lot of things to sabotage it. I thought, 'Fuck this!' I dragged my feet as much as possible, but it still kept happening. So in that way, I was able to filter myself out of it and think it's not me. What a relief!" *See also* CAPTAIN TRIPS; SACRAMENTS.

JERRY'S KIDS • A spoof on the annual Jerry Lewis telethon, conceived and performed by *Saturday Night Live* performers (and longtime Deadheads) Al Franken and Tom Davis, as they emceed several nights of the bicoastal, twenty-three-show acoustic/electric run of three-set shows in the fall of '80 at San Francisco's Warfield Theater and Manhattan's Radio City Music Hall. In the running gag, performed on Halloween night at Radio City, and simulcast across the country to movie theaters, the show was turned into a fund-raiser for a Deadhead "poster child" who had broken his arm scamming into a show. Garcia made an appearance holding a box that purportedly contained his MISSING FINGER, promising it to the highest bidder.

The event was a coup for GD spokesperson-to-be Dennis McNally, who had been trying to have a conversation with Garcia about his own biography of Jack Kerouac, *Desolate Angel,* and went through the motions of auditioning for the part of a "Jerry's kid." "I was already too old and too straight," recalls McNally, "but of course I seized the opportunity to meet Jerry and say to him, 'Did you read my book?,' to which I had the wonderful experience of having him literally jump out of his chair and say, 'You wrote that book? It's the best biography I ever read!' That was in September, and in December, Jerry sent some people to me and said, 'Why don't you do a biography of us?' "

Seeds for the gig had been planted on the two occasions that the band performed on *Saturday Night Live*—11/11/78 ("Casey Jones," "I Need a Miracle"→"Good Lovin' ") and 4/5/80 ("Alabama Getaway," "Saint of Circumstance"). Both band and audience, Franken says, left quite an impression. "Like no other band we've ever had," he says. "Deadheads came out of the wall for that one."

JERRY'S SIDE; THE JERRY SIDE • The right side of the floor, in front of Garcia's position onstage since 4/2/82 at Duke University. Along with THE PHIL ZONE, this is the other major division of what Greg Muck calls "the Dead compass"—verbal mapping of venues, as in, "I'll see you over on Jerry's Side tonight." According to Muck, the "Dead compass" is in effect for Heads even at non-Dead-related events, and Deadheads may kid one another about meeting on the Jerry side of, say, a performance of Wagner's *Parsifal.*

The Jerry Side is sometimes—tongue in cheek—called "the Vince Zone."

JERRYGAPS/BOBBYGAPS 📖 • Pauses in the vocals caused by memory lapses, often followed by bursts of inventive playing. "One night at Shoreline Amphitheater," recalls taper Jeff Althoff, "this guy turns to me and says, 'Have you ever noticed that when Jerry is jamming hard, and the music gets really intense, that he screws up the words?'

" 'You know why that is, right?'

" 'No,' I say.

" 'It's because he's getting the music beamed into him by beings from another planet.'

" 'So, what about the words?'

" 'Well, they don't speak English . . .' "

JOHNNY LAW • Police officers. Used with condescension. "Johnny Law pulled us over for going sixty in a fifty-five. I guess Dead stickers are illegal in Arizona."

The word "Johnny" has been applied contemptuously to policemen since 1850, and is probably a corruption of the French word for police, *gendarmes*. *See* DRUG CHECKPOINT AHEAD!

THE JONES GANG • A one-night-only stage name for the band, conjured up by Lesh during a time-out at Colgate University in Hamilton, New York, 11/4/77. After introducing the "gang"—"Keith Jones [Godchaux], Jerry Jones [Garcia], Bob Jones [Weir], Julius P. Jones [Kreutzmann], Mick Jones [Hart], Phil Jones [Lesh], and Donna Jean Jones [Godchaux]"—he started to make his way through the crew—Harry Jones [Popick], etc.—but was interrupted by a restoration of full audio, at which point the band launched into "Samson & Delilah."

Weir has come up with many goof names for the band onstage, including "The Sunstroked Serenaders"—a product of Weir's overheated imagination under the sun at Ken Kesey's Farm 8/27/72—and the "Just Exactly Perfect Brothers Band," at Winterland 12/9/77. Bill Graham was also fond of introducing the band in creative ways. On 2/28/69 at the Fillmore, the Dead were "the last of the gay desperadoes." *See* BILL GRAHAM; UNCLE BOBO.

JONESIN' • Extreme craving for something, as in, "I'm jonesin' for 'the Dew,' bigtime!" Used by Heads who haven't seen a show in a while, as well as Heads looking for tickets.

From post–World War I addicts' lingo for a heroin habit, a "scag Jones."

JUST DEW IT! • Part of the extensive deadification of Nike slogans and symbols, transforming a motivational sports slogan into a plea for the beloved Garcia-sung ballad "Morning Dew." "Air Garcia" is another popular t-shirt, featuring a silhouette of Garcia leaping with guitar in hand, a joke on the comparative immobility of his stage persona (*see* THE LUNGE).

"Bo knows Jerry" was the instant Head response to the ubiquitous Bo Jackson television campaign.

"When You Absolutely, Positively Have to Be at Every Show" read another sticker, a send-off of the solemn Federal Express oath. Deadhead swipes at popular culture are both a source of harmless PARKING LOT SCENE fun and a way of weaving mainstream cultural images into the fabric of their community. *See also* DEADIFICATION.

KEPLER'S BOOKS & MAGAZINES • A progressive bookstore-café once located on the El Camino Real in Menlo Park, California, and owned by Roy Kepler, who founded the Palo Alto Peace Center. Kepler's was a gathering place for the Beat-influenced artists, musicians, and writers who also frequented clubs like St. Michael's Alley, where Garcia's pre-Dead bluegrass groups like THE WILDWOOD BOYS played. One of its draws was an espresso machine, which lent the establishment a bohemian, North Beach air. In an interview in *The Golden Road,* David Nelson recalled meeting Garcia at Kepler's: "Here was this guy sitting with an open shirt, playing a 12-string, and I think he had a wreath in his hair, like a Greek statue. It was kind of a thing in those days." Garcia played occasional gigs at Kepler's around the summer of '62 on a tiny stage in front of five or six tables, and also was an employee at Kepler's for a while. When asked once what he had learned from taking LSD, Garcia cracked, "I learned I should stop working at Kepler's."

KICK DOWN • To provide. "You've got the kind Veneta bettyboards? Kick down!" *See* SESH.

THE KILLS ✏ • Soundboard tapes of the highest possible sound quality and the most unrelenting performances. "Tapes to die or kill for," explains Charley Wilkins, who relates his friend's regular habit of taking tapes with him whenever leaving his car. " 'They can have my car,' he says, 'but they can't have my kills.' "

"Killer" is the ubiquitous superlative. "Have you checked out that killer 'Eyes' from 2/15/73?"

THE KIND • The good stuff.

Derived from Hawaiian surfing pidgin, "da kine." Among the first surfers, "da kine" was used for everything—even a person whose name you forgot.

"The kind" is used by Heads to praise anything from tapes ("the kind first-gen board") to food ("kind veggie bagels") to performances ("that 'I Know You Rider' was the kind"), and so on. In the parking lot, marketing pressures transform watery spaghetti and tepid Budweiser into "the kind."

When used alone as a noun, "the kind" usually refers to "kind bud," good pot: downy with red or purple hairs, "skunky"-smelling, glittering with resinous crystals, carrying no seeds.

The phrase "Are you kind?" from "Uncle John's Band" was printed on stickers by the MINGLEWOOD TOWN COUNCIL to ask Deadheads to ask themselves if they were being as good to the scene as it had been good to them.

KIND VEGGIE BURRITOS, KILLER STIR-FRY • Heads are able to survive for years of tour on these parking lot

staples, prepared on gas burners or tourbus stoves. Stir-fry —
along with patchouli oil, Nag Champa incense, dogs, beer, and
pot smoke — is one of the primary components of the inimitable
parking lot aroma.

These simple, nourishing foods are easy to prepare and assemble, and the ingredients are available anywhere, which
means that tourheads supporting and feeding themselves by
vending these foods can take advantage of local resources — like
the occasional farmer's market, roadside stand, or organic produce store — and still be able to get by when the only thing open
is a corner grocery.

Many Heads take considerable pride in the foods they vend,
adding freshly diced salsa to plates of nachos, or generous
amounts of their harvest to potent ganja brownies, constructing
elegant dinners on paper plates of lasagna, tossed salad, and
garlic bread. Certain vendors — like the celebrated "Burrito
People," or Paul Goeltz (whose oatmeal-chocolate-chip-raisin-
banana cookies are legendary), or the cheerful egg-roll man
outside of '80s shows at Oakland's Kaiser Auditorium — become
parking lot legends. In the late '80s, a vanload of Heads from
France drew crowds in the parking lot by selling hot buck-
wheat crepes rolled on a traditional crêpe stone and soaked in
Grand Marnier and sugar, under a sign, "Hell in a *Crêpe.*"

KNOTS • A Garcia metaphor for the challenge he faces
nightly. "For me, playing is like unraveling a whole bunch of little knots," he says. "Some shows I never get past the knots. I
spend the whole night trying to untie them, and my consciousness never breaks through to the first person out there."

KREUTZMANN, BILL • Drums and percussion. Born
on May 7, 1946, in Palo Alto, California.

Since day one, Bill Kreutzmann has been the steady backbeat of the Grateful Dead. "He was blessed with an ability to
find the beat and lock onto it," said Mickey Hart. "He was naturally smooth and in time, which made him irreplaceable. He
was the center pole that allowed the rest of us to go roaming off
the edges."

Kreutzmann's mother was a dance teacher at Stanford Uni-

versity, who occasionally enlisted her son's help in keeping the
beat on an Indian tom-tom while she notated choreography at
home or in class. When Kreutzmann was twelve, he studied
with a drum teacher named Lee Anderson, who taught on
Perry Lane—coincidentally, right next door to where Ken Kesey was writing his first, unpublished novel, *Zoo*. In those days,
record stores offered glassed-in booths for listening to records,
and Kreutzmann spent hours in those booths.

He joined a few rock and roll bands—like the Legends, that
played Chuck Berry tunes at Y dances, and another called the
Sparks. By the early '60s, various permutations of THE WILD-
WOOD BOYS and MOTHER MCCREE'S UPTOWN JUG CHAMPI-
ONS were playing at the local hootenannies in places like the
Tangent, and Kreutzmann became a regular. "My heart just
said, 'This music is really cool.'"

Kreutzmann met Garcia at Dana Morgan's Music Store in
'62, when he sold Garcia a banjo. Soon, Garcia was working
there too, Weir was hanging around playing hooky from high
school, and Kreutzmann had a new band: the Zodiacs, with
PIGPEN blowing harp, Garcia on bass, and Troy Weidenheimer
on guitar. By '65, the band had become THE WARLOCKS, and
Kreutzmann's new friend Phil Lesh was turning him on to the
volcanic polyrhythms of Elvin Jones, over which John Coltrane was laying down his "sheets of sound."

"I just bit on that," Kreutzmann recalled to Blair Jackson. "I
thought, 'I've gotta learn to play this stuff!'"

The Warlocks played five sets a night, six nights a week, for
six weeks at the In Room in Belmont starting in September of
'65. The music was already starting to stretch: "The weekends
were all these heavy straight juicer types," says Kreutzmann.
"They'd be looking up at us as we played all these long, long
songs."

After the Warlocks had become the Grateful Dead, and Hart
was a member of the band, the two drummers set about to becoming as closely locked in as possible. Hart hypnotized
Kreutzmann at least once, and in practice sessions at the
Potrero Theater in San Francisco, the drummers would prac-

tice what they called "going out," riding the cascading climaxes of "The Other One" for hours at a time. Their mind-melding interaction—the word Hart uses is "entrainment"—is breathtaking on "The Eleven" from *Live/Dead* (with Kreutzmann in the left channel and Hart in the right), the result of long hours of playing odd time-signatures till they became as natural as breath.

When Hart left the band in '71, Kreutzmann once more became the only drummer, and the next four years were a peak of the Dead's ability to jam like the jazz groups Kreutzmann had so admired years before, with Kreutzmann in intimate dialogues with each bandmember, *simultaneously*. To David Gans, what defines this period was "clarity, flexibility, exploration. Everybody was awake, and you could hear everything perfectly. There was a soulfulness to the performances, everybody had their place in the audio spectrum, and there was one drummer, who could turn on a dime. Everybody had their place in the pulse of the music, and it went *everywhere*. When Mickey came back, the band lost the ability to corner readily. And that changed everything. It's not to say it changed it for the worse, but it changed it."

One way it changed it was by opening up the drum solos into drum *showdowns*, percussion as a martial art, with the two drummers doing symbolic battle. A good example of the classic Kreutzmann/Hart percussion-as-concussion workout is "Parallelogram" on INFRARED ROSES (*see DRUMS*).

Though as much of a drummer, Kreutzmann is less of a showman than Hart, and a very humble and private man. "Sometimes virtuosity is lost on me," he says. "So that guitarist can play two million notes—big deal, did he play any music, anything that hit you in the heart, and grabbed you and moved you?"

Kreutzmann is an avid kayaker, and runs the Lost Coast Kayak Adventures company. Kreutzmann and his wife, Shelley, have two children, Stacey and Justin. They live on a Mendocino County ranch, raising horses and Rottweilers.

LAKE ACID • The town of Lake Placid, New York, after Deadheads had passed through. As the band and fans trucked into Lake Placid for a gig on 10/17/83, Heads blocked out many of the *"Pl'*s" from city signs, including the Hilton.

LAMINATES • BACKSTAGE PASSES good for more than one show, sealed in plastic, assigned to family and friends of the band and crew. The word "laminate" can apply to the passes themselves, or to the holders of them, as in, "All the laminates got in early and saved seats." Laminate passes, or "lammies," often worn on a cord, are dispensed by THE OFFICE.

In the old days, laminates were given only to bandmembers and their friends. As more and more Heads per show were granted backstage passes, two classifications of laminate were instituted—one for insiders and the other for "friends of friends," with writing on the back that determined the bearer's status (e.g., "GDP—Jerry's Guest"). On rare occasions, laminates have been counterfeited.

THE LAST ONE • Printed on the tickets for October 20, 1974, the closing night of a five-night run at Winterland, before the band's announced "retirement" from touring. Until the band launched a tour in June of '76, Heads referred to the run as "the last five nights."

'74 had been a difficult year for the band, though they were playing well. Following the release of *From the Mars Hotel* and the radio popularity of "Scarlet Begonias" and "U.S. Blues," the band was being booked into larger and larger coliseums and stadiums, and the bandmembers were disillusioned with the kind of "success" that meant "billions of cops and people getting busted at your gigs," as Garcia put it. Hunter had warned in a Dead Heads' Newsletter in '73 of a self-perpetuating cycle (which he called "Urobouros," after the serpent that feeds off its own tail) of larger halls requiring a larger sound system, which would require larger gigs to pay for it. Pigpen had died a year earlier; and the Dead's music—as *Blues for Allah* would show—was about to change. It was time to reflect, retract.

The scene backstage during the "last run" was *electric* in more ways than one. Cameramen were filming *The Grateful Dead Movie*. Stephen Barncard, the producer of *American Beauty*, remembers that to get onstage you were encouraged to "lick a puddle of acid off your wrist," dropped there by a member of the road crew. "I was off and on that stage about fifteen times, which would have been OK, but I was smoking the hash oil too, so I was stupid *and* in outer space. People couldn't figure out why I wasn't saying anything. I *couldn't* say anything."

For the final entrance, Bill Graham, in white top hat and tails, introduced the band with a simple tribute: "As it should be on a Sunday night in San Francisco, the Grateful Dead."

Mickey Hart, who had left under a cloud three years earlier, sat back down in the big chair facing Kreutzmann, and brought down the old thunder for the second-set opener, "Playin' in the Band," as Heads ticked off the songs they might never hear live again. The cameras roamed around while Boots—the band's "pyrotechnician"—sent lighter-fluid firesigns to the rafters in time to the music.

The notion that Winterland would be the Dead's last stand, however, was dispelled quickly by the bandmembers' eagerness to play. By January of '75, they were recording *Blues for Allah*, and by March, they were rehearsing aggressive jazzy workouts like "King Solomon's Marbles," with their old friend David Crosby for a benefit for extracurricular activities in San Francisco schools at Kezar Pavilion (the "S.N.A.C.K. benefit") on March 23. By June, they had played another benefit at Winterland, and the "year off" also saw Dead shows at the Great American Music Hall (*see* ONE FROM THE VAULT) and Golden Gate Park, as well as the recording and release of "solo" projects by Garcia, Weir, Hunter, and Hart. For a band that had broken up, they were awfully prolific.

"We're blessed with doing something we can do until we fall over," Weir said in '93, reaffirming the band's determination to keep playing together, and recalling an epiphany he had at a concert by the Count Basie band in San Francisco: "It was a wonderful evening. Three of the four of his original quartet were still playing with him after forty or fifty years and having a ball. A week or two later, Basie went back to his place in Florida, put his feet up, and checked out. I may have seen his last show. He was doing the only thing he could imagine doing, right up until the end. He's a hero of mine for that, and he taught me something really valuable that evening."

THE LEGION OF MARY • The Legion of Mary was a Garcia-band lineup in '74 and '75, consisting of Merl Saunders on keyboards and vocals, John Kahn on bass, Martin Fierro on saxophone and flute, and Paul Humphreys on drums, replaced in '75 by Ron Tutt. The Legion of Mary played club dates at places like the Keystone in Berkeley, the Great American Music Hall in San Francisco, and the Bottom Line in New York. They interspersed reggae covers like "The Harder They Come," Merl-fired funk sweat-raisers like "Expressway to Your Heart" and "Soul Roach," along with Garcia favorites like "Tore Up Over You" and "Let It Rock." *See also* JERRY GARCIA BAND; RECONSTRUCTION.

LESH, PHIL • Bass, vocals, composition. Born on March 15, 1940, in Berkeley, California.

Lesh plays bass as a co-lead instrument rather than strictly a timekeeping one, and his bass lines are contrapuntal, weaving spontaneously composed melodies that can last the length of an entire song, in intimate dialogues with Garcia's lines. Lesh learned how to play bass in THE WARLOCKS, and he has brought to the Dead not only his own distinctive playing style, but interests in music other than rock and roll—such as that of Edgard Varèse, John Coltrane, Charles Ives, Bach, sixteenth-century modal counterpoint, and contemporary composers like Stockhausen and the serialists—which helped create the Dead as a band that reached beyond category.

Lesh's life in music began when he was very young, when his grandmother invited him to listen with her to Bruno Walter conducting Brahms's First Symphony on the radio. "The introduction comes on like the wrath of God," Lesh recalled to David Gans in 1981. "It knocked me against the wall. As soon as I heard that, I knew."

Lesh took up the trumpet when he was fourteen, and was prodigious enough that his parents moved so that he could go to Berkeley High School, where students could take courses in music theory. Lesh got into big-band jazz like Stan Kenton, and at summer music camp, he was introduced to the music of Coltrane and Miles Davis. Around that time—the late '50s— Lesh also met Bobby Petersen, a young poet who turned Lesh on to the novels of Jack Kerouac and Henry Miller, *Howl* by Allen Ginsberg, and marijuana. In 1960, Lesh enrolled at the University of California at Berkeley, where he met TOM CON-STANTEN. Frustrated by a music department that seemed set up to train musicologists rather than composers, Lesh quit in the middle of the semester.

Constanten introduced Lesh to composer Luciano Berio, and Lesh enrolled in Berio's class at Mills College, where he began composing his own pieces. When Berio invited Lesh and Constanten on a tour of Europe with him, they went to Las Vegas to earn the money to do it, where Lesh worked as a keno marker at the Horseshoe Club. Constanten went to Europe with Berio, but Lesh instead headed back to California. He soon met Garcia and Pigpen in Palo Alto. Lesh heard Garcia play banjo at Kepler's Bookstore, and invited him to play on the radio show where he worked as an engineer. The two became friends.

In the early '60s, Lesh moved to the Haight-Ashbury—then still a small, unfamous, hip community—and got an apartment with Constanten, who was back from Europe. Lesh was by that point listening to Bob Dylan's *Another Side of Bob Dylan* and *Bringin' It All Back Home,* and taking acid. He was composing only rarely, but wrote a solo for Constanten's prepared piano that involved shuffling the score before each performance. Lesh hated the Beatles at first, but when he went to see *A Hard Day's Night* at a local moviehouse, "I was the only guy in a theater full of screamin' chicks. I started to grow my hair long."

In '65, Lesh and Weir and Garcia ran into each other at a party at Willy Legate's house in Palo Alto, and went out to Garcia's car to get high. Lesh mentioned to Garcia that he wanted to play an electric instrument—perhaps the bass guitar. The next week, when Lesh went to see the Warlocks at Magoo's Pizza Parlor in Palo Alto, Garcia invited Lesh to take over the bass position in the band from Dana Morgan Jr. Lesh accepted. Shortly thereafter—at the Acid Tests—the music started to open up.

"When we got started," Lesh recalls, "none of us ever really thought of it as a rock band. There was no way to define a rock band then. There were three others—the Beatles, the Stones, and Paul Butterfield's band, and we didn't want to be any one of those. I had experience in avant-garde music, and classical music, and jazz, and it just seemed logical to apply some of those structural techniques. The kind of overlap, simultaneity, that's characteristic of so much classical twentieth-century music seemed ready to hand, and infinitely applicable to the potential we had."

With the introduction of "New Potato Caboose" and "The Other One" in '67, Lesh was established as a co-lead voice. Lesh got Constanten to join the band for the *Anthem of the Sun* sessions, and their ideas about simultaneity—derived from the music of Charles Ives—meshed well with Hart and Kreutzmann's superimposed rhythms. The intimate Lesh/Garcia dialogues were refined during trio sessions with Hart as "Mickey Hart and the Hartbeats" at the Matrix in San Francisco in '68, drifting in and out of "Dark Star," and the bass-driven jam that would become "The Eleven."

Lesh is a power source, the Dead's unsecret weapon, often the leader of the band, thrumming chords at the peak of "Morning Dew," exploding into "The Other One" with a flurry of thick notes, driving the other soloists during "Eyes of the World." Perhaps the highest tribute to Lesh's role in the band is Garcia's: "When Phil's happening, the band's happening."

"Phil Lesh was the band's intellectual," says Hart. "Noise, to him, was dissonance. He knew about the atonal experimentation of Western art music from Schoenberg and Webern on, and he was applying these orchestral techniques to the traditional rock and roll bass line. Phil created a new instrument out of the bass, fanning the strings with dense, thunderous, sensual chords that could rattle your bones. He could see the musical possibilities in anything."

He was the first bandmember to have a side of the audience named after him: THE PHIL ZONE.

Lesh and his wife, Jill, have two sons: Graham and Brian.

🦋 *Rob Wasserman, bassist, collaborator with Bob Weir, on Phil Lesh's approach to the instrument:*

Phil was the first player I noticed, because he was so different from any other bass player I had heard. He's one of the pioneers of the six-string bass. When Phil is shaking buildings with that low note—you can't do that with a four-string bass. Jerry is more like a bass player than Phil is. I hear a lot of bass lines in Jerry's playing. Phil's got his own thing, and it's a counterpoint to Jerry's guitar, or a mirror image. He happens to play bass, but he's more like a horn player, doing all those arpeggios—and he has that counterpoint going all the time.

LINE DONKEYS 📖 • Heads entering a venue with backpack crammed with clothes, food, books, and so on—so loaded down that the friskers are overwhelmed, and the long line stalls while assorted pockets, purses, and carrying bags are emptied, scrutinized, and repacked. Some line donkeys are advocates of "the show is life" philosophy, and try to take it all in with them. Others just don't have cars. *See* RUNNERS.

LINE DUTY • The hours spent waiting on line for tickets, or for the opening of the doors of the venue, especially at general admission shows.

Because the first person who gets through the doors in a group at a show is often responsible for staking out a prime spot with a good view of the stage, the task of line duty is often rotated through a group of "show buddies" in the course of a run.

Bonds of Deadhead community are strengthened on the line. Older Heads share stories of memorable shows past and cultural history and lore with younger Heads, and patient hours of line duty encourage the sprouting of new friendships while sitting together on blankets and newspapers, sharing food and passing pipes. Praise of a jam from a nearby boom box might evolve into a conversation about tapes, leading to the discovery of mutual friends and the swapping of phone numbers. The line is also where Heads try to "call the opener," play games like "Cosmic Wimpout," the Dead triviafest "Head Games," and cards, read, play tapes, guitars, and drums, and catch up on sleep between shows.

LISTS • 1. Written records of songs played, in order of performance, at Dead shows. *See* SETLISTS.

2. Tape lists. The contents of a tape trader's collection—ideally, well-organized and annotated to make tape trading easy and efficient. A typical ad at the back of *Relix* or *Golden Road* will say, "Your list gets mine," an invitation to exchange lists and begin trading.

Many trader's lists are scholarly works in themselves, informing the reader about the contents of the tapes, with mentions of extraordinary jams, notable REVIVALS, or guest musicians. Some traders will rate shows with colorful notes—"4/24/78, an abnormally good night in Normal, Illinois"—or include amusing stage chatter or offstage events.

Traders develop their own rating systems for recording quality, usually using some variation of A, B, C, etc., with pluses and minuses, or numbers. Whether or not a tape is a SOUNDBOARD ("SBD"), a radio broadcast, or an AUDIENCE TAPE ("AUD") is almost always noted, and the numbers of generations from the source tape is often specified. (*See* GEN.)

Many traders supplement their lists with preferences including brand of tape, Dolby or no Dolby, and mailing instructions. Traders on the Net exchange lists as files. *See* DEADBASE.

♣ *Poet and translator Jim Powell's rating system:*

A: perfect very low gen > excellent fairly low gen w/minor defects

B: noticeable but not insistently obtrusive defects: mild > moderate generational deterioration (hiss, faded signal, distortion, breakup) &/or AUD taping problems (audience noise, mushy or boomy hall): listenable with a little patience

C: gettin' kinda grungy: insistently obtrusive defects: muffled sound, moderate to marked generational deterioration, audience &/or hall noise: listening tests your patience

D: poor tape: all of the above and worse: listening requires stinging desire

F: " 'The horror. The horror.' "

A 5.0 > 0.1 rating system seems preferable to an A > F system, however (where 5.0 > 4.0 = A+++ > A---, 3.9 > 3.0 = B+++ > B---, and so on) since it allows closer registration of distinctions between tapes, 10 steps between grades rather than 3 (A+, A, A-). We figure that one decimal point (0.1) equals one generation on optimal analog equipment, with 50 generations to totally obliterate the signal, but we haven't tested this yet.

LIVE/DEAD • Album #4, released in November 1969.

A compilation of live performances from the AVALON BALLROOM (January '69) and the FILLMORE WEST (February and March '69), spliced together to form a single, incandescent set. *Live/Dead* revealed to the record-buying public the Dead at a peak of fearless experimentation and exploration, with Mickey Hart and Tom Constanten on board pushing the envelopes of polyrhythm and tone. The album also represents the end of an era—within a short time after its release, Constanten took his leave, and the band charted a different course, closer to the bandmembers' folk roots.

The inside of the album (or the CD booklet) has a photo taken from the stage at the free concert on Haight Street on 3/3/68, facing east. The marquee of the Straight Theater says "Poet's Theater, Philip Whalen." Whalen was a friend of Jack Kerouac's, and appears in several of Kerouac's novels under

pseudonyms like Ben Fagin and Warren Coughlin. The cover
art is by Bob Thomas, who also designed *History of the Grateful
Dead, Vol. 1 (Bear's Choice)*.

Deadheads who were frustrated for years by having to get
up to flip the record as "Dark Star" segued into "St. Stephen"
were relieved by remastering engineer Joe Gastwirt's stitching
of the album sides into one seamless jam for the CD. *See AMER-
ICAN BEAUTY;* THE HAIGHT-ASHBURY; *WORKINGMAN'S DEAD.*

🍂 *Blair Jackson, editor of* The Golden Road, *on Live/Dead:*
Set and setting. Those were the bywords from none other than Dr. Tim
himself. So when the time came for me to begin my first voyage into the psychedelic otherworld in the fall of '71, there was only one appropriate choice
of music to guide me gently into the unknown: "Dark Star" from *Live/Dead.*
I'd probably listened to the song about a hundred times since I'd picked up
Live/Dead just before Christmas in 1969, yet every time, it felt fresh, new and
alive. I never could quite learn it, never quite remember the exact sequence
of events—whether that shimmering passage that sounded like the petals of
some great metallic flower unfolding came before or after the unsettling ride
through gaseous purple space clouds. There was that moment in there somewhere when a guitar pick slowly crawling up a string felt like having your
backbone slowly removed, and that other passage where Garcia's guitar
sounded like a big fat Siamese cat being squeezed. So those were some of the
signposts I was ready to absorb on Trip #1 that night in my Northwestern
University dorm room.

In the end, as I lay there motionless, headphones on, my eyes closed, it all
went by in the blink of an eye. I remember getting up after the side was over
(teased once again by the "St. Stephen" to come on side two) and saying to
my roommate, "I don't think I feel any differen-a-a-a-au-au-gh-oh my
GOD!"

Set and setting. It was in the grooves, too. The set that the four sides of
Live/Dead chronicled was a sequence of songs the Dead played often in '69,
with occasional variations to keep people guessing. In an era when everyone,
it seemed, was stretching out and releasing endless songs on albums—remember Iron Butterfly's "In-A-Gadda-Da-Vida" or Cream's romp through
"Spoonful" on *Wheels of Fire?* —nothing matched "Dark Star" on *Live/Dead:* It
was twenty-three minutes of utterly unpredictable, constantly shifting musi-

cal energy that poured out of even the shittiest speakers as electro-charged protoplasm, with or without psychedelic assistance. When side two picked up right where "Dark Star" left off, the formlessness gave way to the big rubbery crunch of "St. Stephen," a thousand times more potent than the *Aoxomoxoa* version. Then there was that "William Tell" bridge—was it part of "St. Stephen" or not, I wondered as I sat hour after hour staring at the red, black and white lyric booklet with its cool calligraphy and benign creatures seemingly lifted from the ruins of some imaginary Celtic cathedral. That was followed by "The Eleven," all speedy, swirling circular lines rising and falling in great lonnnnnng breaths, and those lyrics: "Eight-sided whisperin' hallelujah hatrack." Yow!

Side three was Pigpen and the boys playing off that "Lovelight" rhythm in a hundred different ways, with Pig rappin' and howling and screaming and everyone—us, too!—pulled along on a joyous Harley ride. Frankly, side four didn't get a lot of listens in my household, though "Death Don't Have No Mercy" contains one of Garcia's best blues solos ever. "Feedback" took the dark mood to even scarier places (*Pfft,phhttt,zweeeeee!PffttPftttPftt!*), with token light coming out of the blackness just in the nick of time—"We Bid You Goodnight."

In a scene where everyone has a million opinions and there is no consensus about anything, almost everyone agrees that *Live/Dead* is one ba-a-a-a-d motherfucker. For my money, there is no "Dark Star" more sensual, more perfect in its construction, so totally together in its splendid anarchy. And though I suppose I've now heard "better" versions of each of the other tunes, there's something about the ones on *Live/Dead* that just feel right. Maybe it's because the album was there when I needed it (and there when I was ready for it). And now, hearing it as a continuous performance on CD nearly twenty-five years after it was recorded, *Live/Dead* still excites me in a way that no other Dead album does. It remains the absolute apex of psychedelic rock 'n' roll. It is the Dead as a mystical fire-breathing deity, before the distant call of sweet harmonies and shimmering acoustic guitars tamed the savage, beautiful beast.

LOST SAILOR • A Head "severely down on his luck, in a daze, who has lost all sense of reality," according to Maryland Head John Herrold, "usually found on tour in a huddled group, holding up one finger, waiting for a MIRACLE." The term is taken from the Weir/Barlow song of the same name. Also called "scrankers" and "yochies."

LSD • Lysergic acid diethylamide-25, a derivative of ergot, a fungus that grows on ears of rye. LSD is the tool used most often by Deadheads seeking a PSYCHEDELIC experience, a journey of initiation. Deadheads call it by many names, including "acid," "doses," " 'cid," "A," "L," "trips," "hits," "liquid" (when dissolved in liquid form), "blots" (when absorbed into blotter paper), and "sheets" (perforated hundred-hit squares of blotter paper). The form of Grateful Dead music was partially inspired by the Dead's own psychedelic experience at the ACID TESTS.

LSD was first synthesized by Albert Hoffman, a research chemist working at the Sandoz Laboratories in Basel, Switzerland. Hoffman believed that his discovery of LSD was a serendipitous extension of mystical experiences he'd had while young, walking through the Alps. As Hoffman recalled in his memoirs,

While still a child, I experienced . . . deeply euphoric moments on my rambles through forest and meadow. It was these experiences that shaped the main outline of my worldview, and convinced me of the existence of a miraculous, powerful, unfathomable reality that was hidden from everyday sight. . . . Unexpectedly—though scarcely by chance—much later, in middle age, a link was established between my profession and these visionary experiences from childhood.

That link was forged on the afternoon of April 16, 1943, when Hoffman was interrupted in his lab work by "unusual sensations." Unable to work, Hoffman went home, where he experienced "an extremely stimulated imagination . . . an uninterrupted stream of fantastic pictures, extraordinary shapes with intense, kaleidoscopic play of colors." Three days later, Hoffman ingested 250 micrograms of LSD dissolved in water (an infinitesimal amount by non-LSD standards) and embarked on a classic bad trip, with storms of dread, and fear of death, possession, and insanity. The next morning, however, Hoffman awoke "refreshed, with a clear head, though still somewhat tired physically. A sensation of well-being and renewed life flowed through me. When I later walked out into the garden, in which the sun shone now after a spring rain, everything glistened and sparkled in a fresh light. The world was as if newly created."

Sandoz put LSD on the market as an experimental drug to help psychiatrists "gain insight into the world of ideas and sensations of mental patients," under the trade name Delysid. One interested customer was the newly formed CIA. Inspired by Nazi experiments with mescaline in the Dachau concentration camp, for the next two decades, the CIA's project MK-ULTRA tried to find the limits of LSD as a weapon in a "war without death," calculating how much LSD it would take to incapacitate the entire city of Los Angeles, and slipping it to prisoners, addicts, and mental patients.

Pranksterish dosing of agents by agents and rampant "self-experimentation" with LSD became a problem, with a 1954 memo from the Technical Services Staff warning that testing LSD "in the Christmas punchbowls usually present at Christmas parties" was not recommended. Soldiers at Edgewood Arsenal stole the drug for their own purposes, and the word "trip" was coined by Army scientists.

After Dr. Humphrey Osmond, the young Canadian scientist who coined the word PSYCHEDELIC, supervised the mescaline experience of esteemed British author Aldous Huxley, who wrote of his experience of being shown "the miracle, moment by moment, of naked existence" in an essay titled *The Doors of Perception,* LSD was endorsed by bohemian intellectuals like Alan Watts and cultural icons like Cary Grant. LSD was welcomed as a key that might quickly unlock many doors, from a cure for alcoholism, to the treatment of neuroses, to the attainment of a profound understanding of life.

Clinics and research centers employing LSD opened up in several places, including Palo Alto and Menlo Park, where several future members of the Dead were living at the Chateau. Ken Kesey was also in town, a graduate student at Stanford, and enrolled in a research program at the Veterans' Hospital where he was paid $75 a day to take various drugs, including LSD and mescaline. Robert Hunter also took part in these experiments. Soon LSD had found its way back to the circle of Kesey's friends, novelists and musicians living in a group of houses on Perry Lane. The first "electric Kool-Aid" was not Kool-Aid, but dosed venison chili.

On October 24, 1965, THE WARLOCKS dropped acid and spent a day in the woods of Marin County, and then went to one of the Family Dog dances at Longshoreman's Hall to see the Lovin' Spoonful. "It was just really fine to see that whole scene . . . nobody there but heads and this strange rock and roll music playing in this weird building," recalls Garcia. Lesh went up to Ellen Harmon, a member of the Family Dog, and said, "Lady, what this little séance needs is *us.*" With OWSLEY's help to keep dosages up and prices down, LSD became the basis of the psychedelic culture of THE HAIGHT-ASHBURY.

Many have reflected on the uncanny parallels between the structure of a Dead show—especially the second set, moving from structure (the songs) to fertile chaos (DRUMS and SPACE), and back to form—and the LSD journey. "We were improvising cosmically," said Garcia, recalling the Acid Tests. "Being high, each note is a whole universe. And each silence. We're just playing what's there."

For many Heads who "dose" at shows, the Dead's music fulfills the role of a trusted guide through the psychedelic experience. LSD, and the laws against it, also account for many of the difficulties that Heads have, legally and psychologically, inside and outside shows. For many Heads, LSD functions as a SACRAMENT in a religion that has been outlawed. *See* CARRIER WEIGHT LAW, DRUG CHECKPOINT AHEAD!; ROCK MED.

🍂 *John Barlow, lyricist, writing to the* Pinedale Roundup, *Pinedale, Wyoming:*

LSD is a personal, even spiritual, matter. Over the last twenty-five years, I've watched a lot of Deadheads do acid. I've taken it myself. I still do occasionally, in a ritual sort of way. On the basis of their experience and my own, I know that the public terror of LSD is based more on media-propagated superstition than familiarity with its effects on the real world. I know this, and, like most others who know it, I have kept quiet about it.

I've finally realized that if I continue, out of fear, to conceal what I believe in this or any other area of public interest, I participate in a growing threat to the minds of America's young greater than any which acid presents. I mean by that, the establishment of permissible truth in America.

I consider LSD to be a serious medicine. Hey, this stuff can make some people see God. That's serious medicine. LSD is dangerous, but not in the ways generally portrayed. By dressing it up in a Halloween costume of fictitious dangers, we encourage our kids to think we were also lying about its real ones. LSD is dangerous because it promotes the idea that reality is something to be manipulated rather than accepted. This notion can seriously cripple one's coping abilities, though I would still suggest that both alcohol and TV advertising carry it more persuasively than LSD. If you're lightly-sprung, it can leave you nuts. But LSD is not illegal because it endangers your sanity. LSD is illegal because it endangers Control. Worse, it makes authority seem funny. Laugh at authority in America, and you will know risk. LSD is illegal because it threatens the dominant American culture. This is not a sound use of law. Just laws arise to support the ethics of a whole society, and not as a means for one of its cultural factions to impose power on another.

There are probably 25 million Americans who have taken LSD, and who would, if hard pressed in private, also tell you that it profoundly changed their lives, and not necessarily for the worse. I will readily grant that some of these are hopeless crystal worshippers or psychedelic derelicts creeping around Oregon woods. But far more of them are successful members of society, CEOs, politicians, ministers, and community leaders. This is true, whether we want it to be or not.

The fact that so few among these millions dare utter this truth in a supposedly free country, is a symptom of collective mental illness.

THE LUNGE 📖 • Weir's jaunt toward the crowd at the peak of a jam—a distinguishing feature of his onstage theatrics. "I'm the Mr. Show-biz in the group," Weir told David Gans in 1981. "Pigpen was our showman. When he started to slide, I sort of naturally stepped into it. . . . I rather enjoy showboating." (Garcia's onstage dance is generally restricted to gentle rocking during his improvisations punctuated by little wedgings of his glasses up the bridge of his nose before a solo, and affable salutes to the crowd when coming on- and offstage.)

A guaranteed crowd pleaser during "Estimated Prophet," the lunge is "Ace" Weir's addition to the pantheon of high rock and roll drama in the company of Chuck Berry's duckwalk, Pete Townshend's windmilling, and Bruce Springsteen's dancing on top of the piano.

MAGIC • "Few words are as integral a part of the Deadhead lexicon as 'magic,'" wrote Blair Jackson in his essay "Dead Heads: A Strange Tale of Love, Devotion and Surrender," published in *BAM*, a Bay Area music magazine, in 1980. "It is the one term—with all its implications of Merlin, *brujos*, shamen, and psychic legerdemain—that almost every Dead Head will arrive at eventually to explain what it is that separates the Grateful Dead from other bands. 'On a very good night,' comments Mickey Hart, 'the magic will visit us. On other nights, for whatever reasons, it stays away. All we can do, as musicians, is be true to ourselves and play as well as we can and hope that it all meshes and the magic finds us.'"

Garcia's extensive range as a guitarist has been called "Jerry's bag of tricks," and for the poster for the Garcia-on-Broadway run at the Lunt-Fontanne Theater in '87, Garcia posed as a magician, pulling a guitar out of a hat.

Deadheads often speak of "magical" coincidences happening at or around shows; the propitious coincidences of daily life seem intensified by the presence of the Dead and Deadheads, as if the community acted as a kind of focusing lens. "At first, we thought the magic was spiraling out of Jerry's guitar," recalls one of the managers of the Avalon Ballroom. "Then we realized the magic was *us*."

MAIL ORDER • *See* GRATEFUL DEAD TICKET SALES.

THE MAIN TEN • An early title for the instrumental seed of "Playing in the Band," as heard on Hart's first solo album, *Rolling Thunder*, and played live five times notably at the Capitol Theater on 11/8/70. See JAM.

MAXING OUT • Packing a hotel room with tourheads from floor to ceiling with five in the bed, eight on the rug, two in each chair, and one or two in the tub. *See TOUR.*

"MAZEL TOV—[SIGNED] JERRY GARCIA" • The unusually *haimish* autograph Garcia scribed for bat mitzvah girl and burgeoning Deadhead Alexis Rosenfeld, at the request of Garcia's friend, *Saturday Night Live* writer Al Franken. "We took it to a framing place," says Franken, "and of course the guy turned out to be a Deadhead, so he made this incredible tie-dye frame, and didn't even charge us. The kid was amazed." *See* NO SHOWS ON SHABBAS.

MCGANNAHAN SKJELLYFETTI • The pseudonym used in the credits by the band on both the *Grateful Dead* and *Live/Dead* albums for tunes that had been improvised or composed by the entire group: "The Golden Road to Unlimited Devotion," "Cream Puff War," and "Feedback."

The name comes from Kenneth Patchen's novel *Memoirs of a Shy Pornographer*, in which "Skujellifeddy McGranehan" was the protagonist's literary agent: "May I call you Skujellifeddy? Mr. McGranehan's sort of awkward."

MCKERNAN, RON • *See PIGPEN.*

MDMA • Popularly known as "ecstasy," "X," "E," "M" or "double M," MDMA is an amphetamine similar in molecular structure to mescaline, first synthesized in Germany in the

early part of the century and tested for the Army by the Edgewood Chemical Warfare Service in the '50s.

It became a popular recreational drug in the early '80s, when
it was sold to college students in Texas bars. In 1987, in spite of
protests from the psychiatric community, MDMA became the
first drug in history to be made illegal without legislative or ju-
dicial review, under the emergency scheduling power of the
Drug Enforcement Administration.

MDMA is used by some Heads at shows as an "entactogen,"
to increase feelings of empathy, and the sensual enjoyment of
dancing or physical affection. While the drug affects one's feelings about self and other people, it does not especially enhance
perceptions of the music itself. Use of MDMA can temporarily
relax physical boundaries, and the huge HUG CIRCLES that
formed at sunny Frost Amphitheater shows in the mid-'80s
have been partly attributed to the drug. (You'd have to give
Deadheads a drug that *inhibited* hugging, and see if it had any
effect, to prove that true.)

Heads and others have found that MDMA should be used
with caution (beyond the legal considerations), because the
"dosage window"—the difference between an effective dose
and a toxic overdose—is narrow, and overdoses can be fatal
(overdoses of psychedelics like LSD are upsetting, but rarely
fatal). MDMA should *never* be snorted. The street wisdom
is that the drug is hard on the body; exhaustion, back pain,
and increased susceptibility to infection are commonly reported following the experience. Dr. Andrew Weil, author
of *The Natural Mind* and *From Chocolate to Morphine*, advises against frequent, immoderate use of MDMA. A widespread rumor that MDMA use causes a loss of spinal fluid is
false.

**MEET YOU IN FRONT OF THE SOUNDBOARD AT
THE BREAK** • The strategy used commonly to connect with
friends at the show. Other traditional meeting places: the seats
behind the drums, or at the Greenpeace, SEVA, or Wharf Rats
tables. *See* SET BREAK.

MEGA-DEAD PERIOD • A tongue-in-cheek term used by the band and organization for the surge of popularity the band and fans suffered in the late '80s. Often associated with the pop success in the summer of '87 of "A Touch of Grey," a deceptively wry song that captured the imagination of a radio audience.

The Dead scene, which had felt for so many years like an extended family (with the Fillmores, then Winterland, and then Henry J. Kaiser Auditorium in Oakland, as the family living room), was suddenly hot copy in magazines—in *Forbes* yet—and it became permissible to admit on network television that one had been to a show (*see MY LIFE IS SCHEDULED AROUND THEIRS*).

MELONS; MELS • Words used by Garcia for nonhipsters during the *Europe '72* tour. Steve Brown, who worked at Round Records, recalls that if there was a hang-up at the airport, Garcia might snicker, "Oh man, we gotta wait around the lounge with all those *mels?*" Wavy Gravy also remembers Garcia using "melon" to mean someone who is *really* into something: "If you really liked dogs, he'd say you were a *dog melon.*"

MERCY KILLING ✉ • Stealth taper ethics: when the taper gets "nailed" by security guards who demand the tape, and the taper destroys the tape to prevent it from falling into the hands of local bootleggers.

MESCALINE • PSYCHEDELIC extracted from peyote, a slow-growing blue-green cactus with white tufts, native to northern Mexico—in the form of fluffy white or off-white crystals. Peyote is eaten in a sacred manner by the Huichol Indians of northern Mexico and by members of the Native American Church in the American Southwest. Much of what is sold to Heads as mescaline is, in fact, LSD. An active dose of pure mescaline sulfate would fill a large capsule.

The effects of mescaline are similar to LSD and psilocybin mushrooms: intricate displays of color and form (the chief visual designer of Walt Disney's *Fantasia* was attempting to simulate his peyote experiences on film), empathy for other living beings, and a feeling of being in the presence of the sacred. Al-

dous Huxley's influential *The Doors of Perception* was written after a mescaline experience. *See* LSD; SHROOMS.

MIDI • Musical Instrument Digital Interface. A standard
for the exchange of musical information that allows instruments
to communicate with one another, and to sample pre-recorded
sounds from computer disks.

Adopted by the band in the late '80s, MIDI capability enables Garcia to trigger the sounds of a flute from the fretboard
of his guitar, Welnick to play violin or percussion from his keyboard, or Lesh to halo the tones of his bass with a chorus of human voices. The introduction of MIDI to the Dead's setup has
had a more profound effect than any other development since
the Warlocks went electric, adding to the band's vocabulary virtually any sound imaginable.

With the help of the band's MIDI expert Bob Bralove, the
technology became fully incorporated into the band's sound
during the summer and fall tours of '89. The "Dark Star" from
Miami 10/26/89 is a mind-blowing demonstration of it, as the
melody circulates among guitars, virtual oboes and bassoons,
pianos, bass flutes, chimes, bells, kalimbas, typewriters, explosions, steamwhistles, and alarms.

The bandmembers' affinity for "outside" playing makes Dead
shows—especially DRUMS and SPACE—an exceptionally appropriate frontier for exploring the new sonic landscapes MIDI
makes possible. *See MUSIQUE CONCRÈTE.*

🍂 *Bob Bralove on his custom MIDI designs for the band:*

I see much of what I do as *designing virtual instruments*. If you build a guitar,
you can process what it does to make it sound an infinite number of ways.
There's room enough for infinity in any instrument. But in building a virtual
instrument, you create how you produce the sound as well—whether you're
going to pluck it or hit it, what any action is going to do. If you then look at
that virtual instrument as a central brain that can be divided or controlled by
six or seven people simultaneously, you've opened up a whole new conceptu-
alization of what might happen.

I'm trying to build instruments for the Grateful Dead that have built-in infinity for everybody, and at the same time, maintain everybody's power over
their own universe, because that's the nature of this band.

MIDNIGHT SPECIAL • 1. Gert Chiarito's folk music show on Bay Area radio station KPFA, named after a haunting prison lament by Leadbelly.

Lesh worked on the show as an engineer. After meeting Garcia and hearing him play banjo at Kepler's in '62, Lesh successfully landed him an hour special on the show, which was entitled "Long Black Veil," after one of the tunes Garcia was performing at the time. After the special, Garcia became a regular on the show, nurturing a friendship with Lesh that would later lead to an invitation to join the Warlocks.

2. Newsletter for Heads in prison, which keeps Head prisoners informed of Dead scene happenings on the outside while keeping Deadheads in tune with their brethren behind bars. "You have no idea how much it means to hear from you," writes Todd Davidson, New York inmate #13660. "To know we're thought about . . . The little bit of positive energy received in your letters goes a long way."

Another publication, *U.S. Blues*, publishes the poetry of incarcerated Deadheads—sorrowful, often angry, determined to "get by." *See* CARRIER WEIGHT LAWS.

MIKEL • One of the first regular newsletters for tourheads, a labor of love for its creator, Michael Linah, who was a bridge tournament organizer when he wasn't on tour. *MIKEL* vol. 1, no. 1, was published in August 1982 on one side of a Xeroxed sheet, and featured setlists, a summer tour schedule, and an ad for the tenth anniversary celebration of the Springfield Creamery show. *MIKEL* maintained its grassroots handmade feel for three years of issues, with letters from Heads ("After 1st Alpine show Clarkie & I drove out into the cornfields, crashing under a clear blue sky, awakened by three deer next morning," "by the time I got to Austin my brains were the consistency of soggy quiche lorraine," etc.), crossword puzzles (#1 Across: "Eight sided whispering — — —"), press clips, surveys ("Best Venue: Red Rocks"), thumbnail essays ("1984 *Philibuster:* Not since the days of the *Phillmore* has such *philharmonic philanthropy* been seen . . . We Deadheads have *Phil* to thank for such extraordinary doings"), and personal statements from Michael.

Michael also printed up and gave away square stickers commemorating individual runs, illuminated with roses and distinctively trippy lettering, which became treasured additions to many TOURBOOKS. The last issue of *MIKEL* was published in November 1985 by Michael's friends, after Michael himself died of cancer.

MIKEL was an embodiment of the best aspects of Deadhead spirit: creative, idiosyncratic, earnest, bigheartedly enthusiastic about the music and the virtues of the tribe—and free.

MINGLEWOOD TOWN COUNCIL • An effort by Deadheads, with no leader and no formal membership, to address issues plaguing the PARKING LOT SCENE in the post–"Touch of Grey" MEGA-DEAD PERIOD.

"You are all encouraged to join," invited the council's manifesto, handed out at Berkeley's Greek Theater in July '88, and distributed on tour for the next year or two. "The Minglewood Town Council exists as a state of mind whose collective goal is to reach the Deadheads who do not respect the communities we invade for the enjoyment of experiencing a Grateful Dead show."

The manifesto continued: "Concert sites are witness to open drug use, public urination and defecation, complaints from neighbors of Deadheads having sex or sleeping in their doorways. This is not responsible behavior on our part . . . We need to encourage each other. Let's harness the positive energy we collectively hold, and apply it to making the scene a happier, safer, more responsible atmosphere."

One month before, the band had issued an "S.O.S." in concert handouts, implicitly threatening to stop touring if things did not get better. Many Heads have subscribed to the Minglewood Town Council's way of thinking: that it's up to the community itself, rather than local authorities, to maintain an atmosphere where tours can be safe, and minimally onerous to local residents.

MIRACLE SEEKERS • Deadheads near the venue looking for a ticket for the night's show.

The word "miracle," as slang for a ticket, came into Deadhead parlance in '78 on the wings of the Weir/Barlow song "I Need a Miracle." The phrase "I need a miracle!" has become the most common plea for a ticket in the parking lot, both spoken (shouted) and written (colorfully) on cardboard placards in the vicinity of any venue where the band is about to play. "Who's got my miracle?" is a variant. Such pleas have become more common since the band's popularity kicked into overdrive with the pop success of "Touch of Grey" in 1987 and MTV's "Day of the Dead." (*See* MEGA-DEAD PERIOD; TOUCHHEADS.)

The need to quickly capture the attention and sympathy of those holding extra tickets—who may be faced with hundreds of miracle seekers—inspires colorful, idiomatic language: "Hugs for a ticket!" "Need a miracle for my first show!" "Cash or KIND for your extra!" "My VW bug for a ticket." "My girlfriend for a ticket." "My firstborn for a ticket." Even, "Grandma needs a miracle!"

"One people" is Annie Stroukoff's term for miracle seekers taking the subtler approach, circulating silently around the parking lot with one finger held up in the air—the universally recognized sign of needing a miracle. Two fingers = "two people."

While miracle seekers wouldn't exist without the generosity of Deadheads, they have become a symbol of the freeloading aspect of THE PARKING LOT SCENE, and the increase in numbers of Heads "jonesin' for a miracle" since the mid-'80s has been a public relations problem for the band.

MIRACLE TICKET • A ticket for the night's show, usually free.

In the Deadhead spirit of giving, those blessed with EXTRAS will occasionally bestow a ticket on a needy fellow Head with no exchange of funds or goods expected. Tickets may also be bartered for goods, such as handmade t-shirts, Guatemalan pullovers, pipes or something to fill them, food, or transportation. Tapes, understood to be *strictly* free, are almost never bartered.

"Miracle ticket" can also apply simply to any ticket obtained at the last minute for a sold-out show.

MISFIT POWER • Weir's phrase for the particular appeal that the Dead have for those on the fringes of what the straight world defines as the mainstream. The band has always drawn a loyal and passionate constituency from such outlaw communities as the original freaks and hippies and the Hell's Angels, and even as the Dead became "number one top-grossing" entertainers, they maintained their image of outsiders doing it their own way "one of the last bastions of anarchy in America," in the words of spokesperson Dennis McNally.

"The Dead never set out to be revered, they never set out to have a cult," explains Bay Area taper Walter Keeler. "They only set out to be themselves, and that was a shining beacon to the rest of the world. Everybody else who was a little afraid to be themselves could see these weird misfits onstage being weird, having a good time, and making a living at it."

🐾 *Sue Swanson, founder of the Golden Road to Unlimited Devotion fan club, on finding your sisters and brothers:*

That's something that was said to all of us when we were young—"You're not working to your potential." That's what we had in common, and that's why it's been so amazing, such a blessing for us, that we all found each other, and found in each other something that encourages each of us to be ourselves. That's why we *really are* a family. We have biological families, but we are our real family, and we love each other as real brothers and sisters.

THE MISSING FINGER • Garcia is missing the middle finger on his right strumming hand, lost in an accident in the Santa Cruz mountains at age four while chopping wood with his brother, Tiff. An image of Garcia's hand is part of the psychedelic collage on the cover of Garcia's first solo album, and a four-fingered handprint appeared on the promo posters for the album. *See JERRY'S KIDS.*

MOOOOOO • Not a sacred Hindu mantram backward, but an instinctive reaction to being herded in or out of a venue through a narrow passageway.

MOTHER MCCREE'S UPTOWN JUG CHAMPIONS • The bluegrass predecessor to THE WARLOCKS. The first band that included both Garcia and Weir, Mother Mc-

Cree's also included Pigpen on harmonica, guitar, piano, and vocals; Bob Matthews—future recording engineer for the Dead—on guitar, vocals, banjo, and kazoo; Dave Parker on washboard and kazoo; Tom Stone on fiddle; and Marshall Leicester on guitar and mandolin.

The partnership between Garcia and Weir was born out of an impromptu jam one New Year's Eve. Weir recalled to David Gans:

A friend and I were wandering the back streets of Palo Alto. We were way too young to get into any of the hot clubs . . . We walked by the back of this music store that we used to frequent, Dana Morgan Music, and we heard banjo music coming from within. That seemed strange to us, because it was New Year's Eve, so we knocked on the door. It was Garcia. We recognized him from the numerous bands that he was in at the time. He was the local hot banjo player. He was in there playing banjo, waiting for his students to show up. Of course, it was New Year's Eve and absolutely none of them were coming. He was absolutely unmindful of the fact that it was New Year's Eve, so we acquainted him with that information.

They jammed for a while, Weir said, and "by the end of the evening we decided we had enough second-rate talent there to throw together a jug band."

Garcia had been a bluegrass presence in the Palo Alto/Menlo Park area for four years, with membership in bands like the Hart Valley Drifters (with Dave Nelson—future founder of the New Riders of the Purple Sage—on guitar, Robert Hunter on bass, and Ken Frankel on mandolin), the Asphalt Jungle Boys (with Bob Matthews on jug, Dave Parker on washboard, and John "Marmaduke" Dawson on guitar and vocals), THE WILD-WOOD BOYS, and other groups.

MUCHAS GARCIAS • Thanks a bunch. *See* DEADIFICA-TION.

MUSIQUE CONCRÈTE [moo-ZEEK kon-KRET] • Music constructed of sounds that are not usually considered "musi-cal," such as speech, machinery, natural sounds such as thunder or rain, racing car engines, or paper against skin. The term was coined by French radio man Pierre Schaeffer in 1948, the approach pioneered by such composers as John Cage and Steve Reich (a former schoolmate and friend of Lesh's). *Musique concrète* infiltrated the Top 40 in a pop Trojan horse courtesy of John Lennon, who wound lengths of tape around pencils in the studio and other manipulations to produce such eerie masterpieces as "I Am the Walrus."

Garcia's first solo album featured "Late for Supper," successive thunderclaps like pianos being thrown over a high cliff, followed by "Spidergawd," which was haunted by ominous voices Garcia might have remembered from childhood hours spent in front of the radio. Nonmusic music has enriched the Dead's output since the beginning—from FEED-BACK to the Times Square-like cacophonies of "Dark Star" at the Nassau Coliseum on 1/10/79, to Bob Bralove's virtual parking lot on *Infrared Roses.*

This approach allows the bandmembers to welcome *any* sound they can hear or imagine into the music, and encourages Deadheads to hear the sounds of the world as fragments of a great song.

MY LIFE IS SCHEDULED AROUND THEIRS • Proud declaration of Bill Walton, Basketball Hall of Famer and veteran of six hundred shows (including *Egypt '78*), who hopped ON THE BUS in the late '60s while still in high school, and has been friends with the band since '74.

"They're great guys," he says. "Wonderful people—as nice as they are talented. We enjoy each other's company tremendously. The Grateful Dead has meant so much to me in my life." Walton has cultivated a pranksterish talent for sneaking Dead references into his sports interviews. Several years ago, in a postgame interview, CBS's Brent Musberger asked Walton for his thoughts on the team his Celtics had just beat, the Houston Rockets. "Houston, too close to New Orleans," Walton replied, without missing a beat.

An avid collector of more than a thousand tapes, Walton is frequently seen on the side of the stage, and has assisted the band in their radio broadcasts as well. "You're talking to a *hard-core* Deadhead," he explains. "My favorite period of the Dead is the next concert. My favorite song is the next song. I just can't wait for the next one." His favorite spot in a hall: "As close to the speakers as I can get." Walton is much loved among Heads, some of whom have dubbed the towering 6'11" carrottop "Grateful Red."

"I once got into a show because Bill Walton is too tall," explains dancer and gardener Tomlyn Shannon. "He was walking in, and all the guards were looking way up at him, so I slipped right in behind his huge body."

Walton sends his regards to fellow Heads, with the following message: "I'll see them at the next show, and I'm sorry for the people I stand in front of."

MYDLAND, BRENT • Keyboards, vocals, and composition. Born on October 21, 1952, in a U.S. military base in West Germany.

Mydland grew up in Concord, California, and worked professionally with two groups in the '70s—the folk-rock group Batdorf & Rodney, and Silver, a country rock outfit—before being hired to tour in '78 with the Bob Weir Band. A year later, he was invited into the Dead to replace Keith and Donna Godchaux.

From his first show onward—4/22/79, at Spartan Stadium in San Jose, California—Mydland helped breathe new life and color into the band that was worn down by conflicts in the late '70s, bringing fine upper-range harmonies, soulful keyboard dexterity, impassioned original songs, and a flair for choosing covers that *cooked*, like "Hey Pocky Way" and "Gimme Some Lovin'" that were dramatic high points of shows from '79 until his death in '90. In place of Godchaux's grand piano, Mydland brought in several keyboard racks, including the Hammond B-3 organ, which had been a component of the Dead's sound with Pigpen, and synthesizers, which added the sounds of marimbas and strings to the band's sonic vocabulary.

Mydland had been suspended from Liberty High in Brentwood, California, for having long hair. When he was thrown out of the school band for the same reason, he gave up the trumpet and took up keyboards.

In '72, Mydland moved to the Bay Area, and started playing R&B. "We'd have these jams that would turn into parties with three hundred people, and we'd play until the police broke it up." Mydland played in club bands until Silver, which had a successful tour, but was torpedoed by their first single, "Wham Bam Shang A Lang," recorded at the behest of Arista Records president Clive Davis.

He proved his mettle with the Dead early on and, almost astonishingly, settled into a tight musical groove with a band that had been playing together for fifteen years. Mydland's first tours with the Dead were exciting for Heads—the band seemed energized by a new sense of possibility, and on flaming in-the-pocket jams like "China Cat Sunflower"→"I Know You Rider," the musicians seemed to be mining notes between the notes. Mydland added a tropical flair to versions of "Scarlet Begonias"→"Fire On the Mountain" and moaned torn-hearted versions of "Don't Need Love" long after Garcia had walked offstage for the DRUMS.

Mydland was the young man in the band at a time when the Dead was acquiring many younger fans, and his jagged, anguished blues vocals—and dark songs like "Blow Away"—earned him both fans and detractors. "Brent was not an easy person to know," wrote lyricist John Barlow in *The Golden Road* shortly after Mydland's death. "Looking into his core . . . I saw a glistening black thing, coiled up huge, waiting patiently to kill him. And I could tell that neither sweetness nor light would likely dislodge it . . . He was caught between a world which had given him everything and the conviction that he didn't deserve a bit of it."

Mydland's career with the Dead ended in glory, with two of the best tours the band had ever had. Along with the revival of "Dark Star," the band brought back "Death Don't Have No Mercy," with Mydland wailing a verse with hell-hounds on his trail.

He recorded and mastered a solo album in the early '80s that was never released, and also helped out on a number of non–Dead album projects, including Bob Dylan's *Down in the Groove,* and a Joseph Campbell PBS special.

Mydland died of a combined overdose of cocaine and morphine—a "speedball"—in his home on July 26, 1990.

He is survived by his wife, Lisa, and daughters, Jessica and Jennifer.

A selected Brent Mydland non-Dead discography:

Sweet Surprise—Eric Andersen; 1975

Silver—Silver; 1975

Bobby and the Midnites—Bob Weir, Bobby Cochran, Brent Mydland, Tim Bogert, Billy Cobham, Matt Kelly; 1981

🐟 *John Barlow, lyricist, on Brent Mydland:*

Writing songs with Brent was probably the most intimate thing I ever did with a guy. I was trying to write songs with him that would help him see reasons to be alive. All the songs that I wrote with him on *Built to Last* were arguments for life. And the experience of writing songs with Brent was incredibly affirming.

He had a real dissynchrony between the amount of approval he was getting, and the low opinion he had of himself. The more people got into Brent, the harder it was for him. So in an ironic way, by writing songs to help him live, I may have been a contributor to his demise, because they were popular songs, even though they never really developed into what they could have been. It's also hard because when he died, those songs died. The Dead are never going to do those songs.

He was a bigger contributor than anyone was willing to state. He had a genius for providing exactly the right kind of color. He was brilliant, he really was. But there is a coldness about that scene, a permissible range of expression that goes all the way from irony to spite. It's not a place where you can bare your soul safely, which is what makes it so difficult if you're addicted. Getting through an addiction requires you to say what's in your heart, but that's not a place you can do that.

I don't think he got satisfaction out of anything. There was something that was fundamentally unsatisfiable in him.

NETHEADS • One moniker, along with "HOL" (Heads on Line), for the tens of thousands of Deadheads on the Internet. They get there through interactive computer services such as The WELL, America Online, and myriad smaller, local DEAD BOARDS.

Since the mid-'80s, many Deadheads have found themselves comfortably at home in "cyberspace" (a term popularized by William Gibson, the author of *Neuromancer*). For Heads eager to share reflections, passions, and most of all, *information* about the band they love, the opening of the door to Head-to-Head dialogue via modem was the end of isolation between tours, and the beginning of a deep jam among themselves.

On the Net, Heads learn tour dates, both rumored and verified, mail-order info—sometimes ahead of the official hotline announcements—and get setlists and show reports, minutes after the shows are over. They can download text files of band lyrics, interviews, and articles; as well as graphic files of STEALIES, screensavers, and bandmembers' photographs, database software for managing tape collections, even audio files with soundbites of new songs.

The largest assemblage of online Heads—70,000—takes place on an online conference called "rec.music.gdead," which

nearly anyone with an Internet address can read and participate in. Several members of the band and family are online
themselves, including Lesh, Hart, and John Barlow.

See also DEAD BOARDS; DEAD-FLAMES; THE WELL; *APPENDIX
III: HOW TO BECOME A NETHEAD.*

❧ *Jeff "Eagle" Davis, Wyoming Nethead, on online community:*

The bonding force of the Grateful Dead has always been family. A natural
extension of this family occurred as outlaws on the electronic frontier got
loose in cyberspace, and homesteaded in rec.music.gdead. As every acidhead
owes a debt of gratitude to the CIA for the original human experimentation
with LSD, so must one be thankful that the Net, founded by the Department
of Defense as a tool of war and espionage, evolved into a vehicle of global in-
terpersonal communication at the speed of light, and a tremendous force for
peaceful coexistence. The vision of a four-star general in the Pentagon making it possible for Deadheads all over the world to receive setlists and show reviews of the Acid Test house band within minutes of the last chord of the encore has to brighten the eyes of anyone with a touch of outlaw in their heart.

*A sampling from Anthony Fleszar's "You know you're a Nethead
when . . ." (widely available on the Net, naturally):*

1. Your Windows 3.0 background is a picture of Jerry Garcia, your cur-
sor is a Steal Your Face skull, and sometimes you swear it's leaving
"trails."
2. You consider ;-) a new form of punctuation.
3. You remember the Porsche guy.
4. An alarm goes off on your PC when it's time to tape the *Grateful Dead
Hour.*
5. Your email address is something like:

China-Rider@ShakedownStreet.FillmoreWest.GDTRFB.FatmanRocks.OnTour.lsd

NEVER HAD SUCH A GOOD TIME [FROM
"MIGHT AS WELL"] • One of the special class of Dead
lyrics heard by the audience as celebrating the Dead experience, sparking a jubilant roar as they are sung.

Others include: "They're a band beyond description," from
"The Music Never Stopped"; "This space is getting hot," from
"Althea"; "You know it's gonna get stranger, let's get on with the

show," from "Feel Like a Stranger"; "If you get confused, listen to the music play," from "Franklin's Tower"; "Take you to the leader of the band," from "Ramble on Rose"; and "Singing, 'Thank you for a real good time,' " from "Loose Lucy."

NEWBIE • A Deadhead who just got "on the bus." From British schoolboy slang. *See* ON THE BUS; REFORMED DEADHEAD.

NIGHT OF THE LIVING DEADHEADS • Two gatherings for Bay Area Heads in the fall of '86—while Garcia was recovering from his diabetic coma—at Wolfgang's nightclub in San Francisco (Wolfgang's was owned by Bill Graham, whose original name was Wolfgang Grajonza).

"It was a way for the community to get together, for reassurance. Deadheads were hurting, and these events were very healing," explains David Gans, who assisted Bill Graham Productions' Bob and Peter Barsotti in hosting the affairs. Vendors set up booths, and there was dancing to tapes and live bands, like Gans's Crazy Fingers. Interviews with Weir and Garcia videotaped for the event were shown, and a raffle was held to benefit the Rex Foundation.

NITROUS OXIDE • N_2O, the "laughing gas" used commonly as an anesthetic in the dentist's chair. Heads use nitrous, occasionally called "sweet air," for the warm pervasive buzz it induces, its brief duration, a tendency to find everything amusing, and its characteristic effect such that all sounds, including the music the band is playing, are made to ripple and shimmer, like the *whubba-whubba* at the end of "Crowd Sculpture" on *Infrared Roses*. Gray aluminum capsules filled with nitrous oxide ("whippits") are legally available as chargers for devices ("whippetizers") that turn cream into whipped cream.

Nitrous has been enjoyed on both sides of the stage for a long time—there is a hilariously strange "tank party" from the backstage of Winterland depicted in *The Grateful Dead Movie*—and some Deadhead dentists offer their patients a good time with headphones while the necessary work gets done: "Bring in your 2/13/70!"

Nitrous oxide was recognized as a minor PSYCHEDELIC by

writers like William James, who wrote that after inhaling the gas, "depth beyond depth of truth seems revealed to the inhaler. This truth fades out . . . at the moment of coming to; and if any words remain in which it seemed to clothe itself, they prove to be the veriest nonsense." Heads sometimes piggyback these effects on top of the visual effects of LSD and mushrooms.

Once vendors realized that selling balloons filled with the gas could be very profitable, hissing blue tanks in the backs of pickups became fixtures in the parking lot, and a pernicious desire to immediately repeat the experience earned nitrous the unflattering nickname "hippie crack" among Heads.

Nitrous poses several real health hazards. Rapidly decompressing gas inhaled directly from the tank valve can freeze the throat and lungs, suffocating the user. Gas inhaled in an enclosed space displaces oxygen, and an open tank in a sealed vehicle is suicide. Episodes of vomiting, blackouts, and convulsive seizures (which some Heads call "doing the fish" or "fishtailing") are not uncommon. Repeated use of nitrous causes dehydration and inactivates vitamin B_{12}, which can result in irreversible neural damage, causing "the shakes" and memory loss. Hippie crack is also unhealthy for the planet, as nitrous molecules break down the ozone layer, already under assault from CFCs and other pollutants. And nitrous, whether medical grade or industrial, is often contaminated with impurities such as trichloroethylene and toluene, known carcinogens.

Nitrous poses an interesting philosophical quandary to Heads, who are loath to dictate to others how they should enjoy their own neurocircuitry, but Heads who have done a lot of nitrous often express distaste for the drug.

NO, BUT I'VE BEEN TO SHOWS • One common answer to the question "Are you a Deadhead?" Even in a world where the bandmembers are invited to have tea at the White House (and they accept—*see* ONE HEARTBEAT AWAY), many genuine fans of the group's music demonstrate a reluctance to being tagged with the word "Deadhead," not wanting to be lumped into a category with hard-core TOUR RATS, or with the negative portrayals of Heads in the media. "Deadhead? No, but

I like their music. I don't follow them around or anything." *See also* DEAD FREAKS UNITE!; DEADHEAD.

NO SHOWS ON SHABBAS • The bottom line for Orthodox Jewish Deadheads who observe the Sabbath from sundown Friday to nightfall Saturday (twenty-five hours, ten minutes), avoiding all work—including turning on the stove or answering the phone—in keeping with a biblical injunction setting aside one day a week as a time to do nothing but rest, eat, pray, and quietly reflect on what it is to be a Jew. "As wonderful as a show is, it is a distraction," explains Abby Mendelson, Deadhead and *Shomer Shabbas* (observer of the Sabbath). "It's not in the spirit of the Sabbath to go hear the Dead play electric or even acoustic instruments."

While Orthodox Jews conduct their lives within a strict set of rules, there are hundreds of strictly observant Jews who find the time, energy, and freedom to enjoy the band's shows and tapes. Even tapes of Friday-night shows are allowed, Mendelson explains, as long as they aren't made expressly *for* observant Jews.

🍀 *Abby Mendelson, on the relationship between Judaism and the Grateful Dead:*

So much of what Robert Hunter writes in his lyrics is about the fragility of life, about things changing, not knowing what's going on, and having to rely on a higher power. A lot of that is basic Jewish philosophy. *"Once in a while you get shown the light/In the strangest of places if you look at it right." Once in a while—if* you look at it right. That's classic Jewish thought: you don't know exactly where the message is coming from, and you've got to look for it.

"I've stayed in every blue light cheap hotel/Can't win for trying" [from "Stella Blue"]—that's *us!* Knowing failure, getting thrown out of countries, being ravaged and picking yourself up. Bill Graham—he never lost that spirit. Most of his family was destroyed in Europe.

There are times when my family will go home from synagogue and sing "Ripple." It's a wonderful song that reflects a lot of what we feel about life. We also sing a Shabbas song to the melody of "Ripple." I have a friend—another *Shomer Shabbas*—with whom I've seen a number of shows. The first was when his daughter dragged him to Three Rivers Stadium in '90. He was being a good father, so he schlepped out there. He was blown away. Not only by the music, but by the spirituality. Jerry has said that in every generation there are people who hear their message, and for us, the message is very strong.

I know there are other subgroups among Deadheads. It's funny—I see these people and I wonder "what do *they* see in these guys?" How do you get "Stella Blue" if you're *not Shomer Shabbas?* How do *they* get "Franklin's Tower"? For us it strikes a chord. The fragility of life is reflected in everything about the Dead: in the lyrics, of course, but also in the quirky melodies, the odd time signatures, in the band never knowing what it's going to play next. In giving themselves a chance to fail, and having an audience that permits them to fail. To live is not to be a robot, but rather to be spiritual about what you're trying to do. I am constantly amazed at how they tap into that.

Mickey Hart has talked about the healing power of music. "Fire on the Mountain" taps you into that spiritual source. I have many non-Orthodox friends who ask, "What does Judaism do for you?" What it does is that it improves the quality of every aspect of my life. It makes the good times wonderful, and the bad times tolerable. It's not a bunch of people sitting around having fun all the time—*life* is not like that. There are problems with life all the time, but the question is, "How are you going to deal with them?" For me, Judaism is one answer, and in their own way, the Dead are traveling along the same road.

> **NOODLING** • Used by both fans and detractors alike to describe the band's searching excursions during jams and solos, and Garcia's tirelessly inquisitive guitar solos in particular.
>
> What started out as a cliché of negative press coverage has been absorbed and remade by the fans into a term of appreciation for the band's improvisatory spirit, but the word itself is still taken by most musicians as disparaging and inadequate. "I don't think noodling is a flattering term," says mandolin player David Grisman, Garcia's friend and collaborator for thirty years.

🦐 *David Grisman, mandolin player in the Garcia/Grisman Band, on "free music":*
We don't call it "noodling." We call it "free music," or "going into THE ZONE"—the places in music where you can play anything. Only in its worst form would it be noodling. Noodling sounds like you're fidgeting with something. There are places in music where you suspend the structure, trying to create something that has no necessary base or rules. You might be searching for something, or following something. I see it all as composition. You're writing music. It's only a question of speed. If I sat down and spent seven months

writing fourteen bars of music, and play it for somebody, and the next guy makes up fourteen bars of music in the time it takes to play it, the only thing that matters is how that music is, and whether people like it or not. Whether somebody spends all day making a meal, or five minutes making a meal, it's still a meal. How good it is doesn't necessarily have much to do with how long it took to make.

There are a lot of highly developed forms based on the idea of improvisation as composing very rapidly. Garcia's uniqueness is that he applies those ideas to whatever genre he's playing in.

NOSEBLEEDS • Seats in the upper balconies. *See* STUBBING DOWN.

"NOSTALGIA MONGERS" • Music critic Dave Marsh's swipe at the Dead in his 1983 *Rolling Stone Record Guide,* where he pronounced the band's records to be "virtually worthless." After dismissing Garcia's "pedestrian set of chops," Marsh railed against "the group's patchouli-oil philosophy, which does nothing more than reinforce solipsism and self-indulgence in its listeners, except when it's nurturing its Hell's Angels fan club — exactly the sort of stuff that gave peace a bad name."

Mainstream music critics have gotten a lot of mileage over the years bashing the Dead with the charge that they are a retro-'60s band, finding the Dead scene to be a stone against which they may grind axes about drugs, or politics, or fashion — sometimes even music. The fact that the band continued to evolve musically for thirty years — drawing on influences as diverse as jazz, electronic music, contemporary classical, blues, gamelan, and bluegrass, and ranging into new musical territories with a vigor and tenacity paralleled only by Duke Ellington's Orchestra — seemed hidden behind a Tie-Dyed Barrier to everyone but Deadheads.

"Part of what makes me laugh about the Dead's newfound popularity," says *Saturday Night Live*'s Al Franken, "is that Tom Davis and I have been huge Deadheads since the show began. We kept saying, 'Get the Dead on! Get the Dead on!' And they'd laugh at us. People at the show thought we were stuck in the '60s. Now they're the biggest group in the '90s. I feel vindicated." *See* I'LL BE GRATEFUL WHEN THEY'RE DEAD.

NUGGET • A cherished rendition of a tune. Nuggets (or "nugs") are the gold tapers mine their collections for. "Let me SPIN you that 'Cassidy' nug from Meadowlands '85."

THE OFFICE • The home base of Grateful Dead Productions since 1970, in a house on a quiet sidestreet in San Rafael, where the band's management, accounting, and public relations are handled by longtime friends and family members.

A sign on the side of the band members' mailboxes reads, "Do you want to talk to the man-in-charge, or to the woman who knows what's going on?" The Office is primarily the domain of strong, unpretentious women like Eileen Law and her daughter Cassidy, Diane Geoppo, Sue Stephens, Janet Knudsen, Jan Simmons, and Annette Flowers, who do their difficult jobs with sisterly wit and sincere smiles.

The original sketches by Stanley Mouse for *Workingman's Dead* of each of the bandmembers as cowboys, hang above a desk in a room used for interviews, and a sign over the main work area says "Elvis Presley Blvd." The phones ring constantly. Upstairs, Danny Rifkin—who was the manager of the band in the late '60s—coordinates THE REX FOUNDATION, and fields benefit requests; road manager Cameron Sears maps out the band's tours; and Maruska Nelson handles the band's computerized bookkeeping. Downstairs, Dennis McNally talks to the press and the outside world, and Annette Flowers responds to requests for use of Dead lyrics in movies and books on behalf of ICE NINE PUBLISHING.

The Office is also the headquarters of Dead Heads, the band's official mailing list of fans since the days of DEAD FREAKS UNITE! Eileen Law and Diane Geoppo read and answer the incoming mail, and try to keep the list up-to-date. (It was Law's voice on the early GDTS hotline messages, signing off with "Thanks, and stay in touch!") In the early '70s, the band sent out regular mailings to those on the Dead Heads list, which was coordinated by Law and Mary Ann Mayer. These Dead Heads' newsletters had tour dates, family information, and witty, cryptic doodles and poems from Robert Hunter—the so-called Hypnocracy Papers. ("Our freedom shall be to brave the spectre of insanity and make it for the depths—Anyway, you're holding up the train, which means you're either a bandit or a track.")

"We get funny letters," says Law. "The kids will write in saying, 'Could you tell my mom it's OK for me to see shows?' Or, 'Do you *know* the band? Have you *met* them?' So I write back saying, 'Yes, I've known them from the beginning . . .' "

🌺 *Eileen Law, Dead Heads' liaison, on working in the family business:*
They're really a good band to work for. They're just good people. They're always in here—it's not like we work for some band that lives in L.A. I find them very easy to talk to.

The last time I went out on the road with them was in Europe in 1990. I had a real good time, but it is *exhausting.* Traveling, the airports, just dealing with everyone in the outside world. Now they depend on their employees to make things right for them. They have a van waiting for them, cars, planes. Everything is organized, whereas before . . . I remember seeing them in the back of a pickup, driving off to Woodstock.

We laugh, looking back. Things are so serious now. We are *really* busy, doing the lights, the video, the merchandising. It's funny—we all went to those first dances together, and here we are, thirty years later, working together.

Because of that, we know what the band wants, and we know what kind of job they expect from us. We're not gonna sell them out. This job is feelings from the heart.

OH SAY CAN YOU SEE 📖 • Garcia, Weir, and Welnick sang the national anthem at San Francisco's Candlestick
Park for the San Francisco Giants' opening game, April 12,
1993. The Giants won.

ON THE BUS • The moment that you realize you are a
Deadhead is sometimes called "getting on the bus." "I got on the
bus after that Fox show in '77, and started touring heavily." (A
loss of interest is sometimes described as "getting off the bus.")

Most Deadheads recognize the phrase from Weir's lyric to
"The Other One," "The bus came by, and I got on, that's when
it all began—with Cowboy Neal at the wheel of a bus to Never-
Ever Land." "The bus" was the Merry Pranksters' "Furthur," a
renovated and customized 1939 International Harvester,
bought by Kesey in the spring of 1964 for the Pranksters' road
trip to the New York World's Fair, driven by "Cowboy" NEAL
CASSADY.

The bus became a countercultural icon after the publication
of Tom Wolfe's *The Electric Kool-Aid Acid Test*. According to
Wolfe, Kesey first uttered the phrase on the way to Houston,
Texas, as he struggled for an ironic declaration of policy about
what might happen to Pranksters who accidentally got left behind along the way. "There are going to be times when we can't
wait for somebody," Kesey announced. "Now, you're either on
the bus or off the bus. If you're on the bus, and you get left behind, then you'll find it again. If you're off the bus in the first
place—then it won't make a damn."

Deadheads have enlarged on Kesey's declaration, so that the
words mean more than being on a particular bus, and more
than being a Deadhead. The phrase has become a metaphor for
having had a particular insight, a knowledge transmitted
through the music, the experience of shows, psychedelics, and
the community.

"Getting on the bus," says longtime Head Alan Mande,
"means crossing the perceptual threshold, as in Lewis Carroll's
Through the Looking Glass and Joseph Campbell's *Hero With a
Thousand Faces*. 'The bus came by and I got on' is a freeze-frame
of the flashpoint where Grateful Dead music triggers a psy-

chic/spiritual awakening—'the kind of awakening the great religions first intended,' as Campbell said."

ONCE WE'RE DONE WITH IT, IT'S THEIRS • Gar-
cia's articulation of the philosophy underlying the decision to allow Deadheads to record the shows and circulate the tapes
freely on a not-for-profit basis. Garcia himself has traded tapes
of favorite bluegrass and jazz musicians for years. "If the
recording industry had its way," sound man DAN HEALY once
said, "nothing would have a record button. If I had my way,
everything would have a record button." While industry thinking
is still for the most part strongly antitaping, the success of the
Dead's approach in building audiences has impressed a few
other musicians, such as Bruce Hornsby, who instituted a taper's section on his '93 tour. *See* F.O.B.; TAPER'S SECTION.

ONE FROM THE VAULT • Album #23, released in April
1991; recorded at the Great American Music Hall, in San Francisco, on 8/13/75, during the "sabbatical"—the year off from
touring, when the Dead played only four shows. "It seemed like
sort of a little prayer for a smaller time, a more intimate time," said Hunter of the invitation-only performance in
the tiny, ornately decorated club.

🦴 *John Scott, editor of DeadBase, on **One From the Vault:***

This concert was a canny selection for the much-anticipated first release
from the Dead's legendary tape vault. Upon hearing the choice, my immediate reaction was dismay—I had hoped for some undocumented gem from the
late '60s; instead we were being offered a concert of which there were already
good tapes in circulation, as well as a famous (or infamous) bootleg album
(*Make Believe Ballroom*). This disappointment was soon eclipsed by the music
itself, an excellent concert from an exciting and under-documented era in
Grateful Dead evolution. *One From the Vault* also was the belated first release
ever of a complete show.

1975 marked the apex of the Dead's exploration into jazz fusion; and the
nadir of their performing schedule. While the more radical investigations of
that period were merely a moment in the Dead's evolution, the legacy of this
momentous year is alive in some of the most exciting music that the Dead still
grace us with: "Help on the Way"→"Slipknot!"→"Franklin's Tower," "Crazy
Fingers," and "The Music Never Stopped." It was a period of such intense

creative growth that it just might be worth enduring another year of tourless Grateful Dead to engender another artistic leap of this magnitude. The first CD begins, as any truly classic Grateful Dead concert should, with an introduction by Bill Graham.

What follows is one of the most flawless performances in Grateful Dead history. Jumping in with both feet, the band opened with their second public performance of "Help→Slip→Frank." Each was perfect: enigmatic, supple, and joyful in turn. They then debuted "The Music Never Stopped." The music was not only fresh and exciting, but extremely tight. A phenomenally jazzy "Eyes of the World" connects 1974 to the present, and "King Solomon's Marbles" is frenetic ecstasy. The second CD is nearly as wonderful, deftly shifting from a muscular "Other One" to the delicate "Sage and Spirit," then losing itself in the mystical depths of "Blues for Allah." This is one to be savored late at night.

You need not take my word for the majesty of this album. In *DeadBase*, it debuted at number one among our readers, dethroning *Live/Dead*. Don't settle for a tape, buy the album. It is worth owning a pristine copy of this magnificent concert, and we must do everything we can to encourage more frequent releases from the vault.

ONE HEARTBEAT AWAY 📖 • With Al Gore in the number two spot, this is how far we are from our first Deadhead—or at least Dead *fan*—President. While the Veep has "been to shows," and sports J. Garcia ties, the real tourhead-waiting-to-happen on Pennsylvania Avenue is Tipper. A three-show veteran, Tipper took her son, Albert, and her entire White House staff, to a summer '93 show at the RFK. She boogied on the side of the stage, met the band during the break, and, being a drummer herself, was thrilled to stand directly behind Hart during drums.

The Second Lady, whose favorite albums are *Workingman's Dead, American Beauty,* and *Europe '72,* returned the favor by inviting Hart, Garcia, and Weir to the White House for tea. She has "tons" of tapes, she says, and aides report that during the '92 campaign, her bus was a hotbed of tape trading.

OPENER • The first song in a set, as in, "That 'Shakedown' opener at the Garden in '87 blew the roof off!"

Garcia and Weir generally alternate whose song is played as

the opener from show to show, a convention that ensures vari-ety. An unusual song-choice in the opening slot is welcomed by Heads as an announcement that the set will not be business as usual, and the best-loved second-set openers are songs that are gateways to titanic jams, like "Scarlet Begonias" and "China Cat Sunflower."

Heads get a lot of pleasure by attempting to predict which song the band will open a show or set with—"calling the opener"—and one of the few musical parameters that are al-most always in force is that if a "Jerry tune" begins the first set one night, a "Bobby tune" will open the show the next night. "What's the call?" "About due for a 'Jack Straw' to open."

The first show in a tour is also "the opener." *See also* "ALTHEA" AT 3:1, "BUCKET" AT 1:1, "ST. STEPHEN" AT 500:1; BOBBY-TUNES/JERRY-TUNES; PICKY DEADHEADS.

OVER THERE • A World War I–era song about going overseas that was also the alternate title for the album that be-came *Europe '72.* Alton Kelley and Stanley Mouse designed a cover for *Over There,* featuring an Army patch with a lightning bolt. A third unused graphic for the album resembled the cover of *National Geographic,* a concept put on ice by the magazine's lawyers. *See* EUROPE '72.

OWSLEY • Augustus Owsley Stanley, a.k.a. "The Bear." Chemist, sound engineer, jeweler, and artisan, Owsley's name was synonymous with pure and potent LSD in the '60s, both before and after it was declared illegal. Owsley is also the Bear of *Bear's Choice.*

"Without Owsley," writes Jay Stevens in *Storming Heaven: LSD and the American Dream,* "the Acid Tests probably would never have taken place, for the simple reason that LSD was too difficult to obtain." (The only other source was Sandoz Labo-ratories, and the CIA had a virtual monopoly on the Sandoz output. Owsley's acid—which was marketed under names like "Orange Sunshine" and "Mother's Milk"—was said to be purer than that of Sandoz.) For several months in '66, Owsley sup-ported the Grateful Dead with profits from his LSD sales.

Owsley also was a principal advisor and designer of the

Dead's audio equipment for about ten years. "I thought it was absolutely disastrous that we were shooting rockets, building rockets that could deliver atomic bombs to destroy entire cities," Owsley told *Dupree's Diamond News* editor John Dwork, "and musicians were playing on something that looked like it was built in a garage in the '30s."

In 1970, Owsley helped start ALEMBIC, the visionary sound research company that helped develop THE WALL OF SOUND in the early '70s. Owsley was the recording engineer for the *Old and In the Way* album, and STEAL YOUR FACE.

In the early '70s, Owsley began doing fine ornamental metal-work, a craft to which he brought the same meticulous exactitude that he had brought to his chemistry. His STEALIE pendants—depicting the familiar lightning-streaked skull that he designed with Bob Thomas, wrought in fine gold in microscopically precise detail—are prized by Heads.

♣ *Owsley on "the church," in* Dupree's Diamond News:

It wasn't just the Dead. It seemed like every time we went to a concert back in the '60s, it was like a communion. I used to have these arguments on the steps outside the Fillmore with Bill Graham about it: "Come on, Bill, you're running a church here."

I think these experiences go back hundreds of thousands of years. People have always gotten together, and made music, eaten the mystical plants and the sacramental botanicals, and gotten into these states. It's an evolutionary thing. I think it's just something you need. The planet produces these various plants that, when ingested by humans, take their consciousness to another level, and allow them to understand what it all is.

I believe the universe exists in a mind that transcends time and space. There is a transcendent entity, and the world is its dream. Everything fits. Life is inherent in everything.

THE PARKING LOT SCENE • The "show before the show," the nomadic settlement Deadheads create like a circus outside of each venue, tearing it down and setting it up again for each RUN.

At one end of the lot, there's a row of customized tourbuses in various states of repair, hand-painted and festooned with insignia and flags. Heads who live in the buses spread out blankets in front of their rolling homes, offering all manner of wares for sale—from drums, to Guatemalan sweaters, t-shirts, lyric books, plump burritos, jewelry, bongs, incense, photographs, holy images, and "kind imports" (beer).

The main row of vendors is sometimes called "Shakedown Street." The economy of Shakedown Street thrives on barter: a juice for a cookie, a red clay pipe for a pinch of something fragrant to get high, a brass thunderskull buckle for a hand-stitched dress. Cabbage and onions sizzle in woks and felafels tumble into pots of oil, as smoke and steam from camp stoves, mixing with incense, drift over the rows of vendors. Deals are made for tickets—many of the buses have colorful signs on them that say "Need 2 for tonight"—and Heads lounge in and between the vehicles, picking guitars, lofting a Hacky Sack, or hibernating to be fresh for the night's jubilee.

Music streams out of a hundred bus speakers. Walking down

the rows, one passes through the band's history in overlapping crests of melody, a '72 "Big River" washing an '85 "Estimated Prophet" into a '90s "Supplication." Heads who haven't seen each other since spring tour—or the Fillmore—greet one another again. MIRACLE SEEKERS circulate up and down, making requests or offers for tickets—"Cash or kind for your extra!"—or quietly hold up one finger. Scalpers and their runners work the perimeter, often in two-person teams: someone who looks like a Head, asking for extras, and someone behind, reselling the tickets—or counterfeits—at a profit.

Heads in various zones of consciousness—trippers with incandescent eyes and curious smiles, sober WHARF RATS, stoners mellow and adrift—walk around simply observing, or goof on each other, and transactions are made between the cars, in greater secrecy now that there are DEA wolves undercover among the lambs.

Drummers with congas, shakers, and other ancient instruments form a DRUM CIRCLE, drawing dancers in from the lot's far corners, as if the primordial rhythms were a warming fire.

As the sun sets, and ticketholders join the long lines to the doors, the drums' thunder increases, and the cries of the miracle seekers grow more desperate. A few minutes after the show begins, the scalpers lower their prices. While "the Boys" play, the vendors restock their supplies, and the partying goes on.

After the encore, Shakedown Street picks up again, as Heads flow out to the cool air renewed, for something to eat, a t-shirt, or a last dance, and friends and strangers are greeted with a hug and, "Did you have a good show?"

Plans are drawn to meet up later on tour, rides and riders are sought and found, and the village disassembles, to truck on down the road.

"See you at the next one!"

PATCHING IN ↩ • Plugging one tape deck into another tape deck, or directly into the SOUNDBOARD, to record a show.

Though the sea of microphones in the TAPER'S SECTION might make it appear as though each taper has his/her tape deck plugged into its own mics, a closer examination reveals chains of decks wired into one other, with the first one in each chain attached to a set of mics. Under special circumstances—as when the taper's section had to be eliminated because of space limitations—DAN HEALY made available a "board patch" that allowed a few tapers to run cables directly into the mixing board, which were then patched into by other tapers, giving tapers a soundboard of that show.

PEACE • Comparative mythologist Joseph Campbell once said that the Grateful Dead are "the antidote to the atom bomb." The Dead's paradigm of musical cooperation, and the "family groove" of the Dead organization, helps shape the cornerstone of the political philosophy advocated by hundreds of thousands of Deadheads, who attempt to create together a model of a world at peace. "If the world were only filled with Deadheads," says David Djirikian, "imagine how peaceful things would be. (And how impossible to get tickets. But peace may be worth that.)"

Harmony between nations is readily achievable, many Heads believe, if only more will *believe.* The plausibility of peace politics rests on a broad web of personal commitments to the principle that getting along is *the* most important thing. *See* PRACTICE RANDOM KINDNESS AND SENSELESS ACTS OF BEAUTY; THE RAINFOREST TABLE; SEVA.

PEAK • 1. As a verb, to reach the highest moment of an acid trip, or as a noun, the climax of the experience itself. Many psychedelic journeys at shows culminate in a turning point. A peak at a show is often inspired by an intense moment in the music, usually a seamless transition, a crescendo, or SPACE. A shirt that read "I Peaked at the Greek" was popular among Bay Area Heads in the mid-'80s.

The term has been in use at least since the S.F. State Acid Test on 9/30/66 (and undoubtedly before). A poster for the three-day event promised, "Open 3pm Friday, Sept. 30—Peaking Saturday night—Re-entry complete 3pm Sunday."

Of course, Heads and bandmembers also have peak experiences at shows without drugs. "There are times when I come offstage and I swear I've been dosed, but I know I haven't,"

Garcia told Paul Krassner in 1984. "It's happened to all of us in the band—there is some biochemical reality in there. Maybe it has to do with what the East Indians believe about intervals in music containing emotional realities." Hart's conviction that music is "transportation" implies that Dead shows do not depend on drugs to do the work of unlatching the doors of perception. A peak is a *peek* through those opened doors.

2. As a noun, peak is also used to mean the highlight of the show, the set, the run, the tour, the year, the decade. Occasionally used as a suffix, as in "Jerrypeak" or "tourpeak." "That third night at the Garden was the tourpeak."

PHIL BOMBS • Very low notes and chords played by Lesh that can literally cause floorboards and seats to tremble. (The phrase "dropping bombs" was used by early jazz drummers.) "When Phil hits that note that drives a sound wave through your body," explains Tom Bellanca, "that's a bomb." Heads who enjoy being especially close to the speakers often articulate this experience in ways along the lines of Nethead Galen Watts, who speaks of "feeling Phil in your legs" and "sensing Bobby in your chest." *See* DEAFHEADS; THE PHIL ZONE.

THE PHIL ZONE • The left side of the floor facing the stage, so called because of the proximity to Lesh's position onstage. Many longtime Heads are Phil Zone habitués and treasure it as a place for furiously funky dancing. *See* JERRY'S SIDE.

PHIL'S LAST SHOW • A cheeky slogan printed on t-shirts in '90 in reference to pernicious rumors that Lesh was about to announce his retirement from the band. Word to that effect became so widespread that at Cal Expo on June 10 of '90, Lesh announced from the stage: "It's a bullshit lie!" (Garcia quipped, "Yeah—it's the rest of us who are quitting.")

Speculations about the bandmembers' health, personal habits, love lives, and career plans function in the Deadhead community as gossip does in a small town, allowing fans to feel that they are as involved in the bandmembers' lives as the band is in theirs.

PHYSICS FOR DEADHEADS • For Heads in physics class having trouble visualizing the process of a star imploding and becoming a "black hole," vol. 2, issue 3, of the 'zine *Dead Beat* featured this "explanation" by Peter Doherty and Mark Tuchman:

Picture the Dead on the surface of a collapsing object (not the stage at Woodstock!). They are in the midst of playing "Dark Star." . . . As soon as Jerry finishes singing the first verse, Bob's chords begin to sound a little dead, and Jerry's leads become a little flat. When the second verse begins, Jerry is moving much too slow (my old buddy) and the lyrics are drawn out to an almost impossible degree. . . . Everyone onstage is beginning to look tall and thin. . . . The only reassuring thing is that everyone in the audience seems to be sharing this hallucination.

Jerry just shakes his head and keeps playing. The band does not perceive that the music is slowing down or going out of tune, but, in fact, the energy is building until it reaches a climactic burst of cosmic energy, exploding into the hottest "St. Stephen" ever. . . .

If the Dead moved backwards in time by traveling into a black hole and out through a quasar, going from "Dark Star" to "St. Stephen," where would "The Eleven" come in? Before "St. Stephen"? And most disturbing of all, how would you label the tape?

PICKY DEADHEADS • Heads who know the difference between a good performance and a mediocre one, or think they do.

Few Heads think every note the band plays is pure gold. In the same way that family members can be more insulting than friends, Heads "rag on" their favorite band uninhibitedly, cutting down jams, songs, sets, shows, runs, and tours, calling them "weak," "flat," "predictable," and suggesting what should have been played instead. One perennial gripe is that "the new songs suck," though after a few years in THE ROTATION, songs once condemned as non-Deadish (like "Shakedown Street" and "Feel Like a Stranger," both branded "disco Dead" when they were broken out) have gotten so jammed out nearly everyone forgets the time when they were new and undeveloped.

Alan Mande, who was working on the stage crew at the Fillmore East, recalls that after the end of the "Dark Star→Cryptical Envelopment→Lovelight" jam on 2/13/70—considered by most Deadheads to be one of the most intense and lyrical sets ever played—picky Heads were whining that "they just played the album!"

🍂 *Charley Wilkins, on judging shows:*

It can be pretty easy to guess several songs per show. But that doesn't take away from my experience, because who knows how they're going to play the song, or what it will relate to in that moment. I don't care *what* they play as long as they're "on." I'd love to hear a forty-minute "Victim of the Crime," if it's a description of what's happening in the psychic and emotional realms of their lives, because then it will be real, and I can incorporate it into *my* life. Anyone who says, "I can't stand this song"—they're missing what it's all about. I've heard some shitty "Ripples" and some rippin' "Mexicali Blues." If I catch myself stuck in a preconception of whether a song is hot or not, it's better if I just go with the moment. That's why I love the Dead at age twenty-seven more than I did at seventeen—I make it a personal therapy session for myself. It's very freeing and liberating, providing a context to go inside yourself and explore.

PIGPEN (RON MCKERNAN) • Vocals, keyboards, harmonica, guitar. Born Ron McKernan on September 8, 1945, in San Bruno, California; Pigpen was found dead on March 8, 1973.

Pigpen was the Grateful Dead's first frontman, belting "Hard to Handle" with the gruff confidence of a Delta roadhouse singer, stoking "Smokestack Lightning" with staccato harmonica blasts, and whispering husky lowdown come-ons during "King Bee." Pigpen brought to the Dead blues roots, genuine soulfulness, and raunchy and riveting showmanship. His work can be heard on the albums the *AMERICAN BEAUTY; ANTHEM OF THE SUN; VOL. 1 (BEAR'S CHOICE); EUROPE '72; GRATEFUL DEAD; HISTORY OF THE GRATEFUL DEAD; LIVE/DEAD; SKULL FUCK; TWO FROM THE VAULT;* and *WORKINGMAN'S DEAD.*

In the early '50s, Pigpen's father, Phil McKernan, was a blues and R&B disc jockey in Berkeley whose handle on station KRE was "Cool Breeze." When Phil quit radio, the McKernans moved to a working-class neighborhood in Palo Alto that was becoming predominantly black, and young Ron strongly identified with black culture. He began learning blues piano by listening to his father's 78s, and cultivated a biker's image that got him expelled from Palo Alto High. Ron looked and acted older than he was, and at fourteen, he met another local musician with an interest in the blues: Jerry Garcia.

"I was the only person around that played any blues on guitar," Garcia recalls. "He picked up the basic Lightnin' Hopkins stuff, just by watching and listening to me. Then he took up the harmonica, and everybody called him 'Blue Ron'—the black people anyway. They loved that he played the blues. He was a genuine person—he wasn't a white boy trying to be black."

Soon christened "Pigpen" after the unkempt Peanuts comic-strip character, Pigpen began hanging around at the Chateau and the local coffeehouses where Garcia, Robert Hunter, and David Nelson were playing. One night, he got up on stage and blew his harp and sang while Garcia played guitar. "He could sing just like Lightnin' Hopkins, which just blew everybody's mind," Garcia says. Pigpen became a welcome participant in local jam sessions, and in late '62, Pigpen, guitarist Troy Widenheimer (who employed Garcia and Kreutzmann at Dana Morgan's Music Store), drummer Roy Ogborn and Garcia—playing Fender bass—formed the Zodiacs, which played tunes like "Searchin'" at frat parties. (Kreutzmann also drummed with the Zodiacs).

In '64, David Nelson, Bob Matthews, and Bob Weir—who was sixteen—started calling themselves MOTHER MCCREE'S UPTOWN JUG CHAMPIONS, and at the first rehearsal in Garcia's garage, Weir met Pigpen. Hunter—who had been playing locally in THE WILDWOOD BOYS—was impressed by Pigpen, who he felt was "the most professional of anybody in the group." One of Pigpen's most impressive abilities was to improvise blues lyrics on the spot, like the greatest blues singers.

Mother McCree's would occasionally play Jimmy Reed blues, and even an occasional rock and roll tune, and by early '65, Pigpen convinced Garcia to form an electric band, so that

he could play blues organ. THE WARLOCKS played "I Know
You Rider," and Pigpen sang lead on "Big Boss Man" and a
song called "Caution: Do Not Stop on Tracks," with a riff lifted
from an early Van Morrison tune called "Mystic Eyes."

By June of '65, Phil Lesh had joined the Warlocks, and by
the end of the year, they had changed their name to the Grate-
ful Dead, and were playing the Acid Tests (Pigpen preferred
Ripple or Thunderbird wine to LSD.) The band's version of
Wilson Pickett's "In the Midnight Hour"—with a powerhouse
Pigpen rap—was already the climax of the Dead's sets.

In '66, both the Dead and Big Brother and the Holding Company lived in Lagunitas, north of San Francisco, and Pigpen
and Janis Joplin had a summer love affair. That fall, the Dead
took over 710 Ashbury with the help of Pigpen, who sat up
nights drinking in the kitchen with the band's manager until the
other residents moved out. Pigpen met his soulmate, Veronica
Grant, soon after that, and she joined him at 710, where Pigpen
held court, drinking Southern Comfort and playing bottleneck
guitar. When the GOLDEN ROAD TO UNLIMITED DEVOTION fan
club put out its first run of Dead t-shirts, Pigpen's face was on
them.

By '67, Pigpen had added "Smokestack Lightning," "Next
Time You See Me," and "King Bee" to the band's repertoire,
along with Bobby "Blue" Bland's "Turn On Your Lovelight."
"Alligator," A Hunter-Pigpen collaboration, turned into fiercely
psychedelic, percussion-driven jams. (Hart first joined the band
during a two-hour version of it on 9/29/67.) Pigpen's showstop-
ping raps during "Lovelight" were down-and-dirty hybrids of
stage "testifyin' " by soul singers like Wilson Pickett and James
Brown, and the mind-warping hip sermons of Lord Buckley
(also an influence on NEAL CASSADY), who rented yachts in the
mid-'40s and cruised San Francisco Bay with jazz sax great Ben
Webster for MESCALINE parties called "the Church of the Living Swing."

When 710 was busted on October 2, '67, the *Chronicle*'s front-
page story (about "the Dead's way-out 13-room pad," etc.) ran
under a photo of an angry-looking Pigpen. With the incorpora-

tion of Mickey Hart as second drummer in '67, and Tom Constanten's keyboards in '68, the Dead's music became less blues-rooted and more experimental, and Pigpen does not even appear on *Aoxomoxoa*. Though his keyboard playing was not keeping up with the evolution of the music in the studio, Pigpen's command of performance—wading into the crowd to get couples together during "Good Lovin'," urging on his bandmates during "Hard to Handle" with grunts, shouts, and a swagger of his hips—drove the Dead and audiences at shows to ecstatic heights.

In '70, with Constanten no longer in the band, and the Dead reembracing acoustic playing and folk forms like the songs on *Workingman's Dead*, Pigpen returned to a more active role. "Easy Wind," written by Hunter with Pigpen and seminal bluesman Robert Johnson in mind, showcases Pigpen at his mythic American best: a working man "chipping them rocks from dawn till doom," telling his story with indomitable authority.

By '71, the ill effects of Pigpen's years of drinking were taking their toll on his liver, but he was at the height of his rapping powers. The Dead were enjoying a new wave of popularity on college campuses, and two of Pigpen's raunchiest and most imaginative raps electrified the crowd at Princeton University on 4/17/71. Pigpen went out on the fall tour, singing a new Hunter collaboration called "Mr. Charlie" (a slaves' contemptuous term for whites), and an original blues called "Empty Pages." He was playing little, however, and by September, the band was rehearsing with Keith Godchaux as the new keyboard player. Pigpen quit drinking, but the liver degeneration continued.

He went to Europe on the '72 tour, singing a meditative original blues called "Two Souls in Communion," and recording "It Hurts Me Too" and "Mister Charlie" for the album *Europe '72*. On 4/14/72 at the Tivoli Theater in Copenhagen, Pigpen and the band jammed "Good Lovin'," into "Caution," into Bo Diddley's "Who Do You Love," and back into "Good Lovin'," with Pigpen laying down a fierce, dark rap as the bandmembers traded stinging lines.

The bus trips throughout Europe further damaged Pigpen's frail health, and he did not go out on tour again.

The band encouraged him to do a solo album, and in early '73, he began recording piano blues at home on a four-track. "Seems like all my yesterdays were filled with pain," he sang, "there's nothing but darkness tomorrow. Don't make me live in this pain no longer. My poor heart can't stand much more . . ."

Pigpen died of gastrointestinal hemorrhage and cirrhosis of the liver, and his body was found by his landlady on March 8, 1973. A rowdy wake was held at Weir's house, and Pigpen's funeral was attended by Hell's Angels and Merry Pranksters. "He's Gone"—though composed before Pigpen's death—is considered by many Heads, and by lyricist Hunter himself, to be a tribute to Pigpen.

Pigpen is buried in the Alta Mesa Memorial Park in Palo Alto under a gravestone reading: "Pigpen Was and Is Now Forever One of the Grateful Dead."

PIGPEN LOOK-ALIKE CONTEST • Sponsored by Warner Bros. in 1969. An ad in *Rolling Stone* for this unlikely two-part promotional campaign for *Aoxomoxoa* announced that "Part One was a bust. No one has captured the panache, the bravado, the insouciance—the true and utter raunch of Mr. Pen. Just to have a moustache doesn't make it. Just to have long hair doesn't make it. Blondes don't make it. And the pygmy from Venice [Calif.] who wrote that 'contests suck' doesn't make it." The names of the "winners"—if any—are unknown.

THE PINEAPPLE GUYS • David Clark and Mikael Jacobson, two show buddies who give out free pineapple at shows, display setlists, print a newsletter, and put up distinctive $2\frac{1}{4}$ inch-wide canary yellow signs in the strangest of places at West Coast venues.

Clark had been seeing the Dead since '85, and when he and Jacobson went to their first show together in '90, Clark says, "I saw a real difference in the scene. There were a lot of freeloaders, a lot of people needing gas money, a lot of people needing tickets, a lot of people not sending the really good vibes. At that

show, Mikael and I decided that we needed to input something." On a road trip that ended with Clark and Jacobson
scoring tickets for the New Year's '90 show, the Pineapple Guys
were conceived.

Their first signs said simple things like, "Cut Fresh Daily"
and "Pineapple Guys enjoy pancakes," but the signs took on an
uncanny life of their own, especially when improvised—sometimes by a group—one letter at a time, always with Jacobson's
handwritten label: "© *The Pineapple Guys.*"

Experiments in giving out pineapple at places other than
Dead shows met with mixed responses. "Americans are petri-
fied about anything free, especially free food," says Jacobson.
"Especially from two long-haired guys who are smiling *way* too
much."

One of the Pineapple Guys' mottoes is, "We really don't
know what's happening, but it's the greatest."

🍀 © *The Pineapple Guys:*
Start Brain Spew • Days to Melt & Wonder • "Flowed Through"
Creed • Zen Site Bin #22 • Decaf Erases Peanuts • Ideal God
Pile • Prepare to Be Squirted Back to 1948 • It Needs Soup of
Batons • Haiku Fort Bell Shoe • Dr. Ohmy I'm Fun Guy • Tingle Me Pi-
rate or Scram • Imaginary Ranger Station • Implement Boogie • Near
ESP, Y'all Mind • I Strum Elf Plaque • The Psychotic Box Tore
Open • We Meant "Sample From NY" • Some Ultra-Melts? • Plato's
Knit Pancake • Refracting Baklava • Beware Fellow Toast Because Pas-
sionate Invertebrates Are MAD! TOTALLY ABSURDLY VILE!
• Caramels, Monkees, & BATS! • ATOMS • The Pineapple Guys Wel-
come You to This Exact Second

THE PIT 📖 • 1. Slang for the TAPER'S SECTION, before it
was officially sanctioned with taper tickets (in October '84) and
cordoned off behind the board. Mike Yacavone explains: "My
friends and I started taping around '81. The 'pit' was up front,
in the twentieth to thirtieth row. Usually there were a few others wanting to "patch in" and whatnot, so it got to be a scene.
With the mic stands in the air, and the intensity of the compul-
sive behavior about mics and cords and the space around the
mics, and no talking and no clapping, our friends—mostly our

girlfriends—started calling it 'the pit,' and wanted to dance elsewhere. It was a whole different world in the pit. Very male, somewhat macho—'My equipment is better than yours.' "

2. The "moat" in between the stage and the rail. *See* RAILRATS.

PLANET EARTH ROCK & ROLL ORCHESTRA • David Crosby and Paul Kantner's nickname for the cross-fertilization of members of the Dead, Jefferson Airplane, and Crosby, Stills, Nash & Young, playing on sessions for each other's albums circa 1970.

Jefferson Airplane's *Volunteers* and the first "Starship" album, *Blows Against the Empire*—a science-fiction epic about hijacking a starship to found a humane society, inspired by Heinlein's *Stranger in a Strange Land*—were "P.E.R.R.O." projects. Numerous tracks on Crosby/ Nash albums, like "The Wall Song," recorded with the Dead minus Weir, and Nash's "I Used to Be a King" from his *Songs for Beginners*, were other fruits of the informal collaborations that marked these musicians' careers at a time when they had become successful enough in their own bands to exert maximum creative control over the music and the conditions of recording. The P.E.R.R.O. masterpiece was David Crosby's album *If I Could Only Remember My Name.*

Crosby booked Wally Heider's studio in San Francisco for three months, so that he and his friends—like Garcia, Lesh, Kreutzmann, Jorma Kaukonen, Jack Casady, Paul Kantner, Grace Slick, Joni Mitchell, and Neil Young—could drop in anytime and start riffing while producer Stephen Barncard ran tape. Garcia and Lesh darted in and out of Crosby's moodiest, most haunting modal themes; Jorma Kaukonen and Neil Young provided ammo in a song about a cowboy showdown; and Joni Mitchell crested a chorus of harmony singers on Crosby's "Laughing," while Garcia's pedal steel soared. (One of the most lovely tracks cut then, an instrumental fable played by Crosby and Garcia called "Kids and Dogs," is still unreleased.) The album is a group portrait of the best minds of a generation of Bay Area musicians when the "family groove" was strongest. *See* "TEACH YOUR CHILDREN."

🎵 *Steve Barncard, producer, on the **If I Could Only Remember My Name** sessions:*
I was not certain how well the album would sell, and it was obvious that Crosby didn't care. This was his vacation time compared to the main business of CSN. All that mattered was the feeling of the music, that it felt *real*. There was a lot of bartering and trading. Instead of making a guest appearance, and filling out checks—which they hated, 'cause they were all making more money than they could handle—they would do a guest shot in return for another guest shot, or trade a night of studio time. Crosby called it cross-pollinization, which extended far beyond the music.

Those magic melodies, so many of them. "Song With No Words" was recorded on Airplane studio time, with Jack and Jorma, and Michael Shrieve on drums. Some of the instrumentals may have been developed as something that would eventually have words, but they were so beautiful, and the scat-singing worked out so well, that we left them as is. Crosby went very much on serendipity and instinct on that record.

The way that he paid the band at the end—just before Christmas—was that he brought them big bags of green stuff. He'd say, "It's better than checks through the union!"

PLAY LIKE JERRY 📖 • Trying to figure out and emulate *how they play that way* has been an occupation of many Deadhead musicians since the early days. It's also become a cottage industry, with a spate of how-to books, tapes, and craft interviews with the band.

Garcia's Solos: Note by Note is a two-cassette step-by-step demonstration of Garcia's solo work on "Althea," "To Lay Me Down," "Crazy Fingers," and other tunes. In 1993, *Guitar Player* magazine published a book modestly titled *Secrets of the Masters*, which features an interview with Garcia. The December 1987 issue of *Guitar Magazine* includes a similar interview with Weir. ICE NINE, the Dead's publishing company, has published a series of songbooks, including the two-volume *Grateful Dead Anthology*, and *The Music of the Grateful Dead Made Easy for Guitar*.

Guitarist David Fontaine has taken this pursuit a leap further. For more than ten years, Fontaine has been on a relentless pursuit to analyze and duplicate the technical details behind every aspect of Garcia's playing—his fingering, his touch, his tone. Fontaine has spoken at length with GD sound engineers Dan Healy and John Cutler, Garcia's guitar custodian Steve Parish, Alembic co-founder Ron Wickersham, and—in a Providence, Rhode Island, hotel in 1984—Garcia himself, for about an hour.

"I showed Jerry my guitar. He picked it up and played with it a bit, and said the action was a little low. Then I showed him a picture of all the equipment he has, which I also have, down to the bone. He looked at it and said, 'Yep, that's what I use.' I said, 'I'm the only one doing this.' He laughed and said, 'Are you kidding? There are hundreds of you guys out there.' But I'm the only one who's spoken to the guys who wired the equipment."

Fontaine is also the only one who has convinced Doug Irwin, Garcia's guitar craftsman, to make him "Tiger 2," a near-replica of Jerry's original Tiger guitar (*see* THE WOLF). "Doug's guitars are the finest in the world," Fontaine says. "The perfect combination of the Fender Stratocaster and the Gibson SG."

With a near-total replication of Jerry's instrumentation and amplification, Fontaine studies the "Jerry touch" for his Dead cover band, Out of the Blue. He is wary of the copycat tag that people will put on him. "But," he says, "if it weren't for Jerry, I wouldn't be playing guitar right now."

POLIO WEED • A Garcia term from the '70s: marijuana so potent it induces a state of paralysis.

POP THE TABS ✑ • A credo for the Magnetic Tape Generation. Tape traders advise one another to press out the little plastic pieces at the tops of audiocassettes so their (so-called) buddy doesn't accidentally (or so he said) record a fuzzy audience tape of Boreal Ridge (infamously the worst Dead show ever) over a second-gen soundboard of 2/13/70. *See* RETREADING.

POSTSHOW GLOW 📖 • After shows, the crowd is often still tingling with energy and enthusiasm, part of which is dissipated in spontaneous bursts of applause or in chanting THE CHANT ("You know our love will not fade away"). While speed-metal concerts can trigger postshow brawling, Dead shows tend to inspire postshow falafel, snuggling in microbuses, and copious amounts of dubbing.

The downside is postshow burn: raw throat from singing and cheering, lactic acid surplus in the spacedancing muscles, tinnitus in the ears, and general spacedness. One effective prescription for relief: a mound of *pad thai,* a mellow '74 jam, and twelve hours' sleep.

🐞 *Tony Beers, on the postshow recovery:*

I'm an older Deadhead. I don't take drugs anymore. Dancing is my meditation. I dance harder than most eighteen-year-olds out there, and the next day my body is in real pain. I could pull a muscle, or even break a rib from dancing. So I need to stretch out before and after shows. A hot tub and Advil—that would be my dream.

Sometimes after a show, I get an upset stomach. My girlfriend will explain to our friends that this means I had a great time dancing. Once I had to lie down during "Deal"—and I *don't* lie down during "Deal." After a show, my back is killing me. But I'm smiling.

PRACTICE RANDOM KINDNESS AND SENSE-LESS ACTS OF BEAUTY • An invitation by Marin County resident Anne Herbert to join a growing band promoting peace on Earth through acts of guerrilla goodness. "Kindness," she explains, "can build on itself as much as violence can."

Heads have answered her call with a zest for unsolicited acts of goodwill: paying highway tolls for the next three cars in line, donating a used computer to a student who needs and can't afford one, paying for meals for a person with AIDS, and so on. "At '92 Shoreline," admits one anonymous vigilante of virtue, "my family and I handed out tapes to strangers. These were copies of my crispiest soundboards with the j-cards bearing the 'Practice Random Kindness' slogan, along with a plea not to allow the recording to be sold. Our sons were with us, and we let them pick each recipient, walk up to each one to say 'hi,' and hand over a tape. Some folks are so surprised to be given anything by a stranger that they assume you're trying to sell the tapes. It's cool to see that tension break, and the smile set in as they realize it's a no-strings gift. I like to think that by seeing the 'Practice Random Acts of Kindness' slogan on that tape, some of them will decide on their own ways to put the slogan into action themselves."

THE PRE-DRUMS • The songs in THE SECOND SET played before DRUMS and SPACE.

Since the late '80s, the jam on the way into the drums has become one of the most freeform, interactive areas of the music, with long jams out of "Terrapin" evolving into small groupings of the guitarists, drummers, and keyboardists, as the rest of the set has grown tighter, but more predictable.

PRIMAL DEAD • Official Grateful Dead tape archivist Dick Latvala's term for truly transcendent Dead shows. When asked by the band to choose his top three "primal" shows, Latvala selected 2/13/70 at the Fillmore West (one of the most lyrical "Dark Stars" ever played), 10/11/77 in Norman, Oklahoma, and 12/19/73 in Tampa (which became *DICK'S PICKS, VOLUME ONE*).

Another term, "epic shows," is also used by some Heads to denote performances that are the summation and consummation of a particular era of the Dead's evolution. Harpur College 5/2/70 is such a show, consisting of three sets, beginning with a pristine acoustic set sweetened by the harmonizing of the New Riders. In recent years, the "Formerly the Warlocks" show at Hampton on 10/9/89 is considered by many Heads to rate as epic. Primal and epic shows are distinguished by fierce jamming, telepathic ensemble work, and setlists that delve deep into the history of the band. The 10/9/89 show, for example, featured the first "Dark Star" in five years, "Uncle John's Band" SANDWICHED before an old-style "Playin'" reprise, and a gut-wrenching "Death Don't Have No Mercy," with Mydland on vocals. *See also TWO FROM THE VAULT.*

PRODUCTION AIDS • In-studio slang for consciousness enhancers used to maximize productivity or call forth inspiration when recording. "Sometimes," Round Records employee Steve Brown recalls, "production aids were prioritized over recording tape."

For the band's first album, *Grateful Dead*, the production aid of choice was Dexamyl, a dieter's amphetamine. Several tunes on the album blaze at a manic tempo, and the reason for the speed, it turns out, was *speed*. "That's what's embarrassing about that record now," says Garcia. "The tempo was way too fast. We were all so speedy at the time. It has its sort of crude energy, but obviously it's difficult for me to listen to it; I can't enjoy it." (Many Heads *can*, however. *See* GRATEFUL DEAD.)

PSILOCYBIN • *See SHROOMS.*

PSYCHEDELICS • Substances such as LSD, psilocybin mushrooms ("shrooms"), peyote and MESCALINE, and DMT that, when either eaten, smoked, or injected, evoke profound changes of consciousness.

The word was coined by Humphry Osmond in 1957, a combination of two Greek roots, *psyche* and *dê los*, which Osmond translated as "mind manifesting," but could also be translated as "soul clarifying." The other Greek phrases he considered translate as *mind moving, mind rousing, mind molding, mind fermenting, mind bursting forth,* and *mind releasing.*

Another term coined by Osmond, "entheogen," means "summoner of the god within," which is the word closest in sense to the way many Heads use these substances, both inside and outside of shows. Some Heads use psychedelics at shows to experience THE SECOND SET as a journey toward a deep understanding of life.

Psychedelics are reported by some Heads to induce the experience of being in the presence of a "teacher," represented in folk iconography as a wizard, an animal or plant shaman, or a wise crone, occasionally accompanied by wrathful deities. Use of psychedelics to attain audience with this "teacher" is as old as human civilization, though in cultures where psychedelics are used in this way, the journey is guided by tribal elders in a traditional setting, often involving sacred songs, drumming, and tribal imagery. Many of the social forms that have arisen spontaneously at shows—such as the DRUM CIRCLE—can be seen as an attempt by young people to improvise meaningful initiatory rituals in the context of a culture that has little understanding of these experiences.

🍀 *Dee Flanagan on summoning-the-god-within:*

When we started the Dye Works with folks from the Farm in Miami, there were, right there, in the mist of the cow pastures in the warm Florida rain — Mr. Natural would approve, all free — magic mushrooms. We used to bring cow patties (where the mushrooms grow) home in plastic bags, and water them in the backyard. We listened to tunes and made tie-dyes: fabulous woman-art-music-love energy, very very psychedelic.

A busload of folks from the Farm in Tennessee came by our place one day in "the Doggie," a huge old scenicruiser painted jade green, with graceful whales swimming along the sides, and a huge fluke on the back. We sent them on their way with bags of mushrooms for the trip, and felt like we'd created a new destination for them: Further. We started selling our dyes at the Coconut Grove Farmer's Market. Lori's husband at the time, Dean, still sells her stuff direct to the band. The stuff we created then is still a potent visual cue for many people's trips.

To me, "psychedelic" means not a drug, but a *force*, a strength — being able to peer through and beyond and behind What Is Going On, to extract something essential from it, and fuel my life trip with that essence. It means finding out about caring for people, including caring for yourself. It means connecting with other beings, souls, the spirits of rivers, of roads, of clouds, of tunes, an energy/strength/power that is so huge and strong.

I found out when I was having my first kid that you can tap into the Spirit of Life, and there are all these women and babies throughout time who will be at your side, helping you and your baby do the delivery.

This power, though, doesn't come with a set of instructions. I see people at Dead scenes who, all swelled up with psychedelics, tread heavily on other people's lives. Be careful out there.

PUDDLE • *n.* A sizable dose of liquid LSD. Also a verb, "puddle me," or, "I was way puddled for that second set."

THE PYRAMID DIALECT • A rich vein of jargon relating to shows, spoken by an extended family of Heads on tour from the mid-'80s on.

The dialect was named by one of the original users of it, who calls himself the Eye of Horus. After the Dead played at the Great Pyramid in '78, he explains, his friends started referring to taking acid as "going to Egypt." He traces the genesis of the dialect back to St. Paul's school, outside of Concord, New Hampshire. Much of the jargon was compiled there by faculty member Howard Lederer (a.k.a. "Jumbo"), and published in the school newspaper.

"The Dead was revered by a cadre of students who discovered that the music was ideally suited to peaceful listening late at night while **seshing**," explains the Eye of Horus (terms in **bold** are defined below). "Not wanting to **noid** and be busted **deathing**, a terminology was conceived and ritually passed down as a code that could not be interpreted, even if overheard by faculty or narcs. One particular sect revered a tape they called 'The Fox' (Fox Atlanta 11/30/80), and tapes were traded feverishly." (*See* THE FOX'S DEN.)

From there, he explains, the dialect migrated to Trinity College in Hartford, Connecticut, and to Brown University in Providence, Rhode Island, and was refined on all-night drives on tour in the fall of '85 and spring of '86. It spread to Middlebury College in Vermont, and by the summer of '86, to Boston College. By '90, the jargon was in use by a touring "family" who called themselves "The Core."

The Pyramid Dialect:

benji—A $100 bill, reserved for tour emergencies.

biscuit shows—Good shows at out-of-the-way venues, with mainly hardcore tourheads in attendance.

bonus— Extra effort exhibited by the band. For example, when "Deal," which usually ends the set, is followed by "Let It Grow," or when a jam is extended—"THE BOYS seshed the bonus."

bugment—Music so intense it causes your eyes to bug out. "We were subjected to severe *bugment* when they broke out 'Box of Rain.'"

celebrating 365—"A year on tour," celebrated after your 365th show.

civilians—Non-hippies at shows, who will buy only non-tie-dyed t-shirts with cute designs (no skulls or skeletons.)

clandy—Clandestine. "Stash those brews, we gotta be *clandy!*"

coping—The competent state of mind required to function on tour. "Are you *coping?*" can mean "Are you OK?" or "Are you too high to drive?" etc.

crinkly — 1. Music so psychedelic, it pushes the outer envelope. ("Dark Star" Miami 10/26/89 is ultra-crinkly.) 2. The state of mind after a long night of NITROUS OXIDE use.

crisp — 1. A crisp tape is a SOUNDBOARD with no hiss and no saturation. A very flattering term. 2. Similar to #2 definition of "crinkly." Burned out. Not a flattering term. "That guy's *crispy.*"

deathing — Snuffing a bong. Coughing while doing a bong hit may cause one to "whale spout."

de-reek — *n.* Mouthwash or pocket Binaca, remedies for "truck mouth." "Could you sesh me some de-reek?"

de-sesh — *v.* To take something apart, undo, disassemble. "I de-seshed the dishwasher."

the Jerryiott — Any hotel on the tour circuit.

justice — A righteous song choice. "That was *justice* when they broke out 'Dark Star.' "

the Master — Garcia.

message tunes — Songs seen to carry advice from the band to the audience. E.g., "Ship of Fools."

noiding — Paranoia. A heightened sense of awareness of the possibility of being arrested.

outstashed — Hidden so well, no one can find it. "Oh, unkind! I *outstashed* the tickets."

the Pepto pink — Weir's pink guitar.

perma — *n.* Someone who is at every show, a "permanent fixture" on tour. *Mr. & Mrs. Perma* was the honorary title given to a couple who have been on tour since '78 and maintain both East Coast and West Coast tour vehicles. "Perma" can also be an adjective: The *one-stop perma shop* was the Core tour vehicle, vending t-shirts, beer, and parking lot staples.

puppied — So relaxed you want to snuggle.

racking — Sleeping.

randy — A random Deadhead. *Randy B. Crisp* is the guy who shows up in the hotel room after the show to drink beer and borrow tapes, who everyone thinks the *other* guy knows.

rezzie — A "resurrection," the band playing a song that hasn't been played in a long time. *See* REVIVAL.

S.D. — Self-destructive levels of abuse, as in "to be on the S.D. mode," or "I was on S.D. tour."

sesh — *v.* 1. To give, sometimes without expectation of compensation. "*Sesh* me those ultra-crispy Hartfords" is a request for a tape. 2. *n.* Session. To have a *sesh* of smoking pot.

snag — *v.* To steal a major thing.

spinning madly — Copying many tapes.

the super-ultra-mega-majors-death-kind — The most outrageously good thing possible.

teef — *v.* To steal a minor thing. "Dude, did you *teef* my lighter?"

truck mouth — Even more unpleasant than cottonmouth (also, "fur breath").

ultra! — Very good, especially a song that is extremely well-played. "The 'Shakedown' was *ultra!*"

used up — Resources exhausted (can refer to a person, a vehicle, a venue, or a town).

vendorville — a.k.a. "Shakedown Street," the row of vendors in the parking lot.

vids — 1. Hallucinations (from "videos"). "I was having serious *vids* on Mickey's hands." 2. A "scene." "JOHNNY LAW pulled us over and it was a bad *vid.*"

the zacklies — The same as truck mouth, with the feeling of little creatures in your mouth. "I've got the *zacklies.*"

QUAD SPACE • The portion of SPACE during which seismic thunder from THE BEAM, and various sampled and altered sounds, are fed into the arena from additional speakers at the back of the big room, creating, soundman Dan Healy says, "a holographic effect." One of the most interesting uses of this is to produce "dialogues" between the drummers and themselves. This sound-dance is choreographed using a joystick at the soundboard.

"One of the most exciting things about the parts I'm playing, for me," says Bob Bralove, "is that — if we do it really well — that part of the show has the potential of going anywhere, even away from the stage. So you can have a moment in the evening where the performance moves from up there to right here. It's not just that thing spinning around you — we get someplace else."

QUEER DEADHEADS • A social action group for gay, lesbian, and bisexual Heads, founded in San Francisco in March of '93. The group danced down Market Street in the '93 Gay Freedom Day parade, and has grown into an extended "show family," with members in eleven states. (The word "queer," like the word "gay" two decades before it, has been transformed by a new generation of activists from a brand of derision to a badge of defiance.)

"We all had stories to share about it being taken for granted at shows that we were straight," says founding member Layne Ringgenberg. "Within the Deadhead community—a group that has met with much defensiveness and prejudice—there is as much homophobia and prejudice as in everyday life. But when I wear a pink triangle shirt to a show, I'm always greeted by Heads saying, 'I thought I was alone,' or, 'I've never met a gay Deadhead before.' We discovered very quickly that we had more to offer each other than building a float for the parade."
See WE ARE EVERYWHERE.

🍃 *Michael Van Dyke, owner of the Psychedelic Shop in San Francisco:*
To be a Deadhead is to live at the boundaries of social convention, and the status of homosexuals in American culture has likewise largely been that of outlaws. Both Deadheads and queers assert the sovereignty of the individual over society's idea of what it means to be a man or woman, and both are privy to the insights about oneself as an evolving spiritual being that come only from viewing one's own culture from the *outside in.*

The values which appear fixed and rigid to an unquestioning member of the mainstream culture, appear fluid and relative to an outsider. In the instant of seizing the opportunity for personal autonomy, growth, and self-exploration, Deadheads and queers share the transcendent experience of "being in the world but not of it."

QUIETLY FREAKING • Barely coping on the outside, while going gelatinous on the inside. The term belongs to New Yorker David Pelovitz, who recalls a close call at New Jersey's Brendan Byrne Arena. "I was carrying eight joints in a tin of Altoid mints," explains Pelovitz. "They were under tissue paper with a few mints on top. The guard hit the tin in the frisk and checked it out. Since those mints look like pills, I had to convince him they were mints without looking so nervous that he would lift the tissue paper. I had to explain they were just mints totally calmly, and the whole time I was quietly freaking!"

RAILRATS • Those who prefer to see the show as close to the band as possible, "on the rail," the area just below the edge of the stage.

To be on the rail is to be plunged into the music by watching the intricate weaving of a guitarist's fingers, and the ideas and emotion crossing his face; to see the bandmembers think, invent, and react as individuals, by observing their cues and relations with one another.

Railrats must undertake LINE DUTY hours early (sometimes this means the night before); navigate through high crowd densities to reach refreshments or relief; and defend their hard-won REAL ESTATE against "thrashers" who may appear, beer in fist, just as the band comes out for the second set.

For some old-timers who have grown up on the rail, the bandmembers are like old friends, whether they've ever spoken with them or not. "They're the people who are down in front and insist upon being there every show," says Garcia. "We know these people pretty intimately. We look down there and if there's somebody new, we notice them."

THE RAINFOREST TABLE • The Rainforest Action Network outreach post in the halls or on the lawn at venues, offering information and merchandise to raise money for RAN's mission to sound the alarm about the clear-cutting of rainforests in South and Latin America and elsewhere, and the destruction of native cultures by mining, oil, logging, and cattle industries.

RAN has organized Deadhead boycotts of Burger King, Georgia-Pacific, Weyerhaeuser, Mitsubishi electronics and related subsidiaries Nikon, Kirin beer, and Value Rent-a-Car. A RAN demonstration outside of Paramount Studios resulted in a company pledge not to cut endangered tropical wood for movie sets.

The Dead have made table space available at shows for many activist groups, including SEVA; the WHARF RATS; the Further Foundation; and Creating Our Future, a summer camp to train kids to be environmental activists, run by social activist Sat Santokh Singh Khalsa, a former producer of shows at the Avalon Ballroom. *See* SEVA.

🐾 *David Minkow, who has worked the table since February '92:*

For many Deadheads at shows, the Rainforest table is a place of refuge, where you can get setlists or directions to the bathroom or the Wharf Rats, and end up finding out how large the community really is, and what your role could be in preserving an amazing place in the outside world. Deadheads already know they are part of a larger community with certain responsibilities. You'd be surprised to learn how many Deadheads have done work or traveled in the Rainforest.

Some people don't even stop at the table, but I think they're glad we're here — that while everybody cuts loose and dances, the good work is going on.

REAGAN IN CHINA • A current-events theme adopted by the band as a conceptual backdrop for SPACE one night in the early '80s, as part of a band experiment. The approach, explained Garcia in 1984, "provides an invisible infrastructure and a centerpiece for us all to look at. It has provided us more interesting new shapes for the long form music."

"One time," recalled Garcia, "we had the Qaddafi Death Squad as our theme. Sometimes the themes are terribly detailed, sometimes they're just a broad subject. We do this when we think about it. It's made that part of the music at times have some tremendous other level of organization that pulls it together and makes it really interesting."

"We drummers do the same thing," says Kreutzmann. "We'll

be back there saying 'Earthquake!' or 'World War III!' and we'll do bomb shots on the big toms. It's fun to have a theme going through your mind." *See* MUSIQUE CONCRÈTE.

REAL ESTATE • Desired floor space or seats at venues. At West Coast shows, it is considered acceptable to bring a blanket to a general admission show and map out territory for oneself and one's friends; but at East Coast shows, where there is more of a flow of Heads SWIMMING from the front of the venue to the rear and back, saving space is considered rude. *See* EAST COAST DEADHEADS/WEST COAST DEADHEADS.

RECKONING • Album #17, released in March 1981.

Recorded at the same shows as *Dead Set,* in the fall of '80 at New York City's Radio City Music Hall and San Francisco's Warfield Theater.

"*Reckoning* was the result of about three afternoons of rehearsal," Garcia recalls. "That means harmonies, the arrangements—everything. We spent such a small amount of time preparing for that, and it yielded enormous results."

These sixteen songs (or fifteen—"Oh Babe, It Ain't No Lie," found on the original LP, *still* hasn't made it onto CD), are culled from one of the Dead's greatest runs—twenty-five three-set shows (acoustic/electric/electric) performed in just over a month's time in September/October '80. About half—including the Jesse Fuller tall-tale "Monkey & The Engineer" (Fuller also wrote "Beat It on Down the Line"), the old-time "Deep Elem Blues" (referring to the old Elm Street red-light district in Dallas, Texas), the bluegrass classics "Rosa Lee McFall," "Been All Around This World," and "Dark Hollow," and the Garcia/ Hunter Taoist folk anthem "Ripple"—are REVIVALS from the pre-Dead jug band days and from the band's first acoustic effort in 1970. Most of the rest are simply borrowed from the band's electric lineup.

"That's Otis," Jerry's comment between verses on "Ripple," is a reference to Bob Weir's dog, who had wandered onstage.

The first CD issue of *Reckoning* was titled *For the Faithful,* and contained a crude edit of the original two-album set. The album was subsequently remastered and reissued with the original title.

🍀 *David Shenk on* **Reckoning:**

When I close my eyes and think about the Grateful Dead, they are an acoustic band, sitting on stools, weaving through a tender "Bird Song."

The other band—fanned out over a large stage and loaded down with effects pedals, computer-guided MIDI, the Beast, the Beam, and quadrophonic surround-sound—I love. But in my mind's eye, I prefer the stripped-down model—hollow instruments of wood, brass, and leather. The band sharing one Oriental rug, playing—with the crowd's cooperation—a real pianissimo.

In this band, the soundboard is not a fortress of effects, but a simple tool allowing the band to play and sing that much softer and still be heard. Jerry sings at the hushed level his voicebox was built for, and, as he snakes up the neck of his guitar, he gently shakes it to extract the precious reverberations; Bobby lays down a template of rhythm and chords, and then immediately begins to stray, playing ornamental variations on his own theme; Phil plays a minimalist counterpoint to Jerry; Brent tiptoes on his keys, filling in some of Bobby's chords here, dancing up the keyboard for a little color there; Billy and Mickey aren't Rhythm Devils—they're more like Rhythm Gnomes, playing not on thirty pieces but on six between them—two bongos, a snare, a bass, and a couple of cymbals.

Such is my disposition, so I'd probably listen often to *Reckoning* even if it were mediocre. The fact that it's a masterpiece—well, as Jerry says, that's pure gravy.

Reckoning is *my* PRIMAL DEAD, and I've found it a useful Dead *primer* as well. I'll confidently expose any open-eared, not-yet-Head to Jerry's sweet ache on "To Lay Me Down" and "Roses." To hear Jerry trail off the ends of each phrase on "Bird Song" ("All I know, she sang a little while and then flew off.") is to understand his vocal greatness; the same thing can be said about Jerry's leads on "Roses," Bobby's singing on "The Race Is On" and "Dark Hollow," and Brent's work on "China Doll" and "Bird Song."

The magic interaction is here, too. Take a trip to THE ZONE in the "Bird Song" and "Cassidy" jams. This is the Dead in all their mastery, with no straining, no vocal or instrumental clams, no miscues from bandmembers unable to hear each other. While "Dire Wolf," "It Must Have Been the Roses," "To Lay Me Down," "China Doll," "Cassidy," and "Bird Song" are a part of the regular electric lineup, none have ever felt more at home than on this album in this format.

Reckoning is also the Grateful Dead at their risky best, playing in an environment with complete exposure, total vulnerability. That they pull off such a venture makes it all the more satisfying. By the time the album closes with the folk anthem "Ripple," as each set did in the '80 run, we're completely under their spell, slowly nodding our heads to the hopeful "Let there be songs to fill the air" and the sweetly tragic *"If* I knew the way, I would take you home."

Since the album's release in '81, the existential question among die-hard *Reckoning* fans has been "Why don't the Dead play more acoustic sets?" Whatever the reason, let us be thankful that when they did it, they did it right, and that they released at least a portion for us to savor as we wait patiently for the next acoustic run.

RECONSTRUCTION • A Garcia-driven funk/R&B group with fiery horn arrangements that played shows in Bay Area clubs (and two Colorado gigs) from January through September of '79. Reconstruction was a further evolution of the LEGION OF MARY idea of stoking Garcia's exploratory leads with brass, and the band—featuring Merl Saunders on keyboards and vocals, Ron Stallings and Ed Neumeister on sax and trombone, John Kahn on bass, and Gaylord Birch on drums—was much appreciated for the jams that linked Merl-sung celebrations like "Doesn't It Make It Better?" with Garcia workouts like "Struggling Man" and "Dear Prudence."

RED ROCKS • A 9,000-seat amphitheater carved into the granite of the Rocky Mountains near Morrison, Colorado, outside of Denver. The Dead played twenty shows there from '78 to '87, many regarded as classic performances by tape collectors.

🍀 *Blair Jackson, editor of* The Golden Road, *on Red Rocks:*

There's no question that Red Rocks is what Carlos Castaneda referred to in his Don Juan books as a "power spot"—a place imbued with its own mystical energy, spiritually *alive*. It's easy to see why Native Americans gravitated to Red Rocks and considered it a holy place; and easy to understand why the white man would first seek to control it, and later legislate to protect it.

The view from the hillside where the amphitheater sits is magnificent—green and red under an endless azure sky as far as the eye can see. At night, Denver sparkles in the distance like a fantastical Oz. The V-shaped concert site is dwarfed by towering slabs of red rock on two sides, and the surrounding area—all rock and scrub grass and chaparral—looks like something out of a Zane Grey novel. The stage itself is built into the rocks. Getting up the hill from the dirt parking lots in the high altitude (6,000 feet) taxes even the heartiest souls. And there's the weather to deal with—it can be blisteringly hot in the daytime, followed by chilly winds and sudden, intense downpours.

Revered venues like Frost Amphitheater and Berkeley's Greek Theater possess a power and beauty unique to them, but Red Rocks's geological and anthropological history make it more than simply a place to see a show—it's like stepping into pre-history. In retrospect, it's amazing that it wasn't until 1978 that the Dead played there. The fact that the Dead played so many superb shows there only added to its built-in mystique. Among the songs debuted at Red Rocks were "I Need a Miracle," "Shakedown Street," "From the Heart of Me," "Stagger Lee," "If I Had the World to Give" (all '78); "Dear Mr. Fantasy" ('84); the "Hey Jude" coda ('85); and "Knockin' on Heaven's Door" (*sans* Dylan, '87).

Not surprisingly, Red Rocks became one of the Dead world's most renowned pilgrimage spots, and ultimately that proved to be its undoing. By the mid-'80s, thousands of ticketless Heads swarmed over the area around the amphitheater, overrunning the tiny town of Morrison every time the Dead came through. (The Dead's chilly relationship with Denver promoter Barry Fey didn't help matters either.) The Dead haven't played Red Rocks since 1987, but it will always hold a special place in the hearts of Deadheads who were fortunate enough to see a show there. When the lighting was just right, and the sound of the drums would bounce off those rocks, and the puffy clouds over Denver turned silver in an indigo sky . . . well, you had to be there.

REENTRY • The difficult period of transition back to the straight world after ecstatic experiences in Deadland. The term was used as early as '66, on a poster for the Acid Test at San Francisco State.

Many Heads speak of a rough week or so after a run or tour, missing their show buddies, feeling exiled from the place where "magic happens," JONESIN' for the live experience of the music. Tapes help. *See* PEAK.

🎬 *Tony Beers, poet, on going back:*

I get very down on the last show of the tour because I have to face reality, that life is not a Dead show. A lot of times it means schmoozing the boss—I left for three days, and that was two weeks ago. But I always had a job to come back to in Washington. That worked well for a long time, being a bicycle courier and a Deadhead. One company would always take me back.

It's like the worst stormy Monday of your life in quadruple. Even if you don't tour, you're pretty burnt out. Shows are a drug, and afterwards you have a hangover.

REFORMED DEADHEAD • A euphemism for the Head who's become burned out and has traded in touring and the hard-core life for a more rooted existence. Any close-knit subculture is bound to feel claustrophobic to some after a while, and as newbies get their feet wet, some show vets abandon the scene for dinner jazz, Pacifica radio news, and helping to change the world.

🎬 *Scott Meltsner, North Carolinian playwright, on "graduating" from the scene:*

You can't keep touring forever. You're not living your own trip. You can live the band's trip for a while, and feed off that good energy, but you have to fulfill yourself. That scene fit perfectly into a period of my life. You have your time in the womb—safe and secure—and you have your mission, which is to get from show to show, and make sure you have enough money. But there's a whole other world out there for me, and there's important work to do. I'd call that *graduating.*

It's all about the bonds and friendships you make—that's what people get hooked into. Making deep connections with people on a spiritual level. It's a very safe place—you feel very loved, and you feel like you're all in it together. The experience of being human is very isolating, and that's scary to people. Being a Deadhead is a tribal way of living. Everybody has to cope. Everybody is responsible for everybody else.

My old tour friends and I call ourselves a family now, and we're trying to get together and have the same feeling without the Dead. They gave us a place to go and focal point for our energies, but now we do it without them.

If you can stay in that bubble and make it work, more power to you, but for me there's a world of intense problems that you can't ignore. Someone said that to me a long time ago, and it's weird that I'm saying it now. I guess priorities change as you get older.

I don't regret having been in that bubble. It's a part of me. It's a place I can still go to in my mind.

RELIX • If *The Golden Road* is the quintessential "inside" journal for West Coast Heads and *Dupree's* the spiritual conscience of the scene, the bimonthly Brooklyn-based magazine *Relix* is a voice from the East Coast Dead Belt. Its subtitle, "music for the mind," is a statement of conviction that the music produced in the Bay Area in the late '60s was the most "heady" music ever played, a legacy that reached beyond its place and time.

Relix was born in 1974 as *Dead Relix*, edited by pioneer tapers Les Kippel and Jerry Moore. The grassroots aesthetic of *Relix* came out of the early tape-trading underground courtesy of Moore and Kippel, who recorded his second show at the Fillmore East in July '70 with a one-dollar microphone. "I gave the deck to my friends sitting in the front row. All you hear on the tape is my friends saying, 'Hey man, pass the Kool-Aid,'" recalls Kippel. "It got to the point where I had thirteen tape machines running at one time in my house, so we started a magazine that featured articles on equipment, how to smuggle recorders into shows, and lists of good and bad traders."

Kippel and his friends also founded the first Grateful Dead Tape Exchange, a lo-tech precursor of the tape TREES flourishing on the Net. After a few skirmishes with the Dead crew, and one incident in a hotel room where the tapers, spinning madly, were interrupted by an angry BEAR, *Relix* found its niche publishing articles on the shows, favorite tapes, interviews, tour stories, and nostalgic countercultural history and reminiscences. The letters column, and the tapers' and personals ads at the back of the book, have always been a lot of what *Relix* is about: Deadheads seeking community in shared love of the music.

The vision of the magazine strayed a bit during the Reagan Era, but when spreads on Ozzy Osbourne and Joan Jett raised ire, *Relix* returned to its original focus on the Dead, the New

Riders, Jefferson Airplane, Hot Tuna, the Allman Brothers, Commander Cody, and related "Bay Rock" groups. Since the H.O.R.D.E. bands have been taken to the hearts of *Relix* 's readership as keepers of a similar flame, the magazine now also runs features on Phish, Widespread Panic, Blues Traveler, and other psychedelic dharma-heirs. Toni Brown, the editor since 1979, has enlarged the scope of *Relix* to include environmental concerns and social issues like the CARRIER WEIGHT LAW controversy, and Kippel now markets a line of books and CDs called Relix International. *See also* TREES AND VINES.

REPEATS • " 'Corrina' —*again?*" The Dead, by drawing from an active repertoire of over 125 songs, encourages its audience to hear each night as a unique event, and part of what gives a RUN the sense of a tale unfolding over several nights is the lack of repeat performances.

Some Heads become irate when a song is performed more than once in a run. Bob Bralove dismisses the notion that repeats are a violation of unspoken rules governing the feel of a run. "This band doesn't play by any rules," he says. "That's why they're the Grateful Dead." Many Heads would disagree—figuring out the unwritten "rules" of how the band does what it does is part of what being a Deadhead is about.

Some Heads claim that the Dead play more repeats than they used to, but in 1976, the Dead played "Samson and Delilah" on thirty-eight nights of a forty-show tour. *See also* PICKY DEADHEADS; THE ROTATION.

RETREADING ☜ • Taping over a previously recorded tape, presumably one of lower quality. This necessitates putting adhesive tape over the popped "tabs" to unlock the safety catch built into tape decks (*see* POP THE TABS). The slight increase in tape hiss compared to recording on virgin tape means that the pickiest traders will not do this, and prefer not to get retreads in trade.

REVIVAL • When the band plays a tune it hasn't played for several years; also called "resurrection" and "bringing the song back." At Hampton Coliseum on 3/20/86, when the band revived "Box of Rain" for the first time in 777 shows (7/28/73), recalls Charley Wilkins, "I thought the roof was going to blow off." That was nothing, however, compared to the thunder in the same room three years later, when (on 10/9/89) the band woke "Dark Star" from a five-year slumber, and a roaring soared to the rafters that didn't quit until after the first verse.

Over the years, a number of songs have been the object of concerted lobbying for revival, such as the "Cosmic Charlie Campaign" in the mid-'80s. When Eileen Law of THE OFFICE asked Garcia to bring back "Cosmic Charlie," he replied, "Do you know how hard it is to *breathe* between those lyrics?"

REX FOUNDATION • The Dead's in-house charitable foundation, named after deceased roadie Donald "Rex" Jackson, and piloted by a board of directors that includes Garcia, Weir, Hart, roadie Ram Rod, Bill Walton, and manager Danny Rifkin.

Since its establishment in 1983, the Dead have supported the foundation with an annual series of concerts—tickets to which can be written off by Heads as tax-deductible donations. Rex distributes nearly a million dollars each year to mostly small, "close to the bone, low-profile, direct-action" organizations, as Garcia puts it, that address social concerns like AIDS, deforestation, the homeless, concerns of Native Americans, and so on. At Lesh's behest, Rex has also over the years given a number of substantial grants to Ireland's Robert Simpson, and to other avant-garde British composers. Rex grants are generally $10,000 or smaller, and are often granted with no advance notice. "They like to take the Lone Ranger approach," explains GD publicist Dennis McNally. "They jump in, give some money, and they're gone. And people say, 'Who was that?'"

The Dead have a distinguished history of philanthropy that predates Rex. "It's always been our feeling," Weir explains, "that if you're doing well—if you get some—that you give some back. Part of working for a living is working for a world to live in." During their first two decades of philanthropy, McNally explains, the band was never quite satisfied with the results. So they formed their own. "That's the trend in virtually every aspect of their lives," says McNally. "They don't like the way things are run—merchandising, tickets, etc.—so they do it themselves." Another Dead-related group, the Further Foundation, was started by Weir as a way of focusing specifically on the needs of the poor and homeless, with a special emphasis on children. Weir is also involved in the SEVA Foundation, a global health care agency primarily concerned with protecting and restoring sight in underdeveloped countries.

H.E.A.R. (Hearing Education and Awareness for Rockers), another organization with ties to the Dead, is a San Francisco–based outfit that helps educate rock audiences about performance-related hearing loss. Hart, Dan Healy, and *Grateful Dead Hour* host David Gans sit on the board. *See also* SEVA.

🦞 *Bill Graham on the Dead's charitable ways:*

All these years, very quietly, the Dead have probably done more benefits for more varied causes than anyone. There are artists like Graham Nash, Jackson Browne, and Harry Chapin who've helped different causes over the years. But when you get down to the basic simplicity of humanistic tendencies, the Dead were alway there, whether it was voter registration, or a nursery school, a recreation center in Mill Valley, or when the kids were getting busted in the Haight in the late '60s. Nobody has done more than the Dead.

It gets down to, "What do you do with the power you have? What do you do that you don't *have* to do?" The Dead did benefits when they *didn't* have the bread. That's a very significant point. If you asked me for a $500 donation in 1968 when I was close to bankruptcy, it would have been like, "Wait a minute, I have to look after my ass." I know very well how tough things were for the Dead in the early days, and yet they shared when they didn't have that much to share. I just wish there was some way for them to be acknowledged in society at large. Just so the record is set straight.

RHYTHM DEVILS • 1. The term used by the bandmembers for DRUMS, adopted by tape traders in the late '70s for use on setlists and tape covers.

2. The Rhythm Devils were also a recording and performing ensemble consisting of Hart, Kreutzmann, and Lesh, supplemented by other heavyweight percussion demons like Airto, Vince Delgado, Zakir Hussain, vocalist Flora Purim, and various drummers from the Ali Akbar College of Music in San Rafael. They recorded a soundtrack for Coppola's *Apocalypse*

Now (only part of it was used in the film), released in 1979 as *The Rhythm Devils Play River Music.*

The Rhythm Devils played two notable shows at the Marin Veterans' Auditorium in February of '81, mixed in quad. After the show on 2/13—during which Hart and Kreutzmann and two other drummers played the miked floor of the stage, and Lesh soloed by rubbing two basses together—the audience ran up to the edge of the stage and began clapping in complex polyrhythms that lasted for twenty minutes after the show was over. *See also* THE BEAM; THE BEAST; DRUMS.

RIPE • Used to describe a Deadhead-waiting-to-happen: the college freshman who's just picked up "Howl"; the hip kindergarten teacher next door tired of listening to her boyfriend's copy of "Dark Side of the Moon"; or the guy in AP physics who's obsessed with Dungeons & Dragons and *Star Trek: TNG*, thinks the latest hair-farmer band on MTV is too lame for words, and peeks at the older kids tossing a footbag around at lunch with a mixture of fascination and envy.

Along with *The Electric Kool-Aid Acid Test* and *Playing in the Band*, certain *non*-Dead books can serve as catalysts for Deadheads-waiting-to-happen to become happening Deadheads, stepping-stones to climbing on the bus. *See* MISFIT POWER; ON THE BUS.

ROAD BURN • Hair matted, face red, beard and legs unshorn—the stripes of hard tour. "Road burn on certain individuals breeds an almost pious or snobby attitude," explains Nethead Scott Spaid, "since they feel they have gone through a rite of passage to be where they are with the Dead. The Dead scene is the only time I have observed people sharing a common thread of poverty and enjoying it."

ROCK AND ROLL PICASSO • What Hunter once called Bob Dylan, because he brought a "literate authority" to rock and roll.

Much to Hunter's delight, Dylan ended up recording two Hunter tunes for his *Down in the Groove* album. "He just flipped through the songbook that was sitting there at Front Street," Hunter told David Gans in 1988. "He liked these tunes, put them in his pocket, and went off. First time I met him, he said, 'Eh, I just recorded two of your tunes.' I said, 'Neat!'"

"He didn't even ask first?" Gans asked Hunter.

"Bob Dylan *doesn't* have to *ask* a lyricist if he can do his tunes! Come on, man! I've got to say this for the record: You've got your Grammies, you've got your Bammies, and you've got your Rock & Roll Hall of Fame—but as far as I'm concerned, Bob Dylan has done two of my songs, and those other things sound far away, distant, and not very interesting."

ROCK MED • Short for "Rock Medicine," the mobile emergency care clinic which has been providing valuable medical care at Dead shows and other West Coast rock concerts, community events, and festivals for twenty years. "We're like the Deadheads' HMO," says Rock Med's director, Glenn "Raz" Raswyck. The goal of Rock Med, as stated by founding director Skip Gay, is to "take care of the individual, and return him to his friends or family," and to avoid "the necessity of either hospitalization or getting involved with the law." All of the doctors, nurses, paramedics, and staff at Rock Med—outside of the director—contribute their expertise for no pay.

Rock Med was founded in 1972 by folks at the Haight Ashbury Free Clinic, at the behest of Bill Graham, who had seen too many medical needs at Woodstock, and elsewhere, go untreated. "Bill knew that people were going to do what they wanted to do, and you'd better be prepared for it," explains Raswyck. "He felt a moral obligation to be helpful, but also nonjudgmental. At the same time, Bill wanted to put in a safety net, before Heads wound up in local hospitals or jails. As a businessman, he knew when the jails started filling up, officials would start saying, 'You can't do this anymore.'"

On average, Raswyck says, Rock Med cares for seventy or eighty Heads per show, sixty of whom are there for minor matters—cut feet, heat exhaustion, headaches, and so on—but one of Rock Med's areas of expertise is in helping Heads navigate difficult trips: "Intense Psychedelic Reactions." The basic tenets of Rock Med-style "talkdown" are, says Raswyck: "Number one, 'You're OK.' Number two, 'You're in a safe place.' And number three, 'No, we're not going to tell your mom.' " The volunteers are most interested in preventing needlessly dire situations from occurring in the first place. Their brochure advises all Heads to eat nutritiously before shows, and to make sure to drink plenty of nonsugary, nonalcoholic liquids during their journey. And try not to overindulge.

"Abuse," says Raswyck, "gives fun a bad name."

Rock Med lingo:

dugout — The first-aid station located close to the main hall.

field teams — Medics in uniform visibly circulating through the crowd so that they can be flagged down if necessary.

the pit crew — Three-person medic team positioned on the floor near each side of the stage, available for quick aid to overheated or hyperventilating Heads.

space station — The intake room where talkdown happens.

talkdown — Assistance for Heads having difficulty navigating in psychedelic space. "The art of talkdown," explains Steve Anderson in the Rock Med Training Guide, "is the interplay of knowledge, intuition and experience of the guide, varying with individuals, circumstances, substances, and resources available. A tripper is an Id with feet. He has no rules (Superego) or reason (Ego). He is his own universe. We become the rules, and provide an 'alternative ego' until those functions of his character can reassert their own control."

THE ROLL • The thunderous bass intro played by Phil Lesh to kick off "The Other One." The roll has disappeared for years at a time, and its resurrection is always a cause for celebration, as in the titanic crescendo, following space, at Frost Amphitheater on 5/7/89.

ROSEBUD • *See* THE WOLF.

THE ROTATION • The repertoire of songs currently being played by the band. At any given time, there are roughly about 100–125 songs that the band is choosing from at shows, out of over 400 that they have played at one time or another in their career. A Head might say, "We're about due in the rotation for a 'Terrapin,' " meaning that the song is active, but hasn't been played in the last two nights or so.

Certain staples — like "Playin' in the Band" — are always in the rotation. "The Other One" is a warhorse that has stayed in rotation since 11/11/67. "I Know You Rider" and "Morning Dew" have likewise been part of shows since the very early days.

RUN • Several consecutive shows at the same venue. "The Madison Square Garden run in '90 was tasty."

RUNNERS • Heads who go into a general admission venue at the head of the line, unencumbered by backpacks, to stake out the best seats and prime areas of the floor for others in their group. Short, wiry people make the best runners.

The sturdy Heads to the rear, bearing the necessary burden of blankets, water bottles, taping equipment, and food are sometimes referred to affectionately as "mules." *See* LINE DONKEYS; LINE DUTY.

SACRAMENTS • Like members of the Native American Church, some Heads prefer not to call marijuana and psychedelics "drugs," with that term's connotations of illness, abuse, and law enforcement. They prefer the word "sacraments," appropriate to the respect and gravity with which they use these substances. *See* LSD; PSYCHEDELICS.

SANDWICH • As in "musical sandwich," in which the band will play the first part of one tune, drift into another, then maybe another, and eventually return to continue, or reprise, the original. "Some of our songs are meant to be opened up," says Garcia. "They're kind of like loose-leaf files—you open 'em up and stick things in them. They're arranged that way."

"Dark Star" and "Playin' in the Band" are two of the loosest, leafiest of them all, and "Uncle John's Band"—with its driving exploratory jam between the verses—also lends itself to this form of set-building. On 3/23/74, for instance, at the Cow Palace in San Francisco, the band put together a double-decker, opening up the second set with "Playin' in the Band"→"Uncle John's Band"→"Morning Dew"→"Uncle John's" reprise→"Playin'" reprise. The band is so fond of using the parts of "Playin'" as flexible modules, in fact, that "Playin' sandwiches" have been known to stretch them out over entire runs. Some Deadheads joke about an "11-year 'Playin'" that started sometime in '73 where they played only the first part, and ending in Augusta, Maine, in 1984, where they played only the reprise.

🦋 *Elvis Costello on the legacy of the Dead's segues:*

On *Deadicated* [a Dead tribute album, on which he sings "Ship of Fools"], I had originally intended to do "It Must Have Been the Roses" *and* "Ship of Fools," one right into the other, in the spirit of the way they do it. As far as I know, the Dead were the first rock band to ever do that. It's very common in modern rock to have interpolated songs. I suppose that the Dead got it from jazz, but when I first heard them do that, I thought they'd invented it. I've done it throughout my career, and that's probably where I got the notion that it was acceptable.

SCALPERS • Those who purchase tickets for the express purpose of reselling them at a higher price.

As long as the Dead have been selling out shows, Deadheads—known for a willingness to travel great distances to get into a show—have been vulnerable to scalpers and counterfeiters. Heads have long held to an antiscalping ethic: Never sell an "extra" (ticket) for more than "face" (value). Heads have also generally been extremely reluctant to purchase tickets from non-Heads in the lot.

As the Dead's popularity skyrocketed in the late '80s, venerable parking lot ethics were strained by the multitudes of MIR-

ACLE SEEKERS. "As recently as four or five years ago," says Jon Bower, "you could trust most people selling tickets outside the show to not sell for more than face value. Nowadays, people don't think twice about paying fifty dollars for a ticket that's probably not even real." *See also* COUNTERFEIT TICKETS.

SCAMMING IN • 1. Sneaking into a show. Ticketless but resourceful Heads ("scamheads") have come up with hundreds of ways to enter venues, including counterfeiting tickets, jumping fences, "popping" the doors, impersonating arena security, delivering pizzas backstage, climbing in bathroom windows (a bathroom at Winterland was infamous for this), taping together ticket stubs into whole "tickets," and even forging LAMINATE passes.

A "gate rush" is a sort of scam *en masse,* where a sizable horde of ticketless fans overwhelms any physical barriers (and security personnel) and busts into the show. Gate rushes are not common, but they do happen, especially on the East Coast, where crowds are bigger and rowdier and tickets harder to come by.

2. The phrase is also used by F.O.B. tapers both audio and video, to describe smuggling their equipment into the venue. The phrase has passed into very general use among Heads to indicate the use of cunning to getting where one is officially forbidden to go. *See also* F.O.B.

♣ *Steve Marcus, of Grateful Dead Ticket Sales, on scamming in:*

The SPINNERS' big routine would be, they'd go into the show, collect the stubs from people inside the show, then one person would go back out, hand over a couple of hundred stubs, and they'd sit in a circle with a machine that would cut the ends of the tickets flat, and tape all the stubs together. I walked into a circle of about 150 people on New Year's Eve, and I was like, "What are you *doing?*" I walked away with a stack of "tickets" five inches high. The spinners are nice people. But they have a basic attitude that they should get in for free. I get in free now, but I work for the band. In October of 1982, I sat outside one of the shows at Frost Amphitheater, because I could not get a ticket. There were no tickets. I know what it's like to be outside a show. I've been there.

SEASTONES • 1. An album of electronic music, deeply in THE ZONE, released in October 1975, featuring computer music pioneer Ned Lagin, Lesh, Hart, Garcia, David Crosby, Grace Slick, David Freiberg, and Spencer Dryden. (The vocalists spoke "protolanguage," like shards of poetry.) Various smaller groupings of this band played several shows in the Bay Area in '74 — deep-space patrols of the PLANET EARTH ROCK & ROLL ORCHESTRA. In 1991, Rykodisc rereleased the album, with another, leaner version of the piece, from December 1975.

2. A series of performances by Lesh and Lagin — also called "Warp Ten" — at twenty-three Dead shows from 6/23/74 and 10/20/74. The performances at shows, often beginning during the break with the stage lights off, were not well understood by the audience. On 9/14/74, an impatient audience at the Olympiahalle in Munich whistled as a sign of displeasure, and a tape from Winterland on 10/14/74 features someone in the audience yelling "He-e-elllllp!"

SEAT SURFING 📖 • Burying one's ticket stub deep in one's pants pocket, and floating from unoccupied seat to unoccupied seat, each closer to the stage than the last. While it appears anarchic to the ushers, seat surfing is actually a team sport, with thousands playing at the same time. *See* STUBBING DOWN; SWIMMING.

THE SECOND SET • The Main Event. The portion of the show following the break.

A first song leads, ideally without pause, into several other songs linked by highly developed improvisations; the guitarists and keyboard player exit the stage, and the drummers play together (DRUMS); the guitarists and keyboardist return for an exploratory jam by everyone but the drummers (SPACE); the drummers return, and the entire band plays three or four more songs (*see* THE JERRY BALLAD SLOT), often finishing the set with a rager like "Good Lovin'" or "Turn On Your Lovelight"; followed, after a pause, by the ENCORE. (This is a rough map of a form that has evolved gradually over the years, especially since '77 or so.)

The soul of a second set is improvisation. What makes a second set so exciting for Heads is that the band will play to its limits, and build of songs and improvised bridges a new road *somewhere*, if only to SPACE and back. It's the raw act of discovery—for both audience and band—that makes second sets electric.

"Our second half has a shape which is inspired by the psychedelic experience," says Garcia. "It's like a wave form—it has a rise. It's taking chances, and going all to pieces, and coming back, and reassembling. You don't despair about letting yourself go to pieces—you just let it go."

For all the anticipation that leads up to the moment the band walks onstage, the audience is often respectfully quiet. "Scarlet Begonias" or "China Cat Sunflower" or another song announces a groove; forms are established, stretched to their limits or abandoned; new forms arise. When the mojo is working, and the X-FACTOR is in effect, songs that have been played hundreds of times shine as if newly created, and the sequence of songs and jams forms a narrative that touches every human emotion.

The second set is the archetype of Grateful Dead music—a foray into "infinite frontiers," as Blair Jackson put it, by a group musical mind cultivated by playing together for decades, able to draw from many traditions of world music: R&B, jazz, the blues, electronic music, percussion-based tribal musics, and good old American rock and roll, to create something—sometimes only a moment—that is new and alive.

♣ *John Merola, veteran of over five hundred shows, on the second set:*

The Dead weave a cloth of music where there are no holes. The music moves in an upward spiral, growing higher and richer like a form in nature, the way plants grow in spiral shapes so each leaf can catch the most sunlight and nourishment. Listening to the Dead jam, I find inner peace.

SESH • To give without expectation of immediate compensation, as in, "Could you sesh me that crispy board of Harpur '70?" From "session," a gathering of potsmokers. Similar to KICK DOWN. "Sesh me, sesh me, why don't you Phil Lesh me?"

SET BREAK • The intermission between sets. Set break is a time for socializing, fine-tuning setlists, and meeting friends to share the second set with. The hallways fill up with people in various altered states, and circles form for Heads who want to share pipes, backrubs, or conversation (often about the first set). Long lines form in front of the women's bathrooms, and women frequently infiltrate the men's rooms in pairs. Some Heads rest on their backs near the cool of doorways to the outside, while others buy stadium food or share elaborate meals that they have brought in. WHARF RATS hold meetings for sober Heads during the set break, and the DRUM CIRCLES can reach ecstatic peaks as the drumming and chants get louder and louder as the second set nears. *See also* HALFTIME.

SETLIST SHORTHAND 📔 • Abbreviated song titles used on setlists and J-CARDS. Long titles are shrunk to initials ("Goin' Down the Road Feelin' Bad" becomes "GDTRFB"; "Beat It on Down the Line" becomes "BIODTL"), while familiar song-pairings are condensed and joined by an arrow: "Scarlet Begonias"→"Fire on the Mountain" is known commonly as "Scarlet→Fire"; "China→Rider" is "China Cat Sunflower" followed by "I Know You Rider." (The "→" is silent.)

Song titles on setlists get abbreviated because the lists are scribbled in the dark, on tiny pieces of paper, by people who don't want to stop dancing long enough to inscribe " 'Throwin' Stones' followed by 'Not Fade Away' with a jam between them." But the condensation serves another purpose—the use of shorthand and jargon lets you know who is a Deadhead and who isn't, as linguist Natalie Dollar points out in her study of Deadhead speech patterns. It is not difficult to spot novice Heads by their not-yet-compacted litanies of tunes played.

Other common recombinant titles include: "HelpSlipFrank" or "Helpknot" for "Help on the Way"→"Slipknot!"→"Franklin's Tower"; "Estimated→Eyes" for "Estimated Prophet"→ "Eyes of the World"; and "Sailor→Saint" for "Lost Sailor" →"Saint of Circumstance." *See* GOING INTO, COMING OUT OF.

A setlist shorthand primer:

ABBREVIATIONS

BIODTL: "Beat It on Down the Line"

Box: "Box of Rain"

BR × R: "Big Railroad Blues"

BTW: "Black-Throated Wind"

FOTD: "Friend of the Devil"

GDTRFB: "Goin' Down the Road Feelin' Bad"

JBG: "Johnny B. Goode"

LLR: "Looks Like Rain"

LTGTR: "Let the Good Times Roll"

MSWS: "Man Smart, Woman Smarter"

NFA: "Not Fade Away"

Playin' or PITB: "Playing in the Band"

SOTM: "Standing on the Moon"

TLEO: "They Love Each Other"

Touch "A Touch of Grey"

UJB: "Uncle John's Band"

CONDENSED SONG PAIRINGS

Estimated→Eyes: "Estimated Prophet" into "Eyes of the World"

Sailor→Saint: "Lost Sailor" into "Saint of Circumstance"

China→Rider: "China Cat Sunflower" into "I Know You Rider"

Help→Slip→Frank: "Help on the Way" into "Slipknot!" into "Franklin's Tower"

Scarlet→Fire: "Scarlet Begonias" into "Fire on the Mountain"

Playin→Uncle John's: "Playing in the Band" into "Uncle John's Band"

Throwin'→Not Fade: "Throwin' Stones" into "Not Fade Away"

SETLISTS • A record of the songs the band played on a particular evening, in order, written in notebooks—or onto ticket stubs, matchbook covers, grocery receipts, and hands—during the music, and just after the end of sets.

The lists are written while the show is under way because (a) many Heads enjoy perusing the construction of the show as it occurs, and (b) it's the rare Head who can reliably memorize more than a few songs at once (though some, miraculously, remember *everything* about *every* show). Later, the lists are more legibly transcribed into TOURBOOKS and onto hard drives, read over the phone, and emailed around the world for absentees to ponder the most recent addition to band history.

SEVA • A foundation for compassionate social action founded in 1978 by Dr. Lawrence Brilliant, Dr. Girija Brilliant, Ram Dass, WAVY GRAVY and others, to assist communities in need of health and social services. *Seva* means "service" in Sanskrit.

In June '84, the Dead played a benefit for SEVA in Toronto, and bandmembers have appeared at many other SEVA events. "The Dead's management office has been involved in almost every event we've done," says Executive Director Amy Somers. "They've donated amazing amounts of time and other resources to us." Along with Greenpeace and other charitable organizations, SEVA is granted a table at Dead shows, so that they may educate Heads during the set break.

In its first fifteen years, SEVA's efforts focused on the curing of blindness in the Third World, spending nearly $25 million on cataract operations, and the construction of eye clinics in Nepal and elsewhere. Having nearly achieved their goal of having the clinics become self-sustaining, the organization has diversified its resources, and is presently involved in Native American health concerns, Guatemalan and Mexican refugee assistance, and developing alternatives to incarceration with the warden of San Quentin prison.

SHAKEDOWN STREET • Album #15, released in November 1978. The album was produced by Lowell George, the late witty bottleneck-guitar genius of Little Feat. *Shakedown Street* features studio versions of "Fire on the Mountain," "I Need a Miracle," and the title track. The anticipated collaborative fire between band and producer was damped by George's "health problems" (*see* WHITE POWDERS), but the guitars have an *etched* quality that still sounds bright, and the versions of "Fire on the Mountain" and "Good Lovin'" simmer on precision and percussion. There is a haunting drummer's desert groove before "Fire on the Mountain" called "Serengetti."

♣ *Steve Silberman on Shakedown Street:*

I remember the night the college radio d.j. announced he'd gotten an advance copy of *Shakedown Street.* I packed my pipe, knowing that I was going to have only one chance to hear the new Dead album for the first time.

I liked the snap of the drums in "Good Lovin' "—an old friend in a new zoot suit saying that things were not what they used to be, but this is how they *are.* I remember the excitement of hearing Garcia start cooking in the middle of "France"—as if they were going into "Uncle John's Band"—but it faded out. A long silence followed.

Then those first chords of "Shakedown"—the "fate" chords—rang in my room. It was an announcement of a new sensibility: urbane, and slightly jaded, until you noticed the chorus was about rediscovering wonder. (Years later, when the song came into its own in thunderdomes like Madison Square Garden, the riff gave Garcia a showcase for funk so nasty it was *promiscuous,* with its repeated dare: *"Don't tell me . . . Don't tell me . . .* BLAM," while Lesh carpet-bombed the Phil Zone.)

Then word came from Chicago that the Dead had set up acoustic in a student lounge at Loyola, and played "Whinin' Boy Blues" and "Big Boy Pete." The tourheads pulled into Oberlin two days after that, and on 11/20/78, about forty of us drove up to Cleveland, chewing that clean Red Dragon blotter.

The Cleveland Music Hall was the kind of place that was so intimate you didn't want to talk, because you'd be afraid the band would hear what you were saying.

During the break, the drummers strolled out, and half the people in the room thought the band was still tuning by the time Garcia had gone off into that deep, deep landscape that is so much a part of him, that to us will always be home. The songs—"Jack-a-Roe," "Playin'," "Shakedown"—surfaced and submerged back into that river of jamming in which songs are islands. We swam. After "Shakedown," Garcia began singing about loving someone so much you wanted to give them the world, the song we were calling "Serenade"—"If I Had the World to Give." Weir rang keening tones with his slide, and the two guitarists began coiling over and over around that elegiac descension, sad sirens from the Zone.

The band slipped seamlessly back into "Playin'." The moment had been made.

"SHIT HAPPENS" • An outtake from the *Built to Last* sessions that may have become an anthem of Deadhead fraternities (*see* HOUSE OF JERRY), but never made it out of the studio. A studio rehearsal tape has a take of "Shit Happens" between a slow, fragile version of "Blow Away" and a drum-machine-driven "Foolish Heart." The song's chorus, "Shit happens—that's all we know! Shit happens, and awa-a-yy we go . . . ," glides on an irresistible hook, and verses are swapped by Weir, Mydland, and Lesh, who sings in a barbershop basso.

SHOW BLANKET • Blankets used to mark off turf and increase comfort at general admission shows. The ideal show blanket is a little tattered, and soft on the soles of dancing feet. Some Heads find that taping down the edges of their blankets prevents others from crowding in the cracks.

SHOWPACK • The small fannypack used to carry the minimum supplies needed during or immediately after a show into the venue: keys, a notebook and pen for the setlist, a pipe and a lighter, a stash, some throat lozenges, and enough money to get home. "I've lost so much stuff over the years at Dead shows," says Glen Goldstein, "that I've learned to strip down to the bare essentials before I go in: car keys, one piece of photo ID—in case they find me wandering through the Mojave with a silly grin on my face—and a ten-dollar bill for emergencies." Also called a "tourpack."

Larger backpacks can also accommodate water bottles, fresh fruit and other nourishments, books and TOURBOOKS, show blankets, and recording equipment (*see* GETTING YOUR DECK IN). *See also* RUNNERS.

SHROOMS • Psilocybin mushrooms. Psilocybin is a PSYCHEDELIC that occurs in nature, producing many of the same effects as LSD, but with a quicker onset (20–30 minutes) and a shorter duration (4–6 hours). Colors and sounds—including music—are intensified, strong emotions may arise, and there may be some stomach discomfort. Abstract geometrical forms and vistas may be seen with the eyes closed or in darkness. Psilocybin mushrooms are used by many peoples of the world in ritual settings.

Psilocybin mushrooms grow wild in many areas of the country, particularly the Pacific Northwest, where whole fields of tiny, potent "Liberty Caps" sprout after rains, but "shrooms" did not become widespread at shows until the late '70s, when methods of indoor cultivation became standardized.

SHUT OUT • To not get tickets to a show or run, either through mail order or by any other means.

SIX PACK • A short six-song first set.

SIX-UP! • A cry warning of the presence of police or "copyright cops," assigned to walk through the parking lot to look for t-shirts or other merchandise that use Grateful Dead trademark imagery—like STEALIES—without a licensing agreement with Grateful Dead Mercantile. *"Six up!* Roll it up!" is what vendors say to help one another avoid getting "popped" (having their merchandise confiscated or being ejected from the lot).

SIXTIES MYTH #73 • In March of '84, *National Lampoon* ran this excerpt from a "memoir" by Vinnie DeMano, debunking "Sixties Myth #73—the coolness of the Grateful Dead":

> I handed Garcia the hit of acid. He stared at it for a while and then asked, "What the hell is this stuff?"
>
> "Acid, man," I responded. "You know, LSD."
>
> He laughed at me and threw the tab over his shoulder. "Hell's bells, sailor, you think we take that shit? We got a band to run here, and I've got a nine thirty appointment with my accountant tomorrow morning. Get me a Bromo, fast."

SKULL AND ROSES (SKULL FUCK) • Album #7, released in October 1971.

While the official title of this album—the band's first gold record—is *Grateful Dead Live,* that name has never been used by the band or Heads. Instead, two nicknames prevail. The first, *Skull and Roses,* is a reference to the Mouse/Kelley cover art; the second, *Skull Fuck,* was the album's working title, nixed by

Warner Bros. as unmarketable. Many members of the organization, along with countless Heads and *DeadBase,* still refer to it as *Skull Fuck.*

The skull-and-roses image was originally a black-and-white illustration by Edmund Sullivan which appeared in a nineteenth-century edition of *The Rubáiyát of Omar Khayyám.* Artists Alton Kelley and Stanley Mouse were smoking pot in a converted firehouse, with the old horse troughs intact, on Henry Street in San Francisco when Kelley discovered the original illustration, realizing it was the perfect icon for the recently renamed Warlocks. The image, with added lettering and color, was used shortly thereafter on posters for a show at the Avalon Ballroom. "Everybody loved the image," recalls Kelley. " 'At least you spelled our name right,' the band said." (An earlier poster had advertised the "Greatful Dead.") The cover of this album also contained an effort to establish communication between the band and its fans. *See* DEAD FREAKS UNITE!

🍀 *John Scott, editor of* DeadBase, *on* **Skull Fuck:**

I can think of no other album that had a greater impact on my musical evolution than *Skull Fuck.* It was pivotal in my development not only as a Deadhead, but as a fan of live music. Once upon a time, I believed that studio albums were inherently superior, cleaner and more carefully considered, showcasing songs at their best. While *Workingman's Dead* and *American Beauty* were near the top of my most-played list, I didn't understand *Live/Dead. Skull Fuck,* a collection of accessible songs, revealed to me the power of live music. I will always be grateful.

Skull Fuck showcased songs that were not available on earlier albums (except for "The Other One"), capturing the best of what the band was doing in 1971. It is noteworthy that nearly every song included continues to be a staple of the Dead's repertoire more than twenty years later. Here were the vinyl premieres of classics such as "Bertha," "Playin' in the Band," and "Wharf Rat," and of the cover standards "Me & My Uncle," "Not Fade Away," and "Goin' Down the Road Feelin' Bad." My only second-guessing of the selection is that in a year of exceptional performances by Pigpen, only one of his songs is included.

Sandwiched between two years boasting better improvisation, '71 saw the Dead investigating a marriage of folk and rock. It was a year better known for raging "Not Fade Away"→"GDTRFB" combos than for long, intricate "Dark Stars." The album begins with "Bertha," an infectious debut. "Playin' " is short, but hints at more involved versions to come, and "Wharf Rat," an empathetic anthem for the downtrodden, sealed my Deadhead fate.

The centerpiece of the album, however, is "The Other One." I was surprised, even disappointed, to find only one song on side three, but on listening to it, I experienced my first musical epiphany. With "Cryptical" excised, the recording begins with a drum solo, then travels a rollercoaster ride through verses, jams, and space as the song stretches to an impressive eighteen minutes, a powerful reminder that extended improvisations were not neglected entirely in 1971.

My newfound appreciation for live music was solidified by the seamless transition from "Not Fade Away" into "Goin' Down the Road." Until Walkmans were outlawed on the slopes, this jam was my music of choice for skiing bumps. With this combination, the Dead taught me to ski in the moment (ski here now), and revealed to me the magic and freedom inherent in live music.

"SLIPKNOT!" • One of the most demanding and satisfying compositions in the band's music, a sequence of complex unison passages and dramatic scales used as a transition between "Help on the Way" and "Franklin's Tower," credited on *Blues for Allah* to the entire band. "Slipknot!" is an instrumental, and Heads have speculated that the title may refer to the knottily precise unison passages, but the original source may be this verse written by Hunter in the studio during the sessions: "beautiful lie/you can pray/you can pay/till you're buried alive—/blackmailer blues/everyone in the room owns a part of the noose—/slipknot jig slipknot jig slipknot jig/did someone say—help on the way—/well I know—yeah I do—/that there's help on the way." *See* DOORWAYS AND SPLICES.

SMALL HALLS • Venues more intimate than, say, a hockey rink or a 75,000-seat football stadium. Until the late '80s, the Dead had a distinguished history of playing smaller venues like the Berkeley Community Theater and Radio City Music Hall, even though they often could have made more money playing the larger arenas: halls like the moorish, atmospheric Fox Theaters in St. Louis and Atlanta, the Starlight in

Kansas City, the Stanley Theaters of Pittsburgh and Jersey City, Boston's Music Hall, and New York's Beacon Theater, built with superb acoustics in mind, as opposed to airplane hangars, erected for the sake of most seats having a clear sight line to the ice. *See* FANTASY VENUES; MEGA-DEAD PERIOD.

🍀 *John "Tex" Coate, on seeing Garcia at the Family Dog at the Great Highway in San Francisco:*

I loved that venue—it was the best of them all. That's where the Dead would float their little experimental things: Bobby Ace and the Cards from the Bottom of the Deck, Mickey Hart and the Hartbeats. One time I was there, and I was quite wrecked, and I was standing five feet away from Garcia. The stage was just a riser that went up one foot. It was a New Riders' gig, before the first tour, and Jerry was practicing the pedal steel. He played that thing beautifully, soaring out with this really cool music. My eyes were closed, and my head was weaving back and forth. Then he cut in this flanger that gave the music this choked-out gravelly tone. It put my body into shock, and my dancing got totally tweaked. Jerry looked up and went 'Oh, *sorry!*' and turned it off. That's how down-home things were in those days.

THE SOUNDBOARD • The main control center for the sound system and lighting, located in the center of the arena, that has evolved over the years into an island of computer screens, equipment, and personnel. At the front of the soundboard, the mixer toward the stage over the audience from behind a fifty-input Gamble console, with a smaller board to his left that handles the drums and percussion, and racks of processing equipment. Also on the island, in their own stations, are CANDACE BRIGHTMAN and her assistants directing the lights, Howard Danchik of UltraSound running the soundboard tapes of the show, and others. The collaborative process that makes Dead shows beautiful is not restricted to the stage—when the Dead head into THE ZONE, the rest of the crew are *all* "playing in the band," helping to create the magic in their own ways.

SOUNDBOARD TAPES (SBDs) ⌐ • Tapes in circulation copied from master tapes made by crew members at the SOUNDBOARD from the direct stage feeds, as opposed to AUDIENCE TAPES, made with microphones by those in the TAPER'S SECTION or F.O.B.

Crisp, free of audience noise, with vivid stereo separation, "soundboards" or "boards" are usually the tapes most sought after by traders, as in, "I'll dub you the Winterland 10/17/78 boards if you spin me the board of that '78 Cleveland Music Hall." Often traders will seek to upgrade from an audience tape to a board of the same show. There are excellent audience tapes available from certain shows, however—Hollywood Palladium 8/6/71 is a classic example—and there are more now than ever, with the advent of portable DAT recorders. Comparatively, some soundboard tapes—especially from the early '80s—sound flat and lifeless. The ULTRA MATRIX method of combining direct board feed and audience miking was developed by Dan Healy to correct this.

SBDs—listed like that on traders' LISTS—are the standard of quality in the trading culture, especially since the dissemination of the BETTYBOARDS, which resulted in a mass raising of trading standards among collectors. *See also* DAT; F.O.B.; PATCHING IN.

SPACE • The freeform musical conversation by the guitarists and keyboardist that follows the DRUMS. "Somewhere in the middle of the second set," writes Bob Bralove in his liner notes for *Infrared Roses*, "the band turns a corner. They enter a musical environment without walls. . . . The song form is abandoned, and the very elements of music may be called into question. The only mandate is to explore new territory . . . where rhythm, tone, color, melody, and harmony can be explored without rules or predetermination."

The seeds of space were sown at the Acid Tests, when *all* premeditated structures—musical or social—were abandoned in favor of plunging into what Blair Jackson calls "the swirl"—"all the players moving inside and outside each other in an intuitive dance." Space is an extension of the raucous FEEDBACK jams of the late '60s, and each night's is different, its own living, breathing personality.

Though the inspiration for the Dead's extraterrestrial excursions is usually traced to free jazz (like Ornette Coleman and Sun Ra), the Dead's ventures into the swirl were also inspired by the tape music experiments of Steve Reich, MUSIQUE CON-

CRÈTE, the compositions of Karlheinz Stockhausen and Béla Bartók, and the American innovations of turn-of-the-century maverick composer Charles Ives. "The idea of Ives's music caught my imagination," Lesh explains, "the simultaneity of it. The metaphor of consciousness—that in our consciousness, we're not only thinking of one thing, but have things in the back and sides of our mind. That our autonomic systems are running our body, while we're blithely thinking about paying the rent. Ives' music was the first music of any kind to address that for me—the simultaneity of experience."

Space has also been the opportunity for some unusual cameo appearances: The taped crooning of Frank Sinatra was siphoned into the mix in Las Vegas one night; roaring Harleys, slot machines, train whistles, Stravinsky's *Rite of Spring*, and Poe's "The Raven" have all made appearances; and Eileen Law remembers one night at the Fillmore when the band miked bacon frying in an electric skillet. ("They were all *really into* bacon then," she recalls.) MIDI has added new pigments to the swirl, and on any given night, one may hear what sounds like a bassoon discoursing with a threshing machine, an underwater spaghetti Western invaded by the Vienna Boys' Choir, or a shoot-out in a holodeck.

Space is not universally appreciated, especially by those who suffer from what Lesh calls "consonance chauvinism" and shout variations on "Play somethin'!" during the full flower of the weirdness.

There is also some controversy over what to call it. In the days of *Live/Dead* it was FEEDBACK; in *DeadBase* it is lumped together with DRUMS as "Drumz"; on a million tape covers it's "jam." In 1980, it appeared on the cover of *Dead Set* as "space."

SPACEDANCING • One style of what writer Shan Sutton calls Deadheads' "bodily conversation with the music"— freeform gestures involving gentle bending at knees, swaying of the arms, and rocking of the head, combined with expressive movements of the hands. Spacedancing is Heads' way of participating in the jam. It may appear to an outsider to be "formless," but close observation reveals that most Heads are responding to subtle gestures in the music with equally subtle gestures. Heads will spacedance *anywhere* — even at concerts by other bands.

"It is very much like the loose-jointed bowing and swaying one·sees in Orthodox Jewish synagogues," suggests Gary Greenberg, "amongst the men who are 'dovening' or praying. One rabbi taught that 'as the soul journeys in the higher realms, it influences the body to make gestures of an entirely uncontrived nature.'" The Hasidim believed that this swaying movement enabled a man to put the whole of himself into his worship, and likened it to a kind of lovemaking with the Divine.

🌺 *Gary Greenberg on spacedancing:*

I think one of the ways to get at what the Dead do is to see them as taking a song and generating sparks with it, one or two of which they then breathe into their own kind of fire. When they are successful, they draw out a moment of creation, the moment that animates all of human action, but which is usually ephemeral and invisible. At those moments, they play the bones of the song, of each other, and of everyone involved. We put the whole of ourselves into our worship, and we sway. *See* HALLDANCING; SPINNERS.

SPIN 🖴 • 1. To tape a show, as in, "Did you spin that '90 Cal Expo?"

2. To copy a tape, as in, "I'll SESH you that Waterbury '72 'Dark Star' if you'll spin me that Lindley Meadow '75."

3. To spacedance energetically (*see* SPACEDANCING; SPINNERS).

SPINNERS • 1. Dancers who twirl energetically to the music, often forming groups in the hallways where their movement won't be obstructed (*see* HALLDANCING). Rapid and prolonged whirling has long been recognized as a way of altering consciousness. Dr. Andrew Weil points out in *The Natural Mind* that turning around until dizzy (whether playing, or on a carnival ride) is often the first means by which a person "gets high." Dead shows — with music continuing for long periods without interruption — offers dancers the chance to spin for hours and attain altered states of consciousness without drugs.

Many religious groups promote spinning and other forms of dancing as a method of entering a blissful state of being. So-called whirling dervishes—Mevlevi Sufis—were inspired by the writings of the thirteenth-century poet Rumi. After hearing praise of Allah in the sound of hammers in a goldbeater's shop, Rumi "unfolded his arms like a fledgling bird, tilted his head back, and whirled, whirled, whirled to the sound of 'Allah' that came forth from the very wind he created by his movement."

With practice, a spinner learns to avoid dizziness, and the motion becomes a *spiraling inward,* deeper into the music.

2. Specifically, "the Spinners" is a nickname for the members of the Family of Unlimited Devotion (formerly "the Church of Unlimited Devotion"), a sect based on a communal farm referred to as "the Land" in Mendocino County, California, until '92.

The Spinners were a striking presence at shows throughout the late '80s and early '90s, young women and men whirling rapidly and gracefully near the hallway speakers in earth-toned cotton dresses, and dropping to the floor in supplication at the end of jams. (The community supported itself by selling the handmade dresses in the parking lot and by mail order.)

Members of the church practiced celibacy, and took formal vows after living in the community for one year, after which they wore habits with roses and crowns of thorns embroidered on them. Church members maintained a daily schedule of prayer, communal work, and religious study; slept on the floor; did not wear shoes; and refrained from all meat, poultry, fish, and eggs, as well as intoxicants, including alcohol, tobacco, and caffeine. "A spirit of asceticism is important in all things," enjoined the credo of the church. "All belongings are the property of the whole community. The members of the order are to live in obedience to the group voice. This obedience is our protection from going astray."

Spinners were encouraged to attend shows as a group, and lack of tickets did not stop them. Spinners became experts at scamming into shows, and there are many reports from Deadheads and GDTS staff of Spinners getting in with Xeroxed tickets, stubs taped together or thrown through the fence, etc.

A common misconception is that the Spinners believe that

"JERRY IS GOD." Church members, however, stress that although the spinning ceremonies every Wednesday and Sunday on the Land were accompanied by live Dead tapes, the God they worship is not one man, but the same "omniscient, omnipresent, and personal" God worshipped by Christians, Jews, Sufis, and Muslims.

The church changed its name to the Family of Unlimited Devotion in April '92 after one of its founders, Joseph Lian, was expelled from the Land on charges that he had committed adultery. Also at that time, the celibacy rule was dropped, and the Family members dispersed into other households.

🍂 *Garcia on the Family of Unlimited Devotion:*

They're kind of like our Sufis. I think it's really neat that there's a place where they can be comfortable enough to do something with such abandon. It's nice to provide that. That's one of the things I'm really proud of the Grateful Dead for. It's like free turf.

SPIRAL LIGHT • "Europe's Grateful Dead Magazine," published since '83 by a team of Deadheads in England including Richard Lee, Rob and Maggie Kedward, Ken Ingham, Jake Frost, Paddy Ladd (one of the instigators of the "Deaf Zone"—*see* DEAFHEADS), and others.

The handsome magazine features interviews, photos, show reports, and setlists like its stateside cousins, but with a dry, distinctly British wit. (In particular, Heads in the U.K. seem less impressed by the Beatles and Who covers than their American equivalents.) The preeminent tone of *Spiral Light* is of passionate appreciation for the band and the culture that produced it. Editor Lee explains that because Euro-Heads rarely get to go to shows, "extensive tape collections abound. U.K. Heads seem to have more of a sense of the band's history." *Spiral Light* thus has several columns of tape reviews, including one, "Plain Rapper," devoted to onstage comments by the band. The magazine also hosts an annual Deadheads party. *Spiral Light* is a marvelous read for American Heads also—an opportunity to see the familiar through new eyes. *See also* DUNKELSTERN!

☘ Spiral Light *on tour to Louisville, Kentucky, "15.6.93":*

We crossed into the Confederate South just before sunset via Cincinnati, which is probably the finest city we saw on the tour; the suburbs set in tree-lined gorges, the city centre full of high-tech glass office blocks, and the river crossing reminiscent of the cover of a 1950s train set with freeways, railways, and waterways intersecting on a multitude of levels. Fears of heavy treatment proved groundless as the local plain clothes constabulary wore matching tie-dyes, and the local populace was very hospitable.

It was still incongruous to find monuments to "our confederate dead" in a city where the main shopping mall is on Mohammed Ali Boulevard . . .

The "Drums" were spirited and traditional, before an excellent "Space" gave way to "The Last Time" and a memorable "Morning Dew." "Gloria" has always struck me as something of an irrelevance, but as with "Saturday Night," it proves to be a revelation live, and the audience mayhem will hopefully be with me each time they encore with this chestnut.

SSSSHHHHHOWTIME! • Music to a Deadhead's ears. Shouted with much backslapping and many soul-shakes at the moment the houselights go down and the bandmembers walk onstage.

STAGE DEMONS 📖 • "I am always battling stage fright," Garcia explained in a 1984 interview. "My whole routine before going into a show is a ritual designed to tunnel-vision myself away from that stage fright. It permeates me. It's a terrible enemy of mine. And it hasn't gotten better over the years. . . .

"It's a funny thing, though, there's a demarcation moment, after the third or fourth song, where all of a sudden that just disappears, like it was never there. But every night it's the same thing. The night before leaving on a tour, I can't sleep. I'm so nervous and jacked up, thinking about that show."

STARTER TAPE ✑ • A tape meant especially for a RIPE "Deadhead-waiting-to-happen," selected by a veteran who knows where the gold is on old tapes. Starter tapes are best advised to be of excellent sound quality, with the vocals harmonious and jams concise (the "What's Become of the Baby?" marathons can come later).

Harpur College 5/2/70 is a good introduction, with its acoustic first set featuring a mellow "I Know You Rider" building to a crackling "Cumberland Blues," with harmony help on the gospel chestnut "Cold Jordan" from a couple of New Riders of the Purple Sage. Dane County 2/15/73, with an exquisite "Dark Star," complete with a "Feelin' Groovy" jam that evolves into a melodic bass solo, and then into "Eyes of the World" and "China Doll," is hard not to like. A bluegrass fan might be won over by a Warfield '80 "Rosalie McFall," and a jazz lover might be converted by Branford Marsalis's intimate dialogues with Garcia on *Without a Net*'s "Eyes of the World."

STEAL YOUR FACE • Album #13, released in June 1976. Recorded at Winterland, on October 16–20, 1974 (*see* THE LAST ONE.) The album's sound has been much improved by Joe Gastwirt's remastering for the CD.

♣ *David Gans, host of the* Grateful Dead Hour, *on* **Steal Your Face:**

It's hard to imagine what was going through the minds of the Grateful Dead when they put out *Steal Your Face.* Despite several excellent performances, the album is more notable for what was omitted from it than for what was included. There is no collective improvisation on this ostensible document of a very high time in the band's creative history.

Steal Your Face was recorded at the same run of shows that yielded *The Grateful Dead Movie,* and mixed by Bear and Phil. It is not a soundtrack album for the movie, although there is a small amount of overlap between the two. The music in the film is a much better representation of what the band played in October 1974.

Taken out of context, the song selection is abysmal. Of the monumental jams that took place in that five-night run, virtually nothing made it onto *Steal Your Face.* Phil Lesh told me a few years ago that he and Bear considered only material that had not been presented on a live album before. "Truckin'," "Morning Dew," "The Other One," and "Dark Star" had already appeared on various live Dead albums; and it's too bad "Playing in the Band" showed up in rudimentary form on *Skull and Roses,* because by 1974, it was the portal to an exquisite musical space. The omission of "Eyes of the World"→"China Doll" from 10/19, however (to name one outstanding performance from the series), is a damn shame.

Phil and Bear made *Steal Your Face* an album of *songs* as opposed to Grateful Dead music. There are some weird choices; sloppy endings and miscues abound—check out the beginning or end of "Cold Rain and Snow," or the opening of "Beat It on Down the Line." ("Zits and all" was the descriptive phrase attributed to Lesh in *BAM* magazine.)

Fortunately, there are also several excellent performances. "Stella Blue," "Mississippi Half-Step," "Sugaree," and "Big River" are particular standouts.

The album sounds very much like what the Grateful Dead sounded like live in the era of the Wall of Sound. There was a lot of space in the sound, with every instrument occupying its share of the audio spectrum; the ultra-clean P.A. system gave the sound a transparency that comes across nicely in this mix.

The order of songs on the original album, a four-sided vinyl affair, works nicely as four segments. But for continuous listening, try programming this sequence on your CD player: "Promised Land," "Sugaree," "Beat It on Down the Line," "It Must Have Been the Roses," "El Paso," "Mississippi Half-Step," "Big River," "Ship of Fools," "Black-Throated Wind," "Cold Rain and Snow," "Stella Blue," "Around and Around," "Casey Jones," "U.S. Blues."

Like so many Grateful Dead albums, *Steal Your Face* is underrated by fans and band members alike. In 1977, Robert Hunter gleefully quoted the late critic Lester Bangs—"Steal your money is more like it!" Like so many Grateful Dead albums, it could have been a lot better than it is, but it's better than its reputation suggests.

STEALIE • Nickname for the "Steal your face" skull-with-lightning-bolt icon from the cover of the album of the same name. Designed by Bob Thomas, from an idea of OWSLEY Stanley's. Along with the *Skull and Roses* image, stealies have come to be the most pervasive icon on the scene.

The image has spawned a thousand grassroots appropriations (most of them in violation of the band's trademark on the image), all replacing the lightning bolt on the inside with other American icons, such as baseball team emblems, the pink triangle of gay pride, the Batman symbol, dancing bears, and so on. One widespread adaptation called "Space Your Face" has an image of stars inside the stealie's head.

The trademark only applies to lightning bolts with thirteen points.

STEALTH TAPING ☞ • *See* F.O.B.

STUBBING DOWN • One common technique for gaining access to the lower seating levels and floor in a venue, whereby ticket stubs in the better sections are lent to those less fortunate, to get past ushers at the boundary. "We had NOSE-BLEEDS [seats in upper sections] for the first set, but our buddy stubbed us down for the second set." The stubs are either handed over the rails or passed hand-to-hand in the hallway or aisle. A speedy return of the stubs to the rightful owners is proper stubbing etiquette, along with a hug and a "have a great show."

This widespread practice causes problems for the Dead organization, who must obey fire codes limiting floor occupancy (*see* TAKE A STEP BACK), and also annoys some fans, who suddenly find choice mail-order seats swamped with unexpected friends of friends; but it also allows show buddies to enjoy the show together without preplanning, which is only officially possible at general admission shows. *See also* SEAT SURFING.

STYLIES • Caucasian Heads with dreadlocks. Also called "dreadheads."

SUGAR MAGNOLIA • A beautiful female Deadhead, from the spunky muse of the Weir/Hunter song of that title who "jumps like a Willys in four-wheel drive." The term has become popular in personals in *Relix* and other publications: "Kind-hearted Oregon bro seeks sugar magnolia for tours, good lovin' and companionship." Many Heads have marveled over the years at how many beautiful people, both men and women, come to shows.

SWIMMING • Seeing the show from various locations in the venue, moving from the halls to the floor to the rail to the upper levels of seats.

SWINGING • *v.* Vending. "I was swinging t-shirts, and it was really happening, and I sold out at the first show."

THE SWITCH 📖 • For the first decade and a half of the Dead's career, the stage lineup of the band's frontline was, from stage right to stage left, Garcia, Weir, and Lesh. For a brief time in 1978, the right-to-left lineup was Weir, Donna Godchaux,

Garcia, and Lesh (see page 173 of *The Grateful Dead Family Album* for a photo of this configuration in front of the Great Pyramid). Beginning with 4/2/82 at Cameron Stadium at Duke University, Garcia and Lesh switched sides to make better use of the stage monitors, and this arrangement has remained stable to date. *See* JERRY'S SIDE; THE PHIL ZONE.

SYNESTHESIA • The experience of perceiving a sensation with an alternative sensory organ, as when people "see" musical notes or "hear" colors, etc. Many Heads, psychedelicized or not, report that the band's music triggers visual imagery, and bandmembers themselves bear witness to this. "I have always been synesthetic," Hart writes in his book, *Planet Drum*. "A flight of birds . . . can become a rippling rhythm of notes, while a rhythmic pattern played on the Egyptian tar can become a flight of birds riding the desert thermals."

Lesh also has claimed to see music "as notes on spaces, sometimes colored, paisley, sometimes fragmented, and sometimes whirling notes and treble clefs with little feet running around them, but I see the notes we're playing all the time, at least the notes I'm playing, as they are played. Sometimes the register is horizontal; sometimes waving like a flag."

TAKE A STEP BACK • Crowd control, GD-style. This plea for alleviating "the crush" at the front of the stage was issued from the stage by Weir and Garcia dozens of times in the '70s. "All right now," Weir announced in a typical version of the rap at the legendary Cornell show on 5/8/77. "We're going to play everybody's favorite fun game—*Move back.*" As the band riffs behind him, he directs the crowd to "take a step *back*, and take another step *back*, and take yet another step *back*. Everybody feel better? *What do you mean, 'No'?*"

In the bluegrass days, and for the first fifteen years or so of their career, the bandmembers had more of a vocal rapport with their audience, and Pigpen, Weir, Garcia, and Lesh would entertain the crowd with wise-guy comments between songs. "Put your hands in the air and turn around real slow," Weir warned the audience at the Fox Theater in Atlanta, on 5/19/77. "Don't try anything funny, 'cause I got you covered." Weir, particularly, developed an ironic stage persona that made mildly unpleasant tasks seem like part of the fun, while Garcia became increasingly silent onstage as the years passed, with occasional exceptions.

Technical glitches are often the occasion of wit: "Minor technical difficulties, becoming major technical difficulties," groused Lesh, during a lull in the music at the Paramount Theater in Portland in '72. "That's the story of my life."

TAPE COVERS ✏ • *See* J-CARDS.

TAPE EXCHANGES ✏ • Also called "tape clubs," informal organizations of Heads set up in the early '70s to trade tapes person-to-person and through the mail. There were dozens of them, and tapers got to know each other at shows by exchanging business cards with the name of their exchange printed on them. These clubs were the first Deadhead-organized means of increasing one's collection of tapes, and were the first shoots of today's TREES AND VINES.

🦋 *Les Kippel, editor of* Dead Relix, *one of the first publications specifically for tapers:*

When I started seeing the Grateful Dead, I had never experienced anything as *dynamic* as the music that I witnessed there, and I knew I had to be involved. I didn't know how.

After I started taping shows, I could not find anyone else who was recording or had tapes. Me and my friend Arty Carlyle started looking around for people who were taping. We met two others. I had about forty hours of tapes, and they had forty hours. We decided to form an exchange, and I came up with the name, the first Free Underground Grateful Dead Tape Exchange. It was very important for us that we use the word "free." We did not want to buy and sell music—it was bad karma to do so, it wasn't our music. We wanted everything to be based on the concept of "free."

After we formed the Grateful Dead Tape Exchange, Charlie Rosen wrote an article about me in *Rolling Stone* where he called me "Mister Tapes, king of the Grateful Dead Tape Exchange." I got about seventy-five letters from people all over the country who wanted to get involved in collecting tapes. All these people felt the same thing: that the Grateful Dead records that were out at the time did not give a true representation of what the Dead sounded like in concert.

They all started their own tape exchanges, from Harvey Lubar's Hell's Honkies, to the New Jersey Tape Exchange, to the California Tape Exchange. They started forming in every state.

TAPER'S SECTION ✏ • A block of 200 to 250 seats set aside by Grateful Dead Ticket Sales behind the soundboard, where tapers are permitted to set up their decks and microphones, and record audience tapes of the shows for listening and not-for-profit trading.

The Dead's policy of allowing taping is revolutionary, and has had the effect of creating a passionate and loyal constituency of tapers and traders—a lesson not lost on other bands, including several of the H.O.R.D.E. BANDS, Bruce Hornsby, and Metallica (*see* ONCE WE'RE DONE WITH IT, IT'S THEIRS).

The first taper's section was instituted on 10/27/84, at Berkeley Community Theater, after Healy became annoyed by a proliferation of mic stands in front of the soundboard, and reports of tapers' lack of courtesy. "You could stand at the soundboard next to Healy," recalls Steve Marcus, "and literally not see the stage because of all the mic stands. At reserved seat shows, people would show up with their tickets, and tapers would be set up in their seats. That started getting the Dead angry. So I said, "Why don't we put them behind the soundboard?" We never sold the seats behind the soundboard anyway. Then they discussed charging $5 more for taper's tickets, but I said no. So we did an experiment. And it was a hit."

Before the taper's section, taping was officially prohibited, but unofficially tolerated. If you could smuggle your deck into the venue, you could set up your mics. Barry Glassberg—who has taped over three hundred shows—reports that when he ran his reel-to-reel at Roosevelt Stadium in Jersey City in '73, he was the only person he saw taping, but by '74, there was a small cluster of tapers. Steve Marcus estimates that there are now about one hundred tapers who try to go to most shows, and ten to twenty who go to all of them.

The taper's section is, for obvious reasons, one of the quietest places in the audience, with Heads boogieing only very slightly among the coiling cables and towering mic stands. Tapers joke about "taper geeks"—those who become so consumed by their hobby that they forget to enjoy the music—and "taper stress," brought on by such considerations as making sure battery packs are charged, tapes are flipped at the right moment, the cables are plugged in, and equipment is in working order. There is a large body of lore about heroic tapers who have kept decks running without interruption as multiple power supplies failed, beer spilled on decks, etc.

Admittance to the taper's section requires special "taper tickets," by specifying that you want them when mail-ordering from GDTS. From '84 to '86, the taper tickets were stamped with a portrait of "the King of the Tapers" — Richard Nixon. *See also* F.O.B.; GETTING YOUR DECK IN.

🍀 *Taper David Stoller on the taper's section:*

Tapers are strange characters, but true historians. Many tapers have been taping for a very long time, which can make the taping section an intimidating place for newcomers, but the taping section can be a wonderful place to experience the Dead. Most everyone is quiet and concentrating on the music — just remember to watch your step!

There is something magical about driving to the middle of nowhere in Indiana, arriving at a wonderful venue like Deer Creek, heading up to the section, laying back on the grass, and watching a summer sunset, while listening to the show as it's played, through headphones.

I've spent many road trips with a chain of Sony D-5s hooked up in my car, rolling through my friends' collections. At Shoreline in '92, a friend of mine got a box of some great '69 soundboards, and was given the three days until the Vegas shows to copy them. It took the entire trip from San Francisco to Vegas, but we dubbed them all. It's not unusual for a taper houseguest to spend their weekend in town camped out by the tape deck. You can truly call yourself a taper geek when your free time is considered potential dubbing time.

Taping is not for everyone. With good microphones starting at a few hundred dollars, and excellent ones costing a few thousand, it's expensive, time-consuming, and at times, downright tedious. But the results — the ability to preserve the magic of a great show, and share it with others for years to come — make it truly worthwhile.

TAPER TERROR 📖 • *Tapers with high blood pressure would be well-advised to skip this entry.* "Short of erasing tapes by putting electromagnets over every exit," band spokesperson Dennis McNally has said, "taping can't be prevented."

TAPES 🎞 • Recordings of live Grateful Dead, usually on analog cassettes or DATs. Many Heads also refer to them as "bootlegs."

"You trade tapes?" is often one of the first questions in a Deadhead friendship. Tape collecting and trading—strictly not-for-profit—is one of the most durable binding threads in the fabric of the Deadhead community. Most Deadheads begin their listening careers with the official album releases, but quickly find that what draws them in most—extended jamming, multiple versions of beloved songs, interesting sequences of songs in a set—is available on only a few live albums.

"Beyond their role as Makers of Song and Masters of improvisation," writes trader Jim Powell on his LIST, "the Dead are Architects of Sets and Shows." One of the most attractive things about tapes is that they offer whole shows, with mistakes, warm-up tunes, and the spontaneous development of musical architectures intact.

Most importantly, once a Head has "gotten it" at a show, tapes are the most faithful recapturing of the experience.

The number of tapes available to traders is in the thousands, all available for the price of blank tapes, and some postage if trading by mail. Many traders are generous, sharing the fruits of their individual searches for the common good, though there are well-connected taper cliques who trade mostly among themselves. Taper traders meet each other at shows, on the Net, or through tapers' classifieds in magazines like *Relix, Dupree's Diamond News,* and *Unbroken Chain.*

Many collectors take good care of their tape libraries, and it is not uncommon for the racks of tapes to be the most visibly in-order area of a collector's living space. The activity of hunting down obscure tapes, copying them, and logging them onto a list is a school of precision for many young tapers. The lessons of organization learned there are often carried into other areas of their lives, even after they have ceased to be active traders.

☙ *Fred Feldstein, with 2300 DAT hours of live Dead in his collection, on The Hunt:* The first Dead record I owned was *Anthem of the Sun.* I thought, "There must be more of *this!*" The first tape I got, when I was seventeen, was a copy of the Passaic radio broadcast on 11/24/78, with one channel missing, but I loved it. It was live. I hadn't been to a show yet.

You'd start with shitty UD audience tapes, and work your way up to soundboards of Harpur College 5/2/70 and 4/29/71, the last night of the Fillmore East. If you could handle those, it was like your initiation.

When you really got into it, your life would revolve around forty-five-minute intervals of flipping tapes. How much time did I spend taping? How much time *didn't* I spend. I'd go to sleep for forty-five minutes, wake up, flip, pee, and go back to sleep.

The Hunt—with a capital H—was everything. You'd hear about Port Chester or Manhattan Center '71, and you'd start asking around. When you found what you were looking for, you'd listen to it once or twice, and then throw it into your collection. Once you had a tape, it was your clearance to go on and hunt for the next one. You didn't have to worry about it anymore.

I get forty shows at a time. I don't even have a list. The people I trade with don't have lists either. Who needs a list when you've got the *stuff?*

Eventually, I got into jazz CDs. I like jazz—the spontaneity of it. Every session is "live." Now I've started collecting wines, too, calling every winery until I find what I'm looking for. If it doesn't sound good, I don't want to listen to it, and I don't want to taste it if it doesn't taste good. If you appreciate the fine things in life, you can find them—if you're willing to put in some time.

TASTY • One of many culinary adjectives appropriated by Deadheads to describe the pleasure of the experience. " 'Spoonful' was *tasty.*" "Second set Tuesday in Philly was *sweet!*" Verbal SYNESTHESIA. *See* HOT.

TATTOOS • The tribal sign written in the flesh.

Tattoos are a badge of initiation behind bars, where—according to Pat, a young Haight survivor with *Grateful Dead* in pot leaves across his belly—tat guns are jerry-rigged out of Walkman motors and guitar strings.

T.C. • *See* TOM CONSTANTEN.

"TEACH YOUR CHILDREN" • Garcia plays the pedal steel guitar on this '70 pop anthem from Crosby, Stills, Nash & Young's *Deja Vu,* making it the most widely recognized piece of music he may likely ever—nearly anonymously—be a part of. Garcia's bright melodic riffs are the song's fourth voice, providing a lyrical counterpoint to Nash's soothing harmonized homilies that spanned a hit-radio bridge over the much-hyped "gen-

eration gap." When Garcia recorded the track, he'd been playing the pedal steel for all of two weeks.

Garcia's pedal steel also graced Nash's "I Used to Be a King,"
and has been given cameos on dozens of albums by Jefferson
Airplane, the New Riders of the Purple Sage (of which Garcia
was a founding member), Robert Hunter, and others. In 1987,
Garcia brought sit-down cowboy grandeur onto the stage for
the tour with Dylan, and the pedal steel is also the lead voice of
the studio version of "The Wheel" on Garcia's first solo album.
Garcia has said his own favorite pedal steel track can be found
on David Crosby's "Laughing," on *If I Could Only Remember My
Name. See* PLANET EARTH ROCK & ROLL ORCHESTRA.

🎸 *Steve Barncard, producer, on the recording of "Teach Your Children" at Wally
Heider's studio in San Francisco:*

Graham played the song acoustic, walking in and out of the studio singing
like a troubador. David and Stephen came over and worked out their parts,
and next thing you know, there were microphones in front of them. This all
happened within a day.

Graham instigated it, "We need a steel guitar player." It was Crosby who
said, "What about Garcia?" They were all staying at the Red Lantern Inn,
with junkies hanging around outside the studio. Garcia came in with Steve
Parish. We went into the back room, and Bill Halverson, who was the engineer, wasn't there for some reason. The band said, "Well—get it *goin'!*" I'd
been there about ten days, I'd never done eight- or sixteen-track recording,
so I was like, "Oh—*here's* the monitor system." But I got the limiter in there,
and cranked it, and Garcia put the echo on it. We did it in two takes. The vocals were already there. Garcia was very funny, and Crosby and Garcia had
their usual banter, tossin' around bats [joints] the size of Camels. You could
expect a night of good weed, good music and good humor when those guys
were together.

TEASE • False hint of a song during tuning or a jam-in-
progress. Teases are occasionally frustrating to fans, especially
when the song teased is a very desired one, like "St. Stephen."

A show at Meadowlands Giants Stadium on 6/17/91, referred to by collectors as the "Dark Star Tease" show, featured
glimmers of the "Dark Star" theme—instigated by Hornsby—
in at least three points during the first and second sets.

Many Heads can "call" a song from the subtlest of clues during tuning, which can appear, to a non-Deadhead, like a form of E.S.P.

TECHNO-SHAMANISM • The marriage of technology and essence. The Dead were exponents of this aesthetic long before it was named and popularized by Terence McKenna and the Acid House generation, and many Heads find themselves equally at home at Rainbow Gatherings, and in cyberspace.

TERRAPIN STATION • Album #14, released in July 1977. *Terrapin Station* features a slick studio version of "Estimated Prophet" with sax and a disco-fied "Dancin' in the Streets," as well as the Lesh rocker "Passenger." (Another Lesh tune, "Equinox," with Garcia on lead vocals, was not released.)

The second side of the album is given to the long suite "Terrapin Station," recorded with a full choir and orchestra, scored by Paul Buckmaster. The opening of the suite, "Lady With a Fan," is among the most exquisite pieces of music the Dead have recorded, with diamond-bright guitars woven as tight as a Celtic knot. A Hart *timbale* duet with Garcia was wiped from the master by producer Keith Olsen. Hart said later, "Olsen was a good producer, and a good engineer. But he had a problem: He didn't know the Grateful Dead, and he wanted to mold the Grateful Dead in his own image." Still, the complex interweaving of lyric and melodic motifs gave "Terrapin" a sweep and scale the Dead hadn't attempted in the studio since *Anthem of the Sun.*

🦋 *Susan Dobra on "Lady With a Fan":*

The poet of ancient times sang to the soul of his audience. Invoking mythical or historical heroes and monsters, gods and demons, he conjured archetypal visions in the minds and hearts of his rapt listeners. Those who listened were carried beyond the everyday limitations of time and space to where they witnessed the reenactment of apocalyptic battles, revelations, victories, and defeats, realms where fortunes rise and fall, illuminated by the mutually creative act of artist and audience.

The studio version of "Terrapin Station" consists of seven interconnected parts. The familiar opening, a sparkling five-note guitar riff, is like the opening of a treasure box, setting the mood for the first part of the story, "Lady

With a Fan." The first four lines of the song follow the classical poetic tradition of an invocation, used by Homer, Milton, and epic poets in many cultures, to call upon the Muses to guide the poet through the telling of the story: "Let my inspiration flow/in token rhyme suggesting rhythm/that will not forsake me/till my tale is told and done." It is characteristic of the worldview of Robert Hunter that no actual deity is invoked; he calls upon the power of poetic imagination itself. The invocation apparently worked; Hunter describes the writing of this cycle—of which the album contains only a small part—as a transmission, saying it "came in on a pure beam."

The poem begins with a fire already burning, casting shadows out of which the shapes of the story's characters materialize. The characters that emerge are a sailor and a soldier, given sparse description. A third character emerges: "While the storyteller speaks/a door within the fire creaks/suddenly flies open/and a girl is standing there." It is an age-old motif: the love triangle. She challenges both men to become her lover, by tossing her fan into "the lion's den." To win her, you must prove yourself by taking the chance of being eaten alive. The soldier passes, but the sailor tries. And here the story comes to an end, with the storyteller commanding the listener to decide "if he was wise." It is a device reminiscent of the traditional tale "The Lady or the Tiger?" in which the ending is left to the reader/listener. "The storyteller makes no choice/soon you will not hear his voice/his job is to shed light/and not to master." This abdication of responsibility for the outcome of the story makes the song an invitation to collaborative creativity, the modus operandi of the Grateful Dead. It is the community, the generations after generations of listeners, who will provide the sense of the story, adapting it to the changing conditions of their culture. "Lady With a Fan" is a celebration of the creative act, and an exploration of its mysteries and communal character.

TERRAPIN TAPES • A mail-order business specifically geared toward Deadhead tapers and tape collectors. "About ninety-five percent of our customers are Deadheads," says proprietor Ken Hays, who runs the service out of his Stamford, Connecticut home, and offers rock-bottom prices on audio tape and equipment. They also sell *DEADBASE* and Dead-related computer software.

In the spring of '93, this promising business was threatened by a much larger, non-Head firm offering even lower prices. Hays responded by appealing to his customers in an open letter, explaining that, based on the competitor's history, those prices would remain low only long enough to drive Terrapin out of business. "Once we're gone, they crank up their prices," he advised.

Word got around quickly, and in a robust display of community as well as intelligent consumerism, Heads overwhelmingly rallied to Terrapin's side. "Since that letter," Hays says, "things have really turned around. Our business is better than ever. The letters I've received are emotional and inspiring. People know I'm a Deadhead. They know I'd never rip them off, and would never sell their name to a mailing list. That's an important element—knowing where your dollars are going."

🌿 *Ken Hays on Deadheads as customers:*

We do about 20 percent of our business through personal checks, and since day one, we've only had one check bounce that was never recovered. That's phenomenal. That's well below national statistics. In three years of processing credit card receipts, we've had *zero* chargebacks—claims by customers that they never got the merchandise. In mail order the national average is about 15 percent—it's a huge area of fraud. But we've had no theft at all.

When I went to apply for a merchant Visa/MasterCard account, I went to six banks, all of whom were interested until the identity of our customers was revealed. Every time I mentioned Deadheads or the Grateful Dead, the application was terminated, citing a high-risk clientele. It was incredible prejudice.

Three years later, when our bank reviewed our records, they were shocked by the absence of fraud. They asked me, "What are you doing? How are you able to have no theft?"

It's really important to show the honesty and loyalty of Deadheads, when they're so often thought of as being drugged-out, long-haired hippies from the '60s. Quite simply, we're dealing with a clientele that is the coolest customer base of any company in the world. *See also* I'LL BE GRATEFUL WHEN THEY'RE DEAD.

TERRAPIN TRAILWAYS • An outrageously "deadicated" '48 White Motor Company bus, owned by Norm Ruth, which has ferried many Heads in high style from its home base near Rio Rancho, New Mexico, since 1982. River-blue with Klaxon horns, emblazoned with the compleat Dead zodiac of "Shakedown dude," Space Your Face, flying eye, and indigo rose, Terrapin Trailways is Deadhead aesthetics worthy of the Smithsonian, and makes a "long strange trip" look *comfortable*.

Calico—durable Hog Farmer, champion of bus living, and Deadhead tribal elder—nominates Terrapin Trailways for "Best Bus in the Lot," and one rider, Jeffro, talks about what happens when the bus pulls into town: "Necks crane and people change lanes to scope the full view as it lumbers down the highway. Tourists pull their camcorders away from Canyon de Chelly to capture a truly American phenomenon, and the local kids wave hello and start flashing peace signs. In the heart of the wilderness, old-timers come to check out the '48 White, oblivious to the paint job: 'Pa's comin' downstairs—he ain't been out of bed for weeks.' A parks employee grabs his guitar, comes back to the bus, and sings decades-old self-penned Vietnam protest songs as we cook chili cheeseburgers. Terrapin Trailways transcends Deadheadness, and legitimizes a healthy chunk of weirdness." *See* TOURBUS.

❧ *Norm Ruth, owner of Terrapin Trailways:*

Terrapin Trailways and I first crossed paths in the spring of 1982, while I was apprenticing as a blacksmith in a small town in New Mexico. It became my home, and the bus has taken me on many wondrous adventures.

Her original owner was Uncle Sam, the Atomic Energy Commission in Utah. The military olive-drab appearance quickly gave way to a vibrant display of nature's colors. Terrapin Trailways is a flagship, representing what I believe are the freedoms and values shown to us by the Dead. The bus is a visual, real-time experience, a psychedelic ballroom on wheels—that thing you saw on the road at night, but can't quite describe to your friends the next morning. The bus has a spirit that calls to me, and has become my life's work, bringing me more happiness and fun and pleasure than I could have imagined. It has also been the source of more heartbreak and anguish than I care to remember. Just like life, when the sun shines, it shines brightly, and when it rains, it rains hard; and there are the days between. Keeping the "bus trip" together has become—short of my loving family—the biggest joy of my life, natural as breathing, and at other times, a money-sucking, knuckle-bleeding, pain-in-the-ass headache, as hard as the road we travel. May the Road Go on Forever.

THE SHOW • The best show over the course of a run or tour. Also known as "the hot show." Though Dead shows are deeply subjective experiences, making any effort to arrive at a consensus opinion pretty much besides the point, experienced Heads will often be able to say soon afterward which shows will stand the test of time as an important performance.

The elements in the music that make a show *"the* show" are not only earnestness, drive, and experimentation but a setlist that reaches back into the band's history, bringing together songs that are rarely played or exemplary versions of PRIMAL DEAD tunes like "The Other One," "Dark Star," or "Playin' in the Band." Since neither band nor audience can begin to predict when or where *the* show will happen, hard-core Deadheads simply try to see as many shows as possible.

While many Heads will try to catch all three nights of the run in their hometown, and some make it to every show on a tour, straight-world constraints have a way of intervening and forcing a choice, which puts working Heads in the uncomfortable position of having to guess with little if any useful indicators which night will be *the* show.

"Over the years we've gone through hundreds of different theories on how to pick the hot ones," says Glen Goldstein. "Saturday nights. Favorite halls. Cities where they played a hot show last year. Outdoor shows. We're *never* right. I'm averaging only one out of every fifteen shows that I pick being the amazing performance that makes my jaw drop, and leaves me scratching my head for weeks afterward saying, 'What was *that!?*' "

THEY'RE NOT THE BEST AT WHAT THEY DO, THEY'RE THE *ONLY* ONES THAT DO WHAT THEY DO • A proclamation by BILL GRAHAM, displayed on a billboard outside the closing night of WINTERLAND, New Year's Eve, 1978. A makeshift Deadhead banner was held up below Graham's pronouncement that night reading, "1535 days since last SF Dark Star." (At Graham's request, the band did in fact open the third set with it that night. Breakfast was served at dawn.)

The band's two-week run at San Francisco's Warfield Theater in September of '80 was completely sold out by an ad in the *San Francisco Chronicle* that didn't even mention the Dead, but simply had Graham's statement, flanked by skeletons.

THRONES • The single row of high-backed concrete seats around the perimeter of "the pit" at the Greek Theater in Berkeley; very desirable for their good sight lines and back support. *See* GREEK THEATER.

TICKET CHECK • 1. Tickets don't do much good left on the dresser at the Motel 6, so many Heads have learned to ritualize a pocket search as the *last* thing done before leaving for the show. "Back when we forgot to do the ticket check in our hotel at Hampton '86," recalls Charley Wilkins, "I was able to buy a ten-dollar ticket. But that was pre–'Touch of Grey.' Nowadays, ticket check is a little more serious." "Wallet, keys, tickets, doses," checks off one seasoned tourhead. "The essentials."

2. The phrase is also used to describe the pre-entrance security checkpoint where Heads are obliged to raise their tickets in the air in order to proceed to the turnstile. "Have your tickets out and ready!" is the last thing a Head hears in the outside world before entering the gates of Heaven. *See* SCAMMING IN.

TICKETBASTARD • A nickname popular among Heads (along with "SlaveMaster," "TicketMonster," etc.) for Ticketmaster, the nationwide computerized ticket-marketing behemoth known for its exorbitant "service charge" add-on fees. Owned principally by the Chicago billionaire Pritzker family, the company revolutionized the ticket business through computerization, increasing profits for its clients—promoters and arenas—and then using that profit to obtain near monopolies on the tickets. It now controls 85–90 percent of ticket sales for its more than 1,600 clients.

Bob Weir told a California Senate committee that Ticketmaster threatened to stop selling Dead tickets altogether unless the band stopped selling a portion on their own through

GRATEFUL DEAD TICKET SALES, and that the company backed down only in the face of an impending lawsuit. "They are really afraid to go to court right now," Weir told the committee, "because they know that they're going to come up against antitrust laws." Ticketmaster responded to the Weir comment by questioning his qualifications to judge such "complex legal issues."

TIE-DYE • Clothing decorated with swirling, multihued patterns that many Heads have worn to shows since the early '80s.

Though some Heads believe that all hippies in the '60s wore tie-dye, tie-dye was not the costume of the original Haight. Victorian elegance—capes, lace, boots—was the style. At Dead shows, "the dye" was not worn much by Heads until the combined efforts of the Dye Works, and pioneers like Ed Donohue, Mikio, Ralph Mannis, and Phil Brown, produced refinements of design and incandescent colors that raised the craft to an art.

When dye vendors at shows moved from blankets to booths, and Heads set up their own companies (like Liquid Blue and Not Fade Away), tie-dye became big business. The look has become so identified with Deadheads in the media that when a television producer wants to communicate that a character is a Deadhead "type," a tie-dye shirt is all that's required. Though it is common in the press to refer to tie-dye as "the Deadhead uniform," it's extremely important to remember that each hand-dyed garment is unique. Mass-produced, printed pseudo-dyes are shunned.

Tie-dyeing is a very old technique, similar to the Balinese process called *"Ikat."* The first dyers, it is thought, may have gotten the idea from seeing bunched fabric bleached unevenly in the sun. Tie-dye has become a way for Deadheads to recognize one another *outside* of shows as well, though many who sport a dye in the Phil Zone on Saturday night put on a three-piece suit on Monday morning. *See* PSYCHEDELIC; *APPENDIX II: HOW TO TIE-DYE.*

♣ *Rob Lecker's story:*

The morning of my first show at Chula Vista '85, I was walking around in the hills outside the venue when I saw a blind man sitting under a tree wearing a beautiful tie-dye. I sat down and started talking to him. "That's a really beautiful shirt," I told him. "Thanks—my friends buy them for me." "I guess you've never seen what it looks like." "Nope—never seen colors." I traced my hand along the shirt, giving him a map of each color in terms of temperature: "This is *blue*, think of feeling something very cold. This is *red*, like fire—and this part is *yellow* . . ." After I was done, the man said, "Thanks. I never knew tie-dyes had a *pattern* before." [The Dead played "Comes a Time" at that show, with the lines "Comes a time, when the blind man takes your hand, says, 'Don't you see?' "]

THE TIGER • Garcia's GD stage guitar from '79 to '89. The second guitar custom-made for him by Doug Irwin, the Tiger is named for its elaborate inlay of a tiger in ivory and mother-of-pearl. *See* PLAY LIKE JERRY; THE WOLF.

TOUCHHEADS • Short for " 'Touch-of-Grey' Heads," the thousands of new Heads brought into the fold by the band's 1987 hit single "A Touch of Grey," which shot to number 9 on the *Billboard* charts that year, becoming the most successful single the Dead had ever had. The success of "A Touch of Grey" is often cited as the incitement for the influx of younger Heads onto the scene (though Steve Marcus believes it was MTV's "Day of the Dead"). *See* IN THE DARK.

♬ *Steve Marcus of Grateful Dead Ticket Sales on the "Day of the Dead":*
They kept cutting to the parking lot scene at Giants Stadium, saying, *"Cool,* dude, what a *party!"* And a whole shitload of folks came in to party. They didn't even know who the Dead were. You'd see a lot of people in leather with metal studs and pointed hair, 'cause it was "Grateful Dead"—sounds like a metal band! They didn't have a clue. And a lot of the younger ones just didn't have the Deadhead etiquette. When I started working for the Dead in '83, the median age group was twenty-seven years old. By late '87, it was down to about eighteen. That's a hell of a jump. But it's their band too. *See* RIPE.

TOUR • *v.* — To follow the band from venue to venue, seeing as many shows as possible in a series. Most band itineraries are from ten to twenty shows long. Deadheads "tour" or "do tour," as in "Did you do Spring Tour '87?"

Heads who go out on tour regularly are sometimes called TOURHEADS. Heads on tour drive from venue to venue—often all night—living in TOURBUSES, inexpensive motels, or nearby dorm rooms or student co-ops for each run.

"Tour" can also be used as a noun, to describe the community of Heads following the band, like, "Tour is much more paranoid since the DEA started busting Heads."

Heads on tour watch the band's repertoire unfold, and hear songs and jams develop from city to city. Familiar faces are met at each destination, so that the shows themselves—rather than the towns they happen to be in—are "home."

🐌 *Toura Williams, on tour:*

I went on tour by myself, from start to end. Take a train, take a bus, hitch-hike, just to *get there.* It was incredible, the effort I put into following that band. Explaining it to someone who hasn't been on tour is impossible. They think that I'm the only one: "I mean, the band must *know you* by now—don't they see you at every show?"

It is the best way to travel. You get to be a tourist in every city that you visit. Salesmen are the only other people who get to see the world like a Dead-head. Who else do you meet who travels to *Milwaukee?*

That was the magic of tour. Constant movement. And constant waiting. Because to be a Deadhead is to always be on line.

The first night of tour is the most unbelievable energy night. To be *in the room* again, when the lights are still up, the hubbub: *bzzzzzz . . .* It was always the best night to dose. Imagine a map of the United States, or the world, and every Deadhead is a red blinking dot, converging on this little city for the first night of tour.

That's the night of pure celebration.

TOUR FEVER • *See* THE ICK.

TOUR RATS • Hardcore TOURHEADS who live in the parking lot, earning road costs by vending, and waiting—or scamming—for a "miracle." The term is used with outlaw pride when describing oneself, and sarcasm when describing others.

Excerpt from a November '92 study on the homeless population of the Haight-Ashbury, by the San Francisco Department of Public Health:

GROUP 1: Recreational/Touring Homeless—These young people are the traditional Grateful Dead groupies or "dead heads"—a group of youth between 17 and 28 who have dropped out of college or high school to follow the Grateful Dead's concert tour across the country. The

Haight represents but one of many stops for them on a larger sojourn. They are extremely transient and usually come to the area when there are shows in San Francisco or Oakland, and will at times stay between concert dates before moving on either to the next show, a Rainbow Gathering, or a similar counterculture event. Many of these youth are homeless by choice and, for the most part, sustain connections to their family and community of origin. For all their pretensions to difference, they are, in fact, quite tied to a set of middle-class values handed down from their parents. Many will list parents and grandparents among respected and admired individuals and call home for advice about health or personal problems. For many, homelessness is literally a phase.

TOURBOOKS • 1. Many Deadheads keep a journal of the shows they've seen—their own personal *DeadBase*— decorated by hand with setlists, ticket stubs, lyrics, stage banter, hotel receipts, photographs of the show or the friends who were there.

2. Books of tickets for whole tours that were sold by GDTS during the mid-'80s.

TOURBUS • Tipi on wheels, postindustrial folk art, highway Hilton, and "temporary autonomous zone," the tourbus is what makes it possible to *live* tour in communal style. Tourbuses are where many Deadheads learn the nitty-gritty of getting along.

The Merry Pranksters' "Further" may have inspired many a Head to take a great old International Harvester (or a broken-down schoolbus) on the road, but the ideal of tax-free self-sufficiency and follow-your-bliss mobility goes as far back as the nomadic tribes of the Silk Route. With mattresses and glare-easing curtains, portholes, hatchways, and mini-greenhouses poking from sides and roof, and hand-painted roses and skeletons festooning every surface, the tourbus is to a 24-hour-a-day Deadhead what the terraced cliff was to an Anasazi Indian: home. *See* TERRAPIN TRAILWAYS.

TOURHEADS • The especially "deadicated" class of Deadheads who follow the band for most or all of a tour, living along the way in tourbuses, hotels, friends' homes, or local student housing. A 1988 *RELIX* magazine survey states that 91 percent of Deadheads regularly travel away from their home base to attend shows, and most Heads who responded to a survey in *DEADBASE* see an average of seven or so consecutive shows at a time.

According to Steve Marcus of Grateful Dead Ticket Sales, there are approximately two thousand Heads who order tickets for every show, and another five hundred who go to every venue, but don't necessarily try to get in.

TRAILS • Colorful, incandescent paths in the air, seen in the wakes of moving objects by people who have taken psychedelics. Among Heads, the saying "Happy trails!" has an amusing double meaning. Also known as "tracers." *See* ENERGY BALLS.

TREES AND VINES ⌨ • Two extraordinarily efficient systems of disseminating tapes on the Net, originally designed by trader Jeff Loomis, Dan Marsh, and others to get out high-quality copies of Europe '90 soundboards.

In a tree, someone provides a "seed" tape, preferably a low-generation soundboard, to "root" people, who make copies for "branches," who make dubs for "leaves." In a well-organized tree with quality seeds, the leaves, who do the least work and get the tapes with the least quality, get fourth- or fifth-gen tapes. (Inside trading communities, tree metaphors proliferate, with talk of "saplings," "keeping the forest balanced," and so on.)

A slightly slower system, but one that assures higher-quality tapes to everyone, is called a "vine." In this system, the last person on the vine sends blanks to the first person, who copies the source tapes onto the blanks and mails them to the second person. These first-gen copies are then mailed from person to person down the vine, everyone making their own copies of the first-gens. On a vine, no one gets worse than a second-generation tape, and the last person—who provided the blanks and waits the longest for the tapes to come back—gets first-gens.

Trees and vines can theoretically be cultivated in communities with no computers—and tapes were certainly traded efficiently before the Net—but the Net's ability to disseminate information to large numbers of traders quickly has meant a significant upgrading in trading life, with better-quality tapes available to more people. *See* TAPE EXCHANGES.

TRIBE • One way in which Deadheads think of their community—an extended family of people from various classes, races, sexual orientations, backgrounds, and other musical interests.

While "tribe" is normally used to describe a group of people descended from a common ancestor, the tribe of Deadheads is unusual in that membership is *recognized in oneself* rather than inherited. Whether you're a Republican sheep-rancher defending the Constitution in cyberspace, a Radical Faerie, or a neurosurgeon who unwinds with "Terrapin" after a shift in the O.R., for many Heads, sincere appreciation for the music, and sharing it with others, comes before job title, national identity, and political or religious affiliation.

🍂 *Barbara Saunders, writer, on the tribe:*

In most circles, solidarity and brotherly love are apparent only in the worst of times. Years, miles, and generations away from the contexts that gave them meaning, languages, symbols, rituals, and beliefs from all over the world flood our psyches. People occasionally put aside societal roles and rules to band together to fight racism, battle their addictions, or repair the damage caused by great quakes or floods. Rarely do they gather just to weave their particular ways. The Deadhead tribe is centered around what's missing from many ethnic, national, and religious communities: peak experience, that unifies individuals into one people.

Having shared with other Deadheads our most intimate moments and mind-expanding experiments, we expect from each other tolerance, understanding, and unconditional support. Recently, more and more people are gambling on the sincerity of *our* family values—I've seen ads in *Relix* by those who hope to reach black Deadheads and Christian Deadheads, Wharf Rats and gay Deadheads. Our dedication confuses and scares people. Even the most WASPy Deadhead knows firsthand the feelings of being discriminated against, of being closeted, and of coming out. Where the only recognized tribal links are genealogical, a brother/sisterhood among the fans of a rock group makes little sense. But as a friend of mine put it, "We grew up together."

Being ON THE BUS for any length of time includes birthing babies and mourning deaths; watching children grow up; and seeing relationships move from glances exchanged while dancing, to parenting. And through it all the music never stops; doing what moon cycles did for the ancients — providing a touchstone for the passage of time and the stages of our lives.

TRIPPING ON DNA • Going to a show with your parents. *See* FAMILY SHOWS.

THE TRIPS FESTIVAL • Three days of multimedia events, similar to the Acid Tests, at Longshoreman's Hall in San Francisco, the weekend of 1/22 and 1/23/66.

The Trips Festival was organized by Stewart Brand (later the publisher of the *Whole Earth Catalog* and one of the architects of THE WELL), and other representatives of the psychedelic and artistic undergrounds in San Francisco, including Kesey and the Pranksters, and members of the Open Theater and the Tape Music Center.

The Trips Festival featured live bands (including the Dead and Big Brother and the Holding Company), mimes, films, the Ann Halprin Dancers, Don Buchla and his synthesizers, and many other attractions. Handbills advertising the event advised that "Audience dancing is an assumed part of all the shows, and the audience is invited to wear Ecstatic Dress and bring their own Gadgets (A.C. outlets will be provided.)"

The Pranksters' "gadgets" included portapak video cameras that showed the writhing dancers instant images of themselves, as Kesey wrote on an overhead projector things like, "Anybody who knows he is God go up onstage." A shopping bag of Owsley's latest vintage made the rounds, and during the Dead's "set" (to use the term loosely), a champion trampolinist wearing a ski mask dove out of the balcony under a strobe light. It was also at the Trips Festival that Garcia first met Bill Graham.

🌸 *Garcia, on his first impressions of Bill Graham:*

I was having the greatest time in the world. It was like old home week. Every beatnik, every hippie, every coffeehouse hangout person from all over the state was there, all freshly psychedelicized. I had some sense that the Grateful Dead was supposed to play sometime maybe. But it really didn't matter. I was wandering around, and my attention was drawn to this opaque projector projecting on to one of many screens in the place. And the screen said, "JERRY GARCIA, PLUG IN!" I was looking at it and thinking, "Ah, this is an oddly personal thing for it to say. Oh! It must be time to play!"

I get up there on stage and I look at my guitar, and somebody has knocked it over and the bridge is now broken off and it's completely sprung, the strings are sticking out everywhere, the thing is fucked. Then, all of a sudden, here's this guy with the little sweater and the clipboard. He says, "Well, are you the Grateful Dead? You're supposed to be playing now."

I'm sitting on the floor, looking down at the guitar in my lap. I'm holding it like a baby. And Bill looks down at it. Immediately, without saying a word, he falls down and starts picking up pieces. He fumbles around with them, trying to fix it for me. I thought, "What a nice guy." Here's this guy in the midst of all this chaos, trying to fix my guitar for me. I thought it was the most touching thing I'd ever seen.

Always loved him for that, you know.

TROUBLE AHEAD, JERRY IN RED • A popular sticker and bumpersticker during the mid-'80s, after Garcia startled Deadheads by sporting a red t-shirt in lieu of his basic black. The slogan is a tongue-in-cheek alteration of the "Trouble ahead, lady in red" line of the Garcia/Hunter song "Casey Jones."

TRUSTAFARIANS • Derogatory moniker for people with trust funds who dress like hippies and are seen to be hiding their affluence; from "Rastafarian."

Tour offers children of privilege a community that doesn't put a premium on upward mobility, or ask questions about one's family tree or prep-school past. More Heads than would care to admit it put their plane tickets—and hotel suite, show tickets, tape decks, Guatemalan couture, and recreational supplies—on the family tab. A bumpersticker popular circa '90 didn't even have to say "Dead" or "tour" anywhere on it. It had two happy dancing bears, and read: "My Parents Think I'm in College."

TWEAK ☜ • 1. To adjust or fine-tune. A "tweaker" is a taper who is constantly fussing with the recording levels.

2. To freak out.

TWO FROM THE VAULT • Album #25, released in May 1992 as the second in a series of best of live multitrack tapes from THE VAULT, selected by Dan Healy. While editing the muddy-sounding reels of this extraordinary performance for release, engineers Healy and Don Pearson—by analyzing the time difference between the signals from the bass and the drum mics—determined that the road crew, who had not marked the stage the first night, had set up the band's gear the second night a foot off. Healy and Pearson's refinements resulted in a crystalline rendition of the band at the threshold of a major transition into the breakthroughs of *Live/Dead*, recorded six months later.

🎺 *John Dwork, editor of* Dupree's Diamond News, *on* ***Two From the Vault****:*
Dick Latvala, the Dead's tape archivist, has a perfect term for the type of music found on this two-CD concert recording: PRIMAL DEAD, music that seethes with primordial psychedelic energy, painting pictures in the mind's eye of exploding galaxies.

This jewel from the Vault was culled from two concerts, 8/23 and 8/24/68, at the Shrine Auditorium in Los Angeles. The first CD starts with a tight "Good Morning Little Schoolgirl." The "Dark Star" that follows is young and undeveloped compared to mature versions from '69 and beyond; the "St. Stephen"→"The Eleven" is intense, though not as sublime as the version on *Live/Dead*. "Death Don't Have No Mercy," however, is as polished and passionate as the version on *Live/Dead*.

The true magic starts on the second CD with "The Other One"→"New Potato Caboose." "The Other One" is blisteringly hot, but "New Potato Caboose" is beyond description—the Dead at their transportational best. Starting as a beautifully poetic meditation, it rises into a joyous ensemble jam, and when you think the band couldn't become more inspired, Phil erupts into an outrageous lead melody in waltz time. Jerry then launches into *another* jam which builds and builds until he ends the performance with a perfect climax of cascading notes, leaving the listener breathless and grinning.

ULTRA MATRIX 🎗 • A five-year ('86–'91) experiment by GD sound wizard DAN HEALY, who was aiming to enrich recordings of Dead shows by blending the super-clean audio signal from the soundboard feed with the more "alive" P.A. sound that the audience hears (and participates in). Using mics positioned at the front of the soundboard and mixing equipment custom-designed by Ultra Sound, Healy was able to synch the board-feed with the later-arriving signal from the mics. The result was spectacular, as tape collectors who prize "Healy Ultramatrix" or "Ultramix" tapes have discovered.

"To my ears," says *Grateful Dead Hour* host David Gans, "a properly done Ultra Matrix tape is the best possible concert tape." Although Healy agrees with this assessment, he abandoned the process in 1991, in favor of recording the show both ways separately.

UNBROKEN CHAIN • A six-times-a-year Deadhead 'zine from Richmond, Virginia, edited by Laura Smith. *Unbroken Chain* incorporates press clippings, Dead-related comics, tour photos, and columns like "Grateful Gourmet," to present an overview of Deadhead culture from all angles. The journal also includes setlists, record reviews, a letters column called "Chain Reaction," and lists of Deadheads in jail seeking contact.

Started as a xeroxed newsletter in '86, *Unbroken Chain* is a handsome thirty-two-page magazine that still feels like it's put together by a group of friends. In 1993, editor Smith and photographers Tim Ashbridge and Steve Deems collaged a 20- × 30-inch poster of Deadhead vanity plates after three years of taking photos in the parking lot, from AIKO to WORLOX. (*See* GRTFLDED.)

Though Deadhead culture moves with the band, each of the long-lasting Dead-related magazines has the flavor of a particular region (*THE GOLDEN ROAD*, the West; *RELIX*, the East; and *DUPREE'S*, the cosmos), and *Unbroken Chain* is as comfortable as a Virginia porch swing.

UNCLE BOBO • An affectionate nickname for the late Bill Graham, which Graham never liked. "It's a special night tonight," Bob Weir announced onstage at Winterland on 1/8/78. "Aside from being Sunday, it's also Uncle Bill's birthday. And it kind of caught us by surprise, so we didn't have any time to go out and buy anything special or elaborate for him. The best we could do on short notice was to give him a new name. And so now, instead of Uncle Bill Graham, it's *Uncle Bobo* Graham." The band then played "Happy Birthday."

Graham was not amused. "I came off the stage and I said, "How would you like to be called 'Uncle Bobo'?" recalled Graham to biographer Robert Greenfield. "It happens at every Dead show. At least half a dozen times, I say, 'Do me a favor. Don't call me that.' I loathe the name. It's like 'Uncle Shit.' I've asked Bob Weir, 'Please, at some birthday, give me another present. Give me *my* name back.' " *See* BILL GRAHAM.

"U.S. GREYS" • The working title in the studio for "U.S. Blues." Another early version, played live with different lyrics, is called "Wave That Flag" on '70s setlists.

USELESS DEAD STATS • A computer program designed in 1989 by Nethead Eric Simon, as a graduate school exercise in Fortran programming, to tabulate extremely minute Dead show statistics. This online cousin to *DEADBASE* is maintained on an Internet computer server (gdead.berkeley.edu) and can break down any given group of setlists into an elaborate chart of song occurrences, set timings, openers, closers, and encores. "The name is intended to emphasize what I already know," says Simon. "That my compilations are silly." In its first year, however, Simon reports that the program was being used two hundred times a month. Each year, Simon and Randy Jackson use the program to tabulate and electronically post a GD "Year in Review," read widely on the Net. Heads' enthusiasm for stats is at least as passionate as baseball fans'. *See also* NETHEADS; *APPENDIX III: HOW TO BECOME A NET-HEAD.*

USELESS SMILE • "Someone whose ingestion of tiny pieces of paper has rendered them incapable of mundane skills like speech and rational thought," explains Michael Murphy. "As in, 'Two hours into the show, I was a *useless smile.*'"

THE VAULT • The Dead's own collection of recorded shows, in a couple of different rooms at CLUB FRONT, cool but not temperature-controlled, with unpainted plywood shelving along the walls loaded with Ampex and Scotch reels, and boxes of DATs and cassettes.

There are several different areas in the main vault, for live tapes, studio projects, and individual projects by bandmembers. The vault is well organized—all the reels from '73 and '74 are filed neatly in gray boxes along one wall, for instance—and

Dick Latvala is slowly cataloging it all onto a database. There's an overwhelming amount of creativity preserved in those rooms, even beyond the over 2,200 Dead shows on the shelves that will be meat for future scholars and stardust for future Heads. The Dead's collection is not complete—there are collectors who have tapes the Dead don't have—but tape archivist Dick Latvala, an ex-trader himself, won't discuss which shows are missing. "I'd like to maintain the sense of mystery," he says.

Among the earliest tapes in the vault is a recording of "Cat on a Hot Tin Roof," featuring Lesh on lead trumpet, from 5/21/59. On the same tape, there's a version of "I'll Remember April," a lilting jazz standard recorded by Miles Davis, performed by Lesh in September of '59, at a tryout for the College of San Mateo band. In the same cardboard box of "prehistoric masters" (as they are labeled) is a tape of an original work by Lesh titled "Finnegan's Awake." There's a tape of a bluegrass group called the Sleepy Hollow Hog Stompers, featuring Garcia on guitar and banjo, playing "Chuck a Little Hill," "Billy Grimes," "Cannonball Blues," "Devilish Mary," and "Buckdancer's Choice," with Garcia on lead vocals. There's a recording from July of '61 of the "Ellen Smith Blues"—a duet by Garcia and Hunter on guitar and mandolin—made at a coffeehouse called the Boar's Head at the Jewish Community Center in Belmont, California, and "Deep Elem Blues," which became an acoustic Dead favorite, recorded a year later. A tape of "Will the Circle Be Unbroken" from the College of San Mateo Folk Festival on 11/10/62 features Garcia, Hunter, and David Nelson, who went on to found the New Riders of the Purple Sage. These tapes—jazz, bluegrass, a few originals—are where Dead history begins.

The individual bandmembers' areas trace the careers of inquisitive minds at large, ranging among the sounds of the world with the talent, the time, and the money to follow through their inspiration. There's an unreleased Garcia session from Wally Heider's studio on 5/31/74 featuring a cover of "Some Enchanted Evening," along with songs few people have heard since, like "Cardiac Arrest." There are also reels on Garcia's shelf from a bluegrass festival on 4/27/74; a tape from the sessions for Garcia's first solo album, featuring Garcia on trumpet; and never-released studio versions of "Dear Prudence," "Diamond Joe," and "Simple Twist of Fate," from '79. On Hart's shelf, there are outtakes from his first solo album, *Rolling Thunder*, sessions for *Planet Drum*—a summit meeting of the greatest drummers in the world—and a tape labeled "BEAM for Whales."

An area in another room catalogs ongoing projects by Bob Bralove, John Cutler, and Jeffrey Norman, and outside the vault door, piled in the hallway, are boxes of reels by the New Riders and the Quicksilver Messenger Service.

The taping of Dead shows by the band was done haphazardly in the early days. Kidd Candelario ran two-tracks after the Europe tour in '72 until '74, but was also responsible for Keith Godchaux's equipment, so if anything demanded Candelario's immediate attention, the reels might not have been flipped, and some scrap of music lost. Another complication is that the old analog reels are decomposing, and some of them can only be played once more before disintegrating. A process of heating the tapes, called "baking," allows the tapes to be played, and eventually Latvala hopes to install a CD writer in the studio, so a CD can be pressed instantly from a tape.

The band takes its live recording much more seriously now, and as of the summer tour of '92, Healy has been running "A-DATs" of every show, a process that records eight digital tracks onto a single super-VHS tape, three at a time, taking up fifteen to eighteen tapes per show.

It is also Latvala's job to make dubs on cassette for anyone in the band or staff who wants to hear the shows, and in his office at the rear of Club Front is a machine called a "KABA" that makes ten simultaneous cassette copies from a single DAT.

Latvala has become much more selective in what he thinks is a good recording of the band, since his days in Hawaii when he hiked four miles to the post office hoping a hissy audience tape of some Carousel "Anthem" jam would be there waiting for him; but he is not a jaded man. "Sometimes I get overwhelmed by the spiritual heaviness of all the magnificent music here," Latvala says, "and all the problems I have yet to solve. But I'm the luckiest guy on Earth."

VELVEETA • A disparaging nickname for the Weir/ Hunter tune, "Corrina." "There's something fun about teasing Weir," laughs John Barlow. "Deadheads are merciless on him. 'The Thin Man Spits.' It's like the way New Yorkers complain about New York. You can get a sense of the dedication of a New Yorker to New York from how relentless his lament is. A really committed New Yorker will not say anything good about the island of Manhattan. But he won't leave it either." *See* THE LUNGE; PICKY DEADHEADS.

VENDORS • Folks who sell goods to finance their way from show to show: "Rasta Pasta," "the kind" grilled cheese sandwiches, beadwork, t-shirts, and so on. Typically honest and very hardworking, they are living exemplars of self-motivation in a free-market economy. "I sell whatever I can vend," says Guy Gimbrone. "Mostly tie-dyes and hemp bracelets. I make food—stir-fry—and sell that all the time. You get back exactly what you put into it. If you want to every night at a show, the potential to make a lot of money is there. But if you just want to make enough dough to get yourself by, and have a little party money, you can do that, too."

Some full-time vendors aren't even Deadheads, but play service-industry Robin to the band's Batman (or suckerfish to the band's tiger shark), making a living by staying tethered to the band's itinerary, selling the basics to TOUR RATS.

VW BUG/VW MICROBUS • Archetypal DEADMO-BILES. "Not the safest cars to drive with kids," admits Tracy Hartman. "But I miss mine dearly. In the '80s, my husband and I were in school. I had a VW bug and he had a VW van. Both were covered in Dead stickers and Cold War era stickers. We have since given the van to friends—it was given to us by friends, and it was given to them by friends too! We couldn't break the tradition."

WAKE OF THE FLOOD • Album #10, released in November 1973.

☙ *Mary Eisenhart, editor of* MicroTimes, *on* **Wake of the Flood:**

Wake of the Flood was the Dead's first studio album since *American Beauty,* and the first offering of Grateful Dead Records. Tired of battling the constraints of the mainstream rock and roll world, which had shown itself monumentally unclear on the concept of what the band wanted to do and why, the GD took advantage of the end of their Warner Bros. contract to start their own record company. The enterprise was fraught with a sense of fateful mission, stubborn integrity, and against-all-odds optimism. Pigpen had died early in the year; Keith and Donna Godchaux had joined the band; the journey continued amid new beginnings.

Full of this spirit, *Wake of the Flood* contains some of the Dead's most beautiful and enduring music. The themes are heavy—mythic journeys, the cycle of the seasons, death and rebirth, a good hard look into the dark unknown—but, as on *American Beauty,* delivered with an indomitably light heart. In Rick Griffin's Düreresque cover art, there's a serenity in the Reaper's face, and a laughing raven evokes the crow's song in "Uncle John's Band": "Like the morning sun you come, and like the wind you go."

Some points of interest:

🔹 "Stella Blue" and "Eyes of the World": Singing and playing, Garcia is at his sweetly plaintive best; Hunter contemplates beginnings and endings, deaths and dissolutions, following the dream, persistence of vision.

THE DICTIONARY ☠ 305

● "Let Me Sing Your Blues Away": This lightweight, bouncy tune is no "Stella Blue," but it's noteworthy as a rare collaboration between Robert Hunter and Keith Godchaux.

● "Weather Report Suite": A thematic companion to "Eyes of the World," this epic celebrates the changes of season, summer emerging from the wind and rain, the flowing of water, the planting and harvest, the cycles of life's journey. Alas, live versions of the first two segments, Weir's instrumental prelude and the Weir/Anderson Part 1, are rarer than appearances of "Cosmic Charlie," but Part 2 ("Let It Grow") is still performed often, usually as a first-set closer. It contains some of John Barlow's most powerful lyrics and, in concert, some of the band's finest jams.

THE WALL OF SOUND • A 641-speaker, 26,400-watt sound system custom designed for the Dead in the early '70s by DAN HEALY, OWSLEY Stanley, and the other engineers at ALEMBIC. The concept was one of radical simplicity: one enormous stack of speakers for each instrument and each microphone, all set up right behind the musicians. No stage monitors, no mixer. "It's like a band playing in a club," explained Owsley, "only *large*. The musicians can adjust everything, including their vocal level."

The three-story-high system was designed and tested at shows throughout '73, and finally brought out in all its towering splendor on 3/23/74, at San Francisco's Cow Palace. Heads raved. With all of Healy's innovations over the years, many who experienced the Wall of Sound swear to this day that it was the best sound system they've ever heard. "It sounded gorgeous," writes David Gans. "The clarity was stupendous."

Part of its brilliance, explains Owsley, was that it emphasized sound projection over mere volume, with the stacks of speakers "coupling like a radio antenna, multiplying their effect far beyond any simple dB of loudness. You could walk right up to the stack and it wouldn't be any louder, and you could walk away from it, and it wouldn't become any less loud for a long way."

Quality and power came at a price, however. The Wall of Sound was extraordinarily cumbersome to haul around, filling five trailer trucks. Because it was so time-consuming to load in and assemble, it was necessary to build *two* of them —with one always leapfrogging ahead to the next gig (with an extra crew). "The thing was such a monster," explains Owsley. "It just became too much. One day the band said, "We can't handle it anymore." With its burdensome expense, the Wall of Sound had become the embodiment of the band's awkward growth spurt in the early '70s and one of the reasons the band decided to tentatively retire from touring at the end of '74 (*see* THE LAST ONE). Those year-end shows were the Wall of Sound's final shows. The system can be seen and heard in *The Grateful Dead Movie,* a filmed account of that final run at Winterland.

The Wall lives on, though, in two ways. First, "I think it raised the consciousness of the industry," says Healy, "and set new standards and exemplified the direction it really should be going in." Second, the band ended up giving most of the Wall of Sound away, Healy says. "There are probably twenty-five little bands running around that got outfitted by that system."

WALSTIB • *See* WHAT A LONG, STRANGE TRIP IT'S BEEN.

THE WARLOCKS • The name adopted in April '65 by the jug band MOTHER McCREE'S UPTOWN JUG CHAMPIONS when they decided to make the transition to electric instruments and dig into R&B. "[Pigpen had] been pestering me for a while," recalls Garcia. "It was just the next step." Soon to become the Grateful Dead, the Warlocks consisted of Kreutzmann, Garcia, Weir, Pigpen, and, after a brief dally with another bassist (Dana Morgan Jr.), Phil Lesh. Lesh had never played bass before.

Their first few gigs were at Menlo College and Magoo's Pizza Parlor in Menlo Park, and included covers of the Rolling Stones' "King Bee," "Little Red Rooster," and "Walking the Dog" and Chuck Berry's "Promised Land" and "Johnny B. Goode."

In September, the band fell into a regular five-set-per-night gig at the In Room, a bar in Belmont, California, which allowed them the opportunity they needed to explore new directions. After playing on acid together one night, recalls Garcia, "We began to see that vision of a truly fantastic thing." With help from Lesh's background in experimental contemporary composition, they began taking the music in the directions implied by that vision. *See also* ACID TESTS; GRATEFUL DEAD.

WARNING! DRIVER MAY BE EXPERIENCING AN AWESOME "CHINA→RIDER!" • One Deadhead answer to the irreverent "Warning!" bumpersticker craze—"Warning! I Brake for Unicorns"—of the late '80s/early '90s. Other Head warning stickers include, "Warning: I Brake For Hallucinations," and "Warning: I Brake Just Like a Little Girl" (cf. Dylan's "Just Like a Woman.")

A Head spoof on the flat '80s class-conscious sticker, "My other car is a Mercedes," reads, "My Other Car Is on Tour." *See* SETLIST SHORTHAND.

WAVY GRAVY • Born Hugh Nanton Romney on May 15, 1936, clown, poet, activist, and advocate of the Wild Good who was a founding member of the Hog Farm, "an expanded family and ex-mobile hallucination" (in Wavy's words) that outlasted the hypes of several eras with "love, slack, and good humor" making decisions collectively. Romney earned his psychedelic handle from bluesman B.B. King at the Texas Pop Festival in 1969.

Wavy earned the original passing grade at the ACID TESTS by navigating through the smoldering psychedelia to assist a tripper who had begun yelling "Who cares?" into a microphone, establishing a compassionate model for talkdown still used today by the ROCK MED emergency medical personnel. Wavy and the Hog Farmers have maintained a long relationship with the Dead, and act as tribal elders, helping to set up campgrounds at venues and taking care of the kids of band and crew backstage at shows, surfing the chaos on a sea of bubbles and face paint. Wavy was a founding member of SEVA, and organizes Camp Winnarainbow in Mendocino, where kids learn clowning, music, yoga, and how to be a good citizen of the planet from such teachers as Mickey Hart. The Hog Farmers maintain collective households in Berkeley and Laytonville, California. *See* SEVA.

🐷 *Wavy Gravy's advice to Deadheads:*

1. We're all the same person trying to shake hands with ourself.
2. Kissing builds up your mouth.

WE ARE EVERYWHERE • The title of a book by one of
the most influential radicals of the '60s, Jerry Rubin. The slogan was picked up by gay rights activists in the early '70s who
printed up stickers with the phrase so that a gay person who
saw one, say, in a conference room at the Pentagon, or in a
sorority house, would know that another proud gay person had
been there.

"We Are Everywhere" stickers began appearing all over
Dead shows in the mid-'80s, and in other places Deadheads frequent, making a similar point: that Deadheads, like gay people,
are *already* participating in every aspect of the human community. *See* QUEER DEADHEADS.

WE WANT PHIL! • A collective cry that, along with "Let
Phil sing!," is heard often from THE PHIL ZONE and elsewhere
in the audience.

During '86 and '87, Lesh started singing again after a few
tours without a vocal mic of his own. (He had damaged his
voice by singing improperly for years.) Lesh responded several
times to the crowd's raucous request by obliging with a "Box of
Rain," "Tom Thumb's Blues," or one other from the Lesh stable.
One night, 5/11/86 at Palo Alto's Frost Amphitheater, Lesh
stepped up to interrupt a pre-show "Let Phil sing!" chant to
banter, "It's not a matter of letting me sing as much as *making*
me sing." To which the crowd quickly rejoined, "Make Phil
sing!" The band opened the show with a Lesh-led "Gimme
Some Lovin'."

WE WILL SURVIVE • Line from the chorus of "A
Touch of Grey," a Garcia/Hunter song introduced in September '82. Heads immediately embraced the declaration
as a motto for the band's and fans' determination to keep
the bus rolling. The line took on special poignancy when
it was sung during the opener to Garcia's post-coma "comeback show" (12/15/86, Oakland Coliseum), and has remained
a powerful symbol of Deadhead community tenacity ever
since.

WEDGERS • People who sleaze ahead in line while the
line is moving. "Back off, you wedgers!"

WEIR, BOB • Rhythm guitar, vocals, composition. Born on October 16, 1947.

Weir is the band's rhythm guitarist and, along with Garcia, co-lead vocalist. "I never wanted to be a lead guitar player," he has said. "My passion is shaping a song."

Weir is a subtle architect of the large forces at play in the Grateful Dead, and it is that mastery of *the shapes of songs*, arrangements and dynamics as dramatic elements, that Weir has brought to the Dead as a composer, in songs like "Let It Grow," "Cassidy," "The Other One," and "Playing in the Band."

Weir has exceptionally large hands, which help him voice chords in unusual ways, and a restless melodic imagination that shuns the familiar or expected, which makes him a driving force in jams, pushing the improvisational envelope, and keeping things off balance in ways that force his bandmates to listen more closely. As a stage presence, Weir stepped to the fore as the band's showman after Pigpen died, and though his dynamic performing style contains elements of showboating, Heads who mistake his stage theatrics for commercial pandering miss the fact that Weir's tunes have always been platforms for some of the most challenging *outside* jamming the band does.

Weir is the adopted son of wealthy professionals from Atherton, California. His father was an engineer, and his mother ran a successful export/import business. "Because of his adoption," says his boyhood chum and longtime song collaborator JOHN PERRY BARLOW, "Weir's always felt himself to be an outsider. I've never seen any size gathering, from five people in a room to the planet Earth, where Weir didn't feel outside of it."

Weir also inherited a severe case of dyslexia, and was unable to keep up in school. Like many of the other bandmembers, he found he didn't fit into mainstream academic life, and became a troublemaker. "Every one of us was nothing but trouble," Barlow says proudly of his fellow Dead comrades as adolescents. "This country was founded by troublemakers. In Weir's case, he's so different fundamentally, that it's not that he didn't want to play by the rules, particularly—he just couldn't understand them. They didn't make sense to him.

"Weir's got a peculiarly focused intelligence," Barlow continues. "Sometimes his insight is just searing. He'll figure something out on a broad intuitive level that escapes everybody else for a long time."

He never did manage to graduate from high school (though he has since received two honorary high school diplomas). But in the early '60s, Weir developed a strong identification with folk musicians like Joan Baez and Reverend Gary Davis (who he later visited to learn Davis's version of "Samson and Delilah.") He took up the acoustic guitar, and started spending time around the Stanford University coffeehouse scene, where he met Garcia, Kreutzmann, and Pigpen. In '64, he formed the jug band MOTHER MCCREE'S UPTOWN JUG CHAMPIONS with Garcia, Pigpen, his high school buddy Bob Matthews, and several others. One year later, the band went electric, becoming THE WARLOCKS.

Like most of the other bandmembers, his life was altered by his experiences with LSD. "The effect psychedelics had on him was profound," Barlow says. "There was a period where he was not on this planet. I don't want to say that he failed the Acid Test, but he certainly got a different score than some folks. There was quite a while there where he was just sort of aphasic. It was like he was really connected on some other level."

The image that I have of that whole period is Bobby living on the second floor of 710 Ashbury Street on the couch there, with all of his worldly goods in a paper bag on the floor. The other person who was in the room all the time was Neal Cassady, because that's where the stereo was. Cassady would come in there about eleven o'clock at night, toss back a couple of bottles of *benzadrina*, take off his shirt, juggle his hammer all night long and shout bebop—just rave scat. Weir would be lying on the couch with eyes open, staring at the ceiling, and it was like he was *dreaming* Cassady somehow. You could see that there was a relationship between this frenetic, powerful energy manifestation, and Weir's utter stillness. That went on for most of the summer of '67.

Weir has been perhaps the most politically active band-member, championing environmental and public health causes with his staunch support of the SEVA Foundation, the Rainforest Action Network, Greenpeace, and others. "I've come to the realization that part of working for a living today is working for a world in which to live," he says. "If we don't stop our ruinous ways, we will end life on this planet in short order." In addition to his support of the band's REX FOUNDATION, he has his own charitable group, the Further Foundation. In '92, he published an op-ed in the *New York Times*, railing against a piece of legislation that would have approved massive deforestation in the United States. *See* SEVA; WEIR/BARLOW.

A selected Bob Weir nonDead discography:

Ace — Essentially the Dead, minus Pigpen, 1972

Kingfish — Kingfish band, 1976

Heaven Help the Fool — Bob Weir Band, 1978

Bobby and the Midnites — Bob Weir ("Midnite the Cat" was on a TV show called *Andy's Gang*, which Weir had watched as a small child), 1981

WEIR/BARLOW • The longtime songwriting collaboration of Bob Weir and John Perry Barlow, born in 1970 with "Mexicali Blues." The Weir/Barlow repertoire includes "Cassidy," "Weather Report Suite," "The Music Never Stopped," "Saint of Circumstance," "Estimated Prophet," and many other Dead classics.

🍃 *John Barlow on Weir/Barlow:*

Bobby's not an easy person to write with. It's like a marriage. For one thing, Weir hates writing. He would rather get a root canal. If Weir's going to do a song, it's going to be under some kind of pressure, like a pending album.

I approach songwriting in a fairly conventional way. My view is, if you start out with something simple and straight ahead, the Grateful Dead will grow their own encrusted stuff on it, and with time it will become a Grateful Dead song, with all its weird labyrinthine characteristics.

Weir's got a completely different approach. He wants it to be *outside* at the get-go. So there's a real dynamic tension that I think is our strength. What we come up with is a hybrid that contains all the energy that comes out of our arguing. We start out with two different objectives and end up with something that neither one of us is all that happy about.

I wish I could see what other people see. I really do. Because I would love to feel prouder of my own work. But I don't. I honestly don't. "Looks Like Rain" sounds maudlin to me. I never liked "Lazy Lightnin' " that much. Hunter is much better at this. Hunter is a true genius, and it's both humbling and humiliating trying to operate in Hunter's shadow all these years.

"Cassidy" is one tune I really feel great about in every respect, and always did. I've come around on a lot of the others. I feel pretty good about "Estimated Prophet," though I hated it so much at the time that I wanted Weir to take my name off of it. I like "I Need a Miracle." I like all of the songs that Weir did on *Heaven Help the Fool* a lot. The others seemed to get framed in a way that bring out my own faults.

Where I've made progress is recognizing that whether I like the work itself, it's been an important contribution, in the sense that if it had just been Hunter, as great as he is, it would have been a mono-culture. It wouldn't have been a complete ecology. And there is something about having both of us there, and the occasional Gerrit Graham and Bobby Petersen, that gives it a much richer dynamic than it would have had otherwise. Also, the fact that you've got Bobby as a central part of the mix instead of a complete focus on Garcia is really healthy. That's an important consideration. So I'm glad that I did it.

THE WELL • The Whole Earth 'Lectronic Link, an online community founded in 1985 by Stewart Brand, Larry Brilliant, and others. The Deadhead conference in The WELL is one of the most articulate and lively Deadhead "neighborhoods" in cyberspace. (There are also many non-Dead related conferences in The WELL.)

The architects of The WELL were veterans of some of the counterculture's most auspicious endeavors. Brand had been a Prankster, organized the TRIPS FESTIVAL, and gave a generation of innovators "access to tools" they needed to effect real change by editing the *Whole Earth Catalog, Co-evolution Quarterly*, and the *Whole Earth Review*. Brilliant was a Hog Farmer (*see* WAVY GRAVY) and an epidemiologist for SEVA, who licensed to The WELL the software that makes the ongoing conversations easier to follow than the rowdier everything-at-once of

DEAD-FLAMES and the Net. The social texture of The WELL was shaped by Matthew McClure and John "Tex" Coate, both alumni of the Farm, the self-sufficient commune in Tennessee that emigrated from the Haight-Ashbury.

David Gans and *MicroTimes* editor Mary Eisenhart were sitting in the balcony of a show at Kaiser Auditorium in November of '85, when the same notion came to them both—that Deadheads were perfect candidates for online community, by virtue of their love of information and communication. Joined in their venture by Deadhead scholar and computer expert Bennett Falk, they passed out flyers at Berkeley Community Theater in April '86, announcing the formation of a "Virtual Village Green" for Deadheads.

"We had envisioned it as a scholarly place, a literary salon" says Gans, "but it turned out to be more rough-and-tumble— more like a *real* village green." The general tone of The WELL, however, is much more like what the founders envisioned than any other Deadhead corner of cyberspace. (Eisenhart has moved on to host the Grateful Dead conference on America Online.)

The conferences in The WELL are organized broadly by subject—like gd—and within subject into topics, like *Deadheads behind the bamboo curtain; Remembering Brent,* or *The soldier, the sailor, and the lady in the fire.* Participants can read everything that's already been written into a topic, and then type in their own responses, called "posts."

The gd conference was so successful that it kept the rest of The WELL afloat while it found its footing, and has since evolved into a virtual archipelago of smaller conferences, including *tapes, tours* (show reports); *deadlit* (books, lyric analysis, philosophy); *tix, feedback* (suggestions to the band); and several private conferences. The presence in The WELL of informed participants keeps unfounded rumors to a minimum, and gives Deadheads a place to get up-to-date information on tour schedules and setlists. *See also* SEVA; *APPENDIX III: HOW TO BECOME A NETHEAD.*

☙ *Steve Silberman, digaman@well.com, on The WELL:*

I am a member of the last American generation to grow up before there were computers in most schools, and many kids' bedrooms. When I was very young, I had a daydream that some day, difficult world problems would be solved by ringing a bell that would summon people to screens located on every street corner. Each person would be given some small part of the larger problem to solve, and when the answers were put together, a bigger thought than any one person could have mustered would have the problem licked.

One of the saddest things about saying good-bye at the end of a show is taking temporary leave of being visibly part of a larger self. Deadheads make tapes and setlists (and books and babies and politics), but the best thing they make is community. A Dead show is like a Shaker barn raising, but the morning after, the real "barn" is not in the venue, or on the tapes, but in the hearts of everyone who was there.

Right after I got over my unnecessary shyness about computers, a friend loaned me a modem, and I remembered something that David Gans had told me years before about a place for Deadheads called The WELL. I dialed the number, and after a few awkward moments of typing and confusion, I opened my eyes in a new world—a place where the dance of ideas about the music, and the world in which the music is made, did not have to end after leaving the parking lot. There, Deadheads talk not only about the band, but what they're reading, who they're loving, the projects they're hopeful about, the things in their lives they need help with. It's not censored, even subtly, the way TV and newspapers (and some other online services) are. It's just a bunch of Deadheads sitting around talking in text—the GROUPMIND made visible.

The WELL, like most good things, has its drawbacks. I earn no aerobics points when I'm logged on, and there are no trees in cyberspace (just tape trees ;-)). It's insidiously addictive. But by now, that sound that my modem makes is like the creaking of a door to the Deadhead clubhouse of my dreams.

Good things are exchanged in The WELL—tapes, extra tickets, and lots of the kind of intelligence about the Dead that rumors only pretend to be. When I can't be at a show, I dip into The WELL about the time I know the show is ending, to watch history advance by an increment as Steve Marcus logs on with the setlist from backstage. And when I go to shows these days, there are all these people to hang out and dance and be with, whose souls I commune with daily; all the other WELLheads, helping to build the real barn, post by post.

WELNICK, VINCE • Keyboards, vocals. Born on February 2, 1951.

Welnick took over the keyboard slot after Brent Mydland's death. His first show was September 7, 1990. (For the first year and a half, the Dead had two keyboardists, the other being BRUCE HORNSBY).

Welnick is a team player, and he has brought a lot of color into the band with the help of Bob Bralove, who has given Welnick Hammond B-3 organ sounds, strings, and horns playable from his MIDI keyboards. Welnick's raucous lead vocals on versions of "Baba O'Reilly" and "Long Way to Go Home" bring ballsy rock and roll flourishes to a band which has traditionally relied on quirkier, subtler dynamics.

Raised in Phoenix, Arizona, Welnick learned to play jazz, blues, and rock from his mother, an accomplished boogie-woogie pianist. He also played classical organ in his local church. His teenage band, the Equations, played double bills with the Spiders, led by Vincent Furnier, the future Alice Cooper.

Welnick first saw the Dead in March 1970 at the Star Theatre, in Phoenix. Around that time, he joined a band called the Beans, and moved to San Francisco with his bandmates, who soon changed their name to the Tubes. The Tubes made a name for themselves playing a gonzo mix of hard rock and jazz fusion, scoring a hit with their debut single, "White Punks on Dope," and earning protests from Moral Majority types for lead singer Fee Waybill's outrageous theatrics.

"I listened to a lot of John Coltrane and McCoy Tyner," Welnick says. "The Tubes used to do a lot of 'Trane's stuff. We played a lot of different genres, so I was familiar with most of the styles the Dead do, except the folkier stuff."

It was a daunting challenge for Welnick to join a band with an active repertoire of more than three hundred songs. He took the albums and tapes home, plugged his keyboard into the stereo, and played along.

"Initially," he said in 1993, "I had every song charted. I took three notebooks with the words, and vague little chord charts.

For about a month, I'd bring the charts out on stage, just so I wouldn't screw up. Now I kind of have a handle on it."

That unspoken communication is a constant challenge. I don't want to get carried away and step on the big boys. A great deal of it is what you don't play. It's a lot more important to listen, more than in any band I've been in. To be aware of what's going on, and not overplay.

If you're listening carefully, there's so much interplay that it gets frightfully exciting. When that happens, there's magic every night. I'm still in complete awe of it. I didn't know how "big time" big time was until I got next to these guys.

WHARF RATS • A group of sober Heads founded by Don B., who, in a 1984 ad in THE GOLDEN ROAD, called for other Heads to "take your 12-step meeting on tour."

The Wharf Rats—named for a Garcia/Hunter song which features an alcoholic character named August West who hopes for a new life—hold lively meetings during the set break at shows. Anyone who thinks sobriety isn't ecstatic hasn't seen the Wharf Rats moshing during "Sugar Magnolia." Their symbol—a yellow balloon—was adopted in 1987, after a Head decorated a balloon with the AA triangle and brought it to a show at Calaveras.

The Rats have developed their own slogans that are Deadified versions of 12-step classics: "Friend of August W.," "Let Go . . . Let Jerry," "Another Dopeless Hope Fiend," and "One Show at a Time." In keeping with the 12-step tradition of being self-supporting, the Wharf Rats declined a grant from the REX FOUNDATION. Since the late '80s, the Dead have set aside an information table at shows for the group.

"For me," explains one Wharf Rat, "giving up drugs is what cleared the path from the music to my head."

☙ *Tommy R., Wharf Rat, The Bus Came By . . . Twice:*
If you are like me, much of your life with the Dead has been spent in an altered state of one sort or another. At some point, you may have wondered if you would get so off on the music, if the drugs weren't there. This thought

troubled my mind on more than one occasion, because I did not want to believe that what had become such a central part of my life, and the focal point
of my spirit, needed to be jump-started by an artificial catalyst.

My father used to irritate me saying, "If you like the music so much, why
do you need the drugs?" My answer to him was, "You don't understand."
There was truth in that, but I knew in my heart that drugs were an integral
part of my experience at shows (and quickly becoming a too-integral part of
my life), and I seriously wondered whether I would enjoy myself as much
without them. I wasn't about to go without them, but I suspected that one day
I would have to stop doing drugs, to see for myself. I only knew that today
was not the day, and neither was tomorrow.

It seems that the Universe was interested to see how I would enjoy a drug-
free life. In 1989, my drug abuse got so bad, I was forced to seek help and go
into rehab. I was told that I would have to stay away from places where I had
had trouble staying sober before. Dead shows certainly fell into this category,
but cutting the Dead out of my life was not an option to me. I had signed on
for the whole trip, and as far as I was concerned, the journey was not over.

Still, I knew I had to stay sober. Drugs had torn me up pretty bad. I will
never regret the experiences, ideas, thoughts, joys, or pain that drugs brought
to my life. I learned a great deal from them. But the simple fact is that when
I stopped learning and it was time to move on, I could not do it. Every time
I got high, this fact rang a little truer.

How was I going to manage this miracle of staying sober at Dead shows?
First, I had to realize that if I didn't drink or take drugs, when the show
ended, I would still be sober. Next, I had to hook up with a support group of
clean and sober Deadheads—the Wharf Rats. It was unbelievable to me that
not only were there others like me at shows, but they staffed an information
table, and gathered for meetings at set break. I was told that to find the meeting, look for the yellow balloons. I thought to myself, "These sick bastards
love the Dead so much that they are willing to risk their sobriety by coming
to shows?" Since then, I have been to over a hundred shows sober. I can honestly tell you that the rapture and joy I knew in the early days is still there for
me sober. Drugs are not a prerequisite to "get it."

Is it the same as it was? Of course not. I am not the same as I was either.

When the bus came by the first time in 1983, I got on with a lot of curiosity.

In 1989, the bus came by again, only this time, a man holding a yellow balloon stuck his head out the back window to tell me there was a nonsmoking section on the bus if I needed it. I smiled and got back on, with a lot of curiosity, and no fear.

WHAT A LONG, STRANGE TRIP IT'S BEEN • The lyric from "Truckin' " that has come to evoke for Deadheads the three-decade journey taken together by the band, the crew, and successive generations of Heads who have grown up together, going to shows, exchanging tapes, ideas, and lore. The line is so familiar to Heads that it can be abbreviated as "WALSTIB" on bumperstickers and license plates. The line earns a cheer for an additional reason at shows: By the time "Truckin' " is played, usually in the second set, those who have taken psychedelics have a lot of light-years of trial and discovery behind them.

WHERE'S THE "DARK STAR"? • An infamously misheard lyric from the Weir/Barlow song "Lost Sailor" that draws howls at shows from Heads who are wondering the same thing. The actual line is, "Where's the Dog Star?"

Hunter's lyrics were printed in a little booklet that came with *Live/Dead*, but for most of the Dead's career, figuring out the exact wording of phrases like "she was too pat to open and too cool to bluff" (from "Scarlet Begonias") was left to solitary guessing or stoned dorm-room committee, and some strange mutations occurred between the band's lips and the fans' ears.

WHAT'S HEARD	ACTUAL LYRIC	THE TUNE
"Rat in a drain ditch, *frog* on a limb"	"Rat in a drain ditch, caught on a limb"	"He's Gone," Garcia/Hunter
"Flashing *my keys* out on Main Street"	"Flashing marquees out on Main Street"	"Truckin'," Garcia/Lesh/ Weir/Hunter ("I once even did some art work with a 'no key flashing' sign," admits Eugene Evon.)
"Mike and Gloria gonna be my name"	"Might and glory gonna be my name"	"Estimated Prophet," Weir/Barlow (Heidi Saller)

"If the thunder don't get you, the *white man* will!"	"If the thunder don't get you, the *lightning* will"	"The Wheel," Garcia/Hunter (a friend of Eugene Evon)
"Takes the wheel when I'm seein' double/*Bakes my chicken when I sleep*"	"Takes the wheel when I'm seein' double/Pays my ticket when I speed"	"Sugar Magnolia," Weir/Hunter
"I told Althea the *treasury* was tearing me limb from limb"	"I told Althea that treachery was tearing me limb from limb"	"Althea," Garcia/Hunter ("I had this one wrong for years," says Jeff Gorlechen. "Even sang it in a band this way [blush].")
"Brown-eyed women *in red leather jeans*"	"Brown-eyed women and red grenadine."	"Brown-Eyed Women" (Heard by Matt McKenzie, coming out of Atlanta's Omni after one of his friend's first shows. "None of us felt compelled to correct her," he says.)
"Several seasons with *that shrinking season*/Wrapped a *bale in sordid covies* . . ."	"Several seasons with their treasons/Wrap the babe in scarlet colors, call it your own"	"St. Stephen" (from the liner notes to a Japanese release of *Aoxomoxoa*)

Newspaper reporters reviewing Dead concerts have reported hearing tunes like *"Mighty Swell"* ("Might As Well"), *"Grow, Jimmy, Grow"* ("Row Jimmy"), and *"Stolen Rain"* (hearing the "Bird Song" line "I'll show you snow and rain" as "I'll show you *stolen rain*"). The publication of the two-volume *Grateful Dead* songbook in the early '70s helped, but the band kept writing new tunes, and Heads wanted to know what the band was singing about *now*. Books of lyrics, caringly transcribed by Heads themselves, became parking lot best-sellers—though the vendors' guesses were not always more accurate than anyone else's.

The task of divining the Dead's lyrics is made even more difficult by the lyricists' attraction to dense, evocative, idiomatic phrasing that does not yield its meaning easily, but reveals "by clews and indirections," as Walt Whitman said. Hunter acknowledged this in the preface to the first edition of his collected lyrics, *Box of Rain*, published in 1990:

Aficionados of the work will find a few unsupposed things lurking in familiar lines. Stranger things thought to have been heard may not be found at all. My inclination has been to forgo printing lyrics on the jackets of recordings and let the songs live out their lives in the listener's ear.

WHIPPITS • *See* NITROUS OXIDE.

WHITE POWDERS • Slang term used by Heads for many different drugs in crystalline form: cocaine, heroin, and amphetamines. "Junk," writes William Burroughs in *Naked Lunch*, "is the ultimate merchandise. No sales talk necessary. The client will crawl through a sewer and beg to buy."

Many of this century's most gifted musicians—Charlie Parker, Bill Evans, Billie Holiday, Keith Richards, Miles Davis—were heroin addicts, and it's no secret that there have been fierce battles with addiction on both sides of "the rail." Eleven-year bandmember Brent Mydland died on July 26, 1990, after a combined overdose of cocaine and morphine. Bullet-shaped cocaine dispensers were not an uncommon sight at shows in the late '70s and early '80s, but as the side effects of these substances became widely known among Heads, and the selfishness and paranoia brought on by these substances helped make them unappealing in a community that prizes generosity and tolerance, many Heads have found a way out of "Jonestown"—while staying on tour—by joining the WHARF RATS.

WHO ARE THE GRATEFUL DEAD AND WHY DO THEY KEEP FOLLOWING ME? • The prince of Deadhead bumpersticker wit. "It says it all," says Erez Kreitner.

In December '87, as part of a cable television pay-per-view broadcast, a Deadhead named Gus put this question to the band. Garcia played along: "We know everything there is to know about you, Gus!" he replied in a mock-conspiratorial tone, and then turned to the rest of the band, slapped his hand to his forehead, and sighed, "Darn it—he found out."

WHO CAN THE WEATHER COMMAND? [FROM "BLACK PETER"] • Miraculous tales of clouds parting the moment a show begins, rainbows appearing during "Terrapin," thunderheads condensing out of clear sky at the drop of a "Looks Like Rain" or rolling away after "Franklin's Tower," constitute a significant body of lore among Heads who want to ascribe supernatural powers to the Dead. A drenched crowd can often expect a sympathetic "Cold Rain and Snow" OPENER.

A spectacular exhibition of the weather becoming a player in the band occurred at the Silver Bowl in Las Vegas on 5/30/92, when Hart traded thunder from THE BEAM with angry anvil clouds, and the crowd gasped as lightning flashed above the stage as the band played "Spanish Jam."

WHO IS THE DOODAH MAN? • One of many questions Deadheads ask themselves and each other about the "real" origins of the tunes, the "doodah man" being the character from the Garcia/Hunter song "Truckin' " who advises the song's narrator that "you got to play your hand."

Figuring out who the characters in the songs were based on is one way for Heads to feel like they have backstage passes to the lyricists' creative process, but the speculations—which run rampant, especially on the Net—are rarely correct. One Head swears that Mr. Benson from "Candyman" was the Dead's accountant, while the doodah man has been traced back to every raffish figure from Ken Kesey to R. Crumb's Mr. Natural.

"Oh, that's just from that song 'Camptown Races,' that goes '_doodah, doodah,_' " explains Hunter. "I wasn't thinking about anybody in particular. Just that gambler on his way home from the game with a pocketful of tin." Sometimes the speculations are as much an act of imagination as the songs themselves.

🐾 _NETHEAD Andrew Shalit's shaggy-dog tale on the origins of "Franklin's Tower":_
"Franklin" is Benjamin Franklin. The Bell is (of course) the Liberty Bell. The tower is a church tower (or watchtower?) in Philadelphia where the Liberty Bell originally (and briefly) hung. When bells are manufactured, the hot

metal is poured into a mold. The mold is removed when the metal is still quite hot (though no longer liquid). The cooling bell is then immersed in water. This process needs to be done very carefully to give a bell a high-quality sound. The dipping process is called "dewing" the bell. The Liberty Bell was quite a large bell for its day and age. There was some question of whether it could survive the dewing process and still produce a good sound. Benjamin Franklin (being the inventor he was) suggested rolling the bell between large tight sheets of cotton immediately after the dewing. This would remove the water (thereby slowing the cooling) and provide a kind of high-tension buffing at the critical stage. He called this process "rolling away the dew." Unfortunately, the bell manufacturers did not take his advice. They did not roll away the dew, and hence when it was hung in the tower, it had only one good ring. Benjamin Franklin's only comment on the matter was "if you plant ice, you're going to harvest wind." The ice refers to an alternate dewing process used at the suggestion of a rival inventor (I'll spare you the details, but he turned out to be quite a Tory). The wind, of course, is the lack of sound from subsequent ring-ings. A second meaning (Hunter's always the punster) relates to Franklin Delano Roosevelt. The musical structure of "Franklin's Tower" is similar to that of "Deal." Hunter was surprised that Jerry would write two such similar songs, and so he considered "Franklin's Tower" a "New Deal." It's really remarkable, the breadth of our culture that Hunter manages to work into his lyrics. By the way, Franklin's Tower (the real one, not the song) has since been converted to a bridge. If anyone's interested in buying it, let me know.

See WHERE'S THE "DARK STAR"?

WHY THE MUSIC NEVER STOPS 📖 • *Garcia, in an interview in '91 with WNEW's Scott Muni:*

Here's the thing. If I stop playing for longer than a month at a time, my chops get so bad I can't stand to listen to myself. For the three months it takes me to recover from that, it's not worth it. So I keep working. If I keep working, I keep playing at a reasonable level.

THE WILDWOOD BOYS • Another of the good-time jug bands that played coffeehouses like the Tangent in Palo Alto and hootenannies on the South Bay Peninsula and in North Beach in '63. At one gig, Robert Hunter introduced his bandmates as, "On banjo, Honest Jerry Garcia, who tunes quite incessantly; Simple Dave Nelson, our Sphinx who never says anything, and wants more than anything to be a *real* boy; and back here we have our bass player, whose name is Norman, and he loves you all. But I don't."

One of the Wildwood Boys' tunes, written by Garcia, was "Jerry's Breakdown"—otherwise known as both "Wilma Gefilte Fish" and "Sweat Trip"—an Earl Scruggs-style banjo speed workout with a minor-key, Middle Eastern flavor. They also played the "Muleskinner Blues" and gospel sing-alongs like "Standing in the Need of Prayer." *See* MOTHER MCCREE'S UPTOWN JUG CHAMPIONS.

WILL SEND BLANKS AND POSTAGE ✎ • Heads just getting started in tape trading will make this offer to traders with larger collections, hoping established traders will agree to record onto blank tapes and seed their collection, preferably with rare, high-quality tapes that have a lot of trading power. In a barter culture, the more you have to offer, the more you can get; beginners must depend initially upon the generosity of more experienced collectors to begin building their collection. The back of Deadhead 'zines like *RELIX* and *THE GOLDEN ROAD* frequently contain classified ads from beginners. *See* TREES AND VINES; YOUR LIST GETS MINE.

WINTERLAND • Bill Graham's 5,400-seat venue in San Francisco's Fillmore district, closed at the end of 1978. There were black lights in the hallways, which bathed white shirts, shoelaces, and skin in a purple psychedelic glow. The much-beloved Bill Graham Productions security guard Clyde Williams—"Willie"—was always at the door, saying, "Have your tickets out and ready!"

A Vietnam vet nicknamed "Joe Tripps" actually lived in Winterland, in a box at the side of the stage. He slept during the shows, and would come out afterwards, as "Greensleeves" played on the P.A., to help clean up. A graffito on the wall said, "You're on the road to heaven." *See* THE LAST ONE; THEY'RE NOT THE BEST AT WHAT THEY DO, THEY'RE THE ONLY ONES THAT DO WHAT THEY DO.

❧ Blair Jackson on Winterland:

Looking back through time from an age when a "small" Dead show takes place in a 14,000-seat hockey arena, it's hard to believe that San Francisco's Winterland was once considered "the big place" where the Dead played. "Absolutely!" remembers Bob Barsotti, a longtime production chief with Bill Graham Presents. "When they started doing shows at Winterland, a lot of people complained about how big it was. And of course it *was* a lot bigger than the Fillmore or the Avalon or the Family Dog. We used to do Thursday at the Fillmore, Friday and Saturday at Winterland, and then go back to the Fillmore on Sunday. We'd move the equipment back and forth on these rolling carts. It took a little while for people to realize that things were only going to get bigger, which they did, of course. And by the time Winterland closed, it seemed like an intimate place."

Located just a block from the Fillmore Auditorium, Winterland was known before the late '60s primarily as the home of the Ice Follies. By the time BGP started putting on occasional shows there in the mid '60s, Winterland was already a decaying old arena. Its acoustics challenged every band that ever played there — DAN HEALY once told me, "Winterland was *awful* acoustically. I'm glad it was like that in a way, though, 'cause that's where we cut our teeth. I was raised in the worst tub going, so by the time I had to venture into bigger halls around the country, I'd lived for so many years with that, the rest of it was a piece of cake." The cavernous arena was particularly cruel to bass frequencies, much to Phil Lesh's chagrin.

Physically, Winterland was not that dissimilar from many older civic auditoriums. It had a high curved ceiling; a small, seven-row lower balcony that rimmed the main dance floor (and even went behind the stage — in those choice seats you could find yourself practically on top of the drummers); a couple of rows of seats right under the balcony; and then a much deeper back balcony that seemed to suck the sound into its vortex. To get up to the balcony, you had to make your way up big switchbacking cement ramps (always quite a freak parade). A small hallway on the lower-balcony level housed a very cool rock memorabilia shop (a real rarity in those days) and what I'm sure was the only organic food concession stand in a major rock venue. For most of the '70s, two *huge* banners hung in the air on either side of the stage: the Dead's skull and roses, and the Rolling Stones' infamous red tongue (left over from the Stones' historic '72 Winterland run).

The human traffic inside Winterland always had a decent flow, even at sold-out gigs, and my (perhaps rosy) memory is that it wasn't even too difficult getting around on the main floor during a show. The maze of big and small rooms and hallways backstage was always a frenetic madhouse. "There were always more people backstage at Dead shows than any other shows," Barsotti says with a laugh. "They always had more complimentary tickets than anyone else—in fact, comps at Winterland was like this *verboten* thing, but somehow they always managed to get in as many of their friends as they wanted. They still do."

If you were moderately determined, you could always score a ticket to a Winterland show: "We always held four hundred tickets at the door, so if you got there at a reasonable hour for any show, you could get a ticket," Barsotti says. "We almost always sold out Dead shows, even in the early days." In the '60s, as often as not, bands like the Jefferson Airplane or Quicksilver (or both) would be on the bill for the big Winterland concerts. "But part of the charm of Winterland, especially early on," Barsotti notes, "is that so many people would go there without really even knowing who was playing there. 'It's Saturday night—let's go to Winterland and see who's there.'"

The Dead played Winterland only sporadically in the late '60s, preferring smaller venues like the Fillmore Auditorium and, after that closed, the Carousel Ballroom. It wasn't until '73 that Winterland became the primary place the Dead played in the Bay Area. By the time the Dead played their final show there, they'd logged sixty-one shows at Winterland—the most they've played in one place (though at their current rate, Madison Square Garden will eclipse that number in a few years).

The building lay empty for a few years, but the Dead found a nice Winterland-equivalent across the bay—the 7,800-seat Oakland Auditorium (a.k.a. Henry J. Kaiser), which served us well until the scene outgrew it, too. In the mid-'80s Winterland was razed and replaced by a condominium development. But it will always live in the hearts of Bay Area rock fans lucky enough to have seen shows there—it definitely had a vibe to it that seemed to bring out the best in every artist who played there, from the San Francisco bands, to the Stones, to Bruce Springsteen, to the Sex Pistols. And fortunately, there will always be one great way to get a little fix of Winterland magic: Watch *The Grateful Dead Movie*, shot there over five nights in 1974.

WITHOUT A NET • Album #22, released in September 1990.

This album documents the tours of late '89 and '90, Mydland's last. Launched by the "Formerly the Warlocks" shows on 10/8 and 10/9/89 at Hampton Coliseum, these tours marked a creative peak for the band, as MIDI added a new spectrum of voices to the musical conversation, and the ensemble sympathies ran deep.

🍀 *Nick Meriwether, historian, on* **Without a Net:**

Without a Net is a meticulous piece of craftsmanship, carefully assembled to approximate a representative live show from the tours that produced it. Those tours left legions of formerly jaded Deadheads awed and reinvigorated: Anyone lucky enough to have seen the Formerly the Warlocks show at Hampton on 10/9/89 will attest to the Dionysian ecstasy that the opening notes of "Dark Star" produced among fans who had spent years listening to *Live/Dead* regretting being born too late. The "Clifton Hanger" to whom the album is dedicated is Brent Mydland, who died right before the album was released. Cover artist Rick Griffin (who did the cover of *Aoxomoxoa*) also died shortly thereafter, and his beautiful graphic for *Without a Net* depicts a circus—a choreographer of adventure and risk—an apt metaphor for a Dead show.

From the opening notes of "Feel Like a Stranger," this virtual show sounds like it's going to be good, with the "Stranger" opener portending a spacy evening, and Garcia's MIDI horn adding a wonderful lushness—"IT" isn't happening yet, but the omens are good. Just before the take-off point of the jam, Brent sings, "It's gonna be a long, long crazy *tour*." This version—from the Formerly the Warlocks show—was the tour opener. The vocals are strong, almost The Band–like in their rough confidence.

The classic Dead shuffle of "Mississippi Half-Step" makes me dance even at home, treated here to its best live performance on an officially released album, with Garcia sounding grizzly as an old prospector. There's a minor vocal slip to lend verisimilitude to the "without a net" vibe. I've always thought the drummers liked "Walkin' Blues" a lot, and their interplay on this serious groove supports that notion.

"Althea" starts strong, with gossamer interplay between four lead players and the drummers. The centerpiece space of "Cassidy" is full of apocalyptic overtones, but never is abstracted too far from the groove. The "Bird Song" jam goes even further, and "Let It Grow" is treated to a letter-perfect performance that makes getting up to put on the second CD difficult until you've had a set break of your own.

There are solid moments in the second set, including a subtle segue between "China Cat Sunflower" and "I Know You Rider," a high-voltage "Help On the Way→Slipknot!→Franklin's Tower," and a powerfully weird "Victim or the Crime." But what makes this disk is Branford Marsalis sitting in on "Eyes of the World" for seamless dialogues with Garcia, who sounds exhilarated to be swapping leads with a melodic mind as fertile as his own, as the band crests wave after wave underneath them. (The entire 3/29/90 tape from which this is taken is worth looking for.)

Brent's cover of Traffic's "Dear Mr. Fantasy"—faded out, unfortunately, to avoid having to pay royalties on the "Hey Jude" that followed it—rounds out the album as a moving tribute. *Without a Net* presents the band at a watershed time in their development, playing a dream setlist. It is an absolutely necessary collection for those interested in the performing history of this band, and for anyone who thinks that older rockers don't take chances anymore.

THE WOLF • First of three celebrated electric guitars custom-designed and built for Garcia by luthier Doug Irwin. Named for its wolf-shaped inlay of ivory and mother-of-pearl, the Wolf was made in '71 from maple and purpleheart, with an ebony fingerboard. In '79, Garcia started playing another Irwin commission, the fourteen-pound "Tiger," made from coca bola, flame maple, and vermilion, with a tiger inlay. The third in the series, "Rosebud," was finished in '90, and became the first Irwin guitar with on-board MIDI (*see* MIDI). Rosebud, which cost Garcia around $13,000, is in-laid with a dancing female skeleton (the "skeleton saint," Irwin says), which some Heads have taken to calling the "Hula Girl." Another Garcia commission, a guitar called Wolf Jr., was finished in '91 but has never made an appearance.

Irwin was nineteen years old and had been making guitars for about a year when Garcia spotted one of his works-in-progress in the legendary Alembic music store, in San Francisco. "I was in the back of the shop charging up some pickups one day when some guy came back and said, 'Hey, Jerry Garcia's out front, and he wants to buy your instrument.' We were always ribbing each other back then, so I didn't believe it. I just laughed. And the guy comes back a few minutes later and says, 'Really—Jerry *is* out there and he wants to buy your instrument.' They finally dragged me out there and sure enough, there he was, and he bought the instrument on the spot. It wasn't even completed. It was all set up, but not yet playable through an amp.

"At the time Garcia was mostly using a Fender Stratocaster. So when he bought that first guitar, he asked me if I would build him a similar guitar, but with Fender pickups and a Fender scale and electronic configuration. That was the Wolf. After I completed it, he asked me to start another instrument for him. He said, 'Look, don't hold back on anything. Do whatever you want.' He gave me an open account."

Irwin, who failed wood-shop in high school, now builds on a commission basis only (*see* PLAY LIKE JERRY), working in the ideal climate of Sonoma County, north of San Francisco. "My style of building really comes from banjo building," he explains. "A lot of hardwoods and very ornate work, and making a quality instrument that will last a long time." He has three guitar projects going for Garcia, all using graphite instead of wood to bring down the weight of the guitar, and is presently training his oldest son, Paul, to follow in his footsteps.

🎸 *Doug Irwin, on the craft of instrument design:*

There is no right or wrong. In fact, there are no rules at all. All musical instruments are tools of the imagination. Even with music itself—there are basic theories of how it works, but you can't spell out in an equation. You can't perfectly calculate a musical scale. When we calculate the scales for the fingerboard, you end up with these fractions of eight or nine points after the decimal.

The average steel string guitar—it's kind of an amazing thing that it stays together. You've got almost five hundred pounds of tension on the top when those brass strings are tuned up, and the wood is only an eighth of an inch thick. You don't want it so stiff that it can't move because you want some acoustic function. But you don't want it going anywhere either. It's a real struggle against a number of things and you're trying to find some sort of balance in there that gives you the best of both.

People end up playing what feels good. They don't want to fight the instrument. If you're wasting your energy balancing the neck, you're not paying as much attention to the music as you want to. Jerry likes a guitar that feels a certain way. He doesn't like an instrument that's too light, but he's developed a permanent curvature of the spine from these heavy instruments. When I built Rosebud, I docked about three pounds off the weight of the Tiger. But most of the weight came back in with the MIDI. This next guitar will hopefully be eight or nine pounds and hopefully still sound the way he wants it to. The way it hangs on you and balances is real important. He's got incredible touch and can really command a lot of subtle differences in his sound with his technique. He's quite the master.

WOODSTOCK • The Aquarian Music and Art Fair, "three days of peace and music," the archetype of the outdoor rock concert as tribal gathering, held on Max Yasgur's farm in the town of Bethel, New York (sixty-five miles from the actual town of Woodstock), on August 15, 16, and 17, 1969. The significance of the festival in retrospect was that of nonconformists of the postwar generation announcing their presence in the world by sheer force of numbers—an audience of 400,000—as champions of peace, community, spirituality, spontaneity, self-determination, and fun. What the Be-In was to the Haight, Woodstock was to the world: a flowering before the scattering of many seeds. Unreconstructed hippies like to look back at the festival, an island of peaceful cohabitation in a violent era, and marvel at how no one was killed—it helped, no doubt, that Wavy Gravy's Hog Farm had been flown in from their Santa Fe commune after they promised to keep the crowd in order with "cream pies and seltzer bottles."

Many groups played well at Woodstock, most notably Jimi Hendrix, Santana, the Who, and Crosby, Stills, Nash & Young. The Dead played just after dark on the second day, and not well, and Deadheads who have heard the stories or the tape have an unusually unromantic view of the event, shared by

Garcia, who once referred to the band's performance there as "the ultimate calamity."

"It was raining," Garcia recalled in 1976, "and there was maximum confusion going on, sound logistics. Really weird. Plus I was high, of course. Huge crowds of people over the stage, and the stage had sheet metal and stuff on it, it's wet, and I'm getting incredible shocks from my guitar. Pretty soon I started hallucinating balls of electricity rolling across the stage, jumping off my guitar. Meanwhile all the little citizens' band radios and walkie-talkies are interfering with the amplifiers, so there are weird voices coming out of the amplifiers. It's dark and you don't see any audience, but you know there's 400,000 people out there.

"Then somebody leans over across the stage, and says the stage is about to collapse. I'm standing there in the middle of this trying to play music. Then they turn on the lights, and the lights are a mile away, monster super troopers, totally blinding, and you can't see anything at all. Here's all this energy, and everything is horribly out of tune, 'cause it's all wet. It was just a disaster. It was humbling." (That's Garcia's voice on the *Woodstock* album before Arlo Guthrie's performance of "Coming Into Los Angeles" saying, "Marijuana — exhibit A.")

WOOKS • From the name of Han Solo's furry comrade, the Wookie. "Hard-core backwoods hippies with hair all over their bodies — back, shoulders, neck, legs, face — wearing shorts and nothing else," says Adam Bluestein. "They have big families with them, and incredible green bud. They're usually very kind."

WORKINGMAN'S DEAD • Album #5, released in May 1970.

🎝 *Blair Jackson, editor of* The Golden Road, *on* **Workingman's Dead**:

Though it was released just five months after *Live/Dead*, *Workingman's Dead* seemed to come from a completely different universe. If the former sounded as if it were laser-beamed from some distant galaxy in the future, the latter rode on into town on horseback from an undefined past. One can certainly overdo the country/rustic analogies when discussing *Workingman's Dead*, but the fact is it did represent a radical departure for the Dead as a recording band. It probably didn't come as too much of a shock for the few people who saw the band often in late '69 and early '70 and heard the gradual shift to shorter songs and more country influences. (At my own first Dead show, at the Capitol Theater in Port Chester, New York, two months before *Workingman's Dead* came out, there had been an entire mini-set of acoustic tunes, including a couple that found there way onto the album.) But it definitely caught more than a few early Dead fans off guard—in fact, one of my best friends in high school essentially abandoned the group at that juncture: "Nah . . . too commercial. No jamming."

It was a different animal, to be sure. "Uncle John's Band" was all over the FM radio dial in the summer of '70, the first Dead song to get any national airplay. With its warm acoustic textures (even down to the snappy percussion) and pleasing harmonies that were like a slightly off-kilter Crosby, Stills & Nash (the reigning harmony kings of the day), the song was an easy listen in the best sense. But the lyrics—a quixotic blend of American mythos and folk wisdom—had a definite edge: "When life looks like easy street there is danger at your door." Robert Hunter has said that listening to the first two records by the Band inspired him to move away from the sort of cryptic word puzzles he constructed for *Aoxomoxoa* and toward a simpler, more direct approach, but the reason it worked (works!) so well is that there were still gossamer veils to be peeled away by the searching listener.

Each song has its own characters and mood, even if the particulars are sometimes elusive. Was there ever a more plaintive slice of country melancholy than "High Time," with its deft intermingling of past, present and future, anticipation and regret, clarity and confusion? What do you make of the mixture of whimsy and dread at the heart of "Dire Wolf"? The bluesy "Black Peter" shivers with the frightening rattle of impending death while curiously offering solace for our own insignificance in the Grand Scheme of Things. On the surface, "Cumberland Blues" is a joyous bluegrass-inspired romp, but the lyrics are all desperation and despair. "New Speedway Boogie," Hunter-Garcia's brooding, churning meditation on the great inescapable Truths of Altamont, is an anthem for the beginning of a new Dark Ages. "Easy Wind" finds Pigpen's hardworking everyman used and abused but defiant as the band, in all its electric glory (no acoustic or steel guitars here!), rumbles underneath, speeding up and slowing down like a drunk trying to pull himself together. And "Casey Jones" has that catchy, slightly annoying smirk to it—lyrically it's a cautionary tale, I suppose, but did anyone ever take it as anything other than a celebration of cocaine? (The band certainly didn't seem to get the "message.") Taken together, the songs form a whole that is actually quite relentless in its darkness, yet there is an unexplainable radiance to the musical arrangements that gives *Workingman's Dead* its "up" feeling—aren't nearly all of your associations with these songs curiously positive?

The process of making *Aoxomoxoa* a year earlier had been nearly as convoluted and Byzantine as its music and lyrics. Likewise, the making of *Workingman's Dead* was as simple—almost casual—as the finished result. The band rehearsed the songs well before going into Pacific High Recording and then cut the songs essentially live (with later overdubs) in the order in which they appear on the album. As a result, it has a natural, unfussed-over feel—rare for a Dead studio record.

The LP became the Dead's first "hit" album, with "Uncle John's Band" even making it up to #69 on the *Billboard* singles chart. *Workingman's Dead* was also the record that first established the Dead as a favorite band among college kids—a position they've held on to ever since. Almost immediately, the success of the album had a noticeable impact on the size of the group's following. In the New York area, where I lived, tickets became harder and harder to get, and inside the halls where they played, cries for "St. Stephen" started to be drowned out by garbled shouts for "Casey-Fuckin'-Joooooooonnnnes!" And that's when I first became a Dead snob: "Oh man, look at the lame-o's who've come into the scene since *Workingman's Dead!*" (Just kiddin', sort of . . .)

THE WORLD ACCORDING TO SHOWS 📖 • Geography lessons courtesy of THE BOYS. "Your whole sense of geography is transformed by your tape collection," explains John Holzman. "Cities that you've previously ignored all of a sudden catch your ear. When someone says they're from New Haven, the first thing you think of is, 'Yale Bowl '71.' "

In addition, Heads make pilgrimages to locales of celebrated past performance. The town of Augusta, Maine, takes on special significance because of the stellar 10/12/84, and Heads that find themselves driving through Normal, Illinois, might stop and dash off a postcard to another devotee of Horton Field

House 4/24/78 (when Garcia hollered, "Whoah, there's a fire," during "Fire on the Mountain").

"When we were visiting our buddy at Cornell," recalls Toura Williams, "we asked him to drive us over to Barton Hall—where they played that show on 5/8/77—so we could bow down." *See* FANTASY VENUES.

X-FACTOR • The term both bandmembers and Heads use for the uncontrollable and unpredictable wild Good Thing that comes into play when the music is at its best. Hart has said "the wolf walked" after certain sets.

The x-factor, like the weather, cannot be commanded, but it can be *invited*. When the x-factor is absent, the bandmembers cast about for a common musical language, tossing out melodic threads that are never picked up and charging up blind cul-de-sacs. When the x-factor is in effect, the jams glide forward like a silver locomotive on frictionless rails, spiriting band and Heads together on that glory ride.

🐾 *Michael Newman, photographer, on naming the nameless:*

It's the elusive musical *anima* that is the difference between the competent and the sublime. When they have practiced their instruments rather than rehearsed their songs; when they are in touch with the dignity and nobility of their tools; when the adventure of risk-taking is inviting, rather than frightening; when they listen; when the new is more interesting than the familiar is safe, *that* is when magic is possible—an allegory from which we can all learn something. Call it the x-factor, call it Godhead, call it THE ZONE, call me when it happens!

YAHSHUAS; THE YAHSHUA BUS • *See* THE COMMUNITY.

YO KINA ZU • This phrase—adapted from Weir's pronunciation of "your kind of zoo" from "Hell in a Bucket"—appeared as the ersatz Latin motto of "Grateful Dead University" on t-shirts in the mid-'80s.

YOU KNOW YOUR KID'S A DEADHEAD WHEN . . . • *Professor of Germanic Languages Paul Roberge reports two telltale signs:*

1. The other night I was reading *The Story of Ferdinand* to my four-year-old daughter. On the page where "five men came in very funny hats to pick the biggest, fastest roughest bull to fight in the bullfights in Madrid," there's a man with a black handlebar moustache and a wide-brimmed hat. Marie pointed out this guy and exclaimed: "Look! It's Pigpen!"

2. A couple of weeks ago, examining a map of the U.S. in the kindergarten classroom, Marie informed some other children: "There's California. That's where the Grateful Dead live." Later, in the library, she discovered a picture book of New York City. When she saw the Statue of Liberty, she broke out in a *sotto voce* but distinctly audible rendering of

"Oooh, freedom! Oooh, liberty!" It would seem that the torch is being passed.

YOUR HANDS • Look at 'em. Weird, huh?

YOUR LIST GETS MINE ☜ • Standard appeal from a tape collector to collectors at large, appearing in classified ads in *Relix* and other Head magazines, and on the Net. Translation: "Send me your list of tapes, I'll send you mine, and we'll see what we can do to round out each other's collections." Once the lists are exchanged and compared, tapers often proceed to trading "a case for a case"—a swap of ten tapes each.

♣ *Anthony Fleszar, on the life of a tape collector:*
You spend all morning looking for this killer "Playin'" jam that you think is on this tape from '72, probably the Fillmore, and you know it's a Maxell with the label on upside down, but it doesn't have a case, and you know the tape starts with "Sugaree" but the last time you think you saw it was in '83, and it was under your friend Brian's refrigerator, or maybe it was just a filler on that Alpine Valley '89 show, which you think you probably listened to in that dude's bus on the way to Deer Creek this year, but his phone number is on the back of the ticket stub that you think is stuffed in your Soundboard of 7/8/78, and you have *no* idea where that is, so you pull out *DeadBase* and start looking for every show since '71 that even had a "Playin'" but by '77 or so you forgot what you were looking for, because you got wrapped up in this version of "He's Gone," where Mickey starts playing the Beam with a dead cat . . .

THE ZONE • The state of being to which bandmembers and the audience "travel" together when the music is at its most intense, exploratory, and collective.

Because Dead music is improvised music, the moment the gate to the zone swings open—when the "rusty strings" are dusted off and shine—always comes as a moment of surprise, of something made new. As Hart says, "Once in the zone, the point is to go somewhere you've never gone before."

The zone was not invented by the Dead, and it's a place people will be able to go to long after the band is gone. Mythographer Joseph Campbell—who only went to one Dead show—recognized that what the band and Heads help create together rhymes with something very old, comparing Deadheads to the ecstatic worshippers of Demeter at Eleusis, the temple of the Mysteries in ancient Greece. "When you see eight thousand kids all going up in the air together, this is more than music. It turns something on in *here* [pointing to his heart]. What it turns on is life energy. This is Dionysus talking through these kids."

The zone is freedom—freedom to spin if you're a spinner, to stand with eyes closed wholly absorbed or flail madly throwing off sweat, to watch the levels on your tape deck dance during one of the great moments of your life. To dance with a child's heart, or drum like a drummer who says, "Your mind is turned off, your judgement wholly emotional. Your emotions seem to stream down your arms and legs and out the mouth of the drum; you feel light, gravityless; your arms feel like feathers. You fly like a bird."

❧ *Three voices from the zone:*

● Helen Rossi

When the Dead are in the zone, the humans onstage surrender their volition to the Whole, and the venue is transported. It's as if the sound is going directly to my subconscious, and instead of hearing music only, I'm having memories, thoughts, and insights.

● Gary Greenberg

The zone is hard to define, but unmistakable when encountered, a sacred space that lies behind and beyond the world we inhabit. It is where the Other lives, a place without time, but filled with consciousness. Certainly Hunter's lyrics are composed of the dust of the zone, poised to catapult you there if you pay enough attention. When I enter the zone, transported there by the Dead, or by drumming, or by making love, or playing the piano, or by good drugs, or any combination, I am a consciousness without an I: the most awesome and liberating experience I have had the good fortune to live through. The zone is as close to pure Being as I have come.

● Gary Burnett

The Dead are a wonderful aggregate of players, and in the normal course of things, that's just what they are—a set of components which add up to a marvelous sum: great music. The zone, however, is that place both within and beyond the music, something that lives beyond musical intention, that speaks directly to the soul of those listening, "a place of first permission," opening into the eternal.

Zs • What every tourhead needs after a long strange trip. At rest stops on the interstate, under buzzing Greyhound depot lights, in bustling train stations and red-eyed on ticket lines, snoozing on hay bales in your backyard or sprawled over sofas in hotel and airport lounges, Deadheads are trying to get some *rest*. Give 'em a break. They need it. *See* DAY OFF.

APPENDICES

I

THE DEAD LINE
(A Selected History)

3/15/40 Phil Lesh, bass and vocals, born
6/23/41 Robert Hunter, lyrics, born
8/1/42 Jerry Garcia, guitar and vocals, born
9/11/43 Mickey Hart, drums, born
3/19/44 Tom (T.C.) Constanten, keyboards, born
8/22/45 Donna Jean Godchaux, vocals, born
9/8/45 Ron (Pigpen) McKernan, guitar, harmonica, rapping, and vocals, born
5/7/46 Bill Kreutzmann, drums, born
10/3/47 John Perry Barlow, lyrics, born
10/16/47 Bob Weir, guitar and vocals, born
7/19/48 Keith Godchaux, keyboards, born
2/2/51 Vince Welnick, keyboards and vocals, born
10/21/52 Brent Mydland, keyboards and vocals, born
11/25/54 Bruce Hornsby, keyboards and vocals, born
6/18/65 Lesh replaces Dana Morgan, Jr., in the Warlocks
12/4/65 Big Nig's Acid Test, first show as the Grateful Dead
9/66 Dead move to 710 Ashbury, Haight-Ashbury, S.F.
1/14/67 Be-In in Golden Gate Park, S.F., first "Morning Dew"
3/17/67 *Grateful Dead* released
6/28/67 Dead play at the Monterey Pop festival
7/23/67 Neal Cassady raps with the Dead at the Straight Theater, S.F.
9/29/67 Hart's first show, at the Straight Theater
10/2/67 Occupants of 710 Ashbury busted for marijuana possession
11/11/67 First "Other One," Shrine Aud., L.A.
12/13/67 First "Dark Star," Shrine Aud.
2/2/68 Neal Cassady dies in Celaya, Mexico
2/3/68 First "China Cat Sunflower," Crystal Ballroom, Portland, OR.
3/3/68 Dead play a free show on Haight Street
6/7/68 First "St. Stephen," Carousel Ballroom, S.F.
7/18/68 *Anthem of the Sun* released
11/23/68 Tom Constanten's first show
6/20/69 *Aoxomoxoa* released

11/10/69 *Live/Dead* released

12/4/69 First "Uncle John's Band," Old Fillmore, S.F.

12/21/69 First "Not Fade Away," at the Old Fillmore

1/26/70 Tom Constanten's last show as a bandmember

5/70 *Workingman's Dead* released

11/70 *American Beauty* released

2/18/71 First "Playing in the Band," "Bertha," "Loser," "Greatest Story Ever Told," "Wharf Rat," "Johnny B. Goode" at the Capitol Theater in Port Chester, NY (first "Bird Song" and "Deal" the next night); Hart takes a hiatus

10/71 *Grateful Dead* (a.k.a. *Skull and Roses* and *Skullfuck*) released

10/19/71 Keith Godchaux's first show

12/31/71 Donna Godchaux's first show

6/17/72 Pigpen's last show

11/72 *Europe '72* released

3/8/73 Pigpen dies

7/13/73 *History of the Grateful Dead* (*Bear's Choice*) released

11/15/73 *Wake of the Flood* released

3/23/74 First "Scarlet Begonias," first "Cassidy," Cow Palace, S.F.

6/27/74 *From the Mars Hotel* released

10/20/74 "The Last One" at Winterland, Hart returns

3/23/75 Dead play SNACK Benefit at Kezar Pavilion, S.F.

6/17/75 First "Help On the Way," "Slipknot!," "Franklin's Tower," "Crazy Fingers," Winterland

9/1/75 *Blues for Allah* released

6/26/76 *Steal Your Face* released

2/26/77 First "Terrapin Station," "Estimated Prophet," Swing Aud., San Bernardino, CA

6/1/77 *The Grateful Dead Movie* released

7/27/77 *Terrapin Station* released

11/15/78 *Shakedown Street* released

2/17/79 Keith and Donna Godchaux's last show

4/22/79 Mydland's first show

4/28/80 *Go to Heaven* released

7/23/80 Keith Godchaux dies

4/1/81 *Reckoning* released

8/81 *Dead Set* released

7/10/86 Garcia falls into a diabetic coma

12/15/86 THE COMEBACK SHOW, Oakland Coliseum, CA

7/6/87 *In the Dark* released

1/31/89 *Dylan and the Dead* released

10/31/89 *Built to Last* released
7/23/90 Mydland's last show
7/26/90 Mydland dies
9/7/90 Welnick's first show
9/90 *Without a Net* released
9/15/90 Hornsby's first show as a bandmember
4/15/91 *One From the Vault* released
10/25/91 Bill Graham dies
11/1/91 *Infrared Roses* released
5/12/92 *Two From the Vault* released
11/1/93 *Dick's Picks, Volume One* released
1/19/94 The Dead are inducted into the Rock & Roll Hall of Fame

II

HOW TO TIE-DYE
A Primer by Glen A. Wagnecz and David Pelovitz

MATERIALS
- Procion MX Fiber Reactive Dyes
- Soda Ash, to help the fabric take the dye
- Synthrapol, a detergent, for precleaning and to prevent backstaining
- Bleach for color removal
- 100% cotton shirts
- Squeeze bottles
- Rubber gloves, filter mask

(One suggested bulk dye/chemical supplier: Dharma Trading Co., P.O. Box 150916, San Rafael CA, 94915. (800) 542-5227.)

CAUTION

Wear rubber gloves and a filter mask whenever working with dyes. Both powder and liquid dyes can become airborne easily and can be quite harmful if you breathe them in.

DYEING

1. Prewash shirts in cold water and Synthrapol.

2. Mix dye as instructed on the package. Set aside.

3. Prepare a presoak solution by adding 1 cup soda ash per gallon of lukewarm water. (One gallon is enough for 10–12 shirts.)

4. Soak the shirts for about 5 minutes in the solution, then wring out excess. A vigorous wringing is crucial.

5. Apply the dye, one color at a time, with liquid soap/hair-dye squeeze bottles (see patterns below). Change gloves and clean work surfaces between color applications.

6. Do not wring out shirts. Place them in a plastic bag and seal. Put it in a warm place for 24 hours—no longer, no shorter.

7. Remove shirt from bag. Before untying string or cutting rubber bands, wash the outside of the bundle with cold water (optional: use rinse cycle of washer, with cold water). Then, keeping shirt under cold running water, remove strings.

8. After about 5 minutes, when water running off the shirt becomes clear, put the shirts into a large tub or laundry sink, filled with cold water (optional: rinse cycle, washing machine). Add Synthrapol, to prevent backstaining. Let shirt sit for about a half hour, occasionally stirring.

9. Wash shirt in full cycle of washing machine (cold water setting).

10. Wear.

11. When washing for the first time, be sure to use cold water. Afterward, treat your tie-dye like any other colored shirt.

DISPOSAL & CLEANUP

1. Soda ash is a mild alkali, and shouldn't be put down the drain without neutralizing. Simply add cider vinegar to bring the solution back to pH neutral, and then pour down drain.

2. Procion Fiber Reactive Dyes contain heavy metals. They should *never* be put down drains. If you have unused liquid dyes that are too old to use for dyeing, store them in glass and mark them as fabric dye. Take old bottles to heavy metal solution reclamation centers.

3. Any spills can be wiped with a mild bleach solution of 1 cup per wash bucket—but keep this solution away from your dyed shirts! Wipe spills quickly, before they have a chance to take.

PATTERNS

"Electric" bunching. Crumple shirt into a ball, using rubber bands or string to hold the shirt in place while the dye is applied. When you take it apart, you get patterns that look like leaves in the fall. Multiple colors should be done in separate steps, with the darkest colors first.

Pleats. Fold shirt like an accordion, into pleats approximately 1-inch wide. You can go up and down the length of the shirt, or diagonally. Different colors are applied across the different pleats (one color per pleat). You get a shirt that has different bands of colors corresponding to the pleats.

Swirl effect. Lay the shirt flat on a piece of plastic-lined cardboard. Keep a similar piece of cardboard handy. Using your index finger and thumb, pinch the shirt where you want the swirl to begin. Then walk around the table while still holding on. The fabric will bunch into a swirl not unlike a jelly roll. Apply each color to a different portion of the swirl. Three or four colors works nicely.

Now put your spare piece of plastic-lined cardboard on top of the shirt, and flip the shirt over. Repeat dyeing procedure.

"Teats." Pinch the shirt and pull up, forming a peak. You can either smooth out any ridges (the smooth cone effect) and then apply dye in a concentric fashion, *or* induce ridges (the pleat effect). Apply dye. If you dye the ridges, you'll get a circle with branches growing out from the middle; if you dye concentrically, you'll get what looks like a bull's-eye.

Batik. Neat effect, but messy. First, dye the shirt using lighter colors like yellow and orange. Then melt wax and apply to the shirt. Allow wax to cool. When you flex the shirt with the cooled wax on it, it cracks, creating a weblike pattern. Excess dye should be rinsed afterward.

For the wax removal, break off as much as possible by hand. The rest can be removed with boiling water (wax will come off and float to the top), or by dry-cleaning shirts.

Reverse dyeing. Bleach can be used to dye an already-colored shirt white. Follow the patterns above, or squirt bleach solution at a colored shirt hanging on a clothesline. Also, bleach can be used like an eraser on a blackboard if your tie-dye is a disappointment and you just want to start over.

No rules are sacred in tie-dyeing. Experimentation is the heart and soul of it. Have fun, and good luck.

III

HOW TO BECOME A NETHEAD

Cyberspace is the online world of people sharing ideas via computer. To join the jam, all you need is a personal computer, a modem, a regular phone line, easy-to-learn communications software like ZTerm or Microphone, and a subscription to an online service like America Online or The WELL, or an Internet account, available to most students for free.

Many Deadheads find themselves comfortably at home in cyberspace. Information about mail order, ticket availability, and setlists circulates rapidly there. It allows Heads to create together in words the kind of community they've been sharing through song and dance for nearly thirty years.

DEAD BOARDS AND ONLINE SERVICES

In addition to the online services mentioned above, smaller local Deadhead bulletin boards (BBS) can provide you with an electronic home base. This is where you will call to log on each day, and where your electronic mail ("email") will be stored while you're offline.

If you don't yet have an email address, a Dead Board can be a good place to start.

Dead-specific BBSs can be accessed by modem through any phone line; the call will cost the same as if you were making a regular phone call — local or long-distance charges, depending on how far you are dialing. National online services such as America Online, The WELL, and Compuserve can provide you with local access numbers from virtually anywhere in the U.S.

Here's a list of Dead Boards we know about. Phone number listed is for modem access, unless specified:

BBS	PHONE	SYSOP	MODEM SPEED (bits per second)
Dead Board	(301) 530-9346	Klaus Bender	9,600
Terrapin Station	(203) 656-0134	"Cap'n Trips"	9,600
Sugar Magnolia	(703) 347-7460	Brian Davidson	14,400
Terrapin Station	(804) 622-4381	Roscoe Primrose	9,600˙
Darkstar Systems	(206) 578-1157	Kay Akagi	14,400

China Cat BBS	(301) 604-5976	Dave Ristau	14,400
Franklin's Tower	(602) 750-1760	Paul Davidson	9,600
Cumberland Mines	(714) 373-1509	Jim Cline	9,600
The WELL	(415) 332-4335 (voice),		
,	(415) 332-6106 (modem), or		
	email:info@well.sf.ca.us		
America Online	(800) 827-6364 (voice)		
Compuserve	(800) 848-8199 (voice)		

DEAD-FLAMES/REC.MUSIC.GDEAD

After you've gotten comfortable navigating the local alleyways of your own online service, you may want to take a leap into the realm of Internet, the information web that links tens of millions of online users. Deadheads from all over the globe use the Internet to congregate in an electronic discussion conference called "rec.music.gdead" or "DEAD-FLAMES."

An estimated 70,000 Heads subscribe to the rec.music.gdead/dead-flames. If your online service has access to Internet newsgroups, ask your sysop (system operator) how to read the rec.music.gdead newsgroup. If your service does not have access to these newsgroups, you should be able to subscribe to a daily digest of the newsgroup by sending a request to:

dead-flames-request@gdead.berkeley.edu

To post a message to all Heads who read rec.music.gdead/dead-flames, send your message to:

dead-flames@gdead.berkeley.edu

But before you post your first message, take stock: Writing to tens of thousands of people at once is not quite like writing a personal letter. You should take care that the information you are *publishing* is accurate.

DEADHEAD SOFTWARE

Another tremendous benefit of cyberspace is the sharing of software, graphics, sound, and text files. Your Dead Board will most likely have dozens of articles about the Dead, tapers' lists, and so on, which you will be able to download onto your computer's hard drive.

Software Primer by Mark Kraitchman

Multimedia files. Many Deadheads design and share various multimedia files, including graphics files in GIF, TIFF, JPEG, PostScript, and X Windows Bitmap formats. (Often these graphics files are obvious GDM and GDP copyright violations.) Most picture files can be viewed on UNIX workstations, Macs, and PCs with the appropriate hardware and software.

Some of these picture files are actually little animations. One of the most widespread mini-animations is commonly referred to as the "Dancing Bear" screen saver. This software is only available for PCs running Windows.

There are also some audio files available, often samples of new Dead tunes. These audio files are available in several formats (au, snd, wav, etc.) and may be played back on NeXT, Suns, Apple, PCs, and Amigas with the appropriate hardware and software. Consult your sysop.

Setlists database. A number of database programs have been written specifically for management of setlists and tape lists. For PCs, there are "WinTaper," "SongTracker PC," and "TaperBase" (a.k.a. "Tbase"). For the Mac, there are John Gilbert's "Stack-O-Dead," a Hypercard database containing setlists, lyrics, graphics, tape-labeling capabilities, and some great soundbites.

GOPHER/FTP

In addition, Internet is a library that contains megabytes of information on the Dead—all free, *if* you can find it and figure out how to get to it. The major site for Dead Internet files is "gdead.berkeley.edu." Gopher and FTP ("File Transfer Protocol") are the two basic procedures for accessing files on the Internet. Ask your sysop about your Internet connectivity—are you Gopher- or FTP-compatible?

If you are a Gopher client, connect with: **gopher gdead.berkeley.edu.**

If you are FTP-compatible, connect with: **ftp gdead.berkeley.edu,** using "anonymous" as the user name.

If you are not FTP-compatible, it is still possible to retrieve files from the gdead.berkeley library. Send email to: **ftpmail@decwrl.dec.com,** with "help" written in the message body. Instructions will be emailed back to you on how to proceed.

NETSPEAK

Here's a Head start on cyber-abbreviation.

BTW: By The Way
FTR: For The Record
FWIW: For What It's Worth
FYI: For Your Information
IJWTS: I Just Want To Say
IMO: In My Opinion
IMHO: In My Humble Opinion
IMNSHO: In My Not So Humble Opinion
JAPD: Just Another Picky Deadhead
MO: Mail Order
NYE: New Year's Eve
ODC: Obligatory Dead Content
OTOH: On The Other Hand
SYF: Steal Your Face, Space Your Face
YATG: Yet Another Ticket Grovel
YMMV: Your Mileage May Vary

IV

PROFILES FROM THE ZONE
(A closer look at some of our sources)

Adams, Rebecca   b.'52   Home base: *Greensboro, NC*
FIRST SHOW: 9/20/70, Fillmore East, NYC
WHEN NOT AT SHOWS: Associate professor of sociology, University of North Carolina at Greensboro; mom

   ♣ "People say Deadheads are throwbacks. I think they're pioneers. They recognize that reality is subjective—there is no *right way*—and have been cognizant of these multiple realities for a lot longer than most other people. This is postmodernism. It's the cutting edge." {pp. xiii, 62, 63, 73, 77, 84, 105, 372, 376}

Beers, Tony   b. '59   Home base: *Santa Cruz, CA*
FIRST SHOW: 7/29/74, Capitol Centre, Landover, MD
WHEN NOT AT SHOWS: Entrepreneur; drug counselor

   ♣ "I dance for meditation purposes, and I go to shows because it's the only place that I can feel safe to express myself. It's very good for my mental health as an ex–drug user." {pp. 46, 158, 229, 244}

Bender, Klaus   b. '59   Home base: *Bethesda, MD*
FIRST SHOW: May 1980, Penn State
WHEN NOT AT SHOWS: Radio communications engineer; BBS sysop; tape collector

   ♣"The scene allows you to be yourself, to be as weird as you want." {pp. 54, 92, 346}

Berliant, Adam   b. '66   Home base: *Seattle, WA*
FIRST SHOW: 6/27/83, Poplar Creek Pavilion, Hoffman Estates, IL
WHEN NOT AT SHOWS: Computer-assisted investigative reporter; jazz fanatic

   ♣ "My commute is precisely forty-five minutes—just long enough for one side of, say, Oakland Aud, 12/31/81. I'll pop it in, and next thing I know, I'm parking the car." {pp. xi, xii, xiii}

Blasik, Scott   b. '78   Home base: *Durham, NH*
FIRST SHOW: Hasn't seen one yet

WHEN NOT AT SHOWS: Student and writer who enjoys being with his friends

☙ "We should enjoy the Dead as long as they are with us, and be grateful there are bands like Phish and Blues Traveler to keep the flame burning after they're gone." {p. 48}

Bluestein, Adam b. '69 Home base: *San Francisco, CA*
FIRST SHOW: 7/12/87, Giants Stadium, East Rutherford, NJ
WHEN NOT AT SHOWS: Writer

☙ "Nothing is true. Everything is permitted."—Hassan-i-Sabbah {pp. 330, 374}

Bobrik, Michael b. '51 Home base: *Arlington, VA*
FIRST SHOW: 6/1/67, Tompkins Square Park, NYC
WHEN NOT AT SHOWS: Chemistry professor, Northern Virginia Community College, Alexandria, VA; performs in acoustic guitar duo, the Wheel

☙ "It was clear right away that this was a very different approach to music. Hearing proto–'The Eleven' in '68 was just amazing. First, they're playing in three-quarter time, almost a waltz. Then, all of a sudden, you noticed they are chopping off one beat. 'Hey—they're playing in eleven-quarter time. *Nobody* plays in eleven-quarter time!' " {p. 88}

Brown, Toni b. '54 Home base: *Brooklyn, NY*
FIRST SHOW: 7/11/69, New York Pavilion, Flushing, NY (site of '64 World's Fair)
WHEN NOT AT SHOWS: Editor/publisher, *Relix;* active in fight to reform mandatory minimum sentences, and in children's issues. {p. 246}

Cecchi, David b. '73 Home base: *Rochester, MN*
FIRST SHOW: "I have never been to a show."
WHEN NOT LISTENING TO TAPES: Geology student, University of Minnesota; "I like to do things outside. I tried to build my own audio speakers. I also like pudding."

☙ "You never find out who your real friends are until you're Dead. Love me, love my tapes."

Clayton, Rick b. '45 Home base: *San Francisco, CA*
("Noodles Romanoff")
FIRST SHOW: 3/10/67, Whiskey-A-Go-Go, San Francisco, CA
WHEN NOT AT SHOWS: Software engineer; Rock Med volunteer

☙ "This goes way beyond being a fan. I'm a part of something. It's the closest thing I have to an ethnic group." {p. 7}

Costello, Elvis   b. '54   Home base: *Richmond, England*
(Declan Patrick Aloysius MacManus)
FIRST SHOW: 5/7/72, Bickershaw Music Festival, Wigan, England
❧ "It was like a revelation. They played all these songs they hadn't recorded—'He's Gone,' 'Tennessee Jed,' 'Ramble on Rose.' And they did Merle Haggard's 'Sing Me Back Home.' That's what I remember most about it. These great songs. Standing in mud and listening to 'He's Gone.'"
WHEN NOT AT SHOWS: Inordinately inventive musician
❧ "I tend not to think about music in literal terms, but in terms of what it conjures up for me. The Dead's music is like a conversation." {pp. 98, 129–30, 163, 253}

Crumlish, Christian   b. '64   Home base: *Oakland, CA*
FIRST SHOW: 6/24/84, Saratoga Performing Arts Center, Saratoga, NY
WHEN NOT AT SHOWS: Freelance writer and editor; painter; cartoonist; video producer; teller of tall tales
❧ "If I go too long without it, I start to need it real bad—to hear the band, to see the people, to be in that environment where anything goes." {p. 87}

Dobra, Susan   b. '54   Home base: *Sudbury, Ontario*
FIRST SHOW: 11/6/77, Broome County Arena, Binghamton, NY
WHEN NOT AT SHOWS: Professor of English
❧ "Turn it on, keep it on." {pp. 283–84}

Dolgushkin, Mike   b. '53   Home base: *San Francisco, CA*
FIRST SHOW: 8/22/72, Berkeley Community Theatre, Berkeley, CA
WHEN NOT AT SHOWS: Artist, Hot Tomato Studios; editor, *DeadBase* {pp. 54–55, 76}

Edwards, Gail   b. '51   Home base: *Boca Raton, FL*
FIRST SHOW: 11/11/71, Atlanta Municipal Auditorium, Atlanta, GA
WHEN NOT AT SHOWS: Computer analyst (specializes in out-of-town assignments near Dead shows); spends "way too much time" on the Internet; likes detective novels, yoga, live music
❧ "Some folks call me 'Gail of the Rail,' others call me 'Butterfly Lady.' One thing's for sure, I'm Dead to the core. Hi Chiefy!" {p. 87}

Eisenhart, Mary   b. '47   Home base: *Oakland, CA*
FIRST SHOW: 12/31/80, Oakland Auditorium Arena
WHEN NOT AT SHOWS: Editor, *MicroTimes* {pp. 86, 304, 375}

Feldstein, Fred   b. '60   Home base: *San Francisco, CA*
FIRST SHOW: 12/12/78, Jai-Alai Fronton, Miami, FL
WHEN NOT AT SHOWS: Haircolorist
🐾 "Don't take it too serious, 'cause the Dead is mysterious." {pp. 280–81}

Flanagan, Dee   b. '61   Home base: *Long Beach, CA*
FIRST SHOW: 7/28/73, Grand Prix Racecourse, Watkins Glen, NY
WHEN NOT AT SHOWS: "I play at the beach, I scramble over mountains, I pour out my heart, I deliver babies, I sing old music, I pray, I color, I watch my children grow."
🐾 "Imagine all the people, sharing all the world." — John Lennon {p. 232}

Fleszar, Anthony   b. '70   Home base: *Houghton, MI*
FIRST SHOW: 7/18/89, Alpine Valley Music Theater, East Troy, WI
WHEN NOT AT SHOWS: Master's student (mechanical engineering-design/dynamic systems), Michigan Technological University; part-time t-shirt salesman
"You know you're a Deadhead when:
🐾 Someone asks you what you do for fun, and you just smile real wide.
🐾 The first entry on your MCI Friend's and Family list is 415-457-6388.
🐾 You try to convince your grandmother 'Aoxomoxoa' is an acceptable play for a Scrabble triple word score.
🐾 Your dog is named Bertha.
🐾 You spend New Year's Eve with your cassette deck instead of your wife.
🐾 Left unoccupied, your hand instinctively taps the beat of 'Not Fade Away.'
🐾 You're still waiting for that second verse of the 'Dark Star' that they started back in May of '73.
🐾 You swear the guy walking by you at the football game just said 'doses.' " {pp. 202, 335}

Fontaine, David   b. '61   Home base: *North Smithfield, RI*
FIRST SHOW: 1/18/79, Civic Center, Providence, RI
WHEN NOT AT SHOWS: Works at Luca Music Store, North Providence, RI
🐾 "I didn't much like the music at first. But the subculture kind of sucked me in. The people are so friendly, you almost want to run away with them." {pp. 227–28}

Fortune, Erik   b. '65   Home base: *San Francisco, CA*
FIRST SHOW: 10/8/84, Worcester Centrum, Worcester, MA
WHEN NOT AT SHOWS: Works at an ad agency; interested in radio production
♣ "For me, the key is balance. The Dead are experiments in controlled chaos." {pp. 65–66}

Gans, David   b. '53   Home base: *Oakland, CA*
FIRST SHOW: 3/5/72, Winterland, San Francisco
WHEN NOT AT SHOWS: Producer and host of the *Grateful Dead Hour;* producer, *Eyes of Chaos/Veil of Order* (going national in '94); author, *Conversations With the Dead, Playing in the Band: An Oral and Visual Portrait of the Grateful Dead* and *Talking Heads: The Band and Their Music* (Avon, 1985); semiprofessional musician playing occasional gigs in the Bay Area {pp. 6, 9–11, 19, 74, 95, 122–24, 176, 186, 196, 203, 248–50, 272–73, 298, 305, 313–14, 374–78, 380}

Goldstein, Glen   b. '59   Home base: *New York, NY*
FIRST SHOW: 6/21/76, Tower Theater, Philadelphia
WHEN NOT AT SHOWS: Public relations executive and amateur pastry chef
♣ "When Phil's in the driver's seat, you got nothin' to worry about." {pp. 261, 287, 377}

Gore, Tipper   b. '48   Home base: *Washington, DC*
FIRST SHOW BACKSTAGE: 6/26/93, R.F.K. Stadium, Washington, DC
WHEN NOT AT SHOWS: Wife of, and assistant to, the Vice-President of the United States {pp. 212, 375}

Gould, Geoff   b. '50   Home base: *San Francisco, CA*
FIRST SHOW: '68, Rob Gym, UC Santa Barbara
WHEN NOT AT SHOWS: Married, father of three; president, Modulus Graphite (guitar/bass maker for Weir/Lesh); volunteer sysop of GD Forum on America Online; plays bass every Sunday at 8:30 A.M. in a lay-led worship service
♣ "When I'm playing music, I'm closer to God."

Gowell, Leslie   b. '61   Home base: *Olympia, WA*
FIRST SHOW: 6/25/78, Autzen Stadium, University of Oregon, Eugene, OR
WHEN NOT AT SHOWS: Mental health professional
♣ "It's a rich subcultural experience that enhances my self-actualization process." {p. 37}

Hartman, Tracy   b. '64   Home base: *Los Altos, CA*
                               (10 mins. from Shoreline)
FIRST SHOW: 2/14/88, Henry J. Kaiser Convention Center, Oakland, CA
☙ "I got on the bus in the first ten minutes. The guys were handing out long-stemmed red roses to all the gals and I was really moved by that."
WHEN NOT AT SHOWS: Human resources representative for a high-tech company
☙ "The Grateful Dead to me is . . . a very comfortable place." {p. 303}

Hays, Ken   b. '65   Home base: *Stamford, CT*
FIRST SHOW: 11/10/85, Brendan Byrne Arena, NJ
WHEN NOT AT SHOWS: Owner, Terrapin Tapes {pp. 284–85, 377}

Hoffman, Paul E.   b. '57   Home base: *Santa Cruz, CA*
FIRST SHOW: 8/16/81, Eugene, OR
WHEN NOT AT SHOWS: Coauthor, *Outside the Show;* professional computer weenie; publisher
☙ "It's all about community. The Grateful Dead and their music are the medium (maybe even the large), but not the message." {pp. 16, 136, 374}

Holzman, John   b. '66   Home base: *New York, NY*
FIRST SHOW: 4/10/83, West Virginia University Coliseum, Morgantown, WV
WHEN NOT AT SHOWS: Works in advertising {pp. xi, 93–94, 332}

Hornsby, Bruce   b. '54   Home base: *Williamsburg, VA*
FIRST SHOW: 9/11/73, William and Mary College, Williamsburg, VA
WHEN NOT AT SHOWS: Musician {pp. 26, 48, 145–48, 157, 211, 278, 282, 315, 340}

Issen, Barney   b. '56   Home base: *Houston, TX*
FIRST SHOW: 7/27/73, Grand Prix Racecourse, Watkins Glen, NY
☙ "I was a half-mile from the stage and hadn't slept in thirty-six hours."
"FIRST SHOW THAT REALLY COUNTS": 7/31/74, Dillon Stadium, Hartford, CT
WHEN NOT AT SHOWS: Father of three; geophysicist; frustrated musician {p. 58}

Kasprzak, Zachary   b. '74   Home base: *Livonia, MI*
FIRST SHOW: 3/24/92, The Palace, Auburn Hills, MI
WHEN NOT AT SHOWS: Civil/environmental engineering major, Michigan State University; manager, Newburgh Swim Club {p. 54}

Keeler, Walter   b. '57   Home base: *San Francisco, CA*
FIRST SHOW: 12/21/78, The Summit, Houston, TX
WHEN NOT AT SHOWS: Computer programmer; taper, trader
    ♣ "There *is* magic in the world, and music plays a big part in it." {pp. 42–43, 195}

Kippel, Les   b. '47   Home base: *Brooklyn, NY*
FIRST SHOW: 5/15/70, Fillmore East, NYC
WHEN NOT AT SHOWS: Former publisher, *Relix;* current president, Relix International; toy collector {pp. 245–46, 277}

Kreitner, Erez   b. '62   Home base: *New York, NY*
FIRST SHOW: 9/2/78, Giants Stadium, East Rutherford, NJ
WHEN NOT AT SHOWS: Independent commodities trader, World Trade Center, NYC
    ♣ "Still looking for that 'Peggy-O.' " {pp. 77, 320}

Kreitner, Roy   b. '66   Home base: *Tel Aviv, Israel*
FIRST SHOW: 10/27/80, Radio City Music Hall, NYC
WHEN NOT AT SHOWS: Student; nitpicker; apostrophist {p. 59}

Lecker, Rob   b. '66   Home base: *San Francisco, CA*
FIRST SHOW: Ventura 7/17/82
WHEN NOT AT SHOWS: "I sit in cafés and have profound philosophical conversations with good friends."
    ♣ "The Deadhead experience taught me the value and the power of a community based on love, compassion, and understanding." {pp. 289–90}

Lester, Jeff   b. '65   Home base: *Hermosa Beach, CA*
FIRST SHOW: 8/28/82, Veneta, OR
WHEN NOT AT SHOWS: Electrical engineer; basketball and volleyball player; avid non–Dead music listener and collector; DAT taper; former guitarist and singer for the band Somewhere Else
    ♣ "I wish I could have been at some '73–'74 shows."

Levy, Dan   b. '58   Home base: *New York, NY*
FIRST SHOW: 5/25/74, UC Santa Barbara
WHEN NOT AT SHOWS: Editor {pp. 80–82}

MacDonald, Jane Williamson   b. '48   Home base: *Penobscot, ME*
FIRST SHOW: 9/27/76, War Memorial Auditorium, Rochester, NY
WHEN NOT AT SHOWS: Crisis therapist; rattle maker (made in the Native

American tradition); number-one fan of Cherry Garcia ice cream {pp. 37–38}

Marks, Jonathan b. '62 Home base: *San Francisco, CA*
FIRST SHOW: 5/4/80, Capitol Centre, Baltimore, MD
WHEN NOT AT SHOWS: Proprietor of Grateful Graphics, San Francisco {pp. 49–50}

McNally, Dennis b. '49 Home base: *San Francisco, CA*
FIRST SHOW: 5/3/68, Low Library Plaza, Columbia University, NYC
WHEN NOT AT SHOWS: *Always* at shows. Publicist and biographer of the Grateful Dead; rare book collector; author of *Desolate Angel*, a biography of Jack Kerouac {pp. 55, 63, 166, 195, 208, 247–48, 279, 372, 374, 376–77, 385}

McVay, Gwyn b. '73 Home base: *Washington, DC*
FIRST SHOW: 9/4/91, Richfield Coliseum, Richfield, OH
WHEN NOT AT SHOWS: Editor by day, writer by night {p. 54}

Meltsner, Scott b. '66 Home base: *Pittsboro, NC*
FIRST SHOW: 4/6/85, The Spectrum, Philadelphia, PA
🕱 "Many people have told me that it was the worst show ever, but I had a blast."
WHEN NOT AT SHOWS: Community playwright
🕱 "I don't tour anymore, but it's a part of me. I have a picture on my wall and it's a place I can still go in my mind." {pp. 244–45}

Mendelson, Abby b. '47 Home base: *Pittsburgh, PA*
FIRST SHOW: 6/10/67, Café-au-GoGo, NYC
WHEN NOT AT SHOWS: Writer, editor, *Shomer Shabbas* Jew
🕱 "When I became an Orthodox Jew, I wrestled with the idea of secular music. I discussed it with my rebbe, and we decided it was not necessary to cast aside music per se. And once you're in the realm of music — it's not like Bach is more kosher than Jerry." {pp. 205–6}

Minkow, David b. '65 Home base: *San Francisco, CA*
FIRST SHOW: 3/22/87, Hampton Coliseum, Hampton, VA
WHEN NOT AT SHOWS: Assistant producer, KQED-FM in SF, show called *Forum*
🕱 "Don't be afraid to get involved. Take the show home with you." {p. 239}

Moyers, Scott   b. '68   Home base: *New York, NY*
FIRST SHOW: 10/9/89, Hampton Coliseum, Hampton, VA
WHEN NOT AT SHOWS: Assistant editor, Doubleday; enjoys collecting records and exploring the caves of the unknown

Murphy, Patrick J.   b. '64   Home base: *Fort Collins, CO*
FIRST SHOW: 7/7/89, JFK Stadium, Philadelphia, PA
WHEN NOT AT SHOWS: Patent attorney, Hewlett-Packard Company, Fort Collins, CO
☘ "Taking a song to the edge and bringing it back—this, for me, is what the Dead are all about."

Newman, Michael   b. '60   Home base: *Topeka, KS*
FIRST SHOW: 7/7/81, Kansas City Municipal Auditorium
WHEN NOT AT SHOWS: Husband, photographer, Deadhead, WELL denizen
☘ "Give me truth before beauty." {pp. 333–34}

Pelovitz, David   b. '64   Home base: *New York, NY*
FIRST SHOW: 3/23/87, Hampton Coliseum, Hampton, VA
WHEN NOT AT SHOWS: Candidate for English Ph.D. (hoping to teach); tie-dyer; onetime *Jeopardy!* participant
☘ "I like innovation, and no one takes risks on a more regular basis than the boyz." {pp. 71, 237, 373}

The Pineapple Guys
Jacobson, Mikael   b. '68   Home base: *Santa Cruz, CA*
FIRST SHOW: '89 {pp. 224–25}

Clark, David   b. '65   Home base: *Carmel, CA*
FIRST SHOWS: '85
☘ "Well, fortunately for the most plious & remarkably resilient spew guy, we feel honored and obliged to say the following: Let all that jazz go for the unattainable C-note blues metal breakfast refraction blossom croissant pipe-flavored quadrant duplex bitter sweet cremation."

Pollock, Jim   b. '71   Home base: *Columbia, SC*
FIRST SHOW: 6/18/92, Charlotte Coliseum, Charlotte, NC
WHEN NOT AT SHOWS: Accountant
☘ "It's an escape, and allows me to find some comfort in an otherwise difficult world."

Shannon, Tomlyn   b. '63   Home base: *Soquel, CA*
FIRST SHOW: 8/4/79, Oakland Auditorium
WHEN NOT AT SHOWS: Community gardener {p. 198}

Shenk, David   b. '66   Home base: *New York, NY*
FIRST SHOW: 4/10/83, West Virginia University Coliseum, Morgantown,
WV
WHEN NOT AT SHOWS: Fishing

Silberman, Jeff   b. '60   Home base: *Mill Valley, CA*
FIRST SHOW: 5/26/77, Baltimore Civic Center, Baltimore, MD
WHEN NOT AT SHOWS: Lawyer, amateur sound recordist {pp. 96, 106}

Silberman, Steve   b. '57   Home base: *Haight-Ashbury, CA*
FIRST SHOW: soundcheck 7/27/73, Watkins Glen, NY
WHEN NOT AT SHOWS: writer, cohost of deadlit, the Dead-related
books conference on The WELL.
🐞 "Angelheaded hipsters burning for the ancient heavenly connection
to the starry dynamo in the machinery of night . . ."—Allen Ginsberg,
"Howl"

Slabicky, Ihor   b. '53   Home base: *Portsmouth, RI*
FIRST SHOW: 4/25/71, Fillmore East, NYC
WHEN NOT AT SHOWS: Editor, *The Compleat Grateful Dead Discography;* col-
lector of "Dark Star" shows
🐞 "Just one more 'Dark Star'!" {pp. 22, 27, 57, 76, 371, 373, 374}

Soucie, Marty   b. '54   Home base: *Luquillo, PR*
FIRST SHOW: 7/27/73, Grand Prix Racecourse, Watkins Glen, NY
WHEN NOT AT SHOWS: Proprietor, Grateful Bed and Breakfast; alternative vacation planner
🐞 "It's taught me that one's work needn't be a drudgery-filled, unre-
warding experience. Find something you feel passionate about, and do it
with all your heart." {pp. 119–20}

Sterns, Stephen   b. '60   Home base: *New York, NY*
FIRST SHOW: 5/11/78, Springfield Civic Center, Springfield, MA
WHEN NOT AT SHOWS: Senior editor, Ballantine Books; reads, cooks, and
trades tapes
🐞 "The Dead are a touchstone—the energy of a show stays with you
long after the show is over." {p. 373}

Stroukoff, Annie   b. '61   Home base: *Cranbury, NJ*
FIRST SHOW: 5/7/80, Barton Hall, Cornell U., Ithaca, NY
WHEN NOT AT SHOWS: Computer graphic artist
☘ "For me, the Dead are a vacation from my day-to-day reality. I work very hard to support myself, my mother, and my two cats. I think I earn my three weeks' vacation, which I take to follow the Dead every chance I get. I tell my co-workers that while they do 'Club Med,' I do 'Club Dead.' " {p. 194}

Swanson, Sue   b. '48   Home base: *West Marin County, CA*
FIRST SHOW: Warlock's second rehearsal, Dana Morgan Music, Menlo Park, CA
WHEN NOT AT SHOWS: A wanna-be international diamond thief {pp. 114–15, 373–74}

Templeton, Matthew b. '71   Home base: *Wilmington, DE*
FIRST SHOW: "Still waiting for a successful mail order!"
FIRST TAPE: 2/13/70, Fillmore East, NYC
IN LIEU OF TOUR: Graduate student {p. 87}

Van Dyke, Michael b. '55   Home base: *San Francisco, CA*
FIRST SHOW: 10/78, Winterland
WHEN NOT AT SHOWS: Owner of the Psychedelic Shop, S.F.
☘ "I bought the Psychedelic Shop eighteen years ago. I was and still am a firm believer in the sacred use of psychedelics. I spend my free time working for the legalization of marijuana (particularly for medical use) in California. I love going to raves. The most important aspect of my life outside Dead shows is the hospice work I do. Working with the dying is the most important part of my spiritual practice, as well as the most rewarding part of my life." {p. 237}

Vickers, Earl   b. '56   Home base: *Campbell, CA*
FIRST SHOW: 9/23/76, Cameron Indoor Stadium, Duke University, Durham, NC
WHEN NOT AT SHOWS: Sound designer for video games; plays in Zilch, a Monkees cover band; writes the occasional piece of short fiction
☘ "I dream about the Dead from time to time. It's cheaper than following them on tour."

Wagnecz, Glen   b. '61   Home base: *Roxbury, NJ*
FIRST SHOW: 5/14/80, Nassau Coliseum, Uniondale, NY
WHEN NOT AT SHOWS: Chemical engineer, employed by Uncle Sam him-

self; "I like hiking, landscaping/gardening, homebrew making, and, of course, tie-dyeing."

🍀 "Being a Head is like having an extended family that you can rejoin from time to time, to take a momentary break from the demands of life. The scene is an amazing balance of people doing their own thing yet not infringing on others. The actual show is just the icing on the cake." {p. 343}

Walton, Bill   b. '52   Home base: *San Diego, CA*
FIRST SHOW: Late '60s, somewhere in California
WHEN NOT AT SHOWS: Basketball Hall-of-Famer (alumnus of the Portland Trailblazers, the LA Clippers, and the Boston Celtics); TV commentator

🍀 "There is no place on earth where the feeling of hope, happiness, community, and the family spirit is higher than it is than at a Dead concert." {pp. 24, 78, 95, 197–98, 247}

Weir, Roberta   Home base: *Albany, CA*
FIRST SHOW: 6/14/68, Fillmore East, NYC
WHEN NOT AT SHOWS: Director, Weir Gallery, Berkeley, CA; painter, sculptor, printmaker, teacher

🍀 "The sage said, 'We try to live according to the Way and have only death. What is there to fear?'" {pp. 159–61}

Wilkins, Charley   b. '66   Home base: *Fairfax, CA*
FIRST SHOW: 9/18/82, Boston Garden

🍀 "I was sixteen and clueless. Bob played drums. Everyone was freaking."
WHEN NOT AT SHOWS: Teaches ninth-grade cultural anthropology and directs the Community Service Department at a Marin County high school; philanthropist, romanticist, and semi-intellectual; plans on changing the world on a large scale {pp. v, 169, 220, 246–47, 288, 372}

Williams, Toura   b. '64   Home base: *Mill Valley, CA*
FIRST SHOW: 4/16/83, Meadowlands Arena, East Rutherford, NJ {pp. 291–333}

Yacavone, Michael   b. '62   Home base: *Lebanon, NH*
WHEN NOT AT SHOWS: Software developer and systems design consultant

🍀 "When they write the history books, the Grateful Dead will be remembered as an ensemble which struggled openly with its music, shining into the shadows of our souls." {pp. 225–26}

V
ACKNOWLEDGMENTS

This book is a quilt of Deadhead intelligence. We would like to extend our deepest appreciation to the hundreds of Heads who articulated, emoted, recalled, searched, and critiqued, so that our book could be an honest reflection of the Deadhead community.

Charley Wilkins brought the authors together, and gave us inspiration and material. His soul is the Deadhead soul: generous, hopeful, and determined. For his efforts and his spirit, he has earned our eternal gratitude, and this book's dedication.

Our forebears Rebecca Adams, Toni Brown, Susan Dobra, Mike Dolgushkin, Natalie Dollar, John Dwork, Mary Eisenhart, David Gans, Paul Hoffman, Blair Jackson and Regan McMahon, Dave and John Leopold, Frederic Lieberman, Dennis McNally, Stu Nixon, Jim Powell, John Scott, Laura Smith, Shan Sutton, and Alan Trist are the Deadhead journalists/archivists/scholars who have pioneered serious study of the band and the community. Their works informed and humbled us daily, and their personal support and contributions to this project were crucial. We will return the favor by following their example, nurturing others' Deadhead projects to come.

For direction, candor, and loads of specific information and criticism in early drafts, a big thanks to Adam Berliant, Alex Blumberg, Paolo Bonetti, Mary Buffington, Chip Callahan, Jon Chalfie, Douglas Conner, Christian Crumlish, Eugene Evon, Jeff Gorlechen, Ben Greenberg, Roy and Erez Kreitner, Jeff Lester, Dan Levy, Ihor Slabicky, David Pelovitz, Walter and Helen Keeler, Jon and Josh Shenk, Todd Vogt, Charley Wilkins, and the aforementioned Gans, Jackson, Eisenhart, Lieberman, and Hoffman.

We are particularly indebted to Ihor Slabicky, Net luminary and author of a 95-page online comprehensive Grateful Dead discography, a brilliant and painstaking labor of Deadhead scholarship, and a major contribution to the community and to this book. Similarly, Nick Meriwether generously offered us access to his unpublished essay, "Bill Graham Presents: A Brief Introduction to the San Francisco Rock Production Company."

SKELETON KEY: A DICTIONARY FOR DEADHEADS is among the contemporary works that owe a debt of gratitude to information technology. The products and services of The WELL, America Online, Microsoft, and Apple allowed us to write this book simultaneously from the Haight-Ashbury and Manhattan, and to efficiently communicate with tens of thousands of Netheads through email.

We are grateful to those thousands of contributors who sent our way inspirational anecdotes and nuggets of information. They came fast and furious, and we tried to keep up. Contributors not already mentioned in the book include Sean Collins, Eric Berlow, Adam Gluckman, Andy Miller, Becky Leyon, Beth Livingston, Bill Moore, Blyth Renate Meier, Bradley Pitt, Brian Markovitz, Brian Zaff, Bruce Higgins, Chip Winger, Chuck Dreyfus, Brian Fancher, Scott Blasik, Chuck Fee, Cormac Burke, Dan Skolnik, Dan Wilson, Daniel Golletz, David Patrick, David Dahl, David Dalto, Tracy Sewell, Ben Karmelich, David Nelson, Donald Meals, Donald Parks, Doug Baker, Elizabeth Converse, Eric Nay, Anton Saurian, Forrest Cook, Gary Clayton, Geoffrey Miller, Hewitt Pratt, "Gonzopolis," Greg Collis, Heidi Saller, Jay Gaines, Jay King, Jeff Gerber, Jeffrey Matthew Ehlinger, Jim Alwan, Jim McVey, Jim Pollock, Joe Troxel, John Duluoz, John Herrold, John Lavalle, John Lee, Marc Geller, Raymond Foye, Allen Ginsberg, Bob Rosenthal, Jeremiah Evans, John Reilly, John Schulien, Paul Goeltz, John Thomas Hardenbergh, "Just Larry," Kate McGurn, Larry Slavens, Lynne Petry, M. J. Knappen, Marc Alghini, Mark Lindley, Mark Paterick, Mark Tanaka, Matt McKenzie, Matthew Peterson, Michael I. Holden, Michael Murphy, Michael Witt, Mike Ells, Mike Frasca, Mike Gardner, Mike Zemke, Anthony Fleszar, John Trevor, Chris Chapell, John Lavelle, Steve Skaggs, Dan Marsh, Ed Perlstein, Rob Cohn, Chris Bucci, Nancy Lee Henning, Neil Rest, Nicholas A. Holmes, Normand Modine, Pat McCuen, Paul Cerra, Pete Sahlin, Rob K., Rob Linxweiler, Robb King, Ron Koslowski, Scott Baldwin (Roserunner), Scott Spaid, Scott Zeller, Sean Kay, Shabtai Klein, Shawna Stewart Anderson, and Tom Donohue. Gratitude to the staffs of Jassajara Bakery and Spinelli's Coffee.

Thanks to players in the band Bob Bralove, Bruce Hornsby, and Tom

Constanten for their time and insider perspectives. We are grateful to David and Jan Crosby for reminding us that music is love.

Special thanks to anyone who has ever suffered "taper stress" in order to make sure that Heads in two hundred years will hear what we hear. You guys are heroes (we promise not to bump the mics).

Everlasting thanks to Bruce Feiler for career support.

Thanks to our parents, Richard Shenk, Betty Ann Shenk, Joanne Cohen, Sidney Cohen, and Donald, Leslie, and Hillary Silberman for their support.

Special thanks to the brothers Shenk, who provided invaluable friendship and advice to both authors.

Alexandra Beers has graced us with patience, wisdom, and much effort.

A deep *gassho* to John Birdsall for his companionship, tolerance, and insight.

A high-five from Steve to Greg Bellatorre, his brother in the Zone. Thanks also to Mark Wilsey and Alan Wasserman.

Bruce Tracy, our editor and benefactor, was and is this book's first and greatest champion. We are profoundly indebted to him for his early enthusiasm, his confidence, and his endless patience. Thanks also to his assistant, Scott Moyers. Jim Trupin, our agent, gave us the first formal professional support for this book, helped us find the right publisher, and helped steered the book all the way to the press and beyond.

Blair Jackson's generosity and Deadhead spirit added immeasurably to the depth of this book.

The intelligence and heart of GD family members Dennis McNally, Gary Lambert, Steve Marcus, Calico, Annette Flowers, Dick Latvala, Eileen Law, and Bill Walton helped guide this book onto the right road.

And, of course, a deep bow of gratitude to the Good Ol' Grateful Dead and crew. Thank you for a real good time.

VI

SOURCES

"Ace Scores a Ticket," by Alex Kolker, from *Tales of Tour*. P.O. Box 3923, Lawrence, KS 66047.

Aharon and Michael of the Community. Author interview (SS), 10/29/93.

Aman, Sally. Author interview (DWS), 1/6/94.

Ashbridge, Tim. "McNally: The Publicist Speaks." (Interview was conducted immediately prior to the JGB show at the Capitol Centre, 11/7/91). *Unbroken Chain.*

Barich, Bill. "Still Truckin'." *The New Yorker*, 10/11/93.

Barlow, John Perry. Author interview (DWS), 3/12/94.

Barlow, John Perry. "The World Without Bill Graham." *The Golden Road.*

Barncard, Steve. Author interview (SS), 12/21/93.

Barrett, Todd. "The Selling of 'The Dead': Much to Be Grateful For." *Newsweek*, 5/30/88.

Beers, Tony, and Tomlyn Shannon. Author interview (DWS), 10/23/93.

Bellanca, Tom. Author interview (SS), 1/14/94.

Blumenfeld, Laura. "The Dead Mystique, Alive and Pulsing: For Deaf Fans, Music That Fuels the Feet and Shakes the Rafters." *Washington Post*, 6/28/93.

Bobrik, Michael. Author interview (DWS), 1/18/94.

Bralove, Bob. Author interview (SS), 10/23/93.

Brandelius, Jerilyn Lee. *Grateful Dead Family Album.* N.Y.: Warner Books, 1989.

Brown, David Jay, and Rebecca McClen Novick. Interview with Jerry Garcia. *Magical Blend* 41 (Jan. 1994).

Brown, Steve. Author interview (SS), 9/27/93.

Bryant, Tim. "DEA Targets Indoor Pot Growers." *St. Louis Post-Dispatch*, 5/9/93.

Calico. Author interview (SS and DWS), 12/13/93.

Clayton, Rick (a.k.a. Noodles Romanoff). Author interview (DWS), 1/21/94.

Coates, John "Tex." Author interview (SS), 1/25/94.

Collins, Sean. Author interview (DWS), 1/19/94.

Collis, Greg. Author interview (SS), 1/5/94.

Constanten, Tom. *Between Rock & Hard Places*. Hulogosi Press, 1992.

Costello, Elvis. Author interview (DWS), 2/25/94.

DeCurtis, Anthony. "The Music Never Stops: The Rolling Stone Interview With Jerry Garcia." *Rolling Stone*, 9/2/93.

Diallo, Yaya, and Mitchell Hall. *The Healing Drum: African Wisdom Teachings*. N.Y.: Destiny Books, 1989.

Duncan, Robert. *The Opening of the Field*. N.Y.: New Directions, 1960.

Dwork, John. "Seek and Ye Shall Find." *Dupree's Diamond News*, summer 1987.

— — —. Author interview (SS), 10/20/93.

— — —. Interview with Vince Welnick. *Dupree's Diamond News* 26 (Nov. '93).

Eisenhart, Mary. Interview with Jerry Garcia, 1987.

— — —. Interview with Robert Hunter, 3/12/88.

— — —. Interview with Robert Hunter, 5/3/91.

— — —. Transcription of press conference with Jerry Garcia and Len Dell'Amico, codirectors of "So Far." Jack Wodell's Screening Room in San Francisco, 10/12/87.

Emshwiller, John R. "Ticketmaster's Dominance Sparks Fears." *Wall Street Journal*, 6/19/91.

FAMM (Families Against Mandatory Minimums Foundation). "LSD Retroactivity." *FAMM-gram*, 12 (July/Aug. 1993).

Fisher, Crystal. Author interview (DWS), 11/23/93.

Fontaine, David. Author interview (DWS), 2/4/94.

Foolish, I. M. "What a Long Strange Trip It's Been: From Touring With the Dead to Touring for the DEA." *Relix* 20, no. 5.

Fortune, Erik. Author interview (DWS), 1/17/94.

— — —. Author interview (SS), 1/21/94.

Franken, Al. Author interview (DWS), 1/18/94.

Gans, David. Author interview (SS), 12/2/93.

— — —. *Conversations With the Dead: The Grateful Dead Interview Book*. N.Y.: Citadel Press, 1991.

— — —. Interview with Don Pearson of UltraSound, recorded live on KPFA, 5/19/93.

Gans, David, and Blair Jackson. "Checking in With Jerry Garcia '81, Part One." *BAM* 111 (8/28/81).

— — —. "Checking in With Jerry Garcia '81, Part Two." *BAM* 112 (9/11/81).

Gans, David, and Peter Simon. *Playing in the Band*. N.Y.: St. Martin's Press, 1985.

Garcia, Jerry. Interview by Paul Krassner, broadcast June 1984.

Garcia, Jerry. J. Garcia Limited Edition Prints. Nora Sage Murray, The Art Peddler, P.O. Box 1371, San Rafael CA 94915. (415) 454-7331.

Garcia, Jerry, Charles Reich, and Jann Wenner. *Garcia: A Signpost to New Space*. N.Y.: Citadel Underground, 1991.

Gimbrone, Guy. Author interview (DWS), 10/23/93.

Glassberg, Barry. Author interview (SS), 1/25/94.

Goldstein, Glen. "Lenny." Unpublished story. Used with permission.

Gowell, Leslie. Author interview (DWS), 11/3/93.

Graham, Bill, and Robert Greenfield. *Bill Graham Presents*. N.Y.: Dell Publishing, 1992.

Grisman, David. Author interview (DWS), 2/4/94.

Gross, Jane. "Deadheads in an Idolatrous Pursuit." *New York Times*, 5/18/88.

Haight, Kathy. "Deadhead Sociology." *Charlotte Observer*, 8/6/89.

Hallsey, Erin. "Grateful Dead Fans Fooled—Bob Weir Impersonator Returns." *San Francisco Chronicle*, 8/90.

Harrison, Hank. *The Dead Book*, Chicago: Links Press, 1973.

Hart, Mickey. *Drumming at the Edge of Magic*. N.Y.: HarperCollins, 1990.

Hart, Mickey, and Fredric Lieberman. *Planet Drum: A Celebration of Percussion and Rhythm*. N.Y.: HarperCollins, 1991.

Hays, Ken. Author interview (DWS), 1/28/94.

Henke, James. "The Rolling Stone Interview: Jerry Garcia." *Rolling Stone*, 10/31/91.

Hippler, Mike. "Gay Deadheads." *Bay Area Reporter*, 8/20/87.

Hoffman, Albert. *LSD: My Problem Child*. N.Y.: McGraw-Hill, 1980.

Hoffman, Paul E., and Cindy Cosgrove. *Outside the Show*. Fleet, CA: Proper Publishing.

Holzman, John. Author interview (DWS), 2/5/94.

Hornsby, Bruce. Author interview (SS), 10/14/93.

Irwin, Doug. Author interview (DWS), 1/22/94.

Jackson, Blair. "Dead Heads: A Strange Tale of Love, Devotion and Surrender." *BAM* 76 (4/4/80).

———. *Goin' Down the Road: A Grateful Dead Traveling Companion*. N.Y.: Harmony Books, 1992.

———. "Listen to the Music Play." Garcia quote from interview with Blair Jackson, 10/28/88. *The Golden Road* 18 (fall 1988).

———. *Grateful Dead: The Music Never Stopped*. N.Y.: Delilah Books, 1983.

Jackson, Blair, and Regan McMahon. "Time Out with Bill Graham." *The Golden Road*, Fall 1985.

Kippel, Les. Author interview (SS), 1/29/94.

Kot, Greg. "Back From the Dead: Guitarist Jerry Garcia Revels in the Rejuvenation of Both Himself and His Band." *Chicago Tribune,* 6/10/93.

Kozinn, Alan. "Churches Increasingly Join the Concert World." *New York Times,* 9/7/93.

Kreitner, Erez. Author interview (DWS), 12/21/93.

Lambert, Gary, ed. *The Grateful Dead Almanac,* Debut Issue. Novato, CA, fall 1993.

Latvala, Dick. Author interview (SS), 11/19/93.

Law, Eileen. Author interview (SS), 2/4/94.

Lieberman, Fredric. Author interview (SS), 10/13/93.

MacDonald, Jane Williamson. Author interview (DWS), 1/31/94.

Marcus, Steve. Author interview (SS), 1/11/94.

Marks, Jonathan. Author interview (SS), 1/20/94.

Martin, Mary Catherine. Author interview (DWS), 10/19/93.

Mattoon, Danielle. Author interview (DWS), 11/23/93.

McKee, James. "Opening Up the 'Oz of Archives': Mickey Hart and the Endangered Music Project." *Folklife Center News.* The Library of Congress, winter 1993.

McNally, Dennis. Author interview (DWS), 10/26/93.

Meltsner, Scott. Author interview (DWS), 1/31/94.

Mendelson, Abby. Author interview (DWS), 1/24/94.

Morse, Steve. "New Age Dead Ready to Play Until They're . . . Dead." *Boston Globe,* 9/28/93.

Muni, Scott. Interview with Jerry Garcia for Arista Records, 9/13/91.

Nash, Michael. "Dan Healy, the Grateful Dead's Wizard of Mix." *Music and Sound Output,* June 1988.

— — —. Author Interview (SS), 1/20/94.

Oxford English Dictionary. Oxford University Press, 1971.

Partridge, Eric. *A Dictionary of Slang and Unconventional English,* 8th ed. N.Y.: Macmillan, 1984.

Perry, Charles. *The Haight-Ashbury: A History.* Vintage Books, 1985.

Pineapple Guys, The. © Author interview (SS), 10/93.

— — —. *The Pineapple Guys© Newsletter.* Carmel, CA, winter 1993.

Powell, Jim. Author interview (SS), 1/4/94.

Raswyck, Glen "Raz." Author interview (DWS), 1/11/94.

Rheingold, Howard. *The Virtual Community: Homesteading on the Electronic Frontier.* Reading, MA: Addison-Wesley Publishing, 1993.

Rock & Roll Hall of Fame Induction, 1/19/94. Transcript provided by Rich Petlock.

"San Franciscan Nights." *Melody Maker,* 9/21/76.

San Francisco Department of Public Health. "Key Participant Interviews Analysis: San Francisco Youth AIDS Evaluation of Street Outreach Project (AESOP)." November 1992.

Santokh, Sat. Author interview (SS), 1990.

Scott, Cindy. "The Further Flavors of Cherry Garcia." *The California Aggie.* University of California at Davis, 4/27/88.

Scott, John. Author interview (SS), 11/16/93.

Shalit, Andrew L. M. "Franklin's Tower." Published on the Net.

Siegel, Buddy. "Bob Weir's Life Beyond Dead." *Los Angeles Times,* 5/6/93.

Silberman, Jeff. Author interview (SS), 10/27/93.

Silberman, Steve. "Transformative Mysteries: A Primer on the Grateful Dead for Aficionados, Initiates & the Wholly Uninformed." *San Francisco Sentinel,* 11/6/87.

— — —. Interview with Robert Hunter. *Poetry Flash,* Jan. 1993.

Slabicky, Ihor W. *The Compleat Grateful Dead Discography,* 11th revision. Copyright © 1983 by Ihor W. Slabicky. Posted electronically on the "rec.music.gdead" files library.

Soucie, Marty. Author interview (DWS), 12/26/93. (Contact GRATEFUL BED & BREAKFAST: P.O. Box 568DI, Luquillo PR 00773. (809) 889-4919.)

Stafford, Peter. *Psychedelics Encyclopedia,* rev. ed. Los Angeles: J. P. Tarcher Inc., 1983.

Sun-downer, Ken, ed. *The Conch-Us Times.* Idyllwild, CA.

Svetkey, Benjamin. "Dead Ahead: Last Year the Grateful Dead Almost Died. Now Jerry Garcia and the Band Are Reborn. (Hold the Mushrooms)." *Entertainment Weekly,* March 1993.

Sutton, Shan C. "The Deadhead Community: A Popular Religion in Contemporary American Culture." Thesis, Wright State University, 1993.

Tawney, Harv. "Waking the Dead." *Crawdaddy,* May 1969.

Troy, Sandy. *One More Saturday Night.* N.Y.: St. Martin's Press, 1991.

Varga, George. "Dead Ahead Newest Band Member Is Grateful for San Diego Ties." *San Diego Union-Tribune,* 12/12/93.

Walton, Bill. Author interview (DWS), 1/14/94.

Wasserman, Rob. Author Interview (DWS), 2/22/94.

Weil, Dr. Andrew. Author interview (SS), 1987.

Wilkins, Charley. Author interview (DWS), 1/30/94.

Wright, Bill. Author interview (SS), 10/22/93.

Zaslow, Jeffrey. "It Doesn't Disturb the Dead at All That Tapers Abound." *Wall Street Journal,* 7/11/86.

Issues of the Dead-related periodicals *The Golden Road,* edited by Blair Jackson and Regan McMahon, and *Dupree's Diamond News,* edited by John Dwork and Sally Ansorge, were invaluable resources.

VII
Notes

Acid Tests — Memories of the tests include those of Carolyn "Mountain Girl" Garcia, as quoted in Sandy Troy's *One More Saturday Night.* Other sources include author interviews with Wavy Gravy, Robert Hunter, Stewart Brand, and Dick Latvala. The CIA connection to the LSD experiments is thoroughly explored in Martin Lee and Bruce Shlain's *Acid Dreams.*

Analy High School — Info from Bill Barich's article "Still Truckin'," *The New Yorker,* 10/11/93, pp. 96–102.

Anthem of the Sun — Remix info from Ihor Slabicky's discography. Title source from Hank Harrison's *The Dead Book;* fire-wheel mandala history from Bill Walker interview in *The Golden Road* #10; Healy quotes from "Dan Healy, the Grateful Dead's Wizard of Mix," by Michael Nash, in *Music and Sound Output,* June 1988; Garcia '72 *Rolling Stone* interview reprinted in *Garcia: A Signpost to New Space,* by Garcia, Reich, and Wenner, 1991.

Aoxomoxoa — Nitrous info from '72 *Rolling Stone* interview reprinted in *Garcia: A Signpost to New Space,* by Garcia, Reich, and Wenner, 1991.

Avalon Ballroom — Graham quote in *Bill Graham Presents,* by Bill Graham and Robert Greenfield, 1992.

balafon — Info from *The Healing Drum: African Wisdom Teachings,* by Yaya Diallo and Mitchell Hall, 1989.

Beam, the — Hart quotes from *Drumming at the Edge of Magic,* by Mickey Hart with Jay Stevens, 1990, p. 185.

Beast, the — Hart quote from *Drumming at the Edge of Magic,* by Mickey Hart with Jay Stevens, 1990, p. 184.

the bogus Bobby — Info from "Grateful Dead Fans Fooled — Bob Weir Impersonator Returns," *San Francisco Chronicle,* Aug. 1990.

Captain Trips — Garcia quotes from '72 *Rolling Stone* interview reprinted in *Garcia: A Signpost to New Space,* by Garcia, Reich, and Wenner, 1991.

Carousel Ballroom — Info from *Bill Graham Presents,* by Bill Graham and Robert Greenfield, 1992.

Cassady, Neal — Garcia quote from *The Holy Goof,* by William Plummer, 1981.

Club Front—Interviews with Dennis McNally and Dick Latvala.

comeback show—"Jerry Garcia Is Taking Care," by Rip Rense. *Mix*, 3/14/87.

Constanten, Tom (*T.C.*)—TC and Lesh quotes from *Playin' in the Band*, page 135. *Fresh Tracks in Real Time* and *OutSides* can be ordered from Tom Constanten: P.O. Box 20195, Oakland, CA 94620. *Heart's Desire* can be ordered from Reckless Records: 1401 Haight St., San Francisco, CA 94117. *Nightfall of Diamonds* can be ordered from Stuff: P.O. Box 2000, Dublin, PA 18917. *Duino Elegies* can be ordered from Hulogosi Press: P.O. Box 1188, Eugene OR 97440. Phone/Fax (503) 688-1199.

crisp—Quote in definition #3 from Charley Wilkins.

dancing bears—Grateful Graphics, (800) 321-9578, 570 York Street, San Francisco, CA 94110.

Dark Star—Hunter quote from author interview.

🍎 *Jim Powell's dozen favorite "Dark Stars":*

There are 199 known Dark Stars by the Grateful Dead (plus two by Kokomo with Kreutzmann and Mydland) and there are tapes of more than 160 of them in circulation, every one containing dazzling passages. This makes selection especially perplexing, but among my favorites I would certainly number: Boston Ark 4/22/69 (31:01); Fillmore East 9/17/70 (25:46); Wembley Empire Pool, London 4/8/72 (31:44); Rheinhalle, Dusseldorf 4/24/72 (42:58 w/insert); Berkeley Community Theater 8/21/72 (35:03 w/insert); Philadelphia Spectrum 9/21/72 (37:22); Palace Theater, Waterbury 9/24/72 (33:30); Winterland 11/11/73 (32:57); Cleveland Convention Center 12/6/73 (42:27); Winterland 10/18/74 (58:04); Miami Arena 10/26/89 (26:00); Madison Square Garden 9/10/91 w/Branford Marsalis (12:29 & 12:40).

day off—Info from Bill Barich's article "Still Truckin'," *The New Yorker*, 10/11/93.

DBA—*The Conch-Us Times* is available by subscription for $8 a year: Box 769, Idyllwild CA 92549.

DeadBase—*Deadbase* can be ordered by writing DeadBase, P.O. Box 499, Hanover, NH 03755; it can also be ordered from specialty retail outlets such as Terrapin Tapes: 1 (800) 677-8650.

Dead Freaks Unite!—"Freak out" from Robert Pitman's article in the *Daily Express*, 3/2/67.

Deadhead—Etymology from the *Oxford English Dictionary*, Oxford University Press, 1971.

Deadhead sociology—Please send academic material to Rebecca Adams, Dept. of Sociology, UNCG, Greensboro NC 27412-5001.

doorways and splices—Garcia quote from Blair Jackson's *Goin' Down the Road*, p. 7.

drums—Hart quote from *Drumming at the Edge of Magic*, by Mickey Hart with Jay Stevens, 1990, p. 185.

DSL (Dead Sign Language)—Info from Bob Bralove and Jim Powell.

DTV (Dead Head TV)—For a broadcast schedule and/or mail-order form to purchase segments, write Dead Head TV, P.O. Box 170642, San Francisco, CA 94117.

Dupree's Diamond News—The Meltzer quote is from *DDN* #23. Info from author interview with John Dwork. To subscribe, write to *Dupree's Diamond News*, P.O. Box 148, Purdys, NY 10578.

Egypt '78—Bill Graham quote from Blair Jackson and Regan McMahon's "Time Out with Bill Graham." Additional info from *BAM*, 11/3/78.

Endangered Music Project—Quote from "Opening Up the 'Oz of Archives': Mickey Hart and the Endangered Music Project," *Folklife Center News*, The Library of Congress, winter 1993.

fantasy venues—Machu Picchu suggested by David Lebow; Herod Atticus Theatre suggested by Stephen Sterns.

Feedback—Hart quote, *Drumming at the Edge of Magic*, pp. 139, 140.

the Fillmore West—First run stats from *DeadBase*. Dosing story and Hart quote from *Bill Graham Presents*, by Bill Graham and Robert Greenfield.

Garcia, Jerry—"In the third grade . . . ," from Garcia, Jerry et al., *Garcia: A Signpost to New Space*. "I was a fuck-up," from *Feature*, via Blair Jackson's *Grateful Dead: The Music Never Stopped;* "wow . . ." and "I was just in heaven . . . ," from *Signpost*. "I just wanted . . ." and "I lasted nine months . . . ," ibid. "Then I heard five-string banjo bluegrass records . . ." from Greg Kot's article in the *Chicago Tribune*. "It just changed everything . . . ," from *Signpost*. Steve Marcus quotes from author interview. Interview with Bob Matthews from the *Grateful Dead Hour*. **Garcia/Grisman** and **Not for Kids Only** can be ordered from Acoustic Disc: 1 (800) 221-DISC.

Godchaux, Keith—Lesh and Weir quotes from David Gans's *Playin' in the Band*, p. 137.

Godchaux, Donna—Elvis Presley, Little Feat, Lynyrd Skynyrd, and Rolling Stones info from Ihor Slabicky's *Grateful Dead Discography*. All quotes from Blair Jackson's *Goin Down the Road*.

The Golden Road—Quote from Slabicky's *Discography*.

the Golden Road to Unlimited Devotion—Author interview with Sue

Swanson. Interview with original club members from *The Grateful Dead Hour.*

Graham, Bill — Quotes from Blair Jackson and Regan McMahon's "Time Out with Bill Graham," and Bill Graham and Robert Greenfield's *Bill Graham Presents.*

Grateful Bed & Breakfast — P.O. Box 568, Luquillo, Puerto Rico 00773. (809) 889-4919.

Grateful Dead — Info from Slabicky's *Discography;* Garcia quote from '72 *Rolling Stone* interview reprinted in *Garcia: A Signpost to New Space,* by Garcia, Reich, and Wenner, 1991.

guitar heroes — Info from Fredric Lieberman.

Gyuto Tantric Choir — Hart quote from Steve Morse's article "New Age Dead Ready to Play Until They're . . . Dead," in the *Boston Globe,* 9/28/93; Steal Your Face watch anecdote reported by Mike Ells.

the Haight-Ashbury — Much of the research, and some of the writing, of this entry was done by Nick Meriwether. Haight Street free show quote from author interview with Steve Brown. The press conference quote is from Hank Harrison's *The Dead Book.* Quote from Garcia '72 *Rolling Stone* interview reprinted in *Garcia: A Signpost to New Space,* by Garcia, Reich, and Wenner, 1991.

halftime — Slam-dunk metaphor from Mike "the Factor" Gardner.

Hart, Mickey — All quotes are from *Drumming at the Edge of Magic:* "acutely aware . . . ," from p. 53. "From the age of ten . . . ," from p. 18. "I remember the feeling . . . ," from pp. 135–136. "Confused, unbalanced . . . ," from p. 145.

the Hippie Highway — Term from Adam Bluestein.

hug circles — Story from Paul Hoffman.

Hulogosi Press — P.O. Box 1188, Eugene OR 97440. Phone/Fax: (503) 688-1199. Rilke's ghost story from author interview with Hunter (SS).

I'll be grateful when they're dead — Info from David Gans and the WELL.

J. Garcia — J. Garcia Limited Edition Prints — Jerry Garcia. Nora Sage Murray, The Art Peddler, P.O. Box 1371, San Rafael CA 94915. (415) 454-7331.

jam — Etymology from an author interview with Clarence Major, author of *From Juba to Jive: A Dictionary of African American Slang.*

the Jerry ballad slot — Garcia quote from interview with Blair Jackson, 10/28/88.

Jerry is God — Garcia interview by David Jay Brown and Rebecca McClen Novick, *Magical Blend* 41 (Jan. 1994).

Jerry's Kids — McNally quote from 11/7/91 interview by Tim Ashbridge, in *Unbroken Chain.*

Johnny Law—Info from *A Dictionary of Slang and Unconventional English*, by Eric Partridge, 1984.

knots—Garcia quote from Blair Jackson's *Goin' Down the Road*, 1992, p. 14.

The Last One—*DeadBase VI*, p. 418; Garcia quote from Blair Jackson, *The Music Never Stopped*, p. 156; Weir quote from Steve Morse's article "New Age Dead Ready to Play Until They're . . . Dead," in the *Boston Globe*, 9/28/93.

LSD—Albert Hoffman quote from *LSD: My Problem Child*, by Albert Hoffman, 1980; Edgewood Arsenal info from *Acid Dreams*, by Martin Lee and Bruce Shlain, 1985; Garcia quote from '72 *Rolling Stone* interview reprinted in *Garcia: A Signpost to New Space*, by Garcia, Reich, and Wenner, 1991; Lesh quote from *The Haight-Ashbury*, by Charles Perry, 1985; second Garcia quote from '72 *Rolling Stone* interview reprinted in *Garcia: A Signpost to New Space*.

magic—Line from Blair Jackson in *BAM* 76, (4/4/80); quote from Sat Santokh.

Mcgannahan Skyjellyfetti—Quote from *Memoirs of a Shy Pornographer*, by Kenneth Patchen, 1945, reprinted by City Lights Press, 1958.

MDMA—DEA info from Kevin Zeese; info from author interview with Andrew Weil.

mescaline—Info from *Psychedelics Encyclopedia*, by Peter Stafford, 1983.

MIDI—Bralove quote from author interview; Vince Welnick interview by John Dwork, *Dupree's Diamond News* 26, Nov. 1993.

Midnight Special—Todd Davidson's address: inmate #13660-018, P.O.B. 901-AUS, Ray Brook NY 12977. For more information, contact Alvin Knox, P.O. Box 1305, Cooksville TN 38503-1305, or Heather Schlesinger, P.O. Box 221973, Chantilly VA 22022-1973.

the Minglewood Town Council—Robert Hunter quote from interview by Mary Eisenhart, 3/12/88.

Mother McCree's Uptown Jug Champions—Weir quote from Gans's *Conversations with the Dead*, pp. 191–92.

Mydland, Brent—"Writing songs with Brent . . . ," from author interview with John Barlow.

oh say can you see—Song info from Reuters.

once we're done with it, it's theirs—Healy quote from "Dan Healy, the Grateful Dead's Wizard of Mix," by Michael Nash, in *Music and Sound Output*, June 1988.

One From the Vault—Hunter quote from interview with Robert Hunter, 5/3/91, copyright © 1991 by Mary Eisenhart. All rights reserved.

one heartbeat away—Tipper Gore info provided by Sally Aman.

parking lot scene — The best description of the economy of Shakedown Street can be found in Alex Kolker's story, "Ace Scores a Ticket," in his self-published book, *Tales of Tour*. Individual copies can be ordered for $6 per copy from Lexman, P.O. Box 3923, Lawrence, KS 66046.

peace — Campbell quote heard 11/1/86 at the Palace of Fine Arts in San Francisco, at a conference featuring Campbell, Garcia, Hart, and others called "Ritual and Rapture"; "family groove" is Dan Healy's phrase.

peak — Garcia quote from Paul Krassner interview, broadcast in June 1984.

Pigpen (Ron McKernan) — Most of the biographical information in this entry comes from Blair Jackson's article "Pigpen Forever: The Life and Times of Ron McKernan," in *The Golden Road* #27. "The Church of the Living Swing" is from *Acid Dreams*.

play like Jerry — Garcia's Solos: Note by Note: Tom Tom Productions, P.O. Box 550, Slatersville, RI 02876. GD books available from Grateful Dead Mercantile: 1 (800) 225-3323.

production aids — Brown quote from author interview with Steve Brown; Garcia quote from '72 *Rolling Stone* interview reprinted in *Garcia: A Signpost to New Space*, by Garcia, Reich, and Wenner, 1991.

quad space — Healy quote from interview on *Dead Head TV*; info from David Gans interview with Don Pearson of UltraSound, recorded live on KPFA, 5/19/93.

railrats — Garcia quote from Henry Allen's article in the *Washington Post*, 6/28/93.

Reagan in China — Garcia quote from Paul Krassner interview, '84. Kreutzmann quote from p. 158 of Blair Jackson's *Goin' Down the Road*.

real estate — Info from Rebecca Adams.

revival — Garcia quote from Eileen Law interview (SS), 2/4/94.

Rex Foundation — McNally quotes from author interview; Garcia quote Press Conference, 10/12/87, transcribed by Mary Eisenhart. Individual donations to these foundations are welcome and tax-deductible. Rex: P.O. Box 2204, San Anselmo CA 94979; Fed. Tax ID #68 0033257. Further: P.O. Box 9357, San Rafael CA 94912. H.E.A.R.: Box 460847, San Francisco CA 94146; 24-hour hotline: (415) 773-9590. Bill Graham quote from Blair Jackson and Regan McMahon's "Time Out with Bill Graham."

rock and roll Picasso — Hunter story from *Conversations with the Dead*, p. 275.

sandwich — Garcia quote from interview with Paul Krassner, broadcast in June 1984.

SEVA — For more information or to make a donation, call 1 (800) 223-SEVA.

the second set — Garcia quote from interview with Paul Krassner, broadcast in June 1984.

"Slipknot!" — Hunter verse from the *Blues for Allah* studio log.

soundboard — Line from David Gans's *Conversations With the Dead*, 1991.

space — First Lesh quote from Gary Lambert's interview, from "Eyes of Chaos/Veil of Order," radio broadcast; second Lesh quote from David Gans's interview, from the *Grateful Dead Hour.*

Spinners — Statement about life on the Land was posted on the WELL. This entry also contains information from author interviews with Steve Marcus and a former member of the Family at Oakland Coliseum, 2/26/94. Garcia quote from interview in *Magical Blend*, Jan. '94.

Spiral Light — For general info, write to Paul Mallett, 48, Allen Road, Fineden, Nr Wellingborough, Northants, England.

stage demons — Garcia quote from Paul Krassner's interview, broadcast in June 1984.

stealie — Owsley comment from interview printed in *Dupree's Diamond News* 26.

the switch — Healy quote from David Gans's *Conversations With the Dead*, 1991.

synesthesia — Lesh quote from *Planet Drum: A Celebration of Percussion and Rhythm*, by Mickey Hart and Fredric Lieberman, 1991, p. 18.

taper terror — McNally quote from Jeffrey Zaslow's article in *The Wall Street Journal*, "It Doesn't Disturb the Dead at All That Tapers Abound," 7/11/86.

"Teach Your Children" — Info from liner notes for *CSN*, 4-CD set, Atlantic 7 82319-2.

Terrapin Station — Hart quote from *Conversations With the Dead*, by David Gans, 1991.

Terrapin Tapes — Info from author interview with Ken Hays at Terrapin Tapes, 1-(800) 677-8650.

the *show* — From Glen Goldstein's unpublished story "Lenny." Used with permission.

They're not the best at what they do, they're the *only* ones that do what they do — Quote and Winterland info from *Bill Graham Presents* by Bill Graham and Robert Greenfield. Warfield story from author interview with Steve Marcus.

TicketBastard — All info obtained from *The Wall Street Journal*, 6/19/91, "Ticketmaster's Dominance Sparks Fears," by John R. Emshwiller.

tourbus — "Temporary autonomous zone" coined by Hakim Bey.

tripping on DNA — The term is Bradley Harrell's.

Trips Festival — Info from *Haight-Ashbury: A History* by Charles Perry, and Garcia quote from *Bill Graham Presents*, by Bill Graham and Robert Greenfield.

Unbroken Chain — To order a sample issue or subscribe write *Unbroken Chain*, P.O. Box 49019, Austin, TX, 78765-9019.

Uncle Bobo — From *Bill Graham Presents*, by Bill Graham and Robert Greenfield, 1992.

the Warlocks — Garcia quote from '72 *Rolling Stone* interview reprinted in *Garcia: A Signpost to New Space*, by Garcia, Reich, and Wenner, 1991.

The WELL — Info on the origins of the WELL comes from *The Virtual Community* by Howard Rheingold. Info on the origins of the GD conferences comes from author interviews with David Gans.

why the music never stops — 9/13/91 interview with Jerry Garcia by Scott Muni of WNEW for Arista Records. Arista turned the interview into a disk that was sent to radio stations to promote the JGB live album.

Woodstock — Garcia quotes from "San Franciscan Nights," *Melody Maker*, 9/21/76.

the zone — Hart quotes from *Drumming at the Edge of Magic*. The phrase "a place of first permission" is from this poem by Robert Duncan, from *The Opening of the Field*:

OFTEN I AM PERMITTED TO RETURN
TO A MEADOW

as if it were a scene made-up by the mind,
that is not mine, but is a made place,

that is mine, it is so near to the heart,
an eternal pasture folded in all thought
so that there is a hall therein

that is a made place, created by light
wherefrom the shadows that are forms fall.

Wherefrom fall all architectures I am
I say are likenesses of the First Beloved
whose flowers are flames lit to the Lady.

She it is Queen Under The Hill
whose hosts are a disturbance of words within words
that is a field folded.

It is a dream of the grass blowing
east against the source of the sun
in an hour before the sun's going down

whose secret we see in a children's game
of ring a round of roses told.

Often I am permitted to return to a meadow
as if it were a given property of the mind
that certain bounds hold against chaos,

that is a place of first permission,
everlasting omen of what is.

VIII
A DEADHEAD'S BOOKSHELF

This list is only a beginning.
Like anything worth loving, the Grateful Dead are a door,
to where other flashing minds are waiting for you.
These books will help see you through.
—Steve Silberman

Small-press books are listed with addresses for ordering. Out of print books can be found in used bookstores, or by mail order from used-book dealers and search services such as Red House Books, P.O. Box 460267, San Francisco, CA 94146, and Water Row Books, P.O. Box 438, Sudbury, MA 01776.

ABOUT THE DEAD AND DEADHEADS
The Grateful Dead Family Album by Jerilyn Brandelius
The Dead family's own tourbook.

Playing in the Band by David Gans and Peter Simon
Brilliantly edited interviews with the band members on the development of their music.

Conversations with the Dead by David Gans
More interviews, including a rare conversation with Owsley.

Drumming at the Edge of Magic by Mickey Hart
Meditations on the ways people of various cultures and eras have used drumming to open the doorway to the spirit, and stories of Hart's own journey with the Grateful Dead, including a frank recounting of his relationship with his father, Lenny.

Garcia: A Signpost to New Space by Charles Reich, Jann Wenner, and Jerry Garcia
A witty interview with Garcia from 1970 by the author of *The Greening of America* and the editor of *Rolling Stone*. Out of print. (Reich's auto-

biography, *The Sorcerer of Bolinas Reef,* out of print, is also worth seeking out.)

"I think of the Grateful Dead as being a crossroads or a pointer sign and what we're pointing to is that there is a lot of universe available, that there's a whole lot of experience available over here. We're kinda like a signpost and we're also pointing to danger, to difficulty, we're pointing to bummers. We're pointing to whatever there is." —Garcia

The Music Never Stopped by Blair Jackson
A well-researched overview of the history, influences, and development of the music, including a vivid description of Deadheads at a show at Ventura in '82. Out of print.

Goin' Down the Road: A Grateful Dead Traveling Companion by Blair Jackson
A selection of articles and interviews from *The Golden Road,* including my own essay "Who Was Cowboy Neal? The Life and Myth of Neal Cassady."

Between Rock & Hard Places by Tom Constanten
T.C.'s erudite memoirs before, during, and after the Dead. A window into the fertile avant-garde Bay Area music scene of the early '60s.

Aces Back to Back: A Guide to the Grateful Dead by Scott Allen
An ambitious attempt to interweave band history interviews and subcultural lore into the narrative of a show. Out of print.

One More Saturday Night by Sandy Troy
Interviews, including Mountain Girl's memories of the Acid Tests.

The Dead, Volume I by Hank Harrison

Bill Graham Presents by Bill Graham and Robert Greenfield
An oral history. The Trips Festival, the Fillmores, Winterland, and beyond.

The Official Book of the Deadheads by Paul Grushkin, Cynthia Bassett, and Jonas Grushkin
The first book about Deadheads, with photos, poetry, clippings, and letters to the Dead Office.

The Water of Life: A Tale of the Grateful Dead by Alan Trist
A retelling of the ancient folktale.
Available from: Hulogosi Press, P.O. Box 1188, Eugene OR 97440.

BY ROBERT HUNTER

Box of Rain: Collected Lyrics by Robert Hunter
Sentinel by Robert Hunter
Contains the long poem "An American Adventure," a memoir of the
Grateful Dead in metaphor. *"It was then that we understood/ we were
dead... but it made/ no difference. The object of our/ faith still showed its beacon
light/ despite the condition of the city."*

Night Cadre by Robert Hunter
Poems.

Idiot's Delight by Robert Hunter
A long poem.
Available from: Hanuman Books, P.O. Box 1070, Old Chelsea Station, New York, NY 10113.

Duino Elegies and *The Sonnets to Orpheus* by Rainer Maria Rilke, translated by Robert Hunter
*"Be, in this immensity of night,/ the magic force at your sense's crossroad; the
purpose of their mysterious plan.// And though you fade from earthly sight,/ declare
to the silent earth: I flow./ To the rushing water say: I am."*
Available from: Hulogosi Press, P.O. Box 1188, Eugene OR 97440.

ABOUT NEAL CASSADY AND THE BEAT GENERATION

Fifteen years before "Cowboy Neal" piloted the Merry Pranksters'
bus Furthur from La Honda to the 1964 World's Fair in New York City,
Neal Cassady was one writer in a group of writers and friends—including Jack Kerouac, Allen Ginsberg, William Burroughs, and others—who
came to be known as the Beat Generation. As the original hippies are to
many young Deadheads, so were the Beats to the original hippies. (Janis
Joplin considered herself a young Beat when she was growing up in
Texas.)

The original Beats met each other in New York City in the late '40s
and early '50s. They took road trips together, hiked into the wilderness,
ate peyote and smoked pot to widen their consciousness, and took each
other very seriously as writers, fellow souls, and cultural innovators, inspired by the rhythms and daring of the explosive new music called be-

bop played in nightclubs by Charlie "Bird" Parker, Thelonious Monk, and Dizzy Gillespie. (An early bebop jam was christened "Kerouac" by Parker, in honor of young Jack, who was always hanging around at the shows.) Though they are referred to as a single "generation," each of the major Beat writers has a distinct voice, from Kerouac's precise and electric panoramas of '40s Denver, to Ginsberg's praise of the magnificence of the real in rhythms echoing Hebrew prayer, to Burroughs's sexually subversive proto-cyberpunk.

The Beats, says poet Michael McClure, "gave each other permission to be excellent," and their enduring intelligence is with us in such diverse places as punk 'zines, meditation halls—and Grateful Dead shows.

The phrase "Beat Generation" was coined by Kerouac, who picked up the word "beat" in 1944 from a heroin addict in Times Square named Herbert Huncke—"Man, I'm *beat*"—hearing in it both an admission of absolute humility, and also "beat" as in *beatitude*, oneness with God.

After a show once, reports Scott Allen, Wavy Gravy ran into Cassady, who had been dancing for three hours. "Boy, are my feet tired," said Neal. "It's a good thing I'm not a foot."

The Portable Beat Reader by Anne Charters

A good selection of writing from most of the major authors of the Beat Generation, including Kerouac, Burroughs, Ginsberg, Cassady, Diane Di Prima, Gregory Corso, and many others, with historical background. Read this book to get an overview, and move on to the individual authors' works.

On The Road by Jack Kerouac

Tender, earnest and smart, crackling with the energy of jazz and the rush of the open road, this story of Sal Paradise (Kerouac himself) and Dean Moriarty (Neal Cassady) has inspired generations of seekers to hitchhike down the highway to look for the lost heart of America. *On The Road* is legendary for having been written in three weeks on a single long roll of teletype paper, but that three weeks followed almost five years of rough drafts, searching for a sound Kerouac found in meeting Cassady.

"Somewhere along the line I knew there'd be girls, visions, everything; somewhere along the line the pearl would be handed to me."

Visions of Cody by Jack Kerouac

The same time period as *On The Road*—the '40s and early '50s—but in more detail. A passionate and honest record of his love for Cassady, unpublished during Kerouac's lifetime, it contains long sections of conversation between Kerouac and "Cody Pomeray" (Cassady) taped while they rolled up fat "bombers" and spun jazz records. *Visions of Cody* is like a hologram of Kerouac's thoughts, memories, and insights into the soul of his best friend; Rudy Rucker calls it "Eternal Mind Transcript."

"I'm completely your friend, your 'lover,' he who loves you and digs your greatness completely."

The Dharma Bums by Jack Kerouac
Does this sound like anyone you know? —

"I see a vision of a great rucksack revolution, thousands or even millions of young Americans wandering around with rucksacks, going up to mountains to pray, making children laugh and old men glad, making young girls happy and old girls happier, all of 'em Zen Lunatics who go about writing poems that happen to appear in their heads for no reason and also by being kind and also by strange unexpected acts keep giving visions of eternal freedom to everybody and to all living creatures . . .

"Ho! What we need is a floating zendo [meditation hall], where an old Bodhisattva can wander from place to place and always be sure to find a spot to sleep in among friends and cook up mush."

Big Sur by Jack Kerouac
Kerouac's alcoholic breakdown and religious conversion.

The First Third by Neal Cassady
The autobiography of Cassady as a young man, growing up in shelters for the homeless in Denver, and teaching himself to write and steal cars. The unself-conscious enthusiasm of the letters collected in this book helped Kerouac find his own voice in *On The Road*.

Grace Beats Karma: Letters from Prison by Neal Cassady

Collected Poems 1947–1980 by Allen Ginsberg
Includes the breakthrough poem "Howl," which Phil Lesh set to music when he was a student, at the College of San Mateo. "Howl" is a blast at hypocrisy and the murder of the spirit by materialism and conformity, and a proclamation of defiance and fellowship during a repressive era. "Howl," "Kaddish," and *The Fall of America* (containing Ginsberg's elegies for Cassady) are also available as City Lights Pocket Poets editions.

Jack Kerouac by Tom Clark

Desolate Angel by Dennis McNally

Memory Babe: A Critical Biography of Jack Kerouac by Gerald Nicosia
Three excellent biographies of Kerouac.

Turtle Island by Gary Snyder
Poetry and essays by one of the writers who helped bring ecological awareness, tribal consciousness, and Buddhism into contemporary life. (Gary Snyder is "Japhy Ryder" in Kerouac's *The Dharma Bums.*

Ring of Bone: Collected Poems 1950–1971 by Lew Welch
Robert Hunter: "Lew Welch was the first poet that I ever seriously read. I thought, 'How long has *this* been going on?' He was to me, what Kerouac was to other people."
Available from: City Lights Books, 261 Columbus Avenue, San Francisco, CA 94133.

SUPPLEMENTARY READING:
Really the Blues by Mezz Mezzrow and Bernard Wolfe
A '30s hipster's search for the deep groove, by the clarinet player and "Johnny Appleseed of weed" who coined the word "pot."

KEN KESEY, THE MERRY PRANKSTERS, AND THE HAIGHT-ASHBURY
One Flew Over the Cuckoo's Nest by Ken Kesey
Kesey's first novel, written while Kesey was a creative writing student at Stanford, living on Perry Lane, and participating in psychedelic experiments at the V.A. hospital. Money from the success of this book helped pay for the Pranksters' house in La Honda and the purchase of the bus called Furthur.

Sometimes a Great Notion by Ken Kesey
Kesey's second novel. The publication party for *Sometimes a Great Notion* was one of three destinations for the Merry Pranksters' cross-country bus trip in '64, the others being the World's Fair and Timothy Leary's League for Spiritual Discovery at Millbrook in upstate New York.

The Demon Box by Ken Kesey
Contains "The Day Superman Died," Kesey's elegy for Speed Limit, the "fastestmanalive" (Cassady).

On the Bus by Paul Perry and Ken Babbs
The bus trip in the Pranksters' own words.

The Electric Kool-Aid Acid Test by Tom Wolfe
A colorful account of the Pranksters and the Acid Tests by a sharp outsider.

Ringolevio: A Life Played for Keeps by Emmett Grogan
An unromantic memoir of the Haight-Ashbury, by one of the founders of the Diggers.

The Art of Rock by Paul Grushkin
The best of the San Francisco psychedelic poster artists' work in color.

The Haight-Ashbury: A History by Charles Perry

The San Francisco Oracle Facsimile Edition edited by Allen Cohen
A collector's edition of the neighborhood newspaper of the Haight-Ashbury, 1966–68.

SUPPLEMENTARY READING:
Stranger in a Strange Land by Robert Heinlein
This science-fiction novel shaped ideas about communal living among the original hippies.

More Than Human by Theodore Sturgeon
A science-fiction novel that influenced Lesh, about the creation of a groupmind.

Journey to the East by Herman Hesse
A mysterious league "on tour" in search of the sacred.

ON PSYCHEDELIC EXPERIENCE
The Doors of Perception by Aldous Huxley
This book, about Huxley's experiences with mescaline, laid the groundwork for the psychedelic revolution.

LSD: My Problem Child by Albert Hoffman

Programming and Metaprogramming in the Human Biocomputer by John Lilly
A compelling model, ahead of its time, for understanding the way LSD works in the "software" of a human mind. Out of print.

Food of the Gods by Terence McKenna
Liberating speculations on psychedelics and history.
"LSD is more than a commodity—it is a commodity that dissolves the social machinery through which it moves."

Acid Dreams by Martin Lee and Bruce Shlain
The secret history of LSD, including the CIA's Project MK–ULTRA.

Storming Heaven: LSD and the American Dream by Jay Stevens
The same subject as *Acid Dreams,* in a more narrative style.

Psychedelics Encyclopedia by Peter Stafford

PiHkal: A Chemical Love Story by Alexander and Ann Shulgin
A complete guide to the class of psychedelics called the phenethylamines—including MDMA and mescaline—contained within a novel by one of the original psychedelic chemists.

Ecstasy: The MDMA Story by Bruce Eisner.

The Natural Mind by Andrew Weil, M.D.

Hallucinogens and Culture by Peter T. Furst
Psychedelics as agents of initiation in traditional cultures. Out of print.
A Huichol Indian's song to the spirit of peyote: *"For shouting and laughing,/ So comfortable, as one desires,/ And being together with all one's companions./ Do not weep, brothers, do not weep./ For we came to enjoy it,/ we came on this trek,/ To find our life."*

ON CYBERSPACE AND VIRTUAL COMMUNITIES
The Virtual Community by Howard Rheingold
An insider's overview of the history and social issues of life online.

SUPPLEMENTARY READING:

T.A.Z. by Hakim Bey

Bey doesn't talk specifically about the Dead, but his idea of "Temporary Autonomous Zones"—cases of uncensored thought and expression, set up like mobile gypsy-camps in temporary gaps in the global net of surveillance—has many implications and resonances for Deadheads.

"The sixties-style 'tribal gathering,' the forest conclave of eco-saboteurs, the idyllic Beltane of the neo-pagans, anarchist conferences, gay faery circles, Harlem rent parties of the twenties . . . face to face, a group of humans synergize their efforts to realize mutual desires, whether for good food and cheer, dance, conversation, the arts of life; perhaps even for erotic pleasure, or to create a communal artwork, or to attain the very transport of bliss . . ."

Available from: Autonomedia, P.O. Box 568, Williamsburgh Station, Brooklyn, NY, 11211-0568.

ON RECOVERY

Alcoholics Anonymous

"The Big Book" of A.A. Available in bookstores and at 12-step meetings. Though not affiliated with A.A., the Wharf Rats can hook you up with the information and community you need to stay sober.

The Zen of Recovery by Mel Ash

The Spirituality of Imperfection by Ernest Kurtz and Katherine Ketcham

The spiritual backbone of recovery, as expressed through many tales and traditions.

" 'Miracle' is simply the wonder of the unique that points us back to the wonder of the everyday."

ABOUT THE AUTHORS

DAVID SHENK is a writer and musician based in New York City. A former producer for National Public Radio, he has also written for *Spy*, *The Washington Post*, *Washington Monthly*, *Mother Jones*, and *Spin*. He is presently writing a book for the University of California Press on democracy in the Age of Information.

STEVE SILBERMAN has spent twenty-one of his thirty-six years in the Phil Zone at Dead shows, dancing through Drums and Space. Steve's essay "Who Was Cowboy Neal? The Life and Myth of Neal Cassady" can be found in Blair Jackson's book, *Goin' Down the Road: A Grateful Dead Traveling Companion*, and his interview with Robert Hunter on poetry, "Standing in the Soul," was published in *Poetry Flash*. Steve studied with Allen Ginsberg at Naropa Institute in Boulder, and he edited Ginsberg's *Snapshot Poetics*. His writings on the Dead and Deadheads, the Beats, Generation X, his own generation, and online community have appeared in *The Golden Road*, *The Whole Earth Review*, *Dupree's Diamond News*, *Sierra*, and *Wired*. Steve is a conference host on The WELL, and lives in San Francisco.

"THANKS, AND STAY IN TOUCH"

If you'd like to keep in touch with us and get onto our *Skeleton Key* mailing list, send a postcard or email with your name and address to:
Skeleton Key 242 W. 104th Street, Suite 3ER, New York, NY 10025.
Email: Skeleton1@aol.com

WHAT DEADHEADS ARE SAYING ABOUT
SKELETON KEY

"Thanks for the fantastic, hilarious neverendingstorybook. Best Dead-book yet, guys!"

—J.W., New York, NY

"I've read other Dead books and this one is right on top."

—J.N., Wynnewood, PA

"Man oh man, do I love *Skeleton Key*. I'm a relative newcomer to the scene, and have been on the bus for 2 or 3 years now. Thanks for such an amazing book."

—L.L., Seneca Falls, NY

"The definitions brought back quite a few memories, smiles, and thoughts of people and places I haven't thought of in quite a while. You helped remind me why I'm there in the first place. Thanks."

—J.M., Jessup, MD

"A tasty, filling book."

—J.D., Brooklyn, NY

"It fills a large void in the Grateful Dead universe."

—B.W., Richmond, CA

"This book has, in my opinion, done the best job to date of documenting in detail the concept of the Grateful Dead scene as a distinct sub-genre of American culture. Not only did I learn a great deal, but I also had the chance to revisit memories that I had forgotten about via certain terms in the book. As I finished reading, I had the vision of an archaeologist 10,000 years in the future uncovering the remains of a VW bus. Inside, that archaeologist finds some dusty cassette covers with, among other words, cryptic symbols like 'BIODTL' and 'GDTRFB' written on it. With the help of an old copy of *Skeleton Key*, he breaks the code and uncovers an entire civilization called The Grateful Dead, and the tales start spinning once again."

—E.Z., Seattle, WA

"I've been into the Dead since 71/72, and the book rings true to my experiences. Postshowglow indeed!"

— M.R., San Jose, CA

"It is wonderful in many expected and unexpected ways. So many great stories from the Show, the Road, the Zone. I love the appendices. I love your tone. The whole book is warm and has made me feel in touch with my family-of-the-spirit."

— J.B., Washington, DC

"Thanks. My 12-year-old son now understands why his dad is on the bus."

— D.T., Seattle, WA

"On the bus this morning I started laughing out loud as I recalled the section from Dead Dreams where that guy yells in his dream, 'Phil likes cheese on his cauliflower!' It's so right on that I've actually cried in a few places. Thanks for the laughter and the tears."

— S.B., Honolulu, HI

"What great reference material for future generations of Deadheads!"

— S.C. & M.R., Tuscaloosa, AL

"I read it from cover to cover in one day! I haven't been into the 'scene' in quite a few years, but your book brought back my enthusiasm for the Dead. Thanks."

— R.K., Hyannis, MA

"I've really enjoyed reading about the Deafheads and Cherry Garcia's alternates and a hundred other stories and quotes that have made me laugh aloud. You've captured a lot of the spirit and feeling and HUMOR of the scene. Thank You (you know, for a real good time)."

— D.S., Providence, RI

"What a great book. I've enjoyed every minute of it. My favorite part is the profiles of the various Deadheads in the appendix."

— Z.K., Gettysburg, PA

"I'm sure you've already received *tons* of mail praising your book, but I'm gonna throw my $0.02 in anyway & say that it's probably the most informative Dead-related book I've read yet. I was more than happy to make a special trip to the ATM to pick up the cash that its purchase required. Here's wishing you tremendous success with the book's sales and good luck in any future endeavors."

—T.G., Cleveland, OH

"Totally indispensable. The route map for everyone on the Grateful Dead bus."

—R.Z., New York, NY

"Can't put it down. I keep running into interesting tidbits which lead to others. *Skeleton Key* is one of the better $15 I've spent. Thanks!"

—H.R., Grand Junction, CO

"I love *Skeleton Key*! Thanks!"

—C.B., Branson, MO

"I started reading your book this weekend and couldn't put it down. Now I'm really jonesin' for a show!"

—B.E., Bloomington, IN

"You gentlemen did a superb job on this book. As a Head since '85, the material is—for the most part—familiar ground, but I am impressed and delighted each time I open it up with the thorough and loving detail to be found in your work. Thanks for adding yet another great edition to the Deadhead Library!"

—D.M., Columbia, SC

"I am a *Skeleton* freak!"

—K.K., West New York, NJ

"Thank you for the book you've written for the world. The *Key* is incredibly well-written and is by far the best addition to our library. We could probably consider it our bible."

—D.C., Tulsa, OK

"I am fifty-one and have been a Deadhead since '69. In my opinion, this is an outstanding reference manual for anybody interested in the Dead — past or present."

—C.S., Ithaca, NY

"Well done! Great facts, humor, insight, stories . . . a must-read for all Heads, newbies and people that want to be more educated on the scene. My mom said that she wanted to borrow it. I said, 'Sure, as long as I get it back.' "

—E.V., New York, NY

"Being somewhat of a 'newbie,' your book has been particularly instrumental in making me feel welcome in a community that holds happiness and love as its unspoken treasure. For that I wish to thank you immeasurably."

—J.L., Madison, WI

"It's a wonderful history lesson and very entertaining. I especially like that it emphasizes the 'family' feeling associated with going to a show. The insight into each of the Dead's albums is also very interesting."

—J.D., Boston, MA

"It's just wonderful and you should be very proud of your literary work of art. I have already passed it on to a friend who attended her 1st show on 8/3/94 in the hopes that she may better understand our tribe."

—K.P., Whereabouts Unknown

"I don't know you guys personally, but you sure know all of us pretty well. Maybe I can lay this on Ol' Pop and see if he can relate. Thanks for the connection."

—S.W.S., Madison, WI

"As hoped for, Jerry Claus left a copy of *Skeleton Key* under our Christmas tree. Let me put it to you this way, I used to consider *DeadBase* the essential book to learning more about the Dead, but now there are two. What *DeadBase* does for the songs, *Skeleton Key* does for the scene."

—D.C., Raleigh, NC

Printed in the United States
by Baker & Taylor Publisher Services